ERROR FREE MENTAL MEASUREMENTS

Applying Qualitative Item Response Theory to Assessment and Program Validation Including a Developmental Theory of Assessment

Robert M. Hashway

ERROR FREE MENTAL MEASUREMENTS

Applying Qualitative Item Response
Theory to Assessment and
Program Validation Including a
Developmental Theory of Assessment

Robert M. Hashway

CXE4

Austin & Winfield, Publishers
San Francisco - London - Bethesda
1998

Library of Congress Cataloging-in-Publication Data

Hashway, Robert M.
    Error free mental measurements : applying qualitative item
    response theory to assessment and program validation including a
    developmental theory of assessment / Robert M. Hashway.
        p. cm.
    Includes bibliographical references and index.
    ISBN 1-57292-111-0 (alk. paper). -- ISBN 1-57292-110-2 (pbk.
    : alk. paper)
    1. Educational testes and measurements--United States. 2. Item
    response theory. 3. Norm-referenced tests--United States.
    4. Educational evaluation--United States. I. Title.
    LB3051.H364   1998
    371.26'0973--dc21   97-50125
                                                                CIP

Editorial Inquiries:
Austin & Winfield, Publishers
7831 Woodmont Avenue, #345
Bethesda, MD 20814
(301) 654-7335

To Order: (800) 99-AUSTIN

This book is dedicated in loving memory of

Victoria Ann Hashway

Table of Contents

Tables

Figures

Preface and Acknowledgements

Since the time of Job, man has attempted to impose an order on the universe. Man has tried to understand what he perceived as his environment. At the beginning of this millennium time traveled at oxen speed. Existence was defined by the environment and superstition where the observable forces of nature and tenants of religion defined reality. It was a time when there was no agreement when the new year started (i.e. 1 January or 15 March) and terror stalked the night. Children were workers; childhood and schooling did not exist; until *circa 1800*, a feudal system and shortage of labor demanded that the young wed and bear children as soon as they were of age (13 to 15 years). *Circa 1300*, the *convivencia* era, European scholars visited Muslim Spain to learn Arabic literature, astronomy and medicine which, coupled with the influence of the Hellenic scholars, led to the Renaissance through classical studies and the European Christians became acquainted with the trappings of culture such as food cooked in oil, spices, literature, art and music. In 1492 the Christian establishment demanded that Jewish scholars and ironsmiths either convert to Christianity or enter exile in Ghettos (iron foundries) and the Jews, primary translators of Arabic and Greek scholarship, rediscovered the geography of Ptolemy which led to the Age Of Discovery and discovery of the Americas. By 1500, millions of books were in print and in 1609 Galileo had confirmed the speculations of Copernicus; 1620, Bacon introduced inductive reasoning and logic; 1700, Descartes and Newton conceived of a pragmatic science leading to the industrial revolution. The evolution of the ''practical arts'' in Europe catalyzed the development of a third world nation developing in the Americas into a technological giant and the evolution of a system of education founded, in part, upon the traditions dating back to A.D. 528 when St. Benedict codified schooling under the 73 articles of the Rule of Benedict including reading, church history and canonical law as well as Charlemagne's first private school for the sons of noblemen in *circa* 830.

Educational theory and practice has paralleled man's perceptions of the physical world and what was necessary to survive within it. The Platonic vs. Socratic approaches to human learning and educational theory parallels the distinction between a pragmatic existential reality and the concept of reality as a social philosophy. The industrial and agrarian man needed to think about reality in certain ways and an educational system to promulgate those philosophies. That way of thinking has led to the production model of education.

As man moved beyond the pragmatic, where robotics and other technologies have antiquated or redefined the concept of human labor and the skills needed to survive in the emerging new world order, the concept of man and how he defines his world has changed. The physical environment is being transformed to a conceptual workplace. Educational theory and practice must evolve in order to meet emerging societal needs. The concept of the educational system as a production system and the student as the product or client of that system is evolving into a new system. The system can no longer be thought of as the provider of a service and the learner as a client or inert recipient of knowledge. The system must evolve along two dimensions. First, the concept of education must evolve into one that facilitates the development of the individual. The purpose of an educational experience is to facilitate the development of individual philosophies of life. Second, the system must take on a Socratic approach where different outcomes from the same experience is not only tolerated; but, encouraged. Educational theory and practice will evolve into a more tolerant structure which will produce thinkers and not worker bees. The society needs individuals who can adapt to a rapidly changing world; not individuals who are prepared to do a particular task which will probably be obsolete prior to the learner entering the work force.

The "great educational debate" is similar to the distinction between the trivium, quadrivium and professional training dating back to *circa* 300 B.C.. Jarvis (1992) suggests a **paradox in being human:** *Human beings have to learn through the experience of living. In An Essay Concerning Understanding ([1690] 1977), Locke argues that human beings are born as tabula rasa-just the opposite of what Plato contends-and acquire knowledge only later...Learning is wider than education; education is only one social institution in which learning occurs, albeit the only one specifically directed toward it...These institutions exist only to facilitate the smooth functioning of the social system, and so they may often constrain learning. Without them, though, there would be a lot less opportunity for human learning and development; this is part of the paradox of being human...Learning, then, is of the essence of everyday living and of conscious experience; it is the process of transforming that experience into knowledge, skills, attitudes, values, and beliefs. It is about the continuing process of making sense of everyday experience-and experience happens at the intersection of a conscious human life with time, space, society, and relationship. Learning is, therefore, a process of* *giving meaning to, or seeking to understand, life experiences* (Jarvis, 1991, p. 9-11). Education in America, dominated by vocationalism, has not evolved from that of a third world nation. In the *America 2000* plan, a program advertised as a major restructuring of the direction of education, President George Bush (1990) indicated that there was a need for fundamental change. *Nations that nurture ideas will move forward in years to come. Nations that stick to stale old notions and ideologies will falter and fail* (Bush, p. 2). Then, within ten short minutes he said: *The corporate community can take the lead by creating a voluntary private system of World Class Standards for the workplace. Employers should set up skill centers where workers can seek advice and learn new skills. But most importantly, every company and every labor union must bring the worker into the classroom and bring the classroom into the workplace* (Bush, p. 7) reverting education in the United States back to the crucible of technocracy and the leadership of self serving industrialists.

I argue the need for a developmental approach to learning throughout the lifespan concordant with the current theories of developmental education (Bryson, 1933; Cross, 1971, 1976; Frazier & Armentrout, 1927; Hall, 1904; Hart, 1927; Harding, 1988; Hashway, 1988; Knowles, 1980; Liveright, 1968; President's Commission, 1947; Rouche & Snow, 1977; Sheldon, 1842). Together with a philosophical redirection is a strong assessment theory corresponding to that redirection. This book attempts to provide direction for that assessment theory.

The first chapter attempts to integrate curricula history into an argument for the need for a developmental approach to human learning. The main body of this book reviews assessment theory and methodologies and error free measurement in particular. Latent trait theory is presented in the second chapter. To provide a frame of reference norm reference and qualitative item response theories are discussed in the next two chapters. Chapters five and six present methods for using assessments for individuals and programs. The remainder of the book provides a new direction in measurement research and utilization. The argument for a time of transition is made in Chapter 8. The principles of developmental learning, qualitative knowledge structures and the differential dynamic nature of human perception and interaction are modeled in the last four chapters. The last third of this book presents new theory and attempts to frame developmentalism into a redcio ad deductit model. This attempt has never been tried before. Working along these lines has led the author to develop two companion volumes *Developmental*

Learning Theory, and *Developmental Curriculum Theory and Methods*; both
of which are anticipated in 1998.

I would be remiss if I did not acknowledge the help of many individuals
either directly or indirectly. It is appropriate that this book was prepared at
Grambling State University, since it houses the only doctoral program in
developmental education in the Americas and Europe. The interaction with
many faculty members was very helpful. In particular, I would like to
acknowledge the discussions of various points with Drs. Vernon Farmer,
Wilton Barham, Olatunde Ogunyemi, and Andolyn Harrison as well as thank
them for kindly listening to my many diatribes on the topic of developmental
learning theory. The early support of former president Harold Lundy, the
former dean of the college of education Burnett Joiner, and the former vice
president of academic affairs Lemore Carter (currently president of Wiley
College) has been an important catalyst to this work. That work would not
have progressed without the continued support of President Raymond Hicks,
Dean Curtis Baham, Acting Vice President J. Copes, Graduate Dean Gerald
Ellis and Trustee President James Caillier. To all of these people, I extend
my gratitude for their support of my vision.

In many efforts of this type there is a class of contributor that often goes
unmentioned. Namely, the army of graduate students who have helped in
many ways. I wish to thank Mr. Mitchel Burchfield, Ms. Karen Sue Cain,
Dr. Lori Hunt, and Ms. Earnestine Bennett-Johnson for commenting on
certain sections of this manuscript as well as Mr. Simon V. Whittaker for his
critical and insightful comments on certain axioms and theorems of
developmentalism. Lastly, I must thank the many students in many of my
classes who have had to labor through some esoteric and protracted diatribes
from time to time.

Reverend Professor Robert Michael Hashway, Ph.D
Grambling, State University
Grambling, Louisiana, 1997

History of Assessment

Educators are facing new kinds of assessment demands generated by new methods for curriculum delivery, changing governmental requirements and a disillusioned public. We no longer assess government officials for proficiency in archery and horse back riding as the Chinese emperors did 4,000 years ago; but, a glance at the Mental Measurement Yearbook (1990) or Tests in Print (1990) shows that a large number of assessment devices are available.

What kinds of assessments are available to meet current educational needs? In what way can educators best use the increasing sophistication of mental measurement? What methodologies are now in use and what kinds of assumptions do they make? In this first chapter, we will begin to examine these questions with a quick look backwards at the development of assessment since ancient China. The focus will be on how broader societal currents shaped assessment philosophy and methods. Next we will look at some special demands developed since the 1960's that educators are dealing with right now and two methodologies available today: Norm referencing (NR) and Item Response models. Finally, I will develop an assessment model predicated upon the theory of developmentalism.

The earliest known written tests were administered by the emperor of China in about 2200 B.C. (Dubois, 1965; Lien, 1976; Ruch, 1929). Unlike most other societies at the time, government officials were chosen based upon performance rather than by a group of aristocrats. Each official was tested every three years and promoted or dismissed based on the results. At the beginning of the Chan dynasty (1115 B.C.), formal procedures for examining political hopefuls were developed. The special needs for which the tests were designed created special criteria. Candidates were required to display proficiency in the ''five basic arts'': music, archery, horse riding, writing, and arithmetic. In addition, candidates had to display a working knowledge of the rites and ceremonies of public life. Two areas of assessment had been distinguished: proficiency and knowledge.

Assessment gradually grew more elaborate. In 165 B.C., five additional ''basic arts'' were added: geography of the empire, civil law, military matters, agriculture, and finance. After 622 A.D., competitive tests were administered on three levels. Candidates first had to pass a local district assessment before they could compete at the provincial capital. Those who passed at the provincial level were honored with a twenty-four hour exam in Peking, after which they went home to await the official report on their place in the ''scale of merit.''

Assessment changed little in the following centuries until the rise of a technocratic civilization. In America, until about 1850, most examinations were limited to recitation and long, difficult essays (Davis, 1971; Lien, 1976). The lack of reliability, implicit in scores from these assessments, was apparent as early as 1845 when Horace Mann argued in favor of the ''new type examinations'' because of their objectivity (Ruch, 1929). However, it remained for researchers in the early 20th century to empirically support Mann's point (Buch, 1916).

Accountability and standardized forms of evaluation quickly became issues in measurement and evaluation. Mann, who was to become a major influence in the development of assessment (Davis, 1971; Ruch, 1929), wanted to develop an instrument that would measure the progress of pupils in the Boston school system. Principals were to be fired if their students did not show satisfactory results on the tests. The wave of immigration into the United States during the mid-19th century exerted a subtle pressure on the development of assessment. There was a desire to sort out the ''rough,'' uneducated new immigrants by using ''scientific'' measurement instruments.

Many educators argued for the development and measurement of educational standards. (Boten, 1932: Buch, 1916; Monroe, De Voss & Kelley, 1917). Tests were developed for spelling, language and arithmetic skills (Boyington, 1932; Buckingham, 1916; Courtis, 1913, 1916a, 1916b, Gray, 1923; Hall, 1911; Monroe, 1923; Pryor, 1923). The ''new type examinations'' estimated a student's knowledge by the number of words spelled correctly or the number of problems completed successfully in a given period (Ebel, 1970; Thorndike, 1911, 1912, 1918; Washburne, 1922).

Psychology at this time was developing into a ''rational science,'' and mathematics as well as statistics began to invade what had been thought of as a purely subjective realm. Inevitably, calls for quantitative and content standards were voiced by well renowned educators (Thorndike, 1911, 1912, 1918; Washburne, 1922). Around the turn of the century, two milestones in modern assessment occurred. In the late 1800's, Francis Galton established his laboratory in South Kensington, England. Galton measured and recorded individual differences in human physical characteristics and sensory and psychomotor responses. His results seemed surprising when published in 1869 and 1883. Individual differences were distributed according to a mathematical model called the ''normal curve of error'' (Harris, 1966;

Hashway, 1977c; Freund, 1962). This discovery led many to believe that mental and physical attributes must also follow the "normal curve." If the results of a assessment were not normally distributed, they inferred that there was something wrong with the test-as opposed to inferring that whatever the assessment was measuring was not normally distributed. Ruch (1929) attributes the normal curve grading scheme to Professor Max Meyer of the University of Missouri and calls it the "Missouri Plan." Remarks by Guy Montrose Whipple (1911) show the intensity of the belief that mental measurements needed to be distributed "normally."

> Finally, we need extended experiments designed to furnish standards of performance in the execution of various mental tests so that ultimately we can compare the performance of the individual pupil in these tests with the normal performance for his age as exactly as we now compare his standing in various physical and anthropometric tests with the norms for those tests. (Whipple, 1911, p.71)

This was the beginning of *norm referenced measurements,* or, as it is also called, *normal curve scaling.* Although many prominent measurement specialists of the time argued against the trend (Thorndike, 1911, 1912, 1918; Washburne, 1922), with the widespread development of intelligence tests after 1905, norm referenced methodology became dominant for many years. The second milestone in modern assessment practice was developed in France by Alfred Binet and Theodore Simon. They produced a series of assessment devices to measure the mental development of young children. Revisions were made in 1908 and 1911 (Binet and Simon, 1916). The original U.S. version, now called the Stanford Binet, was introduced in 1916 by the Stanford University psychologist Louis Terman (Terman, 1916, 1919, 1960). Terman's revision of the Binet & Simon's assessment was the first standardized group assessment.

World War I saw the first large scale application of norm referenced assessment to special social needs. With most men being inducted into the military, the Army needed to develop a group assessment that would classify recruits according to mental ability. A committee of the American Psychological Association, under the direction of Robert Yerkes, set out to develop a assessment that would effectively discriminate recruits according to levels of ability (Yerkes, 1921). Yerkes and Arthur Otis, a student of Terman, produced the first group assessment of intelligence-the *Army Alpha.*

Later, the *Army Beta* version was introduced for those who could not read sufficiently to take the Alpha version.

Since World War I, measurement specialists have developed a large variety of tests. Tests of ability were devised to predict how well a person would succeed at a particular task. Tests of attainment were developed to assess how well, relative to a calibration group, a student attained proficiency of a particular subject. Whether assessing ability or attainment, both were designed to discriminate between individuals (Matarazzo, 1972; Spearman, 1927; Sundberg and Tyler, 1962; Terman, 1916, 1919; Yerkes, 1921).

Specialists have refined these tests over the last century (Carroll, 1950; Lord, 1952; Lord and Novick, 1974; Thurstone and Thurstone, 1941; Wherry and Gaylord, 1944). Assessment event selection techniques were developed which assure a normal distribution of assessment scores (Guilford, 1954; Guilkensen, 1950; Lord and Novick, 1974). However, the basic assumption underlying all these techniques has remained the same: that the "normal-curve" holds true (Lord and Novick, 1974; Matarazzo, 1972).

Finally, modern electronic data processing equipment has had an impact on assessment. The amount of data that could be processed for a large scale assessment was limited by the volume of work required to analyze and report the data. Mechanical sorters were developed, but they were slow and still required much hand work. In the 1950's and early 1960's, computers began to be used in the social sciences, but the machines were still slow. As computer technology and software improved, major new tools became available to the measurement specialist.

Outcome assessment originates from the work of Ralph Tyler at the university level (Madaus & Stufflebeam, 1989; Tyler, 1930, 1942, 1948, 1949, 1950, 1951, 1953, 1959, 1964a, 1964b). In the second and third quarters of this century the focus shifted toward the elementary and secondary sectors with little being done in higher education. Over the last five years higher education has, partially, recaptured the national interest. With its new found importance came a call for accountability models such as outcome assessment (Association of American Colleges, 1985; Bok, 1985; Ewell, 1985; National Endowment for the Humanities, 1984; National Governors' Association, 1986; National Institute of Education, 1984) which is now seen, much in the Tylerian tradition, as a vehicle for developing better students, better teachers, better courses, and better programs (Adler, 1982; Airasian & Madaus, 1976; Boyer, 1983; Carroll, 1990; Cicerelli, 1969; Coleman, 1966; Eisner, 1990; Hashway, 1988, 1989b, 1990; Jackson,

1973; Jencks, 1972; Mackenzier, 1983; Mosteller & Moynihan, 1972; National Governors' Association, 1986; National Institute of Education, 1984; Neill, 1977a, b; Ruffin, 1989; Shanker, 1990; Weisman, 1993). Assessment score decline, as well as other studies, have catalyzed a societal dynamic which stimulated many school systems and colleges to adopt *Back to basics*, or *Competency based* educational programs (Fillbrandt & Merz, 1977; Helper, 1973; Law, 1974; Owen & Ranich, 1977; Wellington, 1977), and education is directed toward a reassessment of entrance standards, program evaluation, and "developmental," "basic," or "remedial" courses. Administrators as well as program implementors are faced with the issue of justifying program costs in terms of outcomes (Hashway, 1989a, b, c).

The question is no longer whether, but how to perform outcome assessments along a continuum from "'procedures that are used to determine the extent to which individual students have met the curricular goals, mastered the prescribed subject matter, and acquired the skills, and characteristics that certify them as having the essential marks of an educated person" (Chandler, 1987, p.12) to a process which can "help identify where things might be done better" (Manning, 1987, p. 32). Recently, a model has been proposed which spans the definitional spectrum (Hashway, 1988, 1990). Regardless of the model, outcome and process assessments are measurement driven.

Modern assessment practice did not evolve from theoretical or methodological concerns. Modern assessment practice emerged from social and public policy debates. Educational assessment practice and methodology evolved as a servant of the prevalent social order. In order to understand how assessment practice evolved an understanding of the evolution of the American curriculum within the social context of a developing third world nation is needed.

ASSESSMENT AS AN AGENT
OF SOCIAL CHANGE

Education in the United States grew rapidly between 1800s and 1900s. During the early and mid 1800s, the main responsibility of educational managers had been to organize the school curriculum, but by the late 1800s, the focus had changed. The influx of immigrants into the United States in the late 1800s resulted in a rapid increase in numbers of students shifting attention from organization and curriculum to seeking ways to accommodate large numbers of students (Hashway, 1988). The percentage of fourteen to seventeen year olds attending high school ranged from 7 in 1840, 11 in 1900, 30 in 1920, and over 51 in 1930. As time marched on cities grew and an identifiable single value structure in any particular city was nonexistent. Education became a mediator between the family and an impersonal societal ordering system where family structures, becoming unstable, were not considered enough to train an individual for the industrial society.

High school principals complained that different colleges had different entrance standards and, because half of the graduating class went on to college, a new standard curriculum was required to meet the needs of the "nontraditional student" (Eliot, 1892a, 1892b, 1905, 1908). He said: *no amount of study in language, natural sciences or arithmetic could protect a man or woman from succumbing to the first plausible delusion or sophism he or she may encounter* (Eliot, 1892b, p. 423). Eliot believed that the ability to express thoughts "clearly, concisely and cogently," the power to reason, moral character, and appreciation of beauty were the purposes of an education. The National Education Association (1893) published its "Cardinal Principles" stipulating that education for life is education for college and that colleges should accept a good education for life as preparation for college studies.

G. Stanley Hall (1904) focusing upon the *"great army of incapables shading down to those who should be in schools for the dullards or subnormal children"* (p. 510) attacked a uniform curriculum as an attempt to impose college domination upon the high school. Eliot (1905) saw that a differentiated curriculum, rather than their capacities, would determine the social and occupational fate of students . William Torrey Harris (1880, 1886, 1888, 1896a, 1896b, 1898a, 1898b) pointed toward vocational training as imposing the values of an industrial society, contending that the purpose of an education was to convey the Western cultural heritage and that each social institution (family, church, industry and school) had a social role. Harris was a leader in moving education from a teacher directed activity to a curriculum directed activity establishing the curriculum and the entire education process as a molecule in the great social milieux.

Curriculum in a State of Flux

The Platoian and Aristilean concepts of mental discipline and a "natural" learning hierarchy formed the organizing curriculum principles (Wolff, 1740). The purposes of education were to discipline and furnish the mind ('Original Papers', 1829) where drill and recitation was predicated upon the "mind is a muscle to be exercised" philosophy (Turbyne, 1962). American educators were interested in the Germanic (Herbartian) concept of education embodying the standard virtues and community values while maintaining discipline for the disorderly and the "dull witted." In 1892 a group of educators who studied in Germany (G. Stanley Hall, John Dewey, Charles DeGamo, etc.) established the Herbart Society for the 'scientific' study of education. Leonard Ayres (1909) and Joseph Rice (1893a, 1893b, 1912) led the movement toward *Scientific Management in Education* (Rice, 1912) guided by Social Control Theory (Ellwood, 1914; Finney, 1928; Ross, 1901; Snedden, 1912, 1915, 1916, 1919, 1921, 1925), believing that *Society is always in the presence of the enemy* (Ross, 1901, p. 190), and that massive intervention and control processes were needed to preserve the society. Frederick Taylor's (1919) scientific management theory gained momentum

Figure 1.1:
American College Test Composite Scores 1964-1989

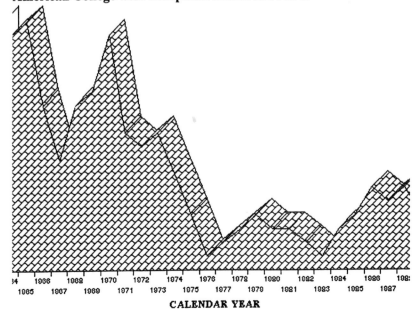

CALENDAR YEAR

in the steel industry (Plunkett & Attner, 1986). Warrett Charters (1923) and Franklin Bobbitt (1918; 1920; 1924) introduced *scientific curriculum development,* using Taylor's methods to decide what to teach (Kliebard, 1987; McNeil, 1977; Tyler, 1949), which resulted in textbooks that stressed skills related to the everyday needs of children and adults.

Eclectic literacy was challenged by Leonard Ayres (1909, p. 5) who published *Laggards in Our Schools* and contended that:

> ...our courses of study as at present constituted are fitted not to the slow child or to the average child but to the unusually bright one...the college preparatory curriculum needed to be replaced by a curriculum attuned to the needs of a new population and a new industrial order...in the country as a whole about one-sixth of all the children are repeating and we are annually spending about $827,000,000 in this wasteful process of repetition in our cities alone.

Ayres developed an index of school efficiency in order to determine the *relation of the finished product to the raw material* which, when coupled with Taylor's (1911) principles of scientific management, led to the adoption of the principle of *The Elimination of Waste In Education* (Bobbitt, 1912, 1918, 1922, 1924, 1926, 1931, 1939, 1946) and the concept of *the superintendent of schools as an "educational engineer" and the school as a "plant."* Bobbitt proposed a system of *education according to need.*

Educators, concerned with the problem of servicing large numbers of students, allowed a leadership abyss to develop and a self serving Black Hand (Sinclare, 1926) to assume control and direction. While educators concerned themselves with counting pupils in individual classrooms, the Black Hand moved the entire system of education from producing literate citizens to producing a nation of drones for the factories. Education changed from a vehicle for protecting individual freedom to a means to a job. The purpose of the entire nation was shifted from providing freedom of thought and expression to providing security and employment.

Figure 1-2:
Scholastic Aptitude Assessment Scores 1956 to 1990

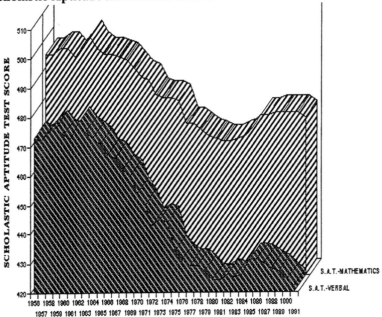

THE BLACK HAND

Industrial and financial Czars, the Black Hand (Sinclare, 1926), controlled the development of education in the United States for personal profit and molded the curriculum so that there would always be an underclass with the modicum of education necessary to perform low level functions in their shops or businesses in sufficient numbers to increase competition; hence, reducing labor costs and a population unable to see that they were being used.

> Next came John H. Francis, and he had a wonderful idea. He was going to have junior high schools all over the city, and the youngsters were to have stenography and typewriting and bookkeeping and manual training-perfect little clerks and shop foremen turned out in two or three years! Francis was a man with a passion for education, a wonderful platform orator; he got his junior high schools, and the fame of them spread all over the

United States. But they cost a pile of money, and they didn't perform the wonders which the business men had hoped for; instead, they got the youngsters interested in music and art and dramatics and debating-and got them organized, so that you couldn't take these things away from them without a riot! So the Black Hand lost all their enthusiasm for Superintendent Francis, and they fired him. (Spencer, 1926, p. 23).

Carnegie Libraries were built by the Black Hand as monoliths to constantly remind the citizens of the cities where his employees lived and worked of his presence and influence at a construction cost of tens of millions of dollars but not a penny for books!

Spencer documented the influence of the Black Hand in every major city in this nation. *The people may have changed but, the Black Hand still influences the direction of education in the United States toward the pecuniary interests of business and finance.*

Bobbitt (1912) exalted the school system developed in Gary, Indiana, a "city having been practically created by the United States Steel Corporation" (p. 259) called the "platoon system" where *the educational engineer at Gary was to formulate a plan of operating his plant during school hours at 100 percent efficiency* (pp. 260-261). The predominant thought of the time concerning curriculum was:

Work up the raw material into that finished product for which it is best adapted...Educate the individual according to his capabilities. This requires that the materials of the curriculum be sufficiently various to meet the needs of every class of individuals in the community; and that the course of training and study be sufficiently flexible that the individual can be given just the things that he needs. (Bobbitt, 1912, p. 269).

Horace Mann had a showdown with a group of Boston school masters where Mann wanted a curriculum that made sense to students, taught in a way that stimulated curiosity and intellectual independence contrasted with the school masters who wanted traditional curriculum taught in traditional authoritarian ways (Cohen, 1990; Cremin, 1957). Social efficiency was the process of scientifically tuning the curriculum to the requirements of the new industrial society led by the Black Hand.

Vocational Education

In the seminal study of vocational education, Dr. Susan M. Kingsbury (1906) found that manufacturers, farmers, representatives of labor unions, and school officials indicated general agreement between the "broader-minded students of education" on the one hand and, on the other, those "men and women who have been brought into intimate contact with the harder side of life"; the "old-fashioned" curriculum was far too removed from the demands of life created by an industrial society and that in practical trade training could be found:

- the fullest development of the individual;
- the reformation of the wayward and vicious; and,
- elevate the Black race in the South.

The Black Hand indicated to the Commission that: *"the processes of manufacture and construction are made more difficult and more expensive by a lack of skilled workmen"* (Kingsbury, 1906; p. 4). The Commission approved the establishment of a new system of education tied to the *callings in life...professional, commercial, productive and domestic* (Kinsbury, 1906, p. 14) and the decline of the apprenticeship system made change a social necessity.

Whereas at one time, the report argued, the system of schooling and the institution of apprenticeship were kept in a kind of balance in terms of their influence on youth, that balance had now been destroyed to the point where a dangerous bias had been created with children and youth devoting their time exclusively to academic studies in school. That balance could be rectified by restructuring the curriculum in schools to include the functions once performed by the apprenticeship system (Kliebard, 1989, p. 101).

The leadership of the organized labor unions believed that an ideal was the creation of their own schools that would serve in place of the old apprenticeship system. The Black Hand made sure that there would be a lack of enthusiasm on the part of the rank and file for that ideal. The Black Hand became so influential that President Theodore Roosevelt found the American school system:

... wellnigh wholly lacking on the side of industrial training, of the training which fits a man for the shop and the farm...We of the United States must develop a system under which each individual citizen shall be trained so as to be effective individually as an economic unit, and fit to be organized with his fellows so that he and they can work in efficient fashion together. (Roosevelt, 1907, p.6).

The early debates reflect uncertainty concerning the form that vocational education should take. Social Efficiency was used by the Black Hand because it afforded the prospect of 'scientifically' attuning the curriculum to industrial and business needs.

Social Meliorists. Lester Ward (1883, 1893) led a movement which included the educational lumanists John Dewey (1896, 1897, 1898, 1899, 1900, 1909) and Herbert Spencer (1865). They believed that: "The denizens of the slums are not inferior in talent to the graduates of Harvard College...Criminals are the geniuses of the slums. Society has forced them into the field, and they are making the best use they can of their native abilities." (Ward, 1893, p. 290). They thought that important curricula questions concerned the theories which give some principle and philosophy to the various subjects: "To study history is not to amass information, but to use information in constructing a vivid picture of how and why men did thus and so; achieved their successes and came to their failures." (Dewey, 1900, p. 199). They believed that systematic grouping of students and selection of teachers served to maintain the existing reward system and that meaningful reform was impossible and contended that a system for social progress was a distribution of the culture through a system of education. They did not imply that education should be a state supported institution in the sense of a school or school building and raised an interesting debate which rages to the current time.

A sad snare would these advocates of legislative teaching betray themselves into, could they substantiate their doctrine. For what is meant by saying that a Government ought to educate the people? Why should they be educated? What is the education for? Clearly to fit the people for social life-to make them good citizens. And who is to say what are good citizens? The Government: there is no other judge. And who is to say how these good citizens may be made? The Government: There is no other judge. Hence the proposition is convertible into this-a Government ought to mold children into good citizens, using its own discretion in settling what a good citizen is, and how the child may be molded into one.

It must first form for itself a definite conception of a pattern citizen; and having done this, must elaborate a system of discipline which seems best calculated to produce citizens after that pattern. This system of discipline it is bound to enforce to the uttermost. For if it does otherwise, it allows men to become different from what in its judgement they should become, and therefore fails in that duty it is charged to fulfil. (Spencer, 1865, p. 158-159).

The social meliorists further contributed to the institutionalization and bureaucratization of education moving it further from the control of the academy.

The Curricula Malaise. While the ideas of leading educators attempted to set the pace for curriculum change, pressure was added by social and economic events of the first half of the 1900s. Two world wars had a tremendous impact on education by creating a new set of students-the service men supported by the G.I. Bill. The communications industry, De Forest's vacuum tube (1096) led to commercial radio stations (*circa* 1920), Zworykins' invention of the iconoscope (picture tube, 1923) led to experimental television (1939) and commercial television (*circa,* 1940), and growth of the communication industry, shifted the locus of control of ideas from the local magnates to the common man who could learn without consulting ward bosses. The beginning of the end of the control of the common man's mind by the wealthy was imminent (Hashway, 1988).

Even though curriculum reform had become a national preoccupation (*circa,* 1930), solutions were not found to problems which were not well definable in a Nation that was in a constant state of social flux. The events that took place in quick succession caught curriculum thinkers in a web which they have not untangled to the present day.

SOCIOPOLITICAL DYNAMICS

Two major social forces have impacted mental measurement: disenchantment with educational quality, and a concern for the needs of the handicapped. Two major educational changes have also had an impact on measurement: programmed instruction and a change in measurement philosophy coupled with the growing awareness of the limitations of norm referenced tests.

Back to Basics

The findings of projects designed to assess school effectiveness in the United States have been disappointing (Jennings and Nathan, 1977). The results of these studies suggest that most variations in achievement scores can be attributed to differences in the home background of students and very little to differences in schools (Airasian and Madaus, 1976; Boyer, 1983; Cicirelli, 1969; Coleman, 1966; Jackson, 1973; Jencks, 1972; Mayeske, et al., 1969; Mosteller and Moynihan, 1972; Neill, 1977b; Rakow, Airasian, and Madaus, 1975). Other studies have suggested that many students have not achieved a level of educational competence associated with minimal life skills (Cook, 1976; Fernandez, 1977; National Assessment for Educational Progress, 1976a, 1976b; National Governors' Association, 1986; National Institute of Education, 1984; Jennings and Nathan, 1977). In addition, college entrance examinations and other types of achievement assessment scores, have been declining since about 1964 (Gilman, 1977a, 1977b; Glennon, 1976; Hashway, 1988, 1989b, 1990; Muller, 1975; Wilhelms, 1975). Awareness of these results catalyzed a movement in many school systems to adopt 'Back to Basics' or 'Competency Based' educational schemes and other, more fundamental, reforms (Carlson, Khoo & Elliot, 1990; Carroll, 1990; Brodinsky, 1977; Educational Assessment Service, 1968, 1977; Eisner, 1990; Fillbrandt and Merz, 1977; Glynn, Yeany & Britton, 1991; Hall, 1975; Handrick, 1975; Helper, 1973; Law, 1974; Mackenzier, 1983; Neill, 1977a; Owen and Ranich, 1977; Ruffin, 1989; Shanker, 1990; Silver & Marshall, 1990; Stensvold & Wilson, 1990; Weisman, 1993; Wellington, 1977; White & Glynn, 1990).

Both forms of education have well defined exit and transitional criteria (California State Department of Education, 1975; Georgia State Department of Education, 1974; Illinois University, 1973; Irvine, 1976). 'Back to Basics,' and 'Competency Based' schemes rely heavily on achievement tests of various types to decide if program objectives have been achieved (Colorado State Department of Education, 1970; Fillbrandt and Merz, 1977; Handrick, 1975; Hawaii State Department of Education, 1972; Hawthorne, 1974; Helper, 1973; Irvine, 1976; Law, 1974; Neill, 1977a).

At some point during the construction of a assessment designed to evaluate attainment of basic life skills or life competencies, the question must be asked: *What are we going to measure?* For example, do we need to know how well a particular student can add fractions compared to other students in the class, school, county, state, or nation? Or, should we be concerned simply with how well a particular student can add fractions? That is, should we estimate the student's ability to solve any addition problem involving fractions that the student could possibly encounter? The major distinction in this argument is between norm referenced and other types of assessment scoring paradigms.

Public Law 94-142

Recently, new regulations were appended to the Education for All Handicapped Children Act (P.L. 94-142). These new regulations provide special education and related services to handicapped children who are not currently being served or are not being adequately served. States were required to provide services to all handicapped children between the ages of six and seventeen years by September 1, 1978. The states were also required to provide services to all handicapped persons between the ages of eighteen and twenty-one years by September 1, 1980. The regulations require that each handicapped child have an individualized program of studies designed by a consortium consisting of at least the parent, the child's teacher, and, where appropriate, the child. The new regulations also require that handicapped children be integrated or educated with nonhandicapped children to the maximum extent possible.

School districts are also required to establish a comprehensive diagnostic assessment and screening program to diagnose specific learning problems. The regulations emphasize that interest should be focused on specific skill areas where a student has not attained mastery. The main measurement issue is the determination of a particular student's competency in a particular subject area. This measurement issue is different from the issue of the relative position of a student with respect to the population of subjects from which the assessment was calibrated. Therefore, the applicability of norm referenced tests to programs mandated by this legislation is questionable.

Programmed Curriculum Delivery

The emergence of individualized curricula have been a major motivational force in the development of domain referenced measures. These programs are designed to allow the student to progress through a precisely defined sequence (Ferguson, 1970; Flanagan, 1967, 1969; Fremer, 1974; Gagné, 1965; Gagné and Paradise, 1961; Glaser, 1961, 1963, 1968, 1971; Glaser and Cox, 1968; Glaser and Klaus, 1962; Glaser and Nitko, 1970, 1971; Nitko, 1968, 1970; Washburne, 1922). This type of curriculum is addressing a question which has plagued the American curriculum for over two centuries, *What is the curriculum and why?* (Bloom, Englehart, Furst, Hill, & Krathwohl, 1956; Bobbit, 1912, 1918, 1922, 1924, 1926, 1934, 1948; Bransferd, Nitsche, & Franks, 1977; Broudy, 1977; Morrison, 1938; Payette, 1969; Rist, 1990; Scandura, 1977, 1976, 1973, 1966; Suppes, 1964; Tyler, 1930, 1942, 1948, 1949, 1950, 1951, 1953, 1959, 1964a, 1964b). The length of time that a student spends on a particular unit is not a prime concern of this type of curricula system. The major concern is whether a student has sufficiently assimilated the subject matter corresponding to the curricula unit he/she is currently working on. [1] Only after displaying sufficient proficiency of the current unit does the student move on to the next unit. An example of this type of system, inappropriately using a nonexistent concept "mastery," is the IPI system (Glaser and Cox, 1968; Glaser and Klaus, 1962; Nitko, 1968, 1970).

AN INDIVIDUALIZED PRESCRIPTIVE INSTRUCTIONAL (IPI) MODEL

The individualized prescriptive assessment model which will be described in this section was formalized by Robert Glaser and his associates (Coulson & Cogswell, 1965; Cox, 1970; Cox & Graham, 1966; Cox & Sterrett, 1970; Flanagan, 1967, 1969; Ferguson, 1970; Glaser, 1963, 1968, 1971a, 1971b; Glaser, Cox, & Vargas, 1966). Although the IPI model, based upon the model developed by Glaser and his associates, is not new and the basic principles were espoused and used for program planning early in the 20th century (Courtis, 1913, 1916a, 1916b; Davis, 1971; Dubois, 1965; Gaines, 1972; Gray, 1923; Haggerty, 1918; Hall, 1911; Hambleton & Gorth, 1970; Monroe, 1917, 1923; Ruch, 1929; Strayer, 1911; Washburne, 1922; Whipple, 1911).

Organization by units is implicit in the model. Each unit is composed of individual skills that must be mastered in order to master the full domain defined by the unit. The IPI assessment model consists of three levels: placement, unit, and curriculum embedded assessments. The placement assessment is administered to all students who enter the program. Initial determination of a student's skill deficiencies, and the selection of a study unit are decided based on the placement assessment. Then, the student is administered a unit pretest. If the student exhibits mastery based on the unit pretest results, an error was made in the placement assessment determination and another unit is selected. If the student does not exhibit mastery on the unit pretest, a learning prescription is developed for one of the skills associated with the unit. When the student completes the skill exercise, the student takes a curriculum embedded assessment (CET). If the student does not pass the CET, another learning prescription is developed. If the student passes the CET, the student goes on to the next skill associated with the unit. When a student completes all skill modules associated with a unit, the student is administered a unit post assessment (UPT). If the student does not pass the UPT, a new learning prescription is devised. If the UPT is passed, the student proceeds to the next unit in the sequence determined by the placement assessment and the learning network until all units are completed.

The programmed instruction sequences outlined above demand a special type of assessment score, one that estimates a particular student's proficiency relative to a specific content area independent of group scores. Here, the norm referenced model does not apply. Another major problem with norm referenced assessments concerns certain undesirable characteristics of the scores themselves. These characteristics and an alternative to norm referenced assessment are described later in this Chapter.

OUT OF THE DEPTHS OF THE
INSTRUCTIONAL MALAISE

A major problem associated with the IPI model is that it was instructional and had limited applicability. It did not focus on the curriculum as an integrative educational vehicle. A global model of curriculum monitoring has been proposed.

Curriculum Development Processes

The curriculum is a *family of educational systems,* a dynamic system meeting societal and personal goals where each part of the learning process must be defined in terms of outcomes, how the learner expends time, and level of acceptable performance. A system specifies the complete learning experience, insuring total system compatibility. Any program so designed is compatible with other courses or programs in the *family of educational systems,* and managed regardless of the number of trainers presenting the materials. Each aspect of a program conforms to a superstructure described in terms of three components: philosophy, system structure and program structure.

Philosophy and Development Process. A *family of educational systems* requires an educational philosophy where the learner is an internalizor and interpreter, integrating events into a world view defining learning environments and outcomes in terms of three types of environmental events: auditory events are received from service providers, media, or other learners; visual events are seen in manuals, demonstrations or course materials; and, activities are individual and group experiences. *Cognitive outcomes* are the set of all rules and processes for determining which rules are required in particular situations. *Affective outcomes* are required for ordered creative thinking, problem solving, teamwork, and leadership. *Psychomotor outcomes* are equipment operation and response skills. Cognitive outcomes (rules and processes) manifest when the learner exhibits a particular predefined response (Scandura, 1966, 1973, 1976, 1977). A *rule* associates a particular event with a response and a *knowledge base* is the set of all rules. *Knowledge is not enough!* A *process* is the skill of determining which class of rules apply to particular situations. The set of all processes is the *application base.* Affective experiences are structured creativity, ordered thinking, and team building. Each program must include *structured creativity* processes for extending or reorganizing knowledge where parameters are identified, characteristics of the solution and knowledge about the parameters defined and organized into a solution process; *ordered thinking* is a methodical attitude toward problem solving; talents, temperaments, and roles in a work team where a person may be a team member or leader are required; teamwork and leadership skills; and, intelligently responding to prompts and retrieving prompts dependent upon the situation and software upon demand are *Psychomotor* outcomes. Once outcomes are defined, experiences which lead to achieving those outcomes are identified. The environment is defined in terms of the three classes of events keyed to specific training outcomes and designed with the philosophy that *for each outcome an activity and for each activity an outcome is defined.* Programs are segmented over time where learners experience individual and group interaction, where the time between training sessions provides learners with opportunities to review materials and contemplate experiences, and the developer attends to time on task and allocation of time to activities.

Innovation through experimentation depends upon many people organized into three areas: direction, development, and delivery. The *program delivery director* is responsible for scheduling courses, material, and facilities as well as faculty. The *program development director* is responsible for defining a program in terms of expected outcomes with the *program development staff*, whose role is to refine outcome statements and develop activities as well as all learner/instructor materials. The *program evaluation director* develops all evaluation protocols as well as evaluates all materials, delivery processes and the extent to which outcomes are achieved. All directors report to the *Vice President for Curriculum* who coordinates development and delivery activities, and reports to the president who is responsible for fiscal and physical affairs. Details of the required documentation, described elsewhere in this Chapter, reflects the developmental philosophy *for each outcome an activity and for each activity an outcome with a means of evaluating performance at each step of the process so that, if necessary, intervention can be provided at the earliest possible point, and learners are provided with continuous progress assessments* (Cross, 1971, 1976; Hashway, 1988, 1989, 1990; Keimig, 1983; Maxwell, 1971, 1979; Nist, 1985).

Curriculum Monitoring

In terms of the societal return per dollar expended, education is expensive. Most schools are involved in curricula delivery with little time for performance monitoring systems, and serve three audiences: administrators require effectiveness and utilization data; instructors need to identify individual strengths, weaknesses, and effective practices; and, learners with timely feedback including indicators of current strengths, weaknesses, and direction. This section describes the latest development stage of a curriculum information system humanistically meeting stakeholder needs (Hashway, 1988, 1990). This holistic model accounts for many factors which affect learners (skill mastery, cognitive style, psychological and social background, and physical disabilities), and is composed of three phases: placement, counseling (which involves proper placement), and intervention to facilitate learning.

In the *placement phase*, a summary report of each learner's status is prepared including cognitive skills, cognitive style, and psychological characteristics. Then, the learner enters the *counseling phase,* where it is recognized that a learner's *persona* is not represented by a limited number of assessment scores and educational decisions are not based solely upon them. Assessments and goal awareness are essential for counselor and learner to select an intervention strategy, considering the learner's personal

Figure 1.3:
Developmental Curriculum Delivery System

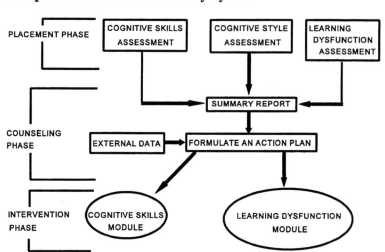

and academic history. Once a plan is formulated, learners enter a *cognitive skills module, learning dysfunction module,* or both. The cognitive skills module attempts to remedy particular skill problems where units and learning tasks in each unit are matched with the cognitive style best suited to each and the learner's cognitive style is mapped against skill levels.

Using both maps, the learner and counselor select a learning program. In the learning dysfunction module an attempt is made to correct for psychological and/or physical barriers to learning. The learner enters a *learning dysfunction center* with a detailed counseling plan, staff and learner develop a learning intervention strategy and after the strategy is executed the learner is re-evaluated. If it is determined that the strategy was not effective, a new plan is devised; otherwise, the learner exits the module. Assessment can provide valuable information for tracking learners through a curriculum and provides data for research as well as program development, validation, audits, and enhancement.

Curriculum Structure Information System (Csis)

More than a database management system, *Csis* structures are included for automatic and empirical modification of curricula sequences and resource-skill-cognitive style associations. Learners are administered a diagnostic assessment battery and performance levels on many domains and courses are generated on paper and on line. Administrators receive reports at aggregate, or learner levels, results are interfaced with registration systems, and learners are processed away from courses that they would not successfully complete.

Figure 1.4:
Curriculum Information System

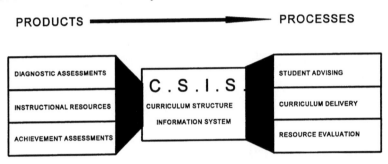

Some believe that locking learners out of courses based upon assessment results is not humane. It is fraud and inhumane to allow a learner to take a course where failure is certain. The humane approach is a program designed for enhancement where success is in the future. Each tutor and curricula manager has profile data for each learner; learning centers and classrooms are organized into multi resource work centers stimulating enhancement through experimentation; diagnostic assessments are administered, processed, and reported immediately; and, the learner has a detailed analysis containing a skill profile, report of the skills to be studied, and resources associated with each skill and cognitive style. There are many advantages to keeping the information on a centralized computer system. *Csis* prepares frequent learner progress reports whereby learners see progress and feel better about themselves and the program. Through *Csis* implementation, learners develop a strong positive attitude toward the curriculum, faculty quickly identify problem areas and improve learner progress plans, administrators receive frequent reports on program progress and *Csis* evaluates resources and resource-skill linkages based on performance data and dynamically modifies them. Over time, *Csis* evaluates and modifies the network of prerequisite skill relationships in the entire multi disciplinary skill bank and evolves presentation sequences (i.e. curriculum or course sequence) and curricula reorganizations representing efficient course design based upon how learners learn.

Education has been criticized for not adhering to an eclectic mission and meeting the needs of at risk students. Each institution must determine its unique belief, purpose, vision, and mission structure. By using the techniques and strategies presented here, a curriculum will be able to "fit" its purpose and mission into the hierarchial framework of the host institution as well as monitor innovation. Once an educational system has defined its beliefs, visions, and missions, objective based planning can be utilized to assure that selected projects have the best possible chance of success by relying upon strategies that will give project ownership to those upon whom success depends. The system must choose a leader according to its beliefs, visions, and missions, and who has the ability to: do and direct research, think and stimulate thinking, and is politically sophisticated. The leader is an advocate for educational advancement through research and a leader in the educational community. The system must choose its service providers according to its beliefs, visions, and mission, they must be innovative thinkers, stimulate thinking in the classroom, and are active in research and professional organizations. Service providers should be in the forefront of producing innovation through experimentation. The process, procedures and systems described here provide a curriculum with the tools and structure for dynamic experimentation and innovation.

For the properly prepared and articulated curriculum *there are no underprepared students, only a curriculum under prepared for those students.* An educational system may consist of different schools, colleges, institutions, and departments; but, those units form a *family of educational systems* existing to meet some societal goal. Until the mission of an educational system is defined and articulated, at risk, under prepared, or talented students are nonsequitors.

OBJECTIVE MEASUREMENT

Norm referenced assessments of ability or attainment are used for many purposes. One is to screen potential candidates to identify those who satisfy the criteria of a particular program. Another is to track learner attainment over time to assess progress. An additional use of norm referenced assessments is to assess the effectiveness of programs. The latter use of norm referenced assessments is often intended to answer one of two questions.

First, is a particular program achieving the objectives for which it was intended? Second, is a particular program or group of programs more successful than other programs designed to achieve the same objectives?

The use of standardized and, in particular, norm referenced scales, has been strongly criticized, (See reviews in Block & Dworkin, 1976). Some of the issues raised will be reviewed later in this volume after the prerequisite technical nomenclature has been described. However, certain social policy decisions have further catalyzed an examination of the philosophical foundations upon which norm referenced tests were predicated.

A court action with important implications for programs for the handicapped is a class action suit, *Larry P. v. Riles*. The lawyers for six minority elementary school students have alleged that their clients were wrongfully placed in classes for the educable mentally retarded on the basis of their clients' scores on norm referenced intelligence tests. The Wechsler, Stanford-Binet, and Leiter tests were specifically mentioned in the suit. These tests are, perhaps, the most commonly used tests of general intelligence. The attorneys for the plaintiffs have attempted to present evidence that the tests are culturally biased in the sense that they reflect "middle-class" experiences exclusive of the experiences of students with different backgrounds. Regardless of the outcome of the San Francisco court action, the testimony presented is likely to have some impact on assessment and evaluation programs.

In addition, assessment use has been criticized on ethnic grounds. In particular, assessment use has been criticized for discriminating against Blacks. An important point is that it is not the instruments themselves, but their use that is being criticized. Although we would like to believe that the last vestiges of discrimination were eliminated in the 1960's, the following affirmative action performance audit indicates that overt, covert, and defacto desegregation remains alive.

Discriminatory Practices

What constitutes a racially distinct institution? The answer to this seemingly obvious question is neither simple nor agreed upon (Olivas, 1989). Case law suggests that, since and before the first challenge to the exclusion of Blacks from the University of Maryland (*Pearson v. Murray*, 168 Md. 478, 182 A. 590, 1936), predominantly White institutions resisted efforts by Black students to enroll. In 1938, the Supreme Court in *Missouri ex rel. Gaines v. Canada*, 305 U.S. 377 (1938) struck down a Missouri directive that did not allow Black residents to attend Missouri law schools; Missouri paid Black residents to attend law schools in another state. Missouri was not the only state that had attempted to carry out such directives. Georgia and other states were carrying out such plans. Ten years later, cf. *Sipuel v. Board of Regents* 332 U.S. 631 (1948), Oklahoma was required to enroll the first Black student in that state's history. Oklahoma, after *Sipuel v. Board of Regents,* admitted Black students, roped them off in a corner and established separate facilities. *The New York Times* (14 October 1948) documented that the first Black student to attend the University of Oklahoma was G. W. McLaurin, a 54 years old Black male who matriculated for a doctorate in education, and his first class was in educational sociology directed by Dr. Frank Balyeat from a desk contained in a specially prepared cloak room. The New York Times reported that the University of Oklahoma assigned McLaurin ''a special desk in the library and a special room in the student union building where he can eat his meals.'' It was not until the early 1950's that Oklahoma, not of their own volition, stopped this practice (cf. *McLaurin v. Oklahoma State Regents,* 339 U.S. 637, 1950 and *McKissick v. Charmichael,* 187 F.2d 949, 4th. Cir. 1951). The state of Texas had the audacity to establish a separate Black law school to serve as an incentive for Blacks *not to attend* the University of Texas law school after the decision against South Carolina in 1947 (*Wrighten v. University of South Carolina,* 72 F. supp. 948, E.D.S.C., 1947). The Texas condition was ruled upon in *Sweatt v. Painter,* 339 U.S. 629 (1950).

    Although the Supreme Court struck down separate but equal practices in *Brown v. Board of Education,* 347 U.S. 483 (1954) and directed any and charged all with the duty to cease and desist such practices with all ''deliberate speed,'' (cf. *Brown v. Board of Education,* 349 U.S. 294, 1955) higher education officials have been negligent in this duty (Entin, 1986; Kujovich, 1987; Morris, 1979; Olivas, 1979, 1989; Preer, 1982). An instance of that recalcitrance was the reason for an independent compliance audit. In January 1969 the Department of Health, Education and Welfare concluded that the State of Louisiana violated Title VI of the Civil Rights Act of 1964 (cf. 42 U.S.C. § 2000d et seq.) by operating a racially segregated system of higher education and requested the submission of a desegregation plan within 120 days or less. It was not until 1973 (cf. *Adams v. Richardson,* 356 F. Supp. 92, 1973) that an injunction was served on the Department of Health, Education and Welfare requiring and enjoining it to: ''within 120 days from the date of this Order to commence enforcement proceedings by administrative notice of hearing, or to utilize any other means authorized by law, in order to effect compliance with Title VI by the states of Louisiana, Mississippi, Oklahoma, North Carolina, Florida, Arkansas, Pennsylvania, Georgia, Maryland and Virginia." The states of Arkansas, Pennsylvania, Georgia, Maryland and Virginia complied with the order. The other states, including the State of Louisiana, had not complied with the order potentially suggesting a deference on the part of the State of Louisiana to the constitution and rights afforded all citizens of the United States.

In *Adams v. Bennett*, 675 F. Supp. 668 D.D.C. (1987), the court recognized the difficulties unique to the desegregation of higher education. Although the court understood the problems, it was not willing to wait for an eternity for a solution to those problems. The recalcitrance of the State of Louisiana and the Department of Health, Education and Welfare to carry out that order exacerbated the problem. It was not until March 14, 1974 that the United States Attorney General attempted to enforce the provisions of the Fourteenth Amendment to the Constitution and Title VI of the Civil Rights Act (cf. *United States of America v. State of Louisiana, et al*, U.S.D.C., 80-3300 §A). The United States alleged that:

> [T]he State of Louisiana and its agents exercising management and control of public colleges and universities, established and have maintained a racially dual system of public higher education in violation of the Fourteenth Amendment and Title VI. The United States further alleged that the defendants had failed to develop and implement detailed plans which "promise realistically and promptly to eliminate all vestiges of a dual system of higher education within the State of Louisiana."

The State of Louisiana denied the allegations and asserted that:

> [P]ublic institutions of higher education in the State of Louisiana are in full compliance with the Fourteenth Amendment and Title VI...have maintained non-racial open admissions policies and non-racial employment policies and have taken other action to comply fully with the letter and spirit of the Fourteenth Amendment and Title VI.

The defendants entered into a so called *Consent Decree* in 1981.

Figure 1.5:
Adjusted Support Ratios for Northern Trustee Universities

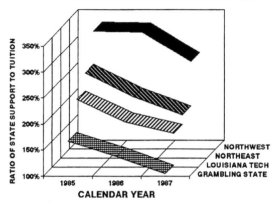

RATIO OF STATE SUPPORT TO TUITION
TRUSTEE SYSTEM - NORTHERN UNIVERSITIES

An independent compliance audit to learn if the State of Louisiana showed good faith compliance with the Fourteenth Amendment and Title VI as amended was conducted (Hashway, 1993). The methodology involved a longitudinal study of data concerning the characteristics of Louisiana' public higher education institutions provided in public documents published by the State of Louisiana as well as data graciously provided by the National Center for Educational Statistics, the U.S. Department of Education Office of Educational Research and Improvement and other federal documents. The educational compliance audit has a long history as a mechanism for educational improvement and policy development (Cronbach, 1963; Dubois, 1970; Ginsberg, 1989; Tyler, 1991, 1950, 1941). The techniques used in this audit not only complied with standard practice (Cronbach, 1991; Metfessel and Michael, 1967; Scriven, 1991; Stake, 1991; Tyler, 1942) but also with the principles for presenting a *preponderance of evidence* in court decisions which have been based, in part, upon behavioral research (*Chance v. Board of Examiners,* 330 *F. Supp.* 203, 1971; *Baxemore v. Friday,* 478 U.S. 385, 1986; Bombey & Saltzman, 1982; Bodner, 1983).

The Boards of Regents and Trustees did not provide Grambling State University with incentive funds. Rather, the operational budget at Grambling was adjusted in such a manner as to equate the student contribution ratio with Louisiana Tech. and, hence, Grambling could either fund enhancements or decrease the burden upon the student. The adjusted

Figure 1.6:
Formula Funding Levels Predicated upon Regent Student Credit Hour Formula and Actual Budget Levels (Budget Levels Beyond 1992-1993 Are Regent Projections)

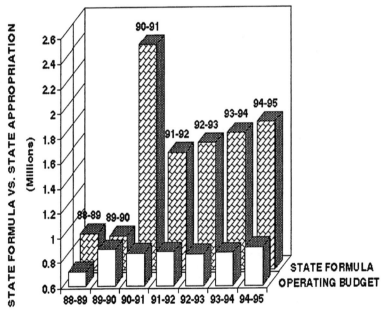

burden ratios indicate that *during the consent decree period the State of Louisiana discriminated between all northern universities.* During the consent decree period, students at Northwestern State University enjoyed a lower burden than students at Northeast. Students at Northeast Louisiana University enjoy a lower burden than those at Louisiana Tech. *During the consent decree period students at Grambling State University experienced the greatest burden in supporting their education-three times that of students at Northwestern, two and a half as much as students at Northeast and twice as much as students at Louisiana Tech. Universities.*

After the consent decree period, all students at the northern universities had to assume a greater proportion of the burden of financing their educations after the consent decree. The magnitude of the change is informative. Students at Northwestern, Northeast, and Louisiana Tech. (predominately Caucasian institutions) had to absorb about a 30% greater burden while Grambling State University (a predominately Black institution) students were required to absorb a nearly 75% increase. In 1988, the year the consent decree ended, Grambling State University students contributed more in fees than the state contributed to the operation of the University! The funding patterns since 1988 indicate that the State of Louisiana appears to be funding northern universities in such a fashion as to equate the burdens of students at Northwestern, Northeast, and Louisiana Tech. Universities and requiring Grambling State University students to assume twice the burden of the students at the other northern Louisiana universities.

Grambling State University students contributed before, during and after the consent decree, between 30 and 350 % more to the support of their educations than students at any other Trustee school. The extent to which the Board of Regents have funded consent decree programs is reflected in how they funded the Ed.D. program at Grambling State University. Although the Ed.D. program at Grambling is the only one of its kind in the United States and has begun to achieve national prominence, it is beginning to decrease in enrolment due to under funding. In addition, the Lincoln Parish Agreement, part of the original consent decree, clearly indicated that if the Board of Regents determined that further education doctorates were needed in Northern Louisiana they would be housed at Grambling State University. Furthermore, the Lincoln Parish Agreement specified specific education doctorates in addition to the existing Ed.D.. As of this time none of the pre-agreed upon doctorates have been implemented at Grambling State University. In addition, although Grambling State University has had exemplary evaluations by NCATE and the Southern Regional Accreditation Association, the Board of Regents, directly after the consent decree ended, determined that other doctorates in education were needed in northern Louisiana and they would be located at Louisiana Tech. and at Northeast Louisiana University.

The last results, combined with an immediate decrease in the state to student contribution ratio the year the consent decree ended, raises serious questions concerning either the understanding or the deliberate intent of, ultimately, the staff and members of the Board of Regents of the meaning and intent of Title VI of the Civil Rights Act of 1964, as amended (Title VI), 42 U.S.C. § 2000d *et seq.* (1982), Title IX of the Education Amendments of 1972, 20 U.S.C. § 1682 *et seq.* (1980), Executive Order No. 11246, as amended by Executive Order 11375, and § 504 of the Rehabilitation Act of 1973, 29 U.S.C. § 794 (1982).

PROGRAM EVALUATION

Beyond the issues outlined above, some researchers criticize the use of norm referenced paradigms for program evaluation. Some of these critics argue that norm referenced assessments tend to assess the abilities within a global content domain too broad to reflect subtle program differences (Airasian and Madaus, 1976; Carver, 1975; Rakow, Airasian, and Madaus, 1976). Others address the issue on psychometric grounds (Cobean, Airasian, and Rakow, 1975; Harney, 1975; Hashway, 1976; Rakow, Airasian, and Madaus, 1975). Norm referenced assessment events are selected in a purposeful fashion (Ahmann & Glock, 1967; Ebel, 1954; Guilford, 1954; Gulliksen, 1950; Lord & Novick, 1974; Nunnally, 1967). The purpose of the selection procedure is to maximally discriminate between individuals (Ebel, 1954; Guilford, 1954; Henryssen, 1971; Lord & Novick, 1974). Hashway (1976) has demonstrated that assessments which maximally discriminate between individuals are totally ineffective for detecting treatment or program differences.

Procedures for program and treatment evaluation continue to be entrenched in statistical models based upon agricultural and biological measurement procedures. Unfortunately, the nature of behavioral measurement is such that the precision of "hard" science data is almost never realized. Statistical treatment of evaluation data is based upon an assumption of measurement precision that is unrealistic. Hashway (1978a, b) has tried to integrate the nature and structure of human measurement models into statistical inference procedures. Some of Hashway's (1978a, b) work will be described and extended to inference models using norm referenced and criterion referenced tests.

Measurement Anomalies

Benjamin Wright (1967) and others have criticized traditionally constructed norm referenced paradigm on two psychometric grounds (Hambleton & Zaab, 1990; Lord, 1980; Rasch, 1980). First, the score received by a particular individual depends on the events used to construct the assessment and, secondly, individual scores depend on the group used to calibrate the assessment. As a corollary, Wright (1967) argues that assessments should produce indicators that exhibit two characteristics: two assessments purporting to assess the same ability or achievement result in the same scores for the same person, and a assessment score should not depend on the group used to calibrate the events included in the assessment.

Consider two traditional assessments, each containing the same number of events, constructed from a group of events associated with the same content domain. Assume that one assessment is composed of very difficult and an other assessment of less difficult events. Assessment scores obtained by a particular individual will depend upon which assessment was administered to that individual. The same individual will obtain a assessment score from the second (easier) assessment that will be numerically larger than the result obtained if the difficult assessment was administered. The two assessments would not be "item-free." A traditional assessment designed to assess achievement in basic algebra is not applicable to high school students if the assessment was calibrated using a sample of elementary school students. Traditionally, if a norm referenced assessment was calibrated using a sample that is not similar to the population for which the assessment was intended to be used, little confidence can be placed in the resulting assessment scores. Traditional, norm referenced tests are not sample-free.

G. Rasch (1966) has presented a selection technique intended to produce assessments with characteristics corresponding to those described by Wright (1967). The Rasch procedure purports to result in assessments that are both sample-free and item-free. That is, the indicators resulting from applying Rasch's paradigm purportedly are not a function of the events used to construct the assessments or the samples used for calibration. The technique is similar to classical Thurstone scaling in that both items and individuals are scaled (David, 1969; Edwards, 1957; Edwards and Kenney, 1965; Edwards and Kilpatrick, 1974; Guilford, 1954; Thurstone, 1927, 1932; Thurstone and Chive, 1929).

Assessments designed to comply with the assumptions of the Rasch paradigm possess two very interesting and useful properties. These properties are discussed in great detail by Wright and others (Forbes, 1976; Forster, 1976; Hashway, 1977, 1978; Mead et al., 1974; Slind & Linn, 1978; Tinsley, 1971; Tinsley & Dawis, 1977; Whitely & Dawis, 1974, 1976; Wright, 1967; Wright & Douglas, 1974; Wright & Panchapakesan, 1969). Instruments constructed using the Rasch paradigm are said to be both item-free and person-free. The instruments are item-free in the sense that two Rasch assessments that contain events assessing the same content domain yield two scores for the same individual that are not appreciably different (Hashway, 1977a, 1977b, 1977c, 1978). It has been shown that the scores obtained for a particular person from two equivalent Rasch assessments differ by an amount appreciably *less* than expected from purely random error of measurement (Hashway, 1977, 1978, 1997). Events that compose a Rasch assessment are said to be person-free in the same sense that the value of the psychometric parameters associated with those events are not dependent upon the population of subjects used to estimate those parameters (Boldt, 1972; Brink, 1972; Forbes, 1976; Forster, 1976; Hashway, 1977, 1978, 1997; Ingebo, 1976; Mead et al., 1974; Tinsley, 1971; Whitely & Dawis, 1974; Willnott & Fowles, 1974; Wright, 1975; Wright & Mead, 1975). Because the scoring formula for Rasch assessments is functionally dependent upon the event parameters, the scoring formula is person-free. It appears that assessments constructed with the Rasch paradigm are viable alternatives to norm referenced assessment.

In conclusion, it has been pointed out that assessments have been in use for a very long time. However, technology is only now beginning to make significant strides in assessment. The remainder of this volume will be concerned with three major issues. One is the construction of Rasch assessments. It should be noted at this time that the Rasch procedure can be used with either norm referenced or criterion referenced assessments. The second major issue is the use of scores derived from these tests for individual and program evaluation. The statistical inference procedures are based on a model of behavioral measurement. In this sense, they are new. The individual and program evaluation procedures presented in this volume are theoretically founded upon the assumptions underlying the measurements for which inferences are to be made. Therefore, they may be in variance with classical inference procedures based on an assumption of "error-free" measurements Thirdly, current assessment technology is predicated upon constructionist concepts which have formed the axioms of education for nearly two millennia. The developmental approach forms a new axiomatic foundation which leads to a different view and technology for both viewing human behavior and constructing assessments.

This volume contains many chapters addressing assessment issues. However, it is conceptualized as being composed of two major sections. The first section describes classical constructionist based assessment construction and assessment paradigms. The second section describes developmental learning theory as well as new instrument construction and assessment technologies as well as methodologies predicated upon that theory.

Notes

1. As we will see later, a major educational policy error has been an over concern with instruction and an over reliance upon sophomoric concepts such as ''mastery.''

2

A Primer on Latent Trait Theory

The assessment development scenario consists of three activities. First, assemble a preliminary set of events. Second, administer a preliminary draft to a sample of subjects. Third, analysis of the preliminary data will provide information to isolate problems in the events themselves, (i.e., previously undetected sources of ambiguity, poor distractors, etc.,) and decide which events seem to fit the particular assessment paradigm. Only after trial data are obtained can it be decided whether the responses to a particular event will fit a specific psychometric model. Before discussing the procedures for deciding the usefulness of an event for a particular model, we have to look at the psychometric models themselves. Since all models are variants of what has been called latent trait theory, this is where we will begin.

The response to an event is the result of a psychological process that is a reaction to the event. An assessment score is an indication of the degree of proficiency in using that psychological process. This description makes a major assumption: *the process that goes on in a respondent's mind when answering a question can be mapped onto a set of numbers.* That is, the underlying psychological process that is a response to the assessment event can be represented by a set of numbers on a continuum that is unidimensional.

The first assumption underlying any assessment is that there exists an attribute to be measured. In the case of psychological and educational assessments, it is assumed that there exists some unseen attribute intrinsic to a respondent and shared by all respondents. This attribute has been called a *latent trait* (Hambleton & Cook, 1976; Hambleton, Swaminathan, & Rogers, 1991; Lord, 1980; Lord & Novick, 1974; Pedhazur & Schmelkin, 1991). The probability that a respondent will respond in the appropriate fashion to an event or group of events is related to the latent trait by a mathematical formula called the *item characteristic function*. The type of function used to define the relationship between the attribute and the probability of success defines the assessment model.

Figure 2.1:
Operant Belief Structure Subsystem

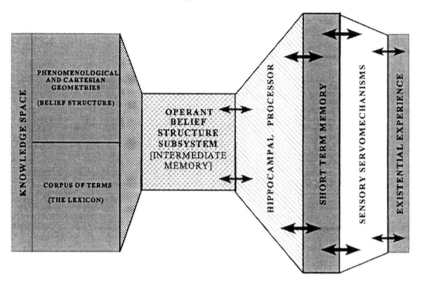

An event is recorded by various sensory processors. Respondents operate in a manner similar to a parallel processor (Rumelhart & McClelland, 1987; Hinton & Sejnowski, 1987) where subsidiary processors transform particular parts of the event data stream. Each sensory servomechanism converts information to and from the senses and muscles with the short term memory. The hippocampal processors interface the short term memory with the long neuron structures which compose the operant belief structure. The operant belief structure is composed of memory atoms associated with the elements of the event and the relationships between those terms which define past experience. The phenomenological and Cartesian nature of the belief space will be discussed later in this book. for the present, we will assume the existence of a latent attribute associated with a set of knowledge elements (atoms) and accepted relations between those atoms.

Associated with a latent trait is a latent trait dimension—a ruler used to estimate a respondent's degree of proficiency in executing the latent trait or underlying behavioral process. A respondent's position on a latent trait dimension is estimated using the responses to the events composing an assessment. For a particular administration, any single respondent is associated with a single point on the latent trait dimension. However, more than one respondent may be associated with a single point. Every point on the dimension is associated with a single level of proficiency.

The content domain consists of a set of atoms and relationships. Those relationships in the content domain define the probability of association between qualitative observations. The sampling domain must be an image of the content space reflecting the events (associations) in the knowledge space. The extent to which the geometries of the content and sampling domains are congruent is a measure of assessment validity.

The space of observations is assumed to be a linear association between the sampling domain and the set of observations. This discussion of classical constructivist approaches to assessment will retain the concept of linearity. Nonlinear relationships will be discussed later in this volume.

Figure 2.2:
Interspacial Endomorphism

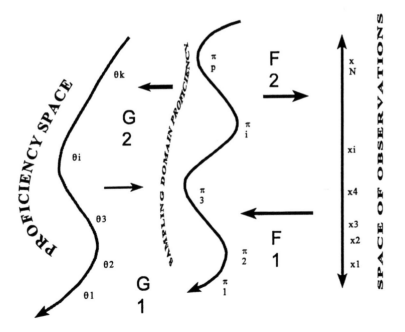

There are assumed to be functions which relate the position of a respondent in a proficiency space to positions in the sampling domain and finally between the sampling domain and the space of observations. Hence, there is an assumed relationship between the *latent trait space* and the *space of manifestations*. Functions are assumed to exist between manifestation, sampling and proficiency domains.

Each of the domains are assumed to be homomorphic, not necessarily isomorphic, representations of each other. There can exist no perfect relationship between the domains. There are three levels of specificity that these functions can assume.

1. ξ: $\Theta \rightarrow \Pi$ is an order preserving transformation where for any two elements $(\theta_1, \theta_2 \in \Theta)$ where $\theta_2 > \theta_1$ there are images such that $\pi_1 = \xi(\theta_1)$ and $\pi_2 = \xi(\theta_2)$ and $\pi_2 > \pi_1$.

2. If Θ and Π are metrizable where σ and μ are the distance functions, respectively, then not only does ξ: $\Theta \rightarrow \Pi$ satisfy 1; but, distance is preserved up to homomorphism. i.e. $\sigma(\theta_1, \theta_2)$ is a linear function of $\mu(\pi_1, \pi_2)$.

3. There is a stronger relationship which may exist between two spaces. There are two functions, $\xi_1: \Theta \rightarrow \Pi$ and $\xi_2: \Pi \rightarrow \Theta$, which exist between two spaces, and the two spaces are strongly related if for all $\theta \in \Theta, \xi_2(\xi_1(\theta)) = \theta$

Most assessments can only hope to satisfy assumption 1. Therefore, the mapping function should be probablistic or qualitative, not deterministic. For any observation, x, there is a function p (π | x) which defines the relationship between the probability that an individual has a latent position, π, given a particular observation, x. The respondent' latent trait score is the value of π which results in a maximum value of p (π | x) for a particular, observed, assessment event sequence, x.

The probability that a respondent will respond appropriately to an event is assumed to vary with the respondent's position on a particular latent trait dimension. An assessment score represents a mapping or association from the categorical set of respondents into the latent trait dimension. This function is called the event's *characteristic function*, and the graph of the function is called the event's *characteristic curve* (Hambleton & Cook, 1976; Hambleton, Swaminathan, & Rogers, 1991; Hambleton & Zaal, 1991; Kifer, Mattson & Carlid, 1975; Lord, 1977, 1980; Lord & Novick, 1974). The mapping function is subject to the constraint that the probability of responding appropriately to an event is a monotonic increasing function of positions on the latent trait dimension (Lord, 1977, 1980; Lord & Novick, 1974; Nunnally, 1967; Guilford, 1954). The constraint implies that the higher a respondent's position on the latent trait dimension the greater the probability that the respondent will respond, appropriately, to any representative event. Equivalently, the lower a respondent's position on the latent trait dimension the lower the probability that the respondent will appropriately respond to any representative event. Two respondents associated with the same position on a latent trait dimension are assumed to have the same response probability.

Assessment events are equivalent to events in the knowledge space in the classical model. The phrases *assessment events* and *test items* will be used synonymously in the discussion of classical models. Also, the words test and assessment will be used interchangably with the understanding that any test is an assessment, yet, an assessment need not be a classical test.

In addition to the probability of an appropriate response, a respondent's position on a latent trait dimension is related to the degree to which a respondent will proficiently execute the particular psychological process considered representative of that dimension. The higher a respondent's position on the latent trait dimension, the greater that respondent's proficiency is assumed to be with respect to the underlying psychological process. The lower a respondent's position on a particular latent trait dimension, the lower the respondent's proficiency is assumed to be with respect to the underlying psychological process.

Position on a particular latent trait dimension should not be confused with process proficiency; they are not synonymous. Psychological process proficiency is a concept. A behavioral process is thought to exist and the degree of proficiency a particular person possesses is assumed to be quantifiable *in terms* of a continuum. The latent trait dimension is also assumed to be metrizable. Distances on the latent trait dimension can be associated with some set of numbers (real, complex, or imaginary)[1]. The latent trait is, at best, homomorphic to the proficiency space.

In addition to the assumptions above, it is assumed that a mathematical function exists which associates positions on the latent trait dimension with the scores obtained from a particular assessment. In this sense, the indicator obtained from a particular assessment for a particular respondent is only one representation of that respondent's position on the latent trait dimension. The score is only a manifestation of the respondent's proficiency in executing the behavioral process assumed to be underlying the responses to the assessment events. A measurement problem is to, first, postulate the functional form of the desired mathematical expression that associates particular assessment indicators with particular positions on the latent trait dimension in a monotonic increasing fashion. Second, it is to decide, from preliminary data, which of the events in the preliminary event pool satisfy the properties implied by the choice of mathematical function. These events form the final assessment. This procedure assumes that the events that correspond to the desired properties derived from one set of respondents will correspond to the same properties when used with a different group. Norm referenced assessments address this assumption by restricting the respondents to those who closely resemble the calibration group.

CHARACTERISTIC FUNCTIONS

The traditional model assumes that the latent trait dimension is unidimensional (Thurstone and Thurstone, 1941). Unidimensionality implies that the latent trait corresponds to a single attribute dimension. Traditionally, the unidimensionality assumption is closely associated with the factor analysis literature. The presence of one common factor explaining a large amount of the observed interitem covariation has been considered an indicator of unidimensionality (Thurstone and Thurstone, 1941). The psychometric difficulties with using factor analysis are described in the literature (Thurstone & Thurstone, 1941; Carroll, 1950, 1974; Wherry & Gaylord, 1944). These psychometric difficulties concern the nature of the correlation coefficients used to calculate the factors and the fact that item level data does not represent a continuous level of measurement. There is a question concerning the use of the factor model that has not been addressed. The mathematics involved in generating the common factors starts with a correlation matrix (Bock, 1975; Finn, 1974; Kleinbaum & Kupper, 1978; Mulaik, 1970; Rummel, 1970; Tatswoka, 1971; Timm, 1975). The results obtained by applying factor analysis are dependent upon the respondents used to generate the event level scores that are, in turn, used to generate the correlation matrix upon which the factor analysis depends (Thurstone, 1938). Therefore, there is no reason to believe that the factor model is any better indication of unidimensionality than any other algorithm.

Norm referenced and most other scaling procedures are based on the assumption that the position of a respondent on a latent trait dimension governs the probability of a subject responding appropriately to an event. The major difference between procedures concerns *how* position on the latent trait dimension is measured (the nature of the metric) and *how* this position is related to the probability of responding correctly to an event. The major difference between assessment construction paradigms rests on the functional equation that defines the action of the constraint.

The function defining the relation between a respondent's position on the latent continuum and the probability of responding correctly to a representative event is unique to each assessment construction paradigm in question. The norm referenced paradigm assumes that the characteristic function is the same for all events. This characteristic function is the cumulative distribution for a Gaussian variable (Guilford, 1954; Lord & Novick, 1974). If P(x) represents the probability that a respondent at position x on the latent trait continuum will respond correctly to an event,

Figure 2.3:
Characteristic Curve of a Norm Referenced Test Item

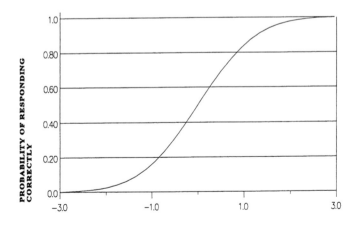

POSITION ON THE LATENT ATTRIBUTE

$$P(x) = \frac{1}{\sqrt{2\pi}} \int_{-\infty}^{x} e^{-\frac{t^2}{2}} dt, \text{ where t is the dummy variable of integration. The}$$

integral on the right of the equation is not expressible in terms of an elementary function. The value of the integral can be approximated using numerical techniques (for an example, see Hashway, 1974). Using numerical approximations, the graph of P(x) vs. x can be drawn. That graph is the characteristic curve assumed to exist for an item selected using the traditional paradigm. The graph is shown in Figure 3.3.

Figure 2.4:
Three One Parameter Logistic Items

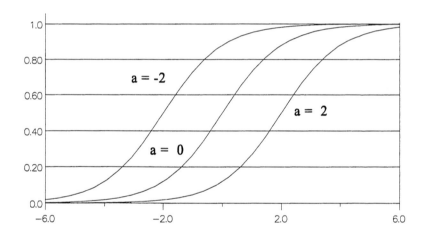

Figure 2.5:
Logistic Characteristic Functions

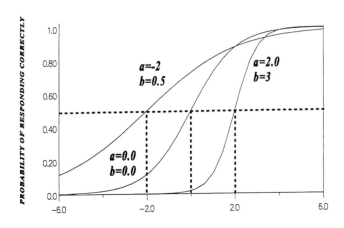

POSITION ON THE LATENT ATTRIBUTE

Rasch (1966) and others have raised some major questions concerning the norm referenced model (Deno, 1985; Gable, Hendrickson, & Stowitschek, 1986; Gallery & Hofmeister, 1977; Jobs & Hawthorne, 1977; Salvia & Ysseldyke, 1985; Stowitschek, Gable, & Hendrickson, 1980; Wallace & Larson, 1977). The norm referenced model assumes that the characteristic function corresponding to each event is the same for all events (see Figure 3.1). This implies that a respondent with a particular latent trait score has the same probability of responding correctly to all events. For a particular respondent, some events may be either more or less difficult than others. For all respondents some events may be more or less difficult than others. Assuming that some events can be more or less difficult than others, the probability of responding appropriately to a set of events is a function of both the respondent' position on the latent trait dimension and the event under consideration. One, two, and three parameter latent trait models assume the existence of a characteristic function that is functionally dependent upon both the position of a respondent on the latent trait dimension and the position of the particular event under study on the same latent dimension.

The *three parameter item response theory model* assumes that the probability of a respondent with ability θ responding appropriately to the i-th. event is $P(x = 1 | \theta, a_i, b_i, c_i), = c_i + \dfrac{1 - c_i}{1 + e^{b_i(a_i - \theta)}}$.

Examples of this function are shown for the special case of the Rasch model in Figure 3.4 and for the general case in Figure 3.5. The index c_i represents the "guessing" parameter, the probability of obtaining an appropriate response from a respondent with "no ability" ($\theta = -\infty$). a_i represents the position of an event in the ability space. If event i is more difficult than event j, then $a_i > a_j$; equivalently, if $a_i > a_j$, event i is more difficult than event j. a_i is called the event difficulty. b_i represents a metric or scaling parameter equivalent to the slope of the characteristic function when $\theta = a_i$. Events with large values of b_i tend to be highly discriminating between ability groups. Events with high b_i are excellent for discriminating between respondents with abilities greater than a_i and those with ability levels below a_i, and is called the discrimination index. Highly discriminating events provide a great amount of information in a small neighborhood centered at a_i; but, little or no information in a neighborhood far from a_i. Assessments consisting of events with high discriminating parameters and all located within a small neighborhood of a_i result in highly precise estimates for respondents also located in that neighborhood with fewer events than an assessment with less discriminating events or events not in a small neighborhood of a_i and are useful for computer adaptive assessment models, and little information for respondents outside a narrow range about a_i . Identifier assessments, developed to locate the general position of a respondent prior to some more precise assessment, should contain events whose positions are representative of a priori assumptions concerning the respondent (s) to be assessed.

The unidimensionality assumption of parametric models seems more global and somewhat more general than the corresponding assumption in the norm referenced model. R.J. Mead (1974) points out that an event that does not fit the Rasch model may not be unidimensional in the sense that a single latent trait is not sufficient to explain the observed response patterns. A strict interpretation of the unidimensionality assumption would imply that an assessment of arithmetic skills would require separate assessments for addition, subtraction, multiplication, etc. This strict interpretation has been empirically tested by Forbes and Ingebo (1975, 1976). They found that it was possible to obtain Rasch event calibrations from a composite event pool without first doing a subscale breakdown. This can be interpreted in two ways: the Rasch model may be sufficiently robust with respect to violations of the unidimensionality assumption, or the unidimensionality requirement is sufficiently broad as to encompass a global latent trait, such as arithmetic skills.

Item response theory assumes that each event occupies a position on the latent trait dimension. The more positive the position of the event, the more difficult the event is considered (measured by the number of respondents who respond appropriately to the event). Each event is considered to have a characteristic function of its own. The characteristic curve corresponding to one event need not be the same as the characteristic curve corresponding to another event. Unlike the norm referenced paradigm, which requires all events to have the same characteristic curve, item response theory takes into account differences that may exist between events (Lord, 1977, 1980; Lord & Novick, 1977; Rasch, 1966, 1980; Wright & Panchapakesan, 1969). The characteristic function corresponding to a particular event is defined by the position of the event on the latent trait dimension and the position of the respondent on the same dimension. If event i is located at position a_i on the latent trait dimension, the probability of an appropriate response to the event, given that a respondent is located at z, is expressed as a function of the distance between the respondent and the event, a_i-z.

The Rasch model is a particular instance of item response theory.

The Rasch characteristic function is: $P(a_i, z) = \dfrac{1}{1 + e^{a_i - z}}$. The

characteristic functions corresponding to three Rasch events located at different positions are shown in Figure 3.4. The previous equation and the curves described by Figure 3.4 indicate that the probability of responding appropriately to an event is a monotonic increasing function of the difference between the position of the respondent and that of the event, a_i-z. Respondents who occupy positions lower than that of the event have a lower probability of responding appropriately to the event than respondents who occupy positions higher than that of the event.

The Rasch model assumes that $c_i = 0$ (no guessing) and $b_i = 1$. The Rasch model has been, erroneously, called the one parameter model. All algorithms for testing the fit of an event to the Rasch model estimate either

a_i and b_i or a_i, b_i, *and* c_i, where after an heuristic is applied by which events for which $b_i \approx 1$ and $c_i \approx 0$ are accepted and others rejected. The Rasch model is not a one parameter model; it is a three parameter model with constraints on two parameters. Furthermore, the two parameter model is a three parameter model where $c_i \approx 0$. The more constraints imposed upon the event the less likely a particular event will meet those constraints. From a given event bank, fewer events will fit the Rasch model than the two parameter model, and fewer events will fit the two than three parameter models.

Once event parameters are estimated, an assessment consisting of a subset of k events is constructed. The usefulness of that assessment at an ability level is reflected in the *test characteristic function*,

$$I_i(\theta) = \frac{\left[\dfrac{\delta P_i(\theta)}{\delta \theta} \right]^2}{P_i(\theta) Q_i(\theta)}$$

and

$$I_T(\theta) = \sum_{i=1}^{n} I_i(\theta)$$

(Reckase & McKinley, 1991). The test characteristic function reflects the amount of information the assessment yields about individuals with ability θ. The assessment that contains a larger number of events in a small neighborhood of θ will yield more information about respondents in that neighborhood than in neighborhoods where there is not a cluster of events. The test information function reflects the distribution of event difficulties and is used to determine if a particular set of events are applicable to a particular respondent or group. An assessment must be sensitive to ability differences [reflected by $I(\theta)$] in the range of abilities in the group or the particular respondent to be assessed. The test information function is useful for tailoring an assessment, or selecting a group of events, to the group or respondent in order to optimize the information obtained from the minimum number of assessment events and assessment time.

Criterion referenced measures obtain estimates (scores) compared with a well defined content domain. The domain is specified by specific behavioral objectives (Airasian, 1971a, b, c; Airasian & Madaus, 1972; Baker & Popham, 1973; Kasecoff, Fink & Klein, 1976; Kriewall, 1969). A process for empirically validating the existence of the unidimensional content domain is the subject of debate. One view, stated previously, is that the use of statistical techniques such as factor analysis is of dubious value due to the metric underlying the data (Thurstone & Thurstone, 1941; Carroll, 1950, 1974; Wherry & Gaylord, 1944). The other side of the issue involves relying entirely upon the process of developing specific performance objectives. Astin (1964, p.811) believes that, "the only method for 'validating' a criterion measure is a logical analysis of its relevance to the conceptual criterion." In addition, Glaser & Klaus (1962, p.449) contend that: " The validity of a proficiency test is primarily a function of the accuracy with which the task has been analyzed and the skill with which the items have been selected."

It is this author's opinion that neither the pure empirical analysis nor the pure logical analysis argument is entirely correct. Assessment events must be constructed so that they correspond very closely to specific performance objectives. However, to rely entirely on the opinions of event authors and screening panels seems to leave much room for conjecture and subjective judgment. If a group of assessment events are highly associated with a specific performance objective, those events should "cluster" together. A different group of events associated with a different specific performance objective should also "cluster" together. Factor analysis was designed to isolate such clusters. However, as previously pointed out, when the data is dichotomous, there are serious questions concerning the calculation of the correlation coefficients upon which a factor analysis is based. Although factor analysis may not be useful, another technique known as *nonmetric multidimensional scaling* may provide the answer (Davison, 1983; Guttman, 1968; Kruskal, 1964a, 1964b; Lingoes, 1973; Shepard, 1957, 1962a, 1962b, 1966; Shepard, Romney & Nerlove, 1972a, b; Young & Hamer, 1987). Multidimensional scaling techniques result in answers to the same questions posed by factor analysis, but are not dependent on the same scaling assumptions. Until empirical evidence is gathered to the contrary, the multidimensional scaling technique is the recommended procedure.

Before the wave of norm referenced assessments, the predominant mode of assessment was, essentially, criterion referenced (Bayles, 1934; Charters, 1923; Courtis, 1916a, 1916b; Gray, 1923; Haggerty, 1918; Hall, 1911; Monroe, 1923; Monroe, Devoss & Kelly, 1917; Morrison, 1926; Otis & Davidson, 1913). The index by which assessment indicators were reported was the proportion of events responded to appropriately within a fixed period. That proportion was assumed to reflect the degree of proficiency a respondent would attain if all events in the domain were responded too. The transition to norm referenced indicators initiated in the late 1920's as a response to a cry for the 'scientific method' still persists today. In the early 1960's, many measurement specialists were arguing for a different type of reporting scheme (Astin, 1964; Davis, 1951; Ebel, 1962; Glaser, 1963, 1971; Glaser & Klaus, 1962). That different type of reporting scheme would support indicants relative to well defined performance criteria. Glaser (1963) called such an assessment an "criterion referenced".

Many researchers interpreted the phrase "relative to a performance criteria" in a particular way. If a respondent obtained an assessment indicator above a cutoff point, the respondent would be considered to have mastered the content domain. On the other hand, if a respondent obtained an assessment index less than the cutoff, the respondent would be considered a nonmaster; thus, the emergence of the *Mastery Test* (Block, 1971a, 1971b; Carver, 1970; Emrick, 1971; Haladyna, 1974; Hambleton & Novick, 1973; Kriewall & Hirsch, 1969; Livingston, 1969, 1970, 1972a, 1972b, 1973).

The major problem with the mastery test is implicit in the concept that such a thing as "mastery" exists, is useful, and the appropriateness of the concomitant use of a cutoff score (Besel, 1973; Carroll, 1970, 1971; Ebel, 1970; Millman, 1970, 1972). First, the choice of a cutoff score is largely a subjective issue. Second, the scores from a mastery test do not make maximum use of the information that could be obtained. Others have interpreted Glaser's (1963) definition of a criterion referenced test in another way. They interpret the phrase "relative to a fixed performance standard" to mean that scores are reported relative to a well specified content domain. These researchers have made complete use of Glaser's (1963) arguments (Brickwell, 1969; Beses, 1973; Davis, 1951; Ebel, 1962, 1970; Glaser, 1963, 1971; Glaser & Cox, 1968; Glaser & Klaus, 1962; Messick, 1975; Meskauskas, 1976; Novick & Lewis 1974). They assume that mastery is not a nonexistent concept. Rather, any single respondent can display a number of mastery states, or degrees of success (Brickwell, 1969; Glaser, 1963, 1971; Novick & Lewis, 1974), and that there exists a continuum ranging from a low of zero to a maximum of 1.0, or some monotonic transformation of that range. The indicator obtained from an assessment is an estimate of the degree of success a respondent would experience if confronted with a representative event from the content domain reflected by the events composing that assessment. Interestingly, assessment has made what seems to be a complete turn around in time back to the pre-1930 era (cf. Thorndike, 1911, 1912, 1918).

Novick & Lewis (1974) have made some strides in defining the distribution of ability relative to criterion referenced indicants. They have applied Bayesian statistical procedures to the problem of estimating a respondent's proficiency level from an assessment consisting of a sample of events representative of the content domain (Freund, 1962; Harris, 1966; Hays, 1973). The Novick & Lewis (1974) approach starts with the assumption that π, each respondent's level of proficiency, can be represented as a proportion on a continuum of proficiency ranging from a low of zero to a maximum of 1.0. A respondent is administered an assessment composed of n events. The collection of n events composing that assessment is considered representative of the domain of interest. After the assessment is administered and scored, it is found that the respondent responded correctly to x events. The problem is to obtain an estimate, π, of the respondent's level of proficiency given that x out of n events were responded to appropriately.

Bayesian procedures use prior information indicating the respondent's proficiency prior to administering the assessment, P. In the case where we would not expect the respondent to have any knowledge concerning the content domain, i.e., before learning occurs, we might assume that P=0. In the case where learning had occurred and it was reasonable to assume that the learning was about eighty percent effective, we might assume that P=0.80. Once P is determined, it is necessary to determine two parameters R and N such that R is greater than or equal to 1.0, N is greater than 2.0 and

$$P = \frac{R-1}{N-2} \text{(see: Hays, 1973). For the case where it is assumed that P=0,}$$

it is only necessary to stipulate R=1 regardless of the value of N that is always greater than 2.0, $\frac{R-1}{N-2} = \frac{1-1}{N-2} = \frac{0}{N-2} = 0 = p$. For the case where P=0.80, one might choose the parameters R=9 and N=12 where $\frac{R-1}{N-2} = \frac{9-1}{12-2} = \frac{8}{10} = 0.80 = P$. Again, for the case where P=0.80, one might choose the parameters R=81 and N=102 where:

$\frac{R-1}{N-2} = \frac{81-1}{102-2} = \frac{80}{100} = 0.80$. The question of what choice of the parameters R and N is appropriate for a given value of P is important. As shown above, for any given value of P, there are many values of R and N

that satisfy the equation, $P = \dfrac{R - 1}{N - 2}$. The particular choice of R and N
have a substantive interpretation. For a fixed value of N, the larger the value
of R the less certain we are in the assumed value of the prior proficiency, P.
For a fixed value of N, the smaller the value of R, the more certain we are
in the assumed value of P. Conversely, for a fixed value of R, the larger the
value of N, the more certainwe are about the assumed value of the prior
proficiency, P. For a fixed value of R, the smaller the value of N, the less
confident we are in the value of P. For example, ifwe felt quite certain that
a reasonable prior expectation after learning, P, is 0.80 the values of the
parameters R and N may be 9 and 12. On the other hand, if we were not
quite as certain that P should be .80, the values of R and N parameters may
be chosen to be 5 and 7 respectively, since $\dfrac{R - 1}{N - 2} = \dfrac{5 - 1}{7 - 2} = \dfrac{4}{5} = 0.80$.

Once the values of the prior probability are chosen, derive a relation
between the probability $P(\pi \mid x)$ that a proficiency value of π given that the
respondent responded correctly to x out of n events. That probability is
expressed in terms of a beta function (Freund, 1962; Harris, 1966; Hays,
1973; Novick & Lewis, 1973). The form of the equation defining that
probability in terms of an assessment of length n is represented by
$P(\pi \mid x) = B^{x+R-1} (1 - \pi)^{n+N-x-1}$;

where,

$$B \equiv \frac{(n + N + R - 1)!}{(x + R - 1)!(n + N - x - 1)!}$$

The major problem that the Bayesian approach and, in particular, this
equation will allow us to solve, is: Given that the observed proportion of
events that a particular respondent has responded appropriately is $\dfrac{x}{n}$, what
can be inferred about the value of the proportion of events, π, which would
have been responded too appropriately if the respondents were asked all of
the events associated with the content domain?

Each model is based on common assumptions concerning the nature of
the measurement process. The difference between the three models stems
from the way in which each defines a functional relationship between
content proficiency and the probability of responding correctly to a
representative event. In practice, the major differences between the models

are the particular characteristic function used by each model which results in model specific sets of events from the same bank, how the characteristic functions are used for constructing assessments, how each model assigns assessment scores to respondents based on those assessments, and how those numbers are used for assessment.

Notes

1. Many authors of statistics books have contended that the domain must be real numbers. However, most texts on the *theory* of measurement do not limit the types of numbers that can be used. The current view of time in the physical sciences is that it is either an imaginary or complex number. If such a basic concept such as time has proved that we have deluded ourselves into believing that the measurement scales upon which measurements in the physical sciences are exclusively real numbers, how can we continue to hold on to the holly grail that the measurement scales for elusive latent constructs in the behavioral sciences must be made using, exclusively, the set of real numbers.

3

Norm Referenced Assessments

Norm referenced event selection paradigms are not dependent upon the content domain for which a assessment is designed. The same event selection procedure is applied in building assessments of ability or attainment. No effort will be made to define the constructs of ability or attainment at this point. The norm referenced measurement model assumes that a latent trait continuum exists. The probability that a respondent will respond appropriately to an event is assumed to depend on the respondent's position on this dimension is known as the normal distribution density function (Nunnally, 1967; Guilford, 1954; Rice, 1893a, 1893b; Thorndike, 1971; Thorndike & Hagen, 1969; Thurstone, 1932, 1937; Yerkes, 1921). The events in a norm referenced assessment are selected so that the score distribution is "spread out as much as possible" (Harvey, 1975; Henryssen, 1971).

The process of assessment construction starts with an initial event bank. Essentially, the process involves a list of specifications or content areas to be included in the assessment. Events that appear upon inspection to be related to the specifications are included in the assessment. This is called face validity (Nunnally, 1967). The set of events forms an initial event pool, or preliminary version, and is administered to a group of subjects. The group of subjects is selected so that they are similar to the group for whom the final version of the assessment is intended.

The initial data are subjected to norm referenced psychometric screening to decide which events conform to the norm referenced model and which do not.

After the screening, events are selected for the final version of the assessment. The fact that a particular event is rejected because it does not fit the norm referenced model does not imply that the event might not be accepted for inclusion in a different kind of assessment. Equivalently, the fact that a particular event is accepted does not preclude using the event for an assessment based upon another psychometric model.

The traditional or norm referenced event selection procedures are described in detail in the literature (Gulliksen, 1950; Guilford, 1954; Nunnally, 1967; Lord & Novick, 1974). The norm referenced model makes certain assumptions concerning the distribution of total scores. Various total score statistics are useful for assessing distributional assumptions and the reliability of the total score, the homogeneity of the event composing the total score, and the error of measurement associated with a particular total score. Event screening and selection procedures as well as total score statistics are also described below.

Once an assessment has been constructed, it is put to use by administering the assessment to samples of respondents. The results of those assessment administrations need to be reported to respondents, administrators, etc. Procedures for reporting those scores will be described. As stated previously, there are certain problems with norm referenced assessments. Some of those problems are discussed in the final section of this chapter.

THE NORM REFERENCED EVENT
SCREENING TECHNIQUE

The process of screening events for norm referenced assessments involves three levels of analysis concerning the structure of the events. The first level attends to whether any poor distractors are present. The second level of analysis is concerned with event homogeneity. That is, are the events highly related to each other and, perhaps, to the same content domain? The third level of analysis is concerned with the difficulty of individual events. The intent of the third analysis phase is to insure that events in a particular spectrum of difficulty are included in the final version of the assessment. Each of the three levels of analysis is outlined in this section.

Distractor Analysis

There are usually two parts of an objective assessment event: the stem and the distractors. The stem presents the respondent with the problem situation or stimulus. The distractors represent a particular subset of all possible responses to that event. Only one distractor is considered the appropriate response to the problem represented in the stem. The proportion of respondent s who respond to each distractor is an indication of the quality of the distractors. If most respondent s choose the appropriate response, either the event is too easy or the distractors are not well constructed. If, for the most part, respondent s select two or three of the possible responses, the remaining distractors are not contributing any information and should be eliminated.

Table 3.1 consists of data obtained from a assessment devised to evaluate the effectiveness of a particular Title I project. The results were generated using a computer program developed by the author (Hashway, 1977a, 1977b, 1978a, 1978b, 1994). Consider the columns headed "percent choosing". The entries in the columns marked "omit", "A", "B, " "C", "D", and "E" are the percent of subjects who choose each distractor or did not respond to (omitted) the event.

Table 3.1:
Event and Distractor Difficulty Indices

EVENT	KEY	OMIT	A	B	C	D	E
1	C	0.0	0.0	0.0	98.0	0.0	0.0
4	B	0.0	18.0	82.0	0.0	0.0	0.0
6	A	2.0	57.0	41.0	0.0	0.0	0.0
7	B	0.0	6.0	94.0	0.0	0.0	0.0
8	B	0.0	14.0	65.0	2.0	2.0	18.0
9	A	0.0	69.0	22.0	10.0	0.0	0.0
10	C	0.0	2.0	24.0	55.0	20.0	0.0
11	D	0.0	6.0	6.0	8.0	78.0	2.0
12	B	0.0	0.0	92.0	2.0	6.0	0.0
14	B	6.0	12.0	49.0	27.0	6.0	0.0
17	A	0.0	63.0	8.0	14.0	14.0	2.0
18	D	2.0	8.0	20.0	4.0	67.0	0.0
23	D	0.0	16.0	12.0	25.0	47.0	0.0
24	B	0.0	16.0	41.0	41.0	2.0	0.0
27	C	2.0	29.0	14.0	47.0	8.0	0.0
29	B	2.0	25.0	59.0	6.0	4.0	4.0
36	E	0.0	4.0	4.0	2.0	29.0	61.0
37	B	0.0	25.0	65.0	0.0	0.0	10.0
38	B	0.0	47.0	41.0	10.0	2.0	0.0
39	C	0.0	27.0	18.0	20.0	31.0	4.0

Consider event 1 in Table 3.1, ninety-eight percent of the subjects responded with the correct answer "C". Clearly, there is a problem with this event. Either the event is too easy for the particular group; the event contains a clue to the correct answer; the other distractors are so poor that they leave the student with only one logical choice; or the distractor "C" contains a clue that makes it stand out as the correct answer. Whatever the cause, this data suggested a problem with either the event stem or the set of distractors. Such an event needs to be either modified and reassessed or discarded entirely.

Consider event 38 in Table 3.1, the percentage of students responding to distractor categories A, B, C, D, and E were 47, 41, 10, 2, and 0, respectively. No subject failed to respond to the event. Since none of the subjects omitted the event, each subject had some idea as to the content domain and, perhaps, the event stem is not faulty. However, although this event is associated with five distractors, it appears as only a two distractor event. Eighty-eight percent of the subjects responded with A or B (A was the "correct" answer). The remaining three distractors did not distract those students who did not know the "correct" answer and thus were not contributing any information about student ability or attainment. In addition, the fact that approximately equal numbers of students answered with A and B suggests a problem with either the event or the distractors. There may be a "clue" in either the event stem or one of the distractors that diverted subjects with high total scores away from the "correct" answer, or both responses "A" and "B" may be equally correct. The latter inference is substantiated based on the event's discrimination index. Event discrimination is discussed in a subsequent section of this chapter.

The correlation between whether a subject selected a particular response and the total assessment score, distractor discrimination, is an indication of the quality of the distractors. Subjects who respond correctly to an event are expected to receive higher total scores than subjects who respond incorrectly to the event. A positive correlation with the total score is expected for the correct response, and a negative correlation is expected for the distractors.

The data in Table 3.2 was generated from the responses to the assessment described previously using the author's computer program. The entries in each of the six right-hand columns are the correlation coefficients between the dichotomous distractor score (chosen/not chosen) and the total assessment score. Each of the six "distractor" categories for each event are listed. Note that "omit" is considered as a separate distractor category.

Consider event 17, the correct response is "A". The correlation coefficients between the total scores and the response categories "omit", "A", "B", "C", "D", "E" are 0.0, .53, -.52, -.08, -.08, and -.45 respectively. This pattern of correlations is reflecting the expected pattern of coefficients if all distractors are behaving properly. The subjects who either failed to respond to the event or selected the incorrect responses tended to obtain lower total scores as indicated by the negative and zero correlations. The subjects who responded correctly to the event also tended to obtain higher total scores as suggested by a response category-total score correlation of .53. Normally, such high correlation coefficients between the correct response and the total score are not expected. This event and set of distractors are exceptional. Under normal circumstances, correct response-total score correlations of .20 or higher are acceptable.

Consider event 38 in Table 3.2, the event response to total score correlation coefficients for each of the six response categories, "omit", "A", "B" "C", "D", and "E" are 0.0, .18, .03, -.13, -.45, and 0.0 respectively. The correct answer is "B". Although the correct response to total score correlation coefficient, *event discrimination*, is positive (.03), it is not appreciably so. The response to total score correlation coefficient for category "A", an incorrect answer, is positive and six times the size of "B". This would suggest that those subjects who responded incorrectly with "A" tended to receive higher total scores than those who did not answer "A". Those subjects who responded with the "correct" category, "B", did not obtain significantly higher total scores than those subjects who did not respond "correctly."

The results concerning event 38 suggest at least two possible problems. First, the event stem may contain a particular word or other source of information that is leading those students with higher total scores to believe that "A" is the correct answer. Second, the correct answer in fact may be "A" and not "B", and the event was miskeyed. If the second possibility is accurate, the event should be rekeyed and all statistics recalculated. If the first alternative is the more plausible alternative, the event should be rewritten and readministered; or, as often happens, rejected in its entirety.

Sophisticated techniques are not needed for this form of event analysis. However, the reader is warned that a quick reading of the data can lead to simplistic conclusions that do not reflect what is really going on with students' responses to an event. For example, consider event 4 in Table 4-2. The response category vs. total score correlation coefficients for the six possible distractors "omit", "A", "B", "C", "D", and "E" are 0.0, 0.17, -0.17, 0.0, 0.0, and 0.0, respectively. An examination of Table 4-1 reveals that eighteen percent (18%) of the subjects selected category "A" and eighty-two percent (82%) of the subjects selected category "B". The subjects did not respond to the other categories and the "correct" answer was considered the response coded as "B". Most of the subjects selected the response "B" and, hence, agreed that it was the correct response. However, this may be collective foolishness, and the data analyst may make an error if the data is not examined in an exploratory fashion (Mosteller & Tukey, 1977; Tukey, 1978). The response category to total score correlation corresponding to the "incorrect" category A of .17 suggests that subjects who selected this response tended to obtain *higher* total scores than subjects who selected the correct response, "B". The response to total score correlation coefficient for category B was -0.17. Subjects who selected the "correct" response tended to receive lower total scores than those subjects who selected the incorrect response. It appears that this event may be miskeyed, or that the event is very ambiguous. In either case the event is in need of further examination.

Table 3.2:
Correlation of the Response Category Scores with the Total Scores

EVENT	KEY	OMIT	A	B	C	D	E
1	C	0.0	0.0	-0.45	0.45	0.0	0.0
4	B	0.0	0.17	-0.17	0.0	0.0	0.0
6	A	-0.14	0.32	-0.28	0.0	0.0	0.0
7	B	0.0	-0.19	0.19	0.0	0.0	0.0
8	B	0.0	-0.31	0.42	0.00	-0.06	-0.23
9	A	0.0	0.23	-0.07	-0.25	0.0	0.0
10	C	0.0	-0.20	0.0	0.25	-0.24	0.0
11	D	0.0	0.30	-0.36	-0.27	0.36	0.06
12	B	0.0	0.0	-0.05	0.19	-0.06	0.0
14	B	-0.03	-0.23	0.18	0.04	-0.12	0.0
17	A	0.0	0.53	-0.52	-0.08	0.08	-0.45
18	D	-0.04	-0.03	-0.03	-0.29	0.41	0.0
23	D	0.0	-0.27	0.06	-0.24	0.37	0.0
24	B	0.0	-0.21	0.13	0.16	-0.49	0.0
27	C	-0.10	-0.20	-0.23	0.37	-0.01	0.0
29	B	-0.10	-0.25	0.63	-0.40	-0.03	-0.47
36	E	0.0	-0.34	-0.07	-0.49	-0.10	0.40
37	B	0.0	-0.27	0.40	0.0	0.0	-0.24
38	B	0.0	0.18	0.03	-0.13	-0.45	0.0
39	C	0.0	0.02	-0.35	-0.02	0.23	0.15

The technique of distractor examination described above involves examining the proportion of subjects who responded to each possible response to total score correlation to detect possible faulty events. Once a distractor analysis is performed and events are eliminated from the event pool because of possible structural flaws, the remaining events are subjected to further analysis. The second level of analysis, outlined below, determines which of the remaining events fit the norm referenced psychometric model.

Homogeneity and Event Discrimination

Traditionally, there are three major areas of concern in screening events: homogeneity, internal consistency, and the maximal dispersion of assessment scores. A group of events is homogeneous if the subjects who respond correctly to an event respond correctly to all other events in the group and receive high total assessment scores; and, if the subjects who respond incorrectly to an event tend also to respond incorrectly to all other events in the group and receive low total assessment scores. A group of events is internally consistent if the probability of successfully responding to an event is a monotonic function of a subject's position on the same latent trait dimension. If subjects with similar positions on the same latent trait dimension respond in similar ways to all events, the group of events is said to be internally consistent. If a assessment is composed of events selected so that the total score variance is larger than for any other set of events, the assessment is said to have maximal total score dispersion (Lord & Novick, 1974).

Event homogeneity can be measured with an event discrimination index. The event discrimination index is, most often, the correlation coefficient between the obtained event scores (correct/incorrect) and the total assessment score. If an external criterion is available, the discrimination index can be defined as the correlation of the event score and the external criterion score. As the discrimination indices of events increase, the resulting assessment becomes more homogeneous (Ahmann & Glock, 1967). The more homogeneous an assessment, the greater the likelihood that the events and the total score are assessing one, rather than more than one, latent trait dimension. If an event pool contains events that are not homogeneous, the discrimination indices of the events can be used to detect those events that, when combined, form a more homogeneous subset of events (Ahmann & Glock, 1967).

For a assessment to result in a reliable assessment score, it is necessary for the events composing the assessment to be internally consistent. Estimates of assessment reliability based upon internal consistency of events are called "internal reliability estimates". Consider a assessment composed of events such that the students respond to any pair of events inconsistently. Since they respond inconsistently to any pair of events they will probably respond inconsistently to any single event if the assessment is administered a second time. There is a large random component in the responses to those events. Consequently, total scores using those events will be unreliable. A assessment is considered reliable when similar total scores are obtained from two distinct administrations of the assessment to the same individual.

There are various indicators of the degree to which a assessment is internally consistent. These indicators are internal consistency reliability estimates. The indices or estimates usually vary from a low of zero to a maximum of one. The higher the internal consistency reliability estimate, the greater the internal consistency of the assessment.

Kuder-Richardson Formula 20. One index of internal consistency reliability is the Kuder-Richardson Formula 20 (KR-20) (Nunnally, 1967). This index is calculated using the number of events composing the assessment, the mean total assessment score, and the total assessment score variance. The KR-20 reliability index is probably the most easily calculated and least accurate of the reliability estimates. It is not directly related to the patterns that may exist between event scores, but it is perhaps the most global estimate of internal consistency. The formula for KR-20 is given by:

$$r_{20} = \frac{N \sigma_x^2 - \bar{x} + \sum p^2}{N \sigma_x^2} \left(\frac{n}{n-1} \right)$$

Split Half Reliability. A less global index of internal consistency, in the sense that it is more sensitive to variations between events, is the split-half reliability index (Gulliksen, 1950). The events are divided into two assessments. The split-half reliability is the correlation coefficient between the total assessment scores obtained from each half. There is a problem associated with using the split-half reliability index, however. Different indices can be obtained depending upon how the events that composed the halves were selected. The correlation coefficient between two halves constructed by randomly assigning events to halves may be a function of the randomization procedure.

Coefficient Alpha. An index of internal consistency that is not as global as KR-20 and does not possess the problem of the split half index is the Kuder-Richardson Formula 21 (KR-21). That formula is:

$$r_{21} = \frac{n \sigma_x^2 - n \bar{x} + \bar{x}^2}{n \sigma_x^2} \left(\frac{n}{n-1} \right)$$. For binary events, KR-21 is equivalent

to Cronbach's alpha coefficient (Anastasi, 1976; Cronbach, 1951; Guilford, 1954; Gulliksen, 1950; Nunnally, 1967), the mean of the reliability estimates obtained over all possible split halves (Guilford, 1954; Lord and Novick,

1974; Nunnally, 1967).

Hoyt's (1941) Reliability Index. Hoyt's reliability index is based on a statistical model which is somewhat different from the Cronbach and Kuder-Richardson indices. This index is based on an analysis of variance model. The procedure partitions the total score variance into contributions due to events and those due to subjects (Alexander, 1947; Guilford, 1954; Hoyt, 1941; Kaitz, 1945; Thorndike, 1971). An example of this partitioning is shown in Table 3.3 where the greatest source of variance was between items indicating that the assessment events were not consistent, perhaps assessing different content areas, and should be carefully examined.

Table 3.3:
Partitioning Variance by the Hoyt Method

Source	SS	df	Mean Square	F-Ratio
Individuals	47.67	50	0.9533	5.7000
Events	116.15	49	14.1732	
Error	393.21	2351	0.1673	
Total	557.03	2450	Hoyt Reliability	0.824

Woodbury's (1951) Tau. The reliability index is a function of the average of the reliabilities of all events that form the assessment, and the number of events included in the assessment. An index of reliability that is invariant to variations in the number of events that form a particular assessment would be useful for comparing two or more assessments consisting of different numbers of events. Woodbury (1951) introduces the idea of *standard length* with a parameter he calls tau, $\tau = \dfrac{n(1-r)}{r}$. Tau varies from zero when the reliability coefficient is 1.0, increases as the reliability decreases, and is unbounded from above. The smaller the value of Woodbury's (1951) tau coefficient, the more reliable the assessment. Tau is n times the ratio of exogenous to true score variance. Since $r = \dfrac{n}{n+\tau}$, $\lim_{\tau \to 0} r = 1$ *and* $\lim_{\tau \to \infty} r = 0$. Since Woodbury's (1951) tau coefficient is functionally related to the reliability, there is no advantage to tau over the reliability coefficient as an indicator of homogeneity.

Lovenger's (1947) Coefficient. A rival to the reliability coefficient as an index of event homogeneity is Lovenger's (1947) coefficient of homogeneity. Lovenger's (1947) coefficient is designed to vary from 0.0 when a assessment is completely heterogeneous to 1.0 when a assessment is completely homogeneous. This coefficient of homogeneity is found using:

$$H_t \doteq \frac{N\left(\sum X_t^2 - \sum X_t\right) + \sum R_i^2 - \left(\sum X_t\right)^2}{2N\left(\sum iR_i - \sum X_t\right) + \sum R_i^2 - \left(\sum X_t\right)^2} =$$

$$\frac{\sigma_x^2 + n\sigma d^2}{2[\bar{I} - \bar{X}] + \sigma_d^2 + n^2 \bar{d}^2 - \bar{X}^2}$$

where H_t = coefficient of homogeneity; N = number of examinees

X_t = total-assessment score

R_i = number of correct responses to i*th* event

i = ordinal number of event where events are arranged in increasing order of difficulty.

n = the number of items; σ_x^2 = the total score variance;

σ_x^2 = the total score variance; $\bar{I}$ = average ordinal number $\sum i\, d_i$; and, $\bar{d}$ = the mean item difficulty.

Lovenger's (1947) coefficient is often much lower than any of the other reliability coefficients reported for the same data. It has been reported that assessments with Kuder-Richardson reliabilities as high as .90 have exhibited homogeneity indices as low as .30 or lower (Lindquist, 1951). Guilford (1954) suggests that the apparent consensus is that the goal of approximating completely homogeneous assessments is a will-o'-the-wisp.

Many assessments that exhibit low values of Lovenger's (1947) homogeneity coefficient may be highly reliable and useful (Guilford, 1954).

Discrimination Theory

The reliability and homogeneity theories assume that obtained scores bear a linear relationship to the latent trait dimension. Ferguson (1949) and Thurlow (1950), the primary exponents of discrimination theory, contend that a linear relationship has not been established and is not necessary. They contend that the rank ordering of individuals should be the chief goal of assessments, and that assessments should be aimed at maximizing discriminations between individuals (Ferguson, 1949; Guilford, 1954; Thurlow, 1950). Individuals are maximally discriminated when no two subjects obtain the same score and are minimally discriminated when all subjects receive identical scores.

Ferguson's (1949) discrimination coefficient is the ratio of the number of discriminations a assessment provides to the maximum number a assessment with the same number of events could provide. The coefficient varies from a score of zero for minimally discriminating assessments to a value of 1.0 for maximally discriminating assessments. It is greatest when the total assessment score distribution is rectangular. The coefficient of discrimination for bimodal or normal total assessment score distributions is smaller than if the total assessment score distribution was rectangular. The formula for the coefficient is

$$\delta = \frac{(n+1)\left(N^2 - \sum f_i^2\right)}{n\,N^2}$$

where δ = coefficient of discrimination, N = number of individuals in sample, f_i = frequency of each score, and n = number of events on the assessment.

An example of each of the previously described reliability estimates is shown in Table 3.4. These indices were derived from the forty event assessment described previously. The author's computer program, *ANALYSIS, V. 14,* was used to compute the indices (Hashway, 1977a, 1977b, 1978, 1994). As seen in Table 3.4, although each of the internal consistency reliability indices mentioned above results in somewhat different numbers, the results are similar. A high internal consistency estimate obtained using one method will usually imply a high internal consistency estimate using another method. The only possible exception, as previously mentioned (Guilford, 1954) is Lovenger's coefficient.

Table 3.4.:
Examples of Homogeneity Estimates

Hoyt Reliability	0.824	KR-21 Reliability	0.781
Cronbach's Alpha	0.831	Woodbury's Tau	10.121
Lovenger's Coefficient of Homogeneity	0.015		
Ferguson's Coefficient of Discrimination	0.952		

EVENT DISCRIMINATION

The reliability of an assessment is closely related to the correlations of the event scores with each other, and with the total score. The more homogeneous a assessment, the greater its internal consistency and the larger the internal consistency estimates. The correlation between event and total scores is defined as *event discrimination*. The higher the discrimination index of each of the events in a assessment, the greater the homogeneity and the larger the internal consistency of the assessment. R. L. Ebel (1954) contends that events with discrimination indices less than .20 should not be included in a assessment. Events with discrimination indices above .20 should be considered for inclusion. Events with discrimination indices above .40 are considered very good events in the sense that they discriminate between adjacent positions on the latent trait dimension (Ahmann & Glock, 1967; Ebel, 1954).

Consider the event discrimination indices shown in Table 3.5, events 4, 12, and 39 are associated with the discrimination indices -.173, -.048, and -.020 respectively. Since these events are negatively correlated with the total score, it can be inferred that subjects who respond *correctly* to these events obtain *lower* total assessment scores. Subjects who respond *incorrectly* to these events obtain *higher* total assessment scores. Such events would not be included in the final version of a norm referenced assessment.

Consider events 4, 7, 12, 14, 24, 36, and 39, each of these events is associated with discrimination indices less than Ebel's (1954) nominal value of .20. The responses to these events are not considered consistent with the other events in the event pool. The inclusion of these events with the other events in one assessment would tend to reduce the reliability, and, consequently, the internal consistency of that assessment. These events would be rejected and not included in the final version of a norm referenced assessment.

Table 3.5:
Event Difficulty And Discrimination Indices

EVENT	DIFFICULTY	DISCRIMINATION
1	58.0	0.453
4	82.4	-0.173
6	56.9	0.321
7	94.1	0.191
8	64.7	0.419
9	68.6	0.229
10	54.9	0.250
11	78.4	0.361
12	92.2	-0.048
14	49.0	0.178
17	62.7	0.527
18	66.7	0.408
23	47.1	0.367
24	41.2	0.131
27	47.1	0.373
29	58.8	0.633
37	64.7	0.395
38	41.2	0.026
39	19.6	-0.020

EVENT DIFFICULTY

Another statistic commonly used to screen norm referenced assessment events is called *event difficulty*. The difficulty index of an event is the proportion of subjects who respond *correctly* to the event. Assessments that contain events whose difficulty levels are all exactly 0.50 have a maximum KR-20 internal consistency reliability index. A compromise between maximum reliability and maximum spread of the observed score distribution is presented as a general rule of thumb. Ebel (1954) says that events should be considered for inclusion in an assessment if their difficulty indices are between .40 and .70. These general selection criteria should result in a assessment with a moderately high internal consistency reliability and a reasonably dispersed observed score distribution.

Consider the events shown in Table 3.5. Events 6, 8, 9, 10, 14, 17, 18, 23, 24, 27, 29, 36, 37, and 38 exhibit event difficulty indices between a low of .40 and a high of .70. The events with difficulty levels between .40 and .70 are considered in the appropriate difficulty range and are candidates for inclusion in the final form of a norm referenced assessment. The events with difficulty indices less than .40 are considered difficult and events with difficulty indices above .70 are considered easy events. Events with difficulty indices either less than .40 or greater than .70 are not considered reflecting the appropriate difficulty range and are not candidates for inclusion in the final form of a norm referenced assessment.

In summary, events selected for inclusion in a norm referenced assessment require certain psychometric properties. These properties ensure that the resultant assessment is homogeneous and internally consistent, and possesses a reasonably well dispersed total score distribution. The point - biserial correlation between the total score and the scores obtained by the subjects in the calibration sample in response to an event should be greater than 0.20. The proportion of subjects in the calibration who respond correctly to an event considered for selection should be between 0.40 and 0.70. For example, of the forty events that compose the previously described assessment, only sixteen events or forty percent (40%) of the events satisfied the event discrimination and difficulty criteria (cf. Table 3.5).

Total Score Statistics

Beyond being internally consistent or homogeneous, norm referenced assessments should also result in scores that are normally distributed. Once the events from the preliminary pool are screened for homogeneity, the assessment constructor can decide if the total assessment score based on the remaining events satisfies the distributional criteria. Statistics by which characteristics of the total score distribution can be detected are described in this section.

DISTRIBUTIONAL STATISTICS

One index that is useful for detecting distributional departures from normality is called the *skewness* index (Bock, 1975; Ferguson, 1971;

Freund, 1962; Harris, 1966; McNemar, 1962). If the coefficient of skewness is significantly less than zero the total score distribution exhibits a greater proportion of low scores than expected from a normal distribution of total scores with the same mean and variance. If the coefficient of skewness is significantly greater than 0 the distribution of total scores exhibits a greater proportion of high scores than expected from a normal distribution with the same mean and variance. The significance of the departure from zero of the observed coefficient of skewness can be ascertained by consulting a table of percentage points for the skewness coefficient, that is, tables found in Pearson and Hartley (1966) if the sample size is greater than 24 and D'Agostino and Tietjen (1966) for sample sizes between 5 and 35.

Another index that is useful for detecting departures from normality is called *kurtosis*. Values of the sample kurtosis coefficient which are significantly greater than zero suggest that the distribution is more peaked with higher tails than expected from a normal distribution. The significance of the departure of the sample kurtosis coefficient from zero can be ascertained by consulting the table of percentage points for the sample kurtosis coefficient (Pearson & Hartley, 1966; D'Agostino & Tietjen, 1971). Bock (1975, p. 162) describes a procedure for converting the deviation of the sample kurtosis from zero to a z-score. The formulas for doing so follow.

$$b_1 = \frac{s^2}{\sigma^3}$$

$$z_s = \frac{s}{\sigma} \sqrt{\frac{(N+1)(N+3)}{6\sigma(N-2)}} \quad and$$

$$b_2 = \frac{k}{\sigma^2}$$

$$z_k = \left(\frac{k}{\sigma^2} - 3 + \frac{6}{N+1} \right) \sqrt{\frac{(N+1)^2(N+3)(N+5)}{24N(N-2)(N-3)}}$$

The significance of the kurtosis coefficient is decided by using the z-score calculated via Bock's (1975) formula and a table of the percentage points of the normal distribution.

Two additional statistics are of use in learning the nature of the total score distribution. The first is the U-statistic proposed by David, Hartley, and Pearson (1954). The U-statistic is the ratio of the sample range to the sample standard deviation, weighted by the number of cases. It is given by the formula:

$$U = \frac{max(x) - min(x)}{N \, \hat{\sigma}}$$

$\hat{\sigma}$ is the unbiased estimate of the variance in the same sample

$$\hat{\sigma} = \sigma \sqrt{\frac{N}{N - 1}}$$

The U-statistic is especially sensitive to outliers (Bock, 1975). Percentage points for U are given in Pearson & Hartley (1966). The second additional statistic is Geary's (1947) A-statistic. Geary's (1947) A-statistic is the ratio of the mean deviation to the standard deviation of total assessment score, $\frac{\sum \left| X_i - \bar{X} \right|}{N \, \sigma}$. According to Bock (1975, p. 163), it is sensitive to kurtosis. Percentage points for Geary's (1947) A-statistic are given in Pearson & Hartley (1966).

The statistics described in this section can be obtained via hand calculation. However, with reasonably large data sets, hand calculation is both laborious and time consuming. To reduce the mundane to the sublime, this author has prepared and published a computer program, called *ANALYSIS [V. 14]* (Hashway, 1994), which calculates the values of all indices described in this section and organizes the output into descriptive tabular formats and many histograms and graphs which ease the exploratory analysis of assessment data (Hashway, 1977a, 1977b, 1978, 1994).

STANDARD ERROR OF MEASUREMENT

As previously stated, it is assumed that there exists a latent trait dimension underlying a subject's responses to a particular assessment. In addition, it is assumed that each subject can be mapped onto one and only one position, t, on that dimension. That position is assumed to be the subject's true score, τ. The true score is operationalized as the mean value of the scores obtained from an infinite number of administrations of the same assessment to the same subject. The observed score, x, is assumed to be an estimate of the true score, τ, corresponding to that measurement. The fundamental measurement model assumes that the probability of obtaining a given observed score, x, from a subject whose true score is τ can be found. The relation defining the association by which the probability can be found is: $x = \tau + \xi$ where ξ is an error term that is normally distributed with a mean of zero and a standard deviation equal to the standard error of measurement, σ_ξ. Two methods for calculating σ_ξ are described below.

There are two theories concerning the procedure used to calculate the standard error of measurement. One is called *classical* and the other *recent*. The recent theory is deliberately *not* called the modern theory. To call the theory most recently discussed in the literature "modern" runs the risk of implying that the recent theory has *superseded* the older or classical theory. This is not true. The newer theory has only recently gained some degree of acceptance and has not superseded the classical theory. In addition, the most recent theory concerning the standard error is exclusively concerned with measurements obtained from achievement assessments and has not been extended to other types of measurements. More often than not, when the standard error of measurement is calculated, the classical approach is employed.

There are two major differences between the classical and recent models. The classical model assumes that the standard error of measurement is constant over all possible values that can be obtained for a particular measurement. For instance, assume that the value of the standard error of measurement for a particular instrument is calculated to be 2.3 for a assessment with two possible values of the measurement (5 and 10). If a particular subject obtains a score of 5, the standard error of measurement associated with the distribution of error corresponding to that particular subject's score is 2.3. If another subject obtained a score of 10 using the same instrument, the standard error of measurement corresponding to the score of 10 is also 2.3. The more recent model assumes that the standard error could vary with the value of the measurement. Measurement nearer the center of the scale of possible measurements would be assigned lower values of the standard error than measurements toward the extremes of the measurement scales. For example, if the possible values that can be assumed by any particular measurement are 2, 5, 6, 7, and 10, the standard errors corresponding to these measurements might be 1.6, .78, .21, .65, and 2.6, respectively. The classical model assumes that the value of the standard error, once calculated, is constant over all observations. The classical model of the standard error is also directly associated with the reliability of an instrument. The idea of reliability of norm referenced assessments was discussed previously in this chapter.

Once the value of the reliability index is known, the value of the standard error is easily calculated using the classical model. The standard error of measurement, SE, is defined classically, in terms of the reliability coefficient, r , and the standard deviation of the population of observed scores, s.

$$\sigma_\xi = s \sqrt{1 - r} \qquad\qquad 3.1$$

Assume that the reliability of a particular instrument is .91 and the standard deviation of the population of observed scores is 15. The value of the standard error is easily calculated by substituting the values of the reliability index (.91) and the standard deviation (15) into equation 3.1.

$$\sigma_\xi = 15\sqrt{1 - 0.91} = 15\sqrt{.09} = 15(0.3) = 4.5 \qquad 3.2$$

The value of the standard error (4.5) calculated above is assumed to be constant despite the value of any particular measurement. If the values of observed scores are 0, 22, 88, or 500 the standard error of measurement associated with each of these scores is 4.5.

The standard error of measurement is classically described as a function of the reliability of measurement and the standard deviation of the population of observed scores. The value of the standard error or measurement is assumed, classically, to be constant for all measurements. The recent theory departs from the classical theory in that the standard error of measurement is not assumed to be constant over all observations.

One recent formulation for the standard error of measurement is proposed by Lord (1952, 1957). A simplified form is presented here. Assume that a assessment composed of N events is administered to a particular individual and that individual responded correctly to X out of the N events. Therefore, an estimate of the proportion of events that a subject would answer correctly if allowed to respond to all events associated with the domain of the assessment is simply $\frac{X}{N}$. Since $\frac{X}{N}$ is a proportion, the standard error of that proportion is: $\sqrt{\dfrac{X(N-X)}{N^3}}$. To convert the standard error from the world of proportions back into the world of total scores, one must multiply the standard error of the proportion by the number of events composing the assessment. The standard error of measurement

$\sigma_\xi(X)$, associated with a particular observed score, X, is $\sqrt{\dfrac{X(N-X)}{N}}$.

Classically, the standard error of measurement is described by

$s\sqrt{1-r}$, implying that the standard error is numerically the same

regardless of the observed score. The formula, $\sigma_\xi(X) = \sqrt{\dfrac{X(N-X)}{N}}$, results

in a fundamentally different implication. By writing the standard error as
$\sigma_\xi(X)$, it is implied that the error associated with a particular assessment
score is a function of that assessment score. The standard error associated
with obtained scores at the extremes of the assessment score range (X = 0 or
X = N) is identically zero. In addition, the standard error is at maximum at
midrange (X = $\dfrac{N}{2}$). It is important to note that the standard error of
measurement is a measure of the error associated with a *particular*
measurement. As such, it should be reported with *each* measurement.

The next section is devoted to a discussion of assessment score reporting
schemes, including procedures for reporting standard errors.

REPORTING NORM REFERENCED
ASSESSMENT SCORES

As pointed out above, two results are obtained from the administration of a
assessment: the observed assessment score and the standard error of
measurement. This section describes various ways in which assessment
scores and standard errors can be reported. Two basic types of reporting
schemes are outlined: *Linearly Transformed Scores* and *Percentile Ranks*.
A separate section is devoted to a discussion of each reporting scheme.

An Understanding Concerning $\sigma_\xi(X)$

σ_ξ and $\sigma_\xi(X)$ symbolize the two types of standard errors of measurement
described previously. The major difference between the two is that σ_ξ is
assumed to have one value for all possible observed assessment scores, X,

and that $\sigma_\xi(X)$ *may* take on different values for each observed assessment score. The fixed standard error model yielding SE as an estimate is a special case of the variable standard error model yielding $\sigma_\xi(X)$ as an estimate of the standard error.

For the moment, we will assume that there is no particular formula associated with SE(X); but, SE(X) symbolizes the idea that the standard error of measurement *may* vary with the observed score. The trivial case of $\sigma_\xi(X)$ is when $\sigma_\xi(X)$ is equal to a constant function for all X. Therefore, the constant standard error model is a special case of the variable standard error model where $\sigma_\xi(X)=\sigma_\xi$ for all possible observed scores, X. The variable standard error model (VSEM) is the most general of the two models. The fixed standard error model (FSEM) is a special case of the VSEM. Therefore, from this point in this chapter, assume that the standard error of measurement is a function of the observed assessment score, that is, VSEM. All statements made concerning the transformation of VSEM scores can be applied to FSEM scores by using the simple equation $\sigma_\xi(X)=\sigma_\xi$ in all formulas.

Linearly Transformed Scores

Linearly transformed scores are precisely what the name implies. The observed scores, X, are transformed to a new set of scores, y, such that the graph of the transformed vs. observed scores is a straight line. Assume that the set of observed scores has a mean of x and a standard deviation of s_x. Assume further that it is desired to transform these scores so that the set of transformed scores, y, has a mean or average of y and a standard deviation of s_y. Each raw score, x, is transformed to the corresponding transformed score, y, by using the first equation and the standard error of y, $\sigma_\xi(y)$, can be calculated using the second equation.

$$y = \frac{s_y}{s_x} x + \overline{y} - \frac{s_y}{s_x} \overline{x} \qquad\qquad 3.3$$

$$\sigma_\xi(y) = \frac{s_y}{s_x} \sigma_\xi(x) \qquad\qquad 3.4$$

For example, assume that a particular set of raw scores had a mean, x of 15 and a standard deviation, S, of 20. Further, it is desired to transform the scores so that the average of the transformed scores, y, is 1000 and the standard deviation is 100. By substitution into equations 3.3 and 3.4 we have:

$$y = \frac{100}{20} x + 1000 - \frac{100}{20}(15) = 5x + 1000 - (5)(15) =$$

$$5x + 925 \ \ and \ \ \sigma_\xi(y) = \frac{100}{20} \sigma_\xi(X) = 5\sigma_\xi(X)$$

For a particular observed score of 20 (X=20) and an associated standard error of 5 ($\sigma_\xi(X)=\sigma_\xi(20)=5$) the transformed score and standard error is found by substitution into each of the previous equations respectively.

That gives

$$y = 5x + 925 = 5(20) + 925 = 100 + 925 = 1025$$

$$and \ \ \sigma_\xi(y) = 5\sigma_\xi(X) = 5(5) = 25.$$

There are essentially three commonly used transformed scores. These are called *z-scores*, *T-scores* and *I.Q.-type* scores. Z-score distributions have a mean of 0.0 and a standard deviation of 1.0. T-scores have a mean of 50 and a standard deviation of 10. Standardized scores have a mean of 100 and a standard deviation of 15. The equations for the transformation of observed scores with a mean of x and a standard deviation of s_x to Z, T, and I.Q. scales, and also equations for calculating the standard error of the transformed score, are shown below.

Transformation to Z-Scores:

$$y = \left(\frac{1.0}{s_x} \right) X - \left(\frac{1.0}{s_x} \right) x \ \ and \ \ \sigma_\xi(y) = \left(\frac{1.0}{s_x} \right) \sigma_\xi(x)$$

Transformation to T-Scores:

$$y = \left(\frac{10}{s_x} \right) X + 50 - \left(\frac{10}{s_x} \right) x \ \ and \ \ \sigma_\xi(y) = \left(\frac{10}{s_x} \right) \sigma_\xi(x)$$

Transformation to I.Q. Scores:

$$y = \left(\frac{15}{s_x} \right) X + 100 - \left(\frac{15}{s_x} \right) x \;\; and \;\; \sigma_\xi(y) = \left(\frac{15}{s_x} \right) \sigma_\xi(x)$$

Given a set of observed scores, x, with a given average, x, and standard deviation, s , that set of observed scores can be transformed to Z, T, and I.Q. Type scores by substituting observed values into these equations.

Percentile Rank

Percentile rank is, perhaps, the simplest assessment score to interpret. A percentile rank is, normally, the proportion of subjects in the *assessment calibration group* that attained a assessment score less than or equal to a particular observed score. For example, assume that a fifty event assessment originally calibrated on a national sample was administered to a group of students. A particular student obtained a score of 45. Upon examination of the data obtained from the calibration sample, it was found that ninety-five percent (95%) of the students in the original calibration sample obtained an observed score less than or equal to 45. Then, the student's percentile rank is 95.

Reporting by percentile rank must allow for the calibration sample. If the sample of students for which the assessment is intended is not very similar to the group with which the assessment was calibrated, the percentile scores based on calibration group data are meaningless. In fact, the event difficulty and discrimination indices calculated using the calibration group data may very well indicate that the assessment events do not fit the norm referenced model within that group.

In most cases, it is more informative from the point of view of curriculum development to report percentile ranks based on the particular group for which the assessment was administered. For example, assume that a assessment was administered to all students enrolled in a particular Title I program. A particular student obtained a assessment score of 23. After examining all of the assessment scores obtained from that Title I group, it was found that forty-three percent (43%) of the students in that group obtained assessment scores less than or equal to 23. Therefore, that student's within-group percentile rank would be 43.

There is at least one major problem with reporting within group percentile ranks. The percentile ranks are not comparable across groups. An observed score of 23 may correspond to a percentile rank of 43 for a Title I group and a percentile rank of 93 for a more advanced Title I group. In addition, unless a different assessment is constructed for each group by performing an event analysis using the data from that group, assessment events may not satisfy the norm referenced criteria. As may be surmised at this point, the standard error of measurement is not easy to calculate for percentile ranks. In fact, there are serious limitations to its use because of the fact that percentile ranks are bounded from below and above. Also, proportions obey a distributional model which is fundamentally different from the model associated with the assessment scores from which they are derived.

PROBLEMS RELATED TO
NORM REFERENCED ASSESSMENTS

This section discusses two problems that are purported to exist with assessments composed of events that are screened using the norm referenced procedure previously described. They are problems which the Rasch model purportedly does not possess, and problems which have arisen within the context of criterion referenced measurement.

All assessments, regardless of event selection procedure, assume that there exists some latent trait dimension which underlies the probability of responding correctly to an event or group of events. A assessment score maps subjects onto a scale considered to be equivalent to the latent trait dimension. A person is assumed to occupy one and only one position on that dimension at any one point in time. Therefore, two assessments constructed from an event pool calibrated on the same set of individuals and considered to map subjects onto the same dimension should result in the same or similar scores for the same individual. Wright (1967) has considered this property to be fundamental to what he calls "objective mental measurement".

It is well known that assessments constructed by traditional or norm referenced means are usually highly correlated. The fact that two assessments are highly correlated implies only that the assessments order subjects in similar ways. There is a difference between similar orderings of subjects and similar scores for the same subject. Similar ordering of subjects means that the position of a particular subject relative to the other subjects in a group is not a function of the assessment used to obtain the subject's score. Similar scores for the same subject mean that the scores derived for the same subject from two or more assessments are not significantly different. Assessments constructed using norm referenced psychometric techniques and representing the same content domain may order subjects in the same way. In most cases, two norm referenced assessments do not result in similar scores for the same subject. The results obtained from traditionally constructed assessments do not correspond to what Wright (1967) has called the event free property. That is, an individual score on a latent train dimension is independent of the particular set of events used to measure that position.

The applicability of a norm referenced assessment to a particular group of individuals is related to the degree to which the group corresponds to the original group used to calibrate the norm referenced assessment. A assessment whose events were screened using an upper middle class sample of subjects may not be applicable to lower class subjects. A assessment designed to assess achievement in advanced calculus whose events were screened using a sample of high school seniors is not applicable to college physics majors. If a norm referenced assessment is administered to a group that does not correspond to the characteristics of the calibration group, the amount of confidence that can be placed on the score originating from that assessment is zero. The scores obtained from norm referenced assessments are not sample free.

The fact that the score obtained from a traditionally constructed, norm referenced assessment is a function of the events used to construct the assessment, and that the meaning that can be associated with a score on an assessment is a function of the group used to calibrate the assessment, has led Wright (1967) to term norm referenced assessment scores ''rubber yardsticks.''

There is another problem with using norm referenced screening procedures which is not associated with the resulting assessment scores. This problem is associated with the use of any psychometric screening procedure at all. We have pointed out that the criteria used to determine whether or not an event is included in the final version of a norm-referenced assessment is based upon certain desired properties of the resulting assessment scores.

Criterion referenced assessment specialists have raised a serious question concerning eliminating events on the basis of certain distributional assumptions (Anderson, 1972; Andrews & Hecht, 1976; Brennan, 1974; Buros, 1977; Cattell, 1944; Cook, 1941; Cox & Vargas, 1966; Cronbach, 1971; Davis, 1971; Ebel, 1961, 1962, 1970; Glaser & Nitko, 1970, 1971; Hively & Page, 1968; Skager, 1978; Starch, 1918; Tiegs, 1931, 1939). The major requirement of a assessment is that the events composing the assessment reflect a *representative sampling* from the event domain. The term "representative" means that the events included in the assessment reflect the *content* inherent in the event domain. Random sampling from a large event domain would be ideal. Representiveness seems to be all that is necessary for practical purposes. The imposition of psychometric criteria on event inclusion may seriously restrict or bias the set of events which are included in the assessment. Therefore, if some psychometric event selection criteria are employed, the *proficiency* estimate obtained from the event satisfying those criteria will be biased. When a particular psychometric criterion is used, the resulting *proficiency* estimate is constrained to proficiency relative to the subset of events satisfying those psychometric criteria as opposed to proficiency relative to the entire domain of events and hence the unrestricted content domain.

VARIANCE AND TREATMENT SENSITIVITY

Precisely what characteristics are necessary in order to guarantee that an assessment will maximally discriminate between individuals. To solve this problem, the criterion of *maximum discrimination between individuals* must be defined. Initially, for the purposes of this book, this criterion will be defined as the sum of squared differences of the total scores between people who are administered the assessment. The summation is taken over all individuals in the norming population, or sample, where x_i^T and x_2^T are the total scores obtained by subjects i and j, N is the number of cases in the norming population, and the index of maximum sensitivity is:

$$M = \sum_{j=1}^{N} \sum_{i<j}^{N} [f(x_i^T) - f(x_i^T)]^2 .$$

Two interesting questions come to mind. (1) What type of function of the total scores, f, will extrimize *M* with respect to the range ($-\infty$, x_N] ? (2) Given the sigma algebra, $\mathfrak{C}^\infty$, of all differentiable functions of the total assessment score on the interval ($-\infty$, ∞), does there exist a function in this algebra which extrimizes, and in particular maximizes, the dispersion criteria, *M*?

Theorem A: Given a fixed range of scores, $(-\infty, x_N]$ where x_N is the maximum total score obtained from a sample of size N, there does not exist a function, f(x), which extrimizes *M*.

Proof: Let g(x) symbolize the probability density function for the total test scores on the interval $(-\infty, x_N]$. The dispersion equation can be written as follows, where the integrals are assumed to be of the Lebague-Stieltjes variety.

$$M = \int_{-\infty}^{x_N} f^2(t)g(t)\,dt - \int_{-\infty}^{x_N} \int^u f(u)f(v)g(u)g(v)\,du\,dv.$$

The fundamental theorem of integral calculus can be used to determine the first and second derivatives of *M*,

$$\frac{\partial M}{\partial x} = f^2 g - fg \int_{-\infty}^{x_N} f(u)g(u)\,du \text{ and}$$

$$\frac{\partial^2 M}{\partial x^2} = 2fgf' + f^2 g' - (f'g - g'f) \int_{-\infty}^{x_N} f(u)g(u)\,du$$

$$- f^2 g^2$$

The solution of the differential equation $\dfrac{\partial M}{\partial x} = 0$ is $f(x) = e^{G(x)}$, where

$$G(x) = \int^x g(u)\,du .$$ G(x) is the cumulative distribution function

of x. Substitution of this result into the equation for the second derivative of the dispersion criteria $\{\dfrac{\partial^2 M}{\partial x^2}\}$, and a little algebra, yields $\dfrac{\partial M}{\partial x} = 0$.

Therefore, there is no function of x_N on the desired interval which extrimizes the dispersion criteria.

Theorem B: Given the sigma algebra, $\mathfrak{C}^{\infty}$, of all differentiable functions on $(-\infty, \infty)$, there does not exist an element of $\mathfrak{C}^{\infty}$ which maximizes the dispersion criteria, M.

Proof: As in Theorem A, let g(x) represent the probability density function of x on $(-\infty, \infty)$. The equations describing the dispersion criteria, and its' first and second derivatives with respect to the total score function, f, over the sigma algebra, $\mathfrak{C}^{\infty}$, in integral (Lebague-Stieltjes) form are:

$$\frac{\partial M}{\partial f} = \frac{f^2}{f}M = \int_{-\infty}^{+\infty} \frac{f^2 g}{f'}\, df - \left[\int_{-\infty}^{+\infty} \frac{f^2 g}{f'}\, df \right]^2 ,$$

$$\frac{\partial^2 M}{\partial f^2} = 2\,\frac{f^2 g}{f'} - \frac{f^2 g f^2}{(f')^3} \int_{-\infty}^{+\infty} \frac{f^2 g}{f'}\, df$$

$$- \frac{2g}{f'} \int_{-\infty}^{+\infty} \frac{f^2 g}{f'}\, df + \frac{2fgf''}{(f')^3} \int_{-\infty}^{+\infty} \frac{f^2 g}{f'}\, df - 2\left[\frac{fg}{f'} \right]^2 .$$

The solution of the equation $\dfrac{\partial M}{\partial x} = 0$ is $f = e^{2\int_{}^{x} g(u)\,du}$. Using the identities $\dfrac{\partial f}{\partial x} = 2fg$, $\dfrac{df}{df'} = 2g$, and $\dfrac{\partial^2 f}{\partial f'^2} = 2fg^2 + 2f\dfrac{\partial g}{\partial x}$, it is easily shown that the five functional entries in the equation for $\dfrac{\partial^2 M}{\partial f^2} = 0$, above, are 1, $\dfrac{f^2 g f''}{(f')^2}$, $-\dfrac{1}{2}$, $-\dfrac{f^2 g f''}{(f')^2}$, and $-\dfrac{1}{2}$ respectively.

Substitution yields the result $\dfrac{\partial^2 M}{\partial f^2} = 0$. Therefore, no functional ransformation over the sigma algebra of the total test score will maximize the dispersion criteria.

An elementary relation, or rule of propositional calculus is that the statement *p implies q* is false if the proposition, *p*, is false. Consider the statement assessments which maximally discriminate between individuals can not reflect treatment differences. It has been demonstrated that, using a particular index of dispersion, total score distributions, and all functional transformations of the total score can not extriize (maximize nor minimize) the dispersion index. Therefore, the statement is logically false. Paradoxically, following the same line of reasoning, the statement assessments which maximally discriminate between individuals can reflect treatment differences is also false!

The research implications of these results are that the presumption that norm referenced assessments can not discriminate between treatment groups is false and that much developmental, and theoretical work needs to be done relative to tests designed to detect treatment effects. The interesting question yet to be solved is "What type of functional transformation of total, or event scores will tend to maximize between treatment effects when maximization is taken over the total score range, over the sigma algebra of all functions?"

The next chapter describes paradigms for assessment construction which were developed to circumvent many of the problems outlined above. The Rasch model was developed in response to the "rubber yardstick" issues raised by Wright (1967). In addition, the Rasch model is used both successfully (Kifer, 1977) and unsuccessfully (Hashway, 1977) in generating criterion referenced assessments.

4

Qualitative Item Response Theory

It was pointed out in the previous chapter that there are some serious problems with assessment scores obtained from norm referenced assessments. Some of these problems have led Wright (1967) to call norm referenced assessments "rubber yardsticks." Item response theory is a psychometric model intended to overcome the rubber yardstick problem. Rasch's model is a special case of what has come to be known as item response theory. As discussed in Chapter III, item response theory assumes that events are distributed on a single dimension corresponding to some latent attribute, and that learners as well as events can be associated with unique positions on that dimension. The position of an individual is a measure of the amount of that attribute that is exhibited by the individual, or the extent to which that individual has successfully executed the underlying process. Events are characterized by three indices. One index, *event difficulty,* is the extent to which that event is either "easy" or "difficult." Events with greater difficulty indices require a greater proficiency on the part of the learner in order to react appropriately than items with lower difficulty indices. Another event index is the "guessing parameter," the probability that a theoretical assessee with no ability or proficiency will respond appropriately. The third index called "event discrimination," the slope of the probability of appropriate response vs. proficiency contour when that probability is $\frac{1 + c}{2}$, where c is the guessing parameter.

The two parameter model assumes that the probability of guessing appropriately is zero (c=0). The Rasch model is a special case of the two parameter model where the discrimination index is assumed to be 1.0 $(b \approx 0)$.

Assessments conforming to the item response model are purported to be both event-free and sample-free (Wilson, 1992). i.e., "objective mental measurements." The assessment scores assigned to a particular student by two parallel assessments constructed via this model are independent of the particular subset of events, selected from a common event pool, composing those assessments. In addition, a particular assessment score has the same substantive interpretation despite the group used to calibrate the event pool.

The assessment scores are expressed on ratio scales. Most often, the logarithm of the assessment score is used and reflects an interval scale. From this point we will assume that all assessment scores are logarithmic *(logit)* and interval in nature. The zero of the ratio scale [1] is operationally defined as the position on the latent trait dimension that corresponds to a zero probability of responding successfully to an event. [2] The assessment scores obtained by two individuals can be directly compared. Two assessment scores obtained from the same assessment can be directly compared.

Research concerning the model has appeared in many research papers and technical journals. The purpose of this chapter is to pull together and summarize the available information. This chapter consists of five major sections. The first section will present a discussion of the theory underlying the model. Procedures for screening assessment events are discussed in the next section. Techniques for reporting the information resulting from the instruments are discussed in the third section. A review of the current research concerning the properties of the model and assessment score results is presented in the next section. Problems related to applying the model to criterion referenced assessments are presented in the fourth and final section.

It was pointed out in the previous chapter that the norm referenced psychometric paradigm assumes that the probability of responding correctly to an event is a monotonic increasing function of the subject's position on the latent trait continuum. The more positive a subject's position, the greater the probability of responding correctly to the event. A higher probability of success suggests that a more positive position on the latent trait dimension is required.

This model presents some major alternatives to the traditional model. The traditional model assumes that the characteristic function corresponding to each event is the same for all events. This implies that a person with a particular latent trait score has the same probability of responding correctly to all events. It is not inconceivable that, for a particular individual, some events may be either more or less difficult than others. It follows that some events are more or less difficult than others. If some events can be more or less difficult than others, it also follows that the probability of responding correctly to a set of events varies with both the subject's position on the latent trait dimension and the event under consideration. Item response theory assumes the existence of a characteristic function that is functionally dependent upon both the positions of a subject and the particular event under consideration on the same latent trait dimension.

Each event is assumed to occupy a position on the latent trait dimension. The more positive the position of the event, the more difficult the event is considered to be in terms of the number of subjects who respond correctly to the event. Each event is considered be described by its own particular characteristic curve. The characteristic curve corresponding to one event need not be the same as the characteristic curve corresponding to another event. Unlike the traditional technique, which requires all seems to have the same characteristic curve and that each event has its own characteristic function allowing for differences that may exist between events (Rasch, 1966; Wright & Panchapakesan, 1969).

The characteristic function corresponding to a particular event is defined by the position of the event on the latent trait dimension and the position of the subject on the same dimension. If event it is at position a_i on the latent trait dimension, the probability of responding correctly to the event, given that a subject is at z, is expressed as a function of the distance between the subject and the event, a_i-z. The probability that a subject at position z on the latent continuum responds correctly to an event at a_i on the same continuum is expressed by:

$$P(a_i, \theta) = \frac{1}{1 + e^{b_i[a_i - \theta]}}.$$

The characteristic functions corresponding to three events at three different positions along the latent trait dimension are shown in Figure 4.1.

The defining equation and the curves described in Figure 4.1 suggest that the probability of responding correctly to an event is a monotonic increasing function of the difference between the position of the subject and that of the event, a_i- z. Subjects who occupy positions lower than that of the event have a lower probability of responding correctly to the event than subjects who occupy positions greater than that of the event.

Figure 4.1:
Three Item Characteristic Curves

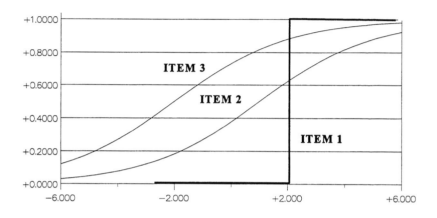

Event Difficulty. The position of an event on the latent trait dimension is called the event's difficulty. The greater an event's difficulty, the more difficult the event appears to be. An event's difficulty is the point on the continuum where it is expected that a subject would have a probability of .50 of responding correctly to the event. For example, three events whose characteristic curves are shown in Figure 5.1 are at positions of -2.0, 1.0, and 2.0 on the latent dimension. Subjects at a position of 2.0 ($z=2.0$) on the latent dimension can expect a 50 Percent Probability of responding correctly to event 1. Subjects at a position of 1.0 ($z=1.0$) on the latent dimension can expect a probability of .50 of responding correctly to event 2. The logistic difficulty index is different from the norm referenced difficulty index. Traditionally, event difficulty is the proportion of subjects responding correctly to the event. The Rasch difficulty index is the position on the continuum where the probability of responding correctly to the event is .50.

Event Discrimination. Another parameter associated with logistically scaled events is called an event's discrimination index. Event discrimination can be thought of as an index of how well the event discriminates between ability levels (Kifer, Mattson, & Carlid, 1975). Indices of event difficulty and discrimination are described in the latent trait literature. The definitions can be found in most standard texts, such as that by F. M. Lord and M. R. Novick (1974). Consider the event characteristic curves described in Figure 4.1, a horizontal line drawn at the probability of success level of 0.50 intersects each of these curves at exactly one point on each curve. The discrimination index for each event is the slope of the characteristic curve at the point where the probability of success is .50. The discrimination indices corresponding to the three events whose characteristic curves are depicted in Figure 4.1 are 99.0 for event 1, 1.0 for event 2, and .50 for event 3. A high discrimination index (much greater than 1.0) suggests that a subject whose position on the latent dimension is greater than that of the event will most probably respond correctly to the event and a subject whose position is less than that of the event's position will respond incorrectly. A low event discrimination (much less than 1.0) suggests that the probability of successfully responding to the event is uniform and that the event does not discriminate well between ability levels. The discrimination index is different from the discrimination index used when events are selected traditionally. The traditional event total score correlation ranges between -1.0 and +1.0. The discrimination index used with the general latent trait model can take on the value of any positive or negative real number. The Rasch model assumes that all events have the same discrimination index, and that the discrimination index is 1.0 for all events. The equality of event discrimination is a consideration in selecting events for inclusion in such a assessment (Wright, 1975; Wright & Mead, 1975; Mead et. al., 1974; Wright & Douglas, 1974; Wright & Panchapakesan, 1969). This topic will be discussed in greater detail in the next section.

CONSTRUCTING ASSESSMENTS
USING ITEM RESPONSE THEORY

The parameters used to select events can be obtained by applying the computer program *ANALYSIS, VERSION 14* (Hashway, 1994) for the 1, 2, or 3 parameter model, or BIGSCALE for the Rasch model to event level data (Wright, Linacr, & Schulz, 1990; Wright & Panchapakesan, 1969; Wright & Mead, 1975). These program obtains maximum likelihood estimates of the event parameters (event difficulty and discrimination) and person parameters (assessment scores). The programs use a classical numerical procedure called the Newton-Rapson method to estimate event and score group parameters. A mathematical function called the log likelihood function is computed. The particular log likelihood function describes the relationship between the observed proportions in the event x score group matrix. The objective is to obtain parameter estimates that extrimise the log likelihood function. The iterative procedure continues until the differences between parameter estimates obtained from two consecutive iterations are negligible. When the likelihood function is extrimised, the cell probabilities calculated from the parameter estimates represent the best fit to the observed probabilities, given the constraints of the particular model.

Fit Mean Square

The first parameter of interest when screening events using this procedure is called the fit mean square. This statistic is a measure of the degree that the event's characteristic function, given the estimated difficulty and discrimination parameters, fits the postulated logistic curve. The fit mean square is a measure of the degree to which the observed event characteristic function conforms to the model represented by the previous equation. The larger the fit mean square obtained for a particular event, the more the event's characteristic curve departs from the two parameter logistic function. The smaller the fit mean square obtained for a particular event, the greater the correspondence between the observed characteristic function and the function postulated by the model. The fit mean square is asymptotically distributed as a F-statistic with N-1 for the numerator, and an infinite number of degrees of freedom for the denominator (where N is the number of score groups used for calibration).

For example, when six score groups are used for calibration, the critical value of the F-ratio at the .05 significance level is 2.2. A value of the fit mean square greater than 2.2 implies a lack of fit between the event's characteristic function and that assumed by the model. A value of the fit mean square less than 2.2 implies that the event tends to fit the model (Wright & Mead, 1957). Thus, if the fit mean square is less than 2.2, the event should be given further consideration.

Table 4.1:
Estimated Two Parameter Logistic Model Parameters for Fifty-five Objectives

OBJEC-TIVE	Event DIFF.	Event DISC.	FIT MEAN SQR.	OBJEC-TIVE	Event DIFF.	Event DISC.	FIT MEAN SQR.
13	+0.97	0.85	0.48	28	+0.12	1.30	3.27
47	-1.15	1.04	0.60	10	-3.02	1.05	3.39
48	-0.59	1.02	0.64	18	-0.61	1.33	1.26
51	+0.44	1.09	0.72	36	+0.50	1.25	4.32
43	-0.27	1.05	0.76	38	-0.21	1.32	4.42
05	-0.83	1.02	0.82	03	-0.89	0.75	4.51
04	-0.21	0.95	0.88	54	+1.02	1.23	4.73
06	-2.36	0.96	0.88	17	-0.58	1.23	4.89
30	+2.19	1.05	1.11	42	-0.58	1.35	5.26
41	+1.50	0.98	1.40	29	+1.65	1.30	5.54
31	+0.04	1.19	1.42	52	+0.61	1.51	6.22
26	+0.79	1.30	1.47	09	+1.86	0.73	6.35
12	-0.26	1.19	1.74	19	+0.77	0.72	6.36
33	+1.14	1.09	1.84	14	+1.33	0.75	6.69
37	+0.23	0.89	1.93	40	-0.12	1.45	7.11
39	-0.49	1.20	1.93	27	+0.08	1.60	7.31
32	-0.70	1.17	2.18	50	-0.75	1.43	7.35
25	+0.06	0.86	2.21	22	-0.10	1.50	7.55
08	+0.07	1.10	2.38	07	+0.43	0.87	7.65
16	+0.47	0.84	2.56	46	-0.04	0.77	7.67
44	-0.78	1.02	2.63	35	+0.85	1.25	8.33
11	-1.16	1.10	2.81	20	-1.00	1.50	8.82
49	+1.25	0.96	2.86	23	+0.81	0.62	9.09
45	+0.76	0.78	2.91	02	-1.11	0.72	13.53
15	-0.53	0.78	2.99	24	-0.47	0.54	16.05
21	-1.82	1.15	3.05	01	-1.58	0.56	22.21
34	-0.46	0.81	3.08	53	+2.31	0.27	39.64
55	+1.62	1.05	3.24				

Consider the event fit parameters (fit mean square) for the fifty-five events shown in Table 4.1. The "events"shown in Table 5.1 were composed of data reported at the objective level from actual event level information obtained by using the *Drumcondra Criterion-Referenced Assessment* (Kellaghan, Madaus, Airasian & Fontes, 1975). The sample used to collect the data upon which the indices in Table 4.1 are based was obtained as part of an experiment to learn the effects of large scale assessment in school settings (Airasian, Kellaghan, & Madaus, 1975). A total of 923 sixth standard students from 30 classes were used for the purposes of objective calibration. The schools in which each class was located were selected as to typify the schools in Ireland, and randomly assigned to treatment groups for the study (Airasian, Kellaghan, & Madaus, 1975). The sample of students used to obtain the calibrations shown in Table 4.1 composed only one (Treatment Group 5) of the treatment groups in the original experiment. To obtain the calibrations shown in Table 4.1, the students were organized into six score groups based on the total number of objectives mastered. The numbers of students in each score group were 153, 149, 152, 163, 151, and 155 respectively from the lowest to the highest total score group. Since six score groups were used to obtain the calibrations, the critical value of the mean square fit parameter is the F-statistic at a nominal .05 confidence level with five and an infinite number of degrees of freedom, 2.20. An objective with a fit mean square greater than 2.20 would not be considered to fit the model. Objectives with a fit mean square less than 2.20 would be considered to fit the model based on the fit mean square parameter and deserving of further consideration.

Eighteen objectives exhibit fit mean square indices less than the critical value of 2.20. The eighteen objectives are objectives 13, 47, 48, 51, 43, 5, 4, 6, 30, 41, 31, 26, 12, 33, 37, 39, 32, and 25 (ordered in terms of increasing mean square fit index). Those eighteen objectives will be considered further. The remaining objectives are not considered to fit the model and are not considered further.

The Rasch Discrimination Criterion

The second criterion for event selection is the discrimination parameter. The Rasch model assumes that all events have the same logistic discrimination parameter, 1.0[3]. An estimate, based upon event data, of the discrimination index for each event is obtained. Because the number of events is finite for any given dataset, there is a degree of error associated with each estimate of event discrimination. That error is operationalized by what is called the standard error of the event discrimination estimate. If the estimated event discrimination plus or minus three standard errors is within the range of 0.80 to 1.20, the event is said to have satisfied the event discrimination criterion.

Each of the eighteen objectives that satisfied the mean square fit criterion also satisfied the event discrimination criteria. It has been that this phenomenon is not unusual. Many events satisfying the mean square fit criterion also fit the discrimination criterion. However, it does not always follow that all events that satisfy the mean square fit criterion also satisfy the event discrimination criterion. Events meeting the event discrimination criteria do not always satisfy the mean square fit criterion. The entries in Table 4.1 demonstrate the last assertion. It has been this author's experience that more events tend to satisfy the event discrimination criterion than the mean square fit criterion.

The Final Event Pool

Events that satisfy both the fit mean square and for Rasch events, discrimination criteria are considered suitable for inclusion in assessments based upon this model. Events that do not satisfy both criteria are not to be included in such assessments. In order for events to be included in the final event pool from which events composing assessments will be chosen, they must exhibit mean square fit statistics less than $F_{\alpha=0.05}$ (df=N, ∞) and event discrimination parameters between 0.80 and 1.20. It has been the author's experience that the Rasch inclusion criteria are conservative. For the typical initial event pool, many events will not find themselves in the final set of events satisfying the Rasch model's inclusion criteria. A series of studies conducted by the author to learn how serious the impact of these criteria is for determining the size of an initial event pool are shown in Table 4.2. The assessment events consisted of events keyed to fifty-five objectives by subject matter experts. For two studies, the events were prescreened using the norm referenced procedure described in the previous chapter. For the other studies, no psychometric prescreening was used. For a third set of studies, data at the level of the objective was used.

* The results after ten studies shown in Table 4.2 suggest that at most fifty percent (50%) and at least eleven percent (11%) of the events initially screened satisfied the Rasch criteria. These results suggest that the assessment constructor should include between two and ten times the number of events required in the final version of the event pool in the initial

event pool, or relax the event inclusion criteria. It is the opinion of the author that both of the alternatives are undesirable to varying degrees depending upon the particular situation. Therefore, it seems that although the properties of the parameter model are interesting and desirable, the model may be so restrictive with respect to event inclusion as to be virtually impractical.

Table 4.2:
Number of Events or Objectives Satisfying the Rasch Criteria

Type of Prescreening	Level of Data	Initial Number of Events	Number of Events Satisfying Criteria [1]	Number of Cases [2]
Norm referenced		82	33 (0.45)	804
and subject	Event			512
matter experts		94	49 (0.53)	
		154	60 (0.40)	683
Subject matter		155	61 (0.40)	804
experts only	Event			
		155	45 (0.29)	924
		154	17 (0.11)	1326
		55	23 (0.42)	668
No		55	18 (0.33)	1221
Psychometric	OBJECTIVE			
Prescreening		55	17 (0.31)	923
		55	13 (0.24)	1196

1. The proportion of initial events satisfying the criteria is shown in parentheses.
2. Number of subjects from which calibration data was obtained.

ESTABLISHING A SCORE FORMULA

Once the events that fit the model have been selected a method of transforming a subject's responses to these events to scores on the latent trait dimension must be devised. The computer algorithms result in indices which describe the relation between total scores (the number of events answered correctly) and the logistic score. The table resulting from the initial screening is not based on only the events that fit the model but on all of the events used. The revised scoring formula is obtained by using the program a second time, considering only those events that fit the model as a result of the initial screening.

Figure 4.2:
A Typical Mapping Function

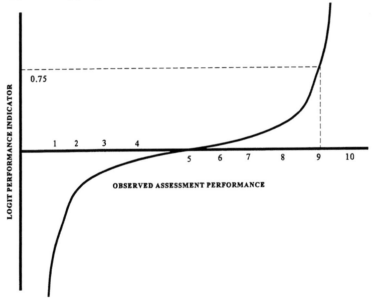

The latent trait model assumes that the latent trait dimension upon which the subjects are mapped is continuous. The position of a subject is found by responses to a finite number of events. The measurement of the position of a subject on some latent dimension is analogous to measuring the length of an object 4.5 inches long with a ruler marked only in inches. It can be learned that the object is greater than 4 but less than 5 inches long. Any attempt at a precise measurement of the length of the object will be the result of some estimating process. Because the procedure assigns scores to subjects and the subjects are assumed to be located on a continuum (using a finite ruler), the question becomes: What is the error of the measurement estimate?

The scoring formula is a mapping from the number of correct responses to a subject's estimated position on the latent trait dimension. An index of the precision of the estimate of the subject's position is also obtained. That index of the precision is called the standard error of the ability estimate. The greater the number of events located about a subject estimated position on the latent trait dimension, the more accurate the estimate of the subject's position and the smaller the standard error of the ability estimate corresponding to that position. This corresponds to measuring the length of a block 4.5 inches long with a ruler marked in 1/8-th inch units as opposed to a ruler marked in 1 inch units. The accuracy of the estimated length with a ruler marked in 1/8 inch units will be greater than the accuracy obtained with a ruler marked in 1 inch units.

The model assumes that a subject's score is not estimable if none or all of the events are answered correctly. It is common practice to obtain a score for a subject who has not responded correctly to any of the events by subtracting one standard error from the score corresponding to a total score of 1.0. The assessment score associated with a perfect score on a assessment composed of k events is found by adding one standard error of the ability estimate the assessment score corresponding to k-1 events answered correctly (Kifer, Mattson, & Carlid, 1975). The mapping of the number of correct responses to logistic scores can be displayed graphically. A typical form of such a graph is shown in Figure 4.2. The number of correct responses forms the horizontal axis and the logistic parameter scores form the vertical axis. To find the logistic score that corresponds to a particular raw score: (1) find the raw score on the horizontal, or raw score, axis; (2) from the point on the raw score axis, draw a vertical line to the graph of the mapping function; (3) from the point where the vertical line intersects the mapping function, draw a horizontal line to the assessment score axis. The point where the horizontal line crosses the assessment score axis is the latent trait score corresponding to the initial raw score. For example, the latent trait score corresponding to a raw score of 9, given the mapping function in Figure 4.2, is +.75.

Once a assessment has been constructed and a scoring formula established, the raw score for each subject can be translated into other assessment score reporting paradigms (for example, stanines, percentile ranks, z-scores) using the same procedures that apply to traditional assessment scores. The transformed scores may be more easily interpreted by the less mathematically sophisticated user. However, all but linear transformations (such as transformations to z-scores or T-scores) will change the interval nature of the logarithmic scale and may result in a noninterval level of measurement. In the case of criterion referenced proficiency estimation, it has been suggested that the ability of a subject with latent score θ and observed score x is estimated by $\pi = \sum_{i=1}^{n} P(x \mid \theta, a_i, b_i, c_i)$.

The major advantages of item response theory lie with its event and sample invariance properties and the interval nature of the measurement scale.

SCORE TRANSFORMATIONS

The range of scores is, in theory, unlimited. Any number between negative infinity and positive infinity can be valid logarithmic scores. Logarithmic assessment scores may take integer values (positive or negative) such as +3, -4, +200, -40, etc. or rational values such as -3.62, 4.17, -27.643, 78.964 or any other values. The range of possible values that a traditionally scaled assessment score can assume is in one-to-one correspondence with the set of positive integers starting with zero and increasing to a maximum equal to the number of events composing the assessment. Scores obtained from a traditional assessment containing 10 events are equivalent or identical to the eleven whole numbers: 0, 1, 2, 3, ..., 8, 9, 10. This model results in assessment scores that are quite different from well known traditional assessment scores. Since these assessment scores are interval scale measurements, various transformations can be performed which map assessment scores onto familiar scales. These transformations do not change the interval character of the scale and will be discussed in this section.

Table 4.3:
The Mean and Standard Deviations of Each of Four Transformed Distributions

	TYPE OF TRANSFORMATION				
	LOGARITHMIC	Z-SCORES	T-SCORES	STANDARD-IZED	W-SCALE
MEAN		0	50	500	
STANDARD DEVIATION	S	1	10	100	a_w S

$a_w = 9.1024$ and $b_w = 100$.

Four types of transformed scores will be discussed in this section: z- scores, T-scores, standardized scores, and W-scores. Z-scores are assessment scores that are distributed with a mean of zero and unit variance. The T-score is distributed with a mean of fifty (50) and a standard deviation of ten (10). The standardized score is distributed with a mean of five-hundred (500) and a standard deviation of one hundred (100). The W-scale score was developed by Woodcock & Dahl in collaboration with Benjamin Wright of the University of Chicago (Hambleton, Swaminathan, & Rogers, 1989; Woodcock & Dahl, 1976). If the mean and standard deviation of the original untransformed Rasch scores are Z and S respectively, the W-scores are distributed with a mean of $9.1024\,Z + 100$, and a standard deviation of 9.1024 S. The mean and standard deviation of each of the transformed distributions are shown in Table 4.3.

Table 4.4:
Transformation Constants

Constant	Z Score	T Score	Standardized	W Scale
a	1/S	10/S	$100 \, / \, S$	9.1024
b	$-\dfrac{\overline{Z}}{S}$	$50 - \dfrac{10\,\overline{Z}}{S}$	$500 - \dfrac{100\,\overline{Z}}{S}$	100

The transformation of a particular score to any of the four scales defined above is accomplished arithmetically by means of what is called a *linear affine transformation*. If F(z) is the transformed score corresponding to the untransformed score, z and Z and S are the mean and standard deviation respectively of the untransformed score distribution, and the relation

between F(z) and z is defined by $F(z) = az + b$. The values of a and b

are constant for a particular transformation and a particular set of untransformed Rasch assessment results. The values of the constants a and b for each transformation are shown in Table 4.4.

Table 4.5:
Distribution of Assessment Scores

ASSESSMENT SCORE	STANDARD ERROR
-4.99	3.33
-1.65	1.11
-0.72	0.88
+0.00	0.83
+0.71	0.88
+1.66	1.11
+4.99	3.33
MEAN ASSESSMENT SCORE	0.807
STANDARD DEVIATION	2.153

The standard error, $\sigma_\xi[F(z)]$, of the transformed score, F(z), is not equal to the standard error, $\sigma_\xi(z)$, of the untransformed logit score, z. The equation, $\sigma_\xi[F(z)]=a\sigma_\xi(z)$ (equation 4.3) describes the relationship between the standard errors of transformed and untransformed standard errors.

The remainder of this section will present examples of these transformations. A set of assessment scores from a particular six event assessment will be used for each example. The logit scores and associated standard errors are shown in Table 4.5.

Transformation to Z-scores. Z-scores are distributed with a mean of zero and a standard deviation of 1.0. $F(z) = az + b$ can be used to accomplish this transformation. The values of the constants, a and b, can be found by using the formulas in the first column of Table 4.4. Since the constant, a, is 1.0/S, and the standard deviation scores shown in Table 4.5 is 2.1537, the value of the constant is 0.991.0/2.1537 or 0.4643. The formula for the constant, b, is b=z/ S. The mean (Z) and standard deviation (S) 0.8073 and 2.1537 respectively. Therefore, the value of b is -(0.8073/2.1537) or -0.3748.

Table 4-6:
Transformation to Z-scores

TYPE OF ASSESSMENT SCORE

UNTRANSFORMED		TRANSFORMED	
Observed Score Z	Standard Error s(Z)	Z-Score F(Z)	Standard Error SE$_F$ (Z)
		0.4643 z - 0.7348	0.4643 s(Z)
-4.99	3.33	-3.05 =0.4643(-4.99)-0.7348	1.55=0.4643(1.55)
-1.65	1.11	-1.50 =0.4643(-1.65)-0.7348	0.52=0.4643(1.11)
-0.72	0.88	-1.07 =0.4643(-0.72)-0.7348	0.41=0.4643(0.88)
0.00	0.83	-0.73 =0.4643(-0.00)-0.7348	0.39=0.4643(0.83)
0.71	0.88	-0.41 =0.4643(-0.71)-0.7348	0.41=0.4643(0.88)
1.66	1.11	0.04 =0.4643(1.66)-0.7348	0.52=0.4643(0.52)
4.99	3.33	1.58 =0.4643(4.99)-0.7348	1.55=0.4643(1.55)

Once the values of the transformation constants have been found these values may be substituted into Equation 4.2 to obtain the transformation equation. For this particular example the transformation equation is $F(z) = 0.4643z-0.3748$ (equation 4.4). Equation 4.3 can be used to define the relation between the standard errors of the transformed and untransformed assessment scores. The equation that describes the relation between the standard errors for this example is $\sigma_\xi[F(z)]=0.4643\sigma_\xi(z)$ (equation 4.5). Consider the assessment score of -0.72 with a standard error of 0.88 (See Table 4.6). The transformed score can be found using Equation 5-4,

F(-0.72) = 0.4643(-0.72)-0.3478=-0.7091 and the standard error is found by using Equation 4.5, 0.4643(0.88)=0.4086. The standardized transformations of each of the scores described by Table 4.5 are shown in Table 4.6.

Transformation to T-scores. Logistic assessment results can be transformed to T-Scores. T-Scores are distributed with a mean of 50 and a standard deviation of 10.0. Equation 4.2 is used to transform the assessment scores. The values of the parameters, a and b, can be found from the sample data by using the formulas shown in Table 4.4. The value of the first parameter, a, is $\frac{10}{S}$ or $\frac{10.0}{2.1537}$ = 4.6432. The formula in Table 4.4 is used to for the value of the parameter, b=50-($\frac{10\ Z}{s}$)=50-3.7484=46.2516. Therefore, the equations transforming the logistic assessment scores and their associated standard errors to T-scores and T-standard errors can be found by substituting the values of a and b into Equations 4.2 and 4.3 respectively. The results of the substitutions are: F(z)=4.6432 Z+46.2516 and $\sigma_\xi[F(z)]$=4.6432s(z).

Consider the untransformed assessment score of 1.66 with the associated standard error of 1.11 as shown in Table 4.5, using Equation 4.8, the corresponding value of the T-score is 4.6432(1.66)+46.2516 or 53.9593. Using Equation 4.9 the standard error associated with a T-score of 53.9593 is: 4.6432(1.11) or 5.1540. The T-scores and standard errors corresponding to the untransformed Rasch scores described in Table 4.5 are shown in Table 4.7.

Transformation To Standardized Scores. Beyond T-scores and standardized scores, logit measurements can also be transformed to standardized scores. These transformed scores are distributed with a mean of 500 and a standard deviation of 100. As with the previous transformations, Equation 4.2 can be used to generate the transformation equation, and the formulas for determining the required parameters (a and b) can be found by using Table 4.4. For the example in Table 4.5 the parameter, a, is equal to $\dfrac{100}{2.1537}$ or 46.432. The remaining parameter, b, is

Table 4.7:
Rasch Measurements after Transformation

Type Of Transformation

Raw Score	Z-Score	T-Score	Standardized	W-Scale
-4.99 (3.33)	-3.05 (1.55)	23.08 (15.46)	231 (155)	54.6 (30.3)
-1.65 (1.11)	-1.50 (0.52)	38.59 (5.15)	386 (52)	84.9 (10.1)
-0.72 (0.88)	-1.07 (0.41)	42.91 (4.09)	429 (41)	93.4 (8.0)
0.00 (0.83)	-0.74 (0.39)	46.25 (3.85)	463 (39)	100.0 (7.6)
0.71 (0.88)	-0.41 (0.41)	49.55 (4.09)	495 (41)	106.5 (8.0)
1.66 (1.11)	+0.04 (0.52)	53.96 (5.15)	540 (51)	115.1 (10.1)
4.99 (3.33)	+1.58 (1.55)	69.42 (15.46)	694 (155)	145.4 (30.3)

equal to 500-(100 ($\dfrac{.8073}{2.1537}$)) or 462.516. The equations relating the standardized transformed measurements and standard errors to the untransformed measurements and standard errors are found by substituting the values of a and b into Equations 4.2 and 4.3. The equations required to transform the data shone in Table 4.5 to SAT scores are $F(z)=46.432z+462.516$ (Equation 4.10) and $\sigma_{\xi}[F(z)]=46.432\ s(z)$ (Equation 4.11). The values of the transformed scores and standard errors corresponding to the data shown in the example of Table 4.5 are shown in Table 4.7.

Transformation to the W-Scale. The transformations of measurements and their associated standard errors are described by Woodcock & Dahl (1976) in terms of the equations $F(z)=9.1024z+100$ (Equation 4.12) and $\sigma_{\xi}[F(z)]=9.1024s(x)$ (Equation 4.13), transcribed into the current notation for convenience. Consider an untransformed score of -1.65 with a standard error of 1.11. The corresponding W-scale score is:

$$9.1024\ (-1.65)\ +\ 100\ =\ -15.0190\ +100\ =\ 84.981.$$

The standard error corresponding to a W-scale score of 84.981 (or, equivalently an untransformed score of -1.65) is: $9.1024(1.11)$ or 10.1037. The measurements and standard errors shown in Table 4.5 have been transformed to the W-scale equivalents in Table 4.7.

In summary, we have seen that logistic measurements may be transformed with an affine transformation without loss of the interval scaling property of the untransformed scale. Procedures and formulae for transforming logarithmic scores and standard errors to z-scores, T-scores, standardized scores and the W-scale have also been presented. The remainder of this chapter will discuss the relevant research. It should be noted that, if a transformed score *and* associated standard errors are used, the inference will be no different than if the untransformed measurement was used. Transformations are used for the ease of human interpretability. The inferential mathematics is not dependent upon the particular transformation (affine) that is selected. This last property is due to the fact that logarithmic measurements are made upon interval scales which is invariant under linear affine transformations. The transformations discussed in this section are all classifiable as linear affine transformation.

TESTING THE ASSUMPTIONS

Two important properties of the logistic model are: event difficulty and total score invariance. Event difficulty invariance implies that the numerical value of the estimate obtained for the position of an event on the latent trait dimension is not dependent upon the sample of subjects used to obtain those estimates. The total score invariance property implies that the estimate of the position on a latent trait dimension for a particular subject is not a function of the particular subset of events drawn from a precalibrated event pool used to obtain that estimate. Since these properties are what Wright (1967) considers the characteristics that place these assessments above or norm referenced assessments, the relevant research should be examined.

The literature can be partitioned into four areas:

1. The underlying theory (Anderson, 1972; Hambleton & Cook, 1976; Hashway, 1977, 1988/1989; Kifer, Mattson, & Carlid, 1975; Wright & Douglas, 1975; Wright & Panchapakesan, 1969);

2. Parameter estimation (Anderson, 1972; Hashway, 1977, 1988/1989; Kifer, Mattson & Carlid, 1975; Wright & Panchapakesan, 1969; Wright & Mead, 1975);

3. Procedures for constructing Rasch assessments (Arneklev, Gee, & Ingebo, 1976; Hashway, 1977, 1988/1989; Ingebo, 1976; Kifer, Mattson & Carlid, 1975; Wright & Mead, 1975); and,

4. The invariance properties (Anderson, Kearny, & Everett, 1968; Forster, 1976; Forbes & Ingebo, 1975; Hashway, 1977, 1988/1989; Willmott & Fowles, 1974; Mead, 1974; Whitely & Dawis, 1974, 1976).

The work concerning the theory underlying item response theory, and procedures for constructing assessments have been outlined previous chapters.

Event Difficulty Invariance

The procedure assumes that both events and subjects occupy positions on the same latent trait dimension. The position of an event is the event's difficulty within the context of the model. Event difficulty invariance means that the position of an event on the latent trait dimension is not a function of the sample of subjects used to obtain estimates of that position.

Forster (1976) investigated the minimum calibration sample required to obtain stable estimates of event difficulty. He randomly selected twenty samples of varying sizes from a population of 1478 fourth grade and 1808 eighth grade students. The students had taken part in the Portland Assessment Program in fourth grade mathematics and eight grade reading. The results suggest that sample sizes of 150 to 200 students result in what Forster (1976) has termed 'stable event difficulty estimates.' The correlation between the event difficulties estimated for the same events from each of two samples was used as the stability criterion. Forster (1976) reports correlations of event difficulty estimates between samples ranging between a low of .9564 and a high of .9910 with a mean of .9797. Forster's (1976) correlations were Pearsonian product moment correlations.

Forbes & Ingebo (1975) have reported the results of a study of the Rasch event difficulty invariance property. These authors were attempting to directly assessment the invariance property. Unlike Forster (1976), Forbes and Ingebo (1975) were not concerned with minimum sample size. Forbes and Ingebo (1975) used seventh grade arithmetic event data. The events were prescreened using traditional difficulty and discrimination criteria. The events that satisfied the traditional criteria were calibrated by the Rasch procedure using each of twelve different groups of subjects. Forbes & Ingebo (1975) report rank difference correlations between the Rasch event difficulty estimates obtained for the same set of events from each of the twelve groups of 1.0.

Anderson, Kearny, & Everett (1968) report that they obtained 'high' Pearson correlations between the Rasch event difficulty estimates obtained using prescreened events with two groups of subjects. The subjects were divided into a 'high' and 'low' group based on the total assessment score. Event difficulty estimates for each event were obtained for each of the samples. Willmott & Fowles (1974) also investigated the event difficulty invariance property. These authors used traditionally screened physics, mathematics, geography and English assessment events and samples of approximately 1,000 students. Two groups of subjects (a 'high' and a 'low' group) were selected based on the total score. These author's report bivariate plots of Rasch event difficulties for the same set of events using each of the two groups as calibration samples. Although the plots reported by Willmot & Fowles (1974) seem to describe a linear trend, no correlation indices were reported. Data sufficient for the calculation of the correlation between event difficulties for one assessment (English) was reported. The correlation between event difficulties obtained from the 'high' and 'low' groups for the English assessment events selected by the Rasch procedure as reported by Hashway (1977a, b) was 0.9727. The slope of the regression of high group event difficulties on low group difficulties was 1.026 (Hashway, 1977a, b). The theoretical value of the regression parameter is 1.0. The use of the regression procedure in this context will be discussed later. Although the correlation of .97 and the bivariate graphs reported by Willmott & Fowles (1974) are impressive, the observed event difficulties for each group and event were not reported. As a result, it is difficult to make any definitive statements concerning event difficulty invariance.

The empirical research reported above concern event difficulty invariance property and can be criticized on at least two points. First, some of these studies present as evidence nothing more than bivariate plots (Willmott & Fowles, 1974). Without some type of assessment statistic one can not ascertain whether the differences observed between event difficulty estimates are significant or merely due to chance. The inspection of a bivariate plot is not sufficient to assessment the event difficulty invariance property. Second, the correlation coefficient is not the appropriate statistic.

Some researchers have reported Pearsonian correlations between event difficulty estimates (Anderson, Kearney & Everett, 1968; Forster, 1976). Others have reported rank difference correlations between event difficulty estimates (Forbes & Ingebo, 1975). The major statistical difference between these two correlational indices is that the Pearsonian assumes that the variables being correlated are sampled from a universe population that is normally distributed while the rank difference correlation makes no distributional assumptions. The reader interested in these differences between the two types of correlation coefficients is referred to the nonparametric statistics literature (Hollander & Wolfe, 1973; Kendall, 1970; Conover, 1971).

The major issue is not with the type of coefficient calculated. It is that the correlation coefficient is not the appropriate statistic. The correlation coefficient is a measure of rank order invariance. If a group of events maintains the same relative rank order based on their difficulty estimates across calibration groups the correlation coefficients (both Pearsonian and rank order) will be high. If events do not maintain the same or similar relative rank orderings both types of correlation coefficients will be low. The event difficulty invariance property requires that the event difficulty estimates are numerically the same for the same event across calibration samples. The existence of a high correlation or similar rank ordering of events across calibration samples is a necessary but not a sufficient assessment of the invariance property. If event difficulty estimates are similar across samples, rank orderings of events based on the estimates will be similar (i.e., high correlations). The existence of similar rank orderings, however, does not imply equivalence of raw scores (McNemar, 1962; Ferguson, 1971).

Given this level of specificity the question now becomes: What is (are) a sufficient statistic(s) for the assessment of the event difficulty invariance property? Fortunately, this question can be answered. Consider the same set of events calibrated using two different groups of subjects. The difficulty estimate obtained for event i using groups j and k will be symbolized by d_{ij} and d_{ik} respectively. If the event difficulty invariance property is operant in the data the two difficulty estimates would be equivalent. Consider the regression equation $d_{ik}=b_1 d_{ij}+b_2$ (Equation 4-14) between the event difficulty estimates. The parameters b_1 and b_2 are called the slope and intercept parameters respectively. *These parameters are estimated using least squares procedures* (McNemar, 1962) for more than one event and two calibration samples. If the event difficulty estimates are equivalent across calibration samples the regression equation obtained from the event difficulties should not be different from the equation $d_{ik}=(1.0)d_{ij}+0.0$. The sufficient condition required to conclude that the event invariance property is operant is that the population parameter corresponding to b_2 is 0.0. The sufficient statistic for assessing the hypothesis that $b_1=1$ and $b_2=0$ is the t-statistic. The t-statistic used is the quotient of the difference between the hypothesized and observed regression coefficient (Heald, 1969; McNemar, 1962; Winer, 1971; Worthing & Giffner, 1943). The regression procedure assessments the property that event difficulty should be invariant across calibration samples.

Whitely & Dawis (1976) report an alternative approach to assessing the event difficulty invariance property. These authors used a prescreened event pool containing 15 events which satisfied the Rasch model assumptions (Tinsley, 1971). Seven alternate forms were constructed. Each alternative form consisted of the 15 Rasch events and 45 events of similar substantive content. Each of the seven forms was administered to groups of high school students ranging in number from 210 to 241. Event difficulty estimates for each of the original 15 events was obtained using the data for each form. Since there were seven forms, seven event difficulty estimates-one using each form-were obtained for each event (Whitely & Dawis, 1976). Whitely & Dawis concluded that event difficulty invariance was a function of the environment of the other events with which the 15 Rasch events were combined.

Whitely & Dawis (1976) used a particular type of one-way analysis of variance procedure to examine their data. The unit of analysis was the event, the dependent variable was the event difficulty estimate obtained using each of the seven assessment forms, the independent variable was the particular form used to figure out the event difficulty estimate (one factor with seven 'levels'). The within cell variance was estimated by: "the squared standard errors weighted by N." (Whitely & Dawis, 1976, p. 334).

The validity of the procedure rests on the assumption that Whitely & Dawis (1976) are correct in their choice of procedure for the calculation of the within cell variance. No rationale or reference was cited in the Whitely & Dawis (1976) paper relative to their choice of the within cell error term. Whitely & Dawis' (1976) procedure is at best questionable at this point because of the lack of rationale for the choice of error term.

Whitely & Dawis' (1976) data was reanalyzed by this author (Hashway, 1977a, b). The average rank difference correlation across forms of event difficulty was .99. The Whitely & Dawis (1976) data, when analyzed in this fashion, seems to negate the conclusions arrived at by the original investigators and to agree with the results reported by Forbes & Ingebo (1976) who report rank difference correlations of 1.00. It seems that event difficulty estimates obtained from either different samples or different forms tend to rank order events in the same way.

We argued previously that the preservation of rank order is a necessary but not sufficient condition for event difficulty invariance. The next step was to determine the slopes of the Rasch event difficulty regression lines. Using the Whitely & Dawis (1976) data, the slopes were calculated by Hashway (1977). The average of the slopes (b_1) and intercepts (b_2) of the regression lines were 1.02 and 0.03 respectively. Each of the slopes and intercepts were assessed for significant departure from unity or zero respectively using a t-statistic (Heald, 1969; Winer, 1971; Worthing & Giffner, 1943; McNemar, 1962). None of the slopes were different from 1.0 (p less than .01) and none of the intercepts were found to be significantly different from 0 (p less than .01). The Whitely & Dawis (1976) data can be seen as confirming the invariance of Rasch event difficulty estimates.

Invariance is not a function of the events that are combined with the Rasch events as the original investigators had concluded. Hashway's (1977a, b) reanalysis indicates that there may be a serious problem with the Whitely & Dawis (1976) procedure. Perhaps, the problem may lie in the selection of the procedure for the calculation of the within cell variance.

Assessment Score Invariance

In addition to the invariance of event difficulty over calibration groups, the item response theory purports the property of assessment score invariance. The score associated with particular people should be invariant with respect to variations of the events making up the assessment upon which that score was based. Specifically, given two assessments where the events forming each assessment were selected from the same set of calibrated events, the scores obtained by the same individual from both assessments should not differ by any more than that which would be expected from random error alone.

Some authors have interpreted score variance to mean that the same total score (number of events answered correctly) obtained from each of two assessments should correspond to the same score (Doherty & Forster, 1976; Wright & Douglas, 1974; Wright, 1967). This interpretation implies that a subject (a) who responds correctly to two events on assessment A should be given the same score as a subject (b) who responded correctly to two events on assessment B. It has been found that the number of correct responses on two assessments constructed from the same event pool correspond quite well (Doherty & Forster, 1976; Slinde & Linn, 1978; Wright, 1967; Wright & Douglas, 1974). Score invariance is more general than described above. There is another dimension of score invariance: the logit score associated with a particular person obtained from two or more assessments, whose events were selected from a calibrated set of events, will be statistically equivalent (Whitely & Dawis, 1974; Wright & Panchapakesan, 1969).

What is a sufficient statistic for assessing this more general score invariance property? Tinsley (1971), using classical statistics, concluded that the ability estimates obtained from Rasch assessments were not invariant over event subsets. Whitely & Dawis (1974) point out that classical statistical procedures end to confound the precision of measurement with statistical equivalency. Assessments of statistical equivalency (classical) are not designed to allow for *known* errors of measurement or limits to precision.

Whitely & Dawis (1974) go on to point out that a assessment of score equivalence must consider the precision of the instrument used to make the measurements. Since assessments consist of a finite number of events, the measurement made using a assessment contains a certain amount of imprecision. The estimate of this uncertainty or imprecision is the standard error of the ability estimate. The assessment statistic proposed by Wright (1967) accounts for the variations inherent in the instrument by means of the standard error of ability estimate. This measure is called the *standardized difference score* (Whitely & Dawis, 1974; Wright, 1967). Assume that assessment scores obtained by person p from assessments 1 and 2 are x_{1p} and x_{2p} respectively. The standard error of the ability estimates corresponding to each of those scores are symbolized by $\sigma_\xi[x_{1p}]$ and $\sigma_\xi[x_{2p}]$, respectively.

The standardized difference score, $z_p = \dfrac{x_{1p} - x_{2p}}{\sqrt{\sigma_\xi[x_{1p}]^2 + \sigma_\xi[x_{2p}]^2}}$,

is interpreted as a z-score (Whitely & Dawis, 1974). The distribution of the population from which z_p is sampled is assumed by Whitely & Dawis (1974) to be normally distributed with zero mean and unit variance.

The *standardized difference statistic* is traceable to Wright (1967) who overlooked an important consideration. If the error is exactly what would be expected from random error alone, z_p is sampled from N(0, 1). However, if the observed score differences are *less* than what would be considered attributable to random error alone, the standardized difference score would be sampled from a normally distributed population, N(0, s^2), where s<1. If the observed score differences are *greater* than what would be considered to arise from random error alone, the population distribution of z_p would be N(M_z, s^2) where $M_z \neq 0$ *or* s>1. Therefore, although the results reported by Whitely & Dawis (1974) tend to agree with their assertion that z_p is sampled from N(0, 1), if the invariance principle is correct, that assertion is generally false.

The Wright (1967) procedure is to sum the standardized difference scores over the population and test this sum for significant departure from zero. The traditional assessment is the t-test (Winer, 1971). The sum of a finite number, N, or unit normal deviates follows a t-distribution with N-1 degrees of freedom (Harris, 1966). However, if the sample distribution is anything other than unit normal, the assessment assumptions are not satisfied.

Hashway (1977) reports the results of a study of the Rasch event-free property. Hashway (1977) used a sample of about 2,000 students from the Republic of Ireland and two assessments constructed from a criterion referenced mathematics assessment which had not been previously psychometrically prescreened. It was found that the distribution of the *standardized difference statistic was not normally distributed,* and the variance of the distribution was *much less than one*. Hashway's (1977) results suggest that assessments constructed, from unscreened event pools, using item response theory are more 'error free' than assessments constructed from traditionally prescreened event pools.

Table 4.8:
A Hypothetical Distribution of Rasch Assessment Scores for Two Individuals and Two Assessments

SUBJECT	ASSESSMENT SCORE		WHITELY & DAWIS (1974) STATISTIC, t_i
	ASSESSMENT 1	ASSESSMENT 2	
1	-0.3536	+0.3536	+0.7072
2	+0.3536	-0.3536	-0.7072
MEAN	+0.0000	+0.0000	+0.0000
	+0.5000	+0.5000	+1.0000

There is another critical problem with the Wright (1967) procedure. It is possible for if to suggest that two assessments are equivalent when in fact the score for the same person on one assessment is the algebraic opposite of the person's score on another assessment. Consider the set of scores in Table 4.8. The mean and variance of the standardized difference scores are 0 and 1 respectively. Therefore, using the Wright (1967) procedure, the conclusion is that these assessments are equivalent. The distribution of scores in Table 4.8 suggests that the two assessments are definitely not equivalent. Although the example cited contained merely two cases, all that is necessary to show that a procedure is erroneous is one counter example. The scores for two assessments that have quite opposite results but satisfy the Wright (1967) equivalence criteria can be easily generated for any number of cases.

Although there are problems with current significance tests concerning standardized difference scores, a method of assessing the score invariance property using these scores can be developed. As stated previously, the major issue concerning the assessing of any hypothesis is: What is the sufficient statistic? A procedure for assessing the score invariance property using the distribution of Wright's (1967) standardized difference scores was developed (Hashway, 1977; 1978). The procedure resulted in a set of sufficient statistics for assessing the score invariance property. That procedure and the sufficient statistics will now be described. The definition of score invariance can be restated in terms of the standardized difference score. The standardized difference score and the procedure used for its calculation were described previously in this section. Two assessments are said to be score invariant if the observed distribution of standardized difference scores can be explained by at most random error. This definition renders a solution to the problem of the choice of a sufficient statistic.

The procedure proposed for assessing the score invariance property involves observing the distribution of standardized difference scores. This is, essentially, a step process. The first step is to compare the observed distribution with the normal distribution function. If it is found that the standardized difference score is due to random error, the score invariance property is operant and the second step can be omitted. The comparison between the observed distribution of standardized difference scores and the expected normal distribution function can be performed using either χ^2 or Kolmogorov-Smirnov statistics (Conover, 1971; Hollander & Wolfe, 1973; Kolmogorov, 1941; Smirnov, 1948). There is some indication that the Kolmogorov-Smirnov assessment is more sensitive to departures from the expected distribution than the chi-square assessment (Massey, 1951). However, Massey's (1951) simulation was performed with large samples of subjects but a small population of samples (46 samples were used). Therefore, the existing evidence in favor of the Kolmogorov-Smirnov assessment over chi-square is not impressive. It is suggested that both assessments be used. If the Kolmogorov-Smirnov or chi-square assessment achieves significance, the hypothesis that the standard difference scores are distributed as the unit normal should be rejected. If the hypothesis that the observed distribution is similar to the unit normal distribution is rejected, the second step in the procedure should be performed.

There are two reasons why the observed distribution would not be non-- normal. First, the observed variation may be greater than expected assuming a normal distribution of error. This situation will result in a probability distribution profile similar to curve B in Figure 4.3. The number of concordant assessment scores will be greater than expected from the error function. Second, the observed variation may be in greater concordance with the invariance property than would be expected from normal error functions. This situation will result in a profile similar to curve A in Figure 4.2. The number of concordant scores would be greater, and the number of discordant assessment scores would be fewer than expected from the error function. It is assumed that two assessments result in Rasch scores that are in greater concordance than expected from random error when three properties are present. (1) The frequency of standardized difference scores centered about zero must be greater than expected from random error alone, thereby indicating a larger than expected frequency of concordant assessment scores. (2) The frequency of standardized difference scores at the extreme ends of the distribution must be less than expected from the error function, and these frequencies approach N(0,1) asymptotically as the value of the observed difference score increases. This suggests that the number of discordant scores is less than expected from the error function. (3) The variance of the standardized difference score should be significantly less than 1.0. This property ensures that the dispersion of difference scores is less than expected

Figure 4.3:
Three Residual Distributions

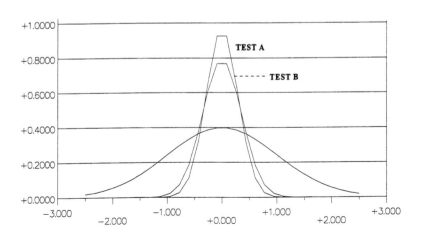

from random error alone.

The first two properties can be determined by examining the observed and expected frequency distributions. The third property can be verified with an F max assessment (Winer, 1971). If any of the three properties are found not to be operant, the score invariance property is not validated. Otherwise, the score invariance property is operant, and the observed score differences are due at most to random error.

The empirical research performed to date seem on the surface to validate the invariance properties. However, certain problems exist concerning the indices used in these studies, indices have been presented which directly test the invariance properties. There is a need for simulations studies where the dimensional and error structures are known before the final page is written on the topic of item response theory.

Notes

1. The least possible logit score in the case of the interval scale.
2. In the case of the three parameter model, where p=c.
3. The general two parameter as well as three parameter models do not constrain the values of any parameter. However, events with negative or zero discrimination indices are of no practical value.

5

Using Assessment Results for Individuals

Three item response theory models and the research associated with them have been discussed and described in the previous chapters. Classical Fisherian techniques have been often used to examine this data. The classical statistical paradigms, based on agricultural research models, assume that the data is obtained without error. Learner behavior is not assessed in deterministic terms. Learner behavior is dynamic in the sense that it is constantly changing and that any point estimate of an attribute is, at best, only an approximation of the position of a moving object on a latent dimension. Since the dimension is latent, we can only assume a direct association with the underlying construct (no error in construct validity). Since the object is dynamic, we can never assume assessment without error unless we adopt a repeated measures design and model the dynamic nature of the learner in the assessment paradigm.

The classical models could be applied if no conceptual errors are present in the assessment (content validity) and the assessment score error is uniformly distributed across the range of possible values. As we have discussed in the previous five chapters, the assessment error is not uniformly distributed across the range of possible values. We know that content validity is strived for; but, the latent nature of the psychological space, renders the assurance of conceptually error free assessment untenable.

We will now use the fundamental theorems of latent trait assessment to present a comparative methodology for learner and group comparison which incorporates the latent nature of the measurement and the variational nature of the error term. Examples of each process will also be presented. Not only has developmental learning theory taken the concept of the learner and the application of assessment results to a new dimension, developmental learning theory has resulted in new data analysis paradigms which will, conceptually, more precisely reflect the characteristics of the learner.

A word on "significance." For the purposes of this discussion we must understand that *significant does not mean important!* The technical term of the word significance only means that we can be reasonably confident that some indicator (assessment score, difference between assessment scores, etc) is not zero. *A nonzero (methodologically "significant") indicator is necessary **but not sufficient** evidence to conclude that the indicator is important!* Importance of a nonzero difference is in the eye of the interpreter.

No paradigm will assess the importance of a, probably, nonzero difference.
That decision is an valuative decision predicated on programmatic,
curricular, and policy parameters which can never be built into a
methodological solution process. Certainly, we must be confident that an
indicator is not zero before concluding that it is significant (important). *A
methodologically significant (nonzero) indicator may not, necessarily, be
substantively large, important, interesting, or otherwise useful (substantively
significant).*

INDIVIDUAL CHANGE SCORES

If a particular individual is administered an assessment on two distinct
occasions and the scores assigned by these assessments to that individual are
not identical, two questions arise:

- Is the observed assessment score difference indicative of a true score
  difference?

- Are the observed assessment score differences due to the dynamic nature
  of the learner and the elusive nature of the domain of assessment
  (previously called measurement error).

The purpose of this section is to present a paradigm for testing the
significance of observed differences in latent trait scores obtained for the
same individual from two or more assessments and is organized in three
parts First, the model for assessing the significance of change scores is
presented. The second and third parts provide examples of increases in
performance.

A Change Model

Let z_1 represent the assessment score for a particular individual at one point
in time and $s_1(z_1)$ correspond to the standard error associated with that
assessment score. Let z_2 represent the assessment for the same individual at
a different point in time and $s_2(z_2)$ correspond to the associated standard
error. Let μ_1 and μ_2 represent the true latent attribute assessment scores
corresponding to the observed assessment scores. The fundamental measurement model can be applied to the data to obtain equations relating the
observed scores as well as the corresponding error components, e_1 and e_2.

$$\left.\begin{array}{l} z_1 = \mu_1 + e_1 \\ z_2 = \mu_2 + e_2 \end{array}\right\} \qquad 5.1$$

The error term, e_1, is normally distributed with a mean of zero and a standard deviation of s_1. The second error term, e_2 is also normally distributed with a mean of zero; but, the standard deviation of the distribution of the second error term is s_2

The null hypothesis is that no change has occurred. The methodological interpretation of the null hypothesis in terms of true scores is that the true scores are equal ($\mu_1 = \mu_2$, or $\mu_1 - \mu_2 = 0$). Applying the null hypothesis, the observed score difference is related to the difference between error components,

$$z_1 - z_2 = (\mu_1 - \mu_2) + (e_1 - e_2) = 0 + (e_1 - e_2) = e_1 - e_2.$$

Therefore, the difference between the observed scores is normally distributed with a mean of zero and a variance of $s_1^2 + s_2^2$ when true scores are iden-

tical. A test statistic, ξ, equal to a weighted difference score and defined by

$\xi = \dfrac{z_2 - z_1}{\sqrt{s_1^2 + s_2^2}}$ (*Equation5.2*), is normally distributed with a mean

of zero and a variance of 1.0 when true scores are identical ($\mu_1 = \mu_2$, or $\mu_1 - \mu_2 = 0$). If ξ is greater than 1.96, the null hypothesis is rejected and it is inferred that a nonzero difference between true scores existed. If ξ is less than 1.96, the null hypothesis is not rejected and it is inferred that the true score difference corresponding to the observed assessment score difference is zero (i.e., $\mu_1 = \mu_2$, or $\mu_1 - \mu_2 = 0$); that is, the observed difference between assessment scores was not sufficiently large to conclude that any true score difference existed.

The mathematical details concerning the assessment of individual change have been described above. The purpose of this paradigm is to determine if an observed score difference for the same individual corresponds to a on zero (not necessarily meaningful) true score difference or merely due to chance. The remainder of this section will be devoted to the presentation of three examples of the application of this paradigm. One example will be concerned with a case where a nonzero increase in true score has occurred. The first example is a case where the null hypothesis is rejected and meaningful gains in true scores exist. The second example concerns a case where the observed score difference does not correspond to a meaningful true assessment score gain. The second example is a case where the null hypothesis is accepted and meaningful (nonzero) true assessment score differences do not exist. The third example is a case where a meaningful decrease in true assessment scores occurred.

Assessing Individual Gains

When a particular student is administered a test at two points in time and the student's assessment score obtained from the second administration is greater than the score obtained from the first administration, two questions arise:

1. Does the gain in observed scores indicate a positive change (gain) has occurred?

2. Is the observed score difference an artifact of assessment error or due to chance; the observed score difference not being indicative of a meaningful positive true score change?

The purpose of this section is to present two examples of the test of observed score gains. The first example concerns a case where a gain is evident. The second example concerns a case where a gain has not occurred.

TRUE SCORE GAIN

In the fall, a student enrolled in an algebra class was administered an assessment designed to assess symbol manipulation skills. An equivalent assessment was administered in the spring of the same year. The logit scores assigned to the student are shown in Table 5.1. Entrance into the next mathematics class in a sequence is based, in part, upon the recommendation of the professor who felt it necessary to determine whether or not meaningful learning had occurred with respect to symbol manipulation before recommending the student for promotion.

Table 5.1:
Logit Assessment Scores

Administration	Assessment Score	Standard Error
Fall	-0.25 (z_1)	0.15 (s_1)
Spring	0.75 (z_2)	0.20 (s_2)

The null hypothesis is that there is no change in true scores between the two administrations ($\mu_{fall} = \mu_{spring}$). The assessment scores and their associated standard errors were substituted into Equation 5.2 to determine the value of the test statistic. The details of that calculation are:

$$
\left.
\begin{aligned}
\xi &= \frac{z_2 - z_1}{\sqrt{s_1^2 + s_2^2}} = \frac{0.75 - (-0.25)}{\sqrt{(0.15)^2 + (0.20)^2}} \\[2mm]
&= \frac{0.75 + 0.25}{\sqrt{0.0225 + 0.040}} = \frac{1.00}{\sqrt{0.0625}} \\[2mm]
&= \frac{1.00}{0.25} = 4.00
\end{aligned}
\right\}
\qquad 5\text{-}3
$$

Because the value of the test statistic (ξ=4.00) is greater than the critical value of the normal deviate at the 95 percent confidence level (1.96), the null hypothesis ($\mu_{fall} = \mu_{spring}$) was rejected. The professor was 95 percent confident that an increase in true score occurred. Equipped with the assessment information and other data the professor gathered throughout the year, the student was recommended for promotion to the next mathematics course.

NON-MEANINGFUL GAINS

It is possible for a student to be administered an assessment on two different occasions in which the score assigned by the assessment on the second administration is greater than the score assigned at the first administration, and no meaningful true score difference occurred.

This occurs when the observed assessment scores are different ($z_1 \neq z_2$; *in this case* $z_1 < z_2$), but that difference is not sufficiently large to infer that any true score difference exists. The purpose of this discussion is to present an example of such a situation.

A particular student is enrolled in a remedial English composition course at a junior college. The student received this distinction by obtaining a score on a preliminary screening examination that was below a cutoff score established by the faculty. The college policy is that any student must repeat a particular unit until nonzero gains are evidenced by pre- and post assessment data. The pre- and post assessment scores obtained by this student are shown in Table 5.2. The instructor's dilemma is to determine whether or not the observed score difference corresponds to a nonzero true score gain. If the observed score difference corresponds to a nonzero true score gain, the student must go on to the next curricular unit in the sequence. If the observed score difference does not imply a nonzero true score gain, the student must be issued another resource related to the curricular unit that the student was previously engaged.

Table 5.2:
Results for a Particular Student from an Assessment of Sentence Structure Proficiency.

Administration	Assessment Score	Standard Error
Preassessment	-1.25 (z_1)	0.60 (s_1)
Post Assessment	-0.75 (z_2)	0.45 (s_2)

The value of the normal deviate, ξ, corresponding to the observed score difference is calculated as discussed previously. The observed score difference is $z_2 - z_1 = -0.75 - (-1.25) = 0.50$. The standard error of this difference is :

$$\sqrt{(0.60)^2 + (0.45)^2} = \sqrt{0.36 + 0.2025} = \sqrt{0.5625} = 0.75 .$$

The value of the appropriate statistic, ξ, is the quotient of the observed score difference and the standard error of that difference ($\xi = \dfrac{0.50}{0.75} = 0.667$).

As the value of ξ is less than the value of the normal deviate a t the 95 percent confidence level (1.96), the inference is that no meaningful true score gains have occurred. The instructor assigned the student to an alternative curriculum unit concerning sentence structure.

ASSESSING NEGATIVE CHANGE

When an assessment is administered to a particular student on two different administrations and the second test score is less than the first, two questions are often asked.

1. Has the student become confused in the intervening period between assessments and is not as operationally functional after the second administration as at the first administration?

2. Is the observed score difference due to assessment misalignment and not indicative of a meaningful true score decrease?

The purpose of this exposition is to present an example of situations reflected by these questions and the application of the confidence testing model to this problem. The first example relates to the situation where a true score decrease has occurred. The second example concerns the situation where an observed score decrease does not correspond to a meaningful true score decrease.

A particular student was involved in a curriculum experiment. The student was administered two treatments. The treatments were sequential in the sense that the student experienced the second treatment after completing the first. An assessment was administered after the student completed each treatment. The reader familiar with experimental design will recognize this as a repeated measures design. The assessment scores are shown in Table 5.3. The question posed is whether or not the observed score difference represents a true score decrease.

Table 5.3:
Results For An Individual In A Repeated Assessment Design

Treatment	Assessment Score	Standard Error
First	$1.50\ (z_1)$	$1.00\ (s_1)$
Second	$1.25\ (z_2)$	$0.80\ (s_2)$

The meaningfulness of the true score difference corresponding to the observed score difference can be assessed using the data in Table 5.3 and Equation 5.2. The absolute value of the difference score is $|\,1.25 - 1.50\,| = |-0.25\,| = 0.25$. The standard error of the difference is the square root of the sum of the squares of the standards errors corresponding to each assessment indicator

$$\sqrt{(1.00)^2 + (0.80)^2} = \sqrt{1.00 + 0.64} = \sqrt{1.64} = 1.281\,.$$

The value of the test statistic, ξ, is the quotient of the absolute difference and the standard error of that difference ($\xi = \dfrac{0.25}{1.281} = 0.195$). Because the observed value of ξ is less than the critical value (1.96) at the 95 percent confidence level, it was concluded that no true score difference was reflected in the data. The data do not support a differential treatment effect for this particular individual.

The mathematical paradigm for assessing the confidence that can be placed in change scores has been presented in this section. In addition, examples of the application of the model to assessment gains and decreases have been presented. The next section will describe paradigms for making inferences concerning group difference.

6

Using Assessment for Program Validation
Examples of Qualitative Data Analysis

Assessment results are often used for the purpose of educational and social program validation as well as criteria in designed experiments. The purpose of this section is to present paradigms by which assessments can be used for the purpose of validation of program outcomes, program evaluation, and as criteria in many experimental designs. The particular designs considered in this section are two group comparisons, preassessment versus post assessment treatment versus control contrasts, repeated assessment designs with k replications, and factorial designs with k levels. Although each design is described in this chapter, no attempt at rigorous design descriptions is attempted. The purpose of this chapter is to describe procedures by which the fundamental assessment model can be applied to each design. The reader interested in the details concerning each design is referred to the experimental design literature (Blalock, 1964; Campbell & Stanley, 1963; Kerlinger, 1973; Winer, 1971). Examples of the application of the theory to each design are presented. In certain instances matrix algebra and vector notation were necessary to specify the model and equations effectively. Vector and matrix arithmetic are often described in a high school modern algebra textbook. The reader interested in presentations of matrix and vector procedures and notation is referred to the many excellent presentations in the literature (Bock, 1975; Finn, 1974; Kerlinger & Pedhazer, 1973; Rummel, 1970).

The fundamental assessment model is extended to group situations. Procedures by which the fundamental assessment model can be used for making inferences between two groups of individuals are described. Next, the application of the fundamental assessment model to situations where two groups of individuals are defined (treatment and control), an assessment administered at the start of the experiment or program, and the same or equivalent assessment was administered at the end of the program or after the treatment was administered to one of the two groups is considered. Subsequently, the situation where the same group of subjects who have been subjected to two or more programs or treatments is discussed. Next, the application of the fundamental assessment model to the situation where two or more groups of individuals are compared to the same criterion or instrument is described. The last section presents applications of the fundamental assessment model to higher order factorial designs.

Fundamental Assessment Model

In the previous section a relation between the observed assessment score, z, for a particular individual, the true score, μ , for that individual and an error component, e, was defined. A true score was defined as an assessment indicator for which the error of assessment was exactly zero (that is, an assessment without error). The observed assessment indicator was defined as the sum of the true score and the error term ($z = \mu + e$). The definition of an observed assessment indicator in terms of a true indicator and an error term is the *fundamental assessment model*. The model further specified that the error term, e, was normally distributed with a mean of zero and a standard deviation equal to the standard error of assessment associated with the observed indicator, s. The purpose of this section is to extend the results obtained by applying the fundamental assessment model with individual assessment scores to aggregated assessment indicators obtained from groups of individuals.

Consider a group of N subjects. The observed assessment indicator for the i-th individual is symbolized by z_i . The true score and error components for the i-th subject are symbolized by μ_i and e_i , respectively. The error component is distributed as $N(0, s_i^2)$, where s_i symbolizes the standard error associated with the assessment score z_i obtained from the i-th individual. Using this notation, the fundamental assessment model implies a specific functional relation between the three quantities, z_i, μ_i, and e_i .

$$z_i = \mu_i + e_i \ where \ e_i \sim \mathbb{N}(0, s_i^2) \qquad 6.1$$

Define the mean or average assessment indicator for the group, $\bar{z}$, as the sum of the observed indicators for each individual composing the group (sum over all i, i = 1, $\cdots$, N) divided by the number of subjects in the group, N. Equation 6.1 can be used to determine the relation between the group mean, the individual true indicators, and the individual error scores.

$$\bar{z} = \frac{1}{N} \sum_{i=1}^{N} \mu_i + \frac{1}{N} \sum_{i=1}^{N} e_i \qquad 6.2$$

Define the mean true score for the group, $\bar{\mu}$, and the mean error component for the group, $\bar{e}$, as the average of the true scores and error components over all individuals composing the group. The mean true score is a single parameter characteristic of the group in the space of true scores or error free measurement. The mean observed score is an estimate of the mean true score. That estimates contains error. Equation 6.2 can be rewritten in terms of the mean true score and the mean error component as
$$\bar{z} = \bar{\mu} + \bar{e} \quad (6.3).$$

To completely specify 6.3 and the associated model, it is necessary to determine the distribution of the mean error term. If it is assumed that the error terms e_i and e_j $(i \neq j)$ are stochastically independent, the distribution of $\bar{e}$ can be completely specified.

Assume that the individuals who compose the group are stochastically independent . Stochastic independence means that the responses, or equivalently the assessment indicators, of any single individual are not necessarily dependent upon the assessment score or responses of any other individual or group of individuals. The fundamental assessment model stipulates that each error term is normally distributed with a mean of zero and known variance, s_i^2 . A well known result of probability theory is that if N stochastically independent random variables, x_i, are distributed as $\mathbb{N}(M, s_i^2)$, then the mean of the random variables is distributed as $\mathbb{N}(M, S^2)$, where S^2 is the mean of the individual variances,

$$S^2 = \frac{1}{N} \sum_{i=1}^{N} s_i^2 .$$ (Harris, 1966; Freund, 1962). Therefore, the mean

error term is normally distributed with a mean of zero and a standard deviation equal to the square root of the mean of the individual error variances.

It is now possible to specify a corollary to the fundamental assessment model. If a group consists of N subjects, the observed, true, and error components associated with the i-th individual are symbolized by z_i, μ_i, and e_i , respectively. The observed indicators are stochastically independent, and $\bar{z}$, $\bar{\mu}$, $and\ \bar{e}$ symbolize the mean observed indicator, true indicator, and error components, respectively, then the mean indicators are related by the following equations.

$$\left. \begin{array}{c} \bar{z} = \bar{\mu} + \bar{e} \\[2ex] where\ \bar{e} \sim \mathbb{N}(0,S^2)\ and\ S = \sqrt{\dfrac{1}{N}\displaystyle\sum_{i=1}^{N} s_i^2} \end{array} \right\} \qquad 6.4$$

This corollary will be called the fundamental assessment model for groups.

A measurement model specifying the relationship between the mean observed, true score, and error components for any particular group has been presented. It has been demonstrated that the group model is a direct extension of the fundamental assessment model discussed in previous chapters. The remainder of this chapter will be concerned with applying this group model to two group comparisons, pre- versus post assessment and treatment versus control group designs, repeated assessment designs, as well as factorial comparisons.

Between Group Comparisons

In many situations the investigator is concerned with comparing two groups of subjects with respect to some criterion. The investigator may randomly assign subjects to one of two groups. One of the groups receives some treatment while the other group does not receive the treatment. An evaluator may be interested in the differences (if any) in achievement exhibited by two groups of students, each group having used one of two texts. Two comparable groups are selected. One group uses one of the two texts while the second group uses the other text. The evaluator compares the two groups with respect to two assessments. The purpose of this section is to present the procedure by which the fundamental assessment model can be applied to this problem.

Consider two groups where group 1 contains $N(1)$ subjects and group 2 contains $N(2)$ subjects. The assessment score, true score, error component, and standard error for the i-th individual in the j-th group (j = 1 or 2 in this case) are symbolized by z_{ij}, μ_{ij}, e_{ij}, and s_{ij}, respectively. The mean assessment indicator, true score, and error components for the j-th group are symbolized by $z_{\bullet j}$, $\mu_{\bullet j}$, and $e_{\bullet j}$, respectively. The standard error of assessment corresponding to the j-th group mean is symbolized by $s_{\bullet j}$. The global group parameters can be written in terms of the components of the observed score for each individual composing the respective groups using the fundamental assessment model for groups.

$$z_{\bullet j} = \frac{1}{N(j)} \sum_{i=1}^{N(j)} z_{ij} \qquad \qquad 6.5$$

$$z_{\bullet j} = \mu_{\bullet j} + e_{\bullet j} \qquad \qquad 6.6$$

$$and \ s_{\bullet j}^2 = \frac{1}{N(j)} \sum_{i=1}^{N(j)} s_{ij}^2 \qquad \qquad 6.7$$

$$\left. \begin{array}{c} z_{\bullet 1} = \mu_{\bullet 1} + e_{\bullet 1} \\[2mm] z_{\bullet 2} = \mu_{\bullet 2} + e_{\bullet 2} \\[2mm] where \ e_{\bullet 1} \sim \mathbb{N}(0, s_{\bullet 1}^2), \ e_{\bullet 2} \sim \mathbb{N}(0, s_{\bullet 2}^2) \\[2mm] and \ s_{\bullet 1} = \frac{1}{N(1)} \sum_{i=1}^{N(1)} s_{i1}^2 \ s_{\bullet 2} = \frac{1}{N(1)} \sum_{i=1}^{N(2)} s_{i2}^2 \end{array} \right\} \qquad 6.8$$

Consider two groups of individuals. The following relations can be written directly from the equations above.

Assume that the group means are not numerically identical $(z_{\bullet i} \neq z_{\bullet j})$. The issue of immediate concern is whether or not the nonzero difference of group means implies a non zero difference of true scores $(z_{\bullet i} - z_{\bullet j} \neq 0 \rightarrow \mu_{\bullet i} - \mu_{\bullet j} \neq 0)$. If the null hypothesis, $\mu_{\bullet i} - \mu_{\bullet j} \neq 0$, is accepted, the observed difference between the group means is due to assessment error. If the alternative hypothesis, $\mu_{\bullet i} - \mu_{\bullet j} \neq 0$, is accepted, the observed nonzero difference in group means is indicative of the potential for a substantively meaningful difference between groups.

Using Equation 6.6 the observed difference can be expressed in terms of a mean true score difference and a mean difference between error components,

$$z_{\bullet i} - z_{\bullet j} = (\mu_{\bullet i} - \mu_{\bullet j}) + (e_{\bullet i} - e_{\bullet j}) \ Equation \ 6.9) \ .$$

If the null hypothesis is true, the observed indicator difference can be attributed directly to assessment error,

$$z_{\bullet i} - z_{\bullet j} = e_{\bullet i} - e_{\bullet j}, \ Equation \ 6.10 \ .$$

Consider the test statistic ξ defined by, Equation 7-14. Because the error components are normally distributed with a mean of zero and their respective error variances, the test statistic, ξ, is distributed as $N(0, 1)$ if the null hypothesis is accurate. Therefore, if ξ is greater than 1.96 (at the 95 percent confidence level) the null hypothesis is rejected and the nonzero difference between group means is attributed to a real difference between true score means ($\mu_{\bullet_i} \neq \mu_{\bullet_j}$). If ξ is less than 1.96, the null hypothesis is accepted at the 95 percent confidence level and any observed differences between group means is attributed to assessment error.

A department in a moderately sized suburban college wishes to make a decision relative to the adoption of two possible textbooks. Initially, sufficient numbers of each book were purchased so that each book could be assigned to one and only one section. Students are alphabetically assigned to sections and the school officials felt that the groups of students were comparable. One group (designated Textbook 1) had 10 students and the second group (designated Textbook 2) had 12 students. An assessment designed to assess the proficiency of students relative to course objectives was administered to each group at the end of the trial period. The mean and standard errors for the two groups were:
$z_{\bullet_1} = 0.8749$ ($s_{\bullet_1} = 0.5058$) and $z_{\bullet_2} = -0.5057$ ($s_{\bullet_2} = 0.3991$).
The difference between group means was $0.8749 - (-0.5057) = 0.8749 + 0.5057$, or 1.3806. The observed difference between group means was not zero. The standard error of the difference in group means was

$$\sqrt{(0.5058)^2 + (0.3991)^2} = \sqrt{0.2558 + 0.1593} = \sqrt{0.4151}, \text{or}$$
0.6443.

The test statistic, ξ, is the quotient of the difference between group means (1.3806) and the standard error of that difference (0.6443), $\xi = \dfrac{1.3806}{0.6443}$, or
2.1428. Because the value of the test statistic is greater than the critical value of a unit normal deviate at the 95 percent confidence level (1.96), the null hypothesis was rejected. These results indicate that there is a true score difference between group means, and the textbooks seem to have a differential impact upon students. In so much as one can ascertain that no difference other than the textbook used existed between groups, the textbook designated as textbook 1 is the better book.

The procedure for comparing two groups of individuals administered the same or equivalent instruments has been presented. An example of the application of that procedure has also been described. The remainder of this chapter will describe the application of the fundamental assessment model to treatment versus control and preassessment versus post assessment, repeated measures, and factorial designs.

Preassessment-Post assessment Two Group Designs

A classical experimental and evaluation design is the treatment control, preassessment-post assessment design. With this type of design two groups of subjects are selected. One group is administered an experimental treatment. The remaining group is not administered the treatment. The group that is administered the treatment is called the treatment or experimental group. The group that is not administered the treatment is designated as the control or reference group. An assessment (such as ability or attainment) relative to experimental or program criteria is obtained prior

Table 6.1:
Notational Scheme for Symbols Corresponding to Aggregated Data for the Preassessment-post Assessment Treatment Versus Control Group Design.

| | Group Designation | | | |
| | Treatment | | Control | |
Index	Preassessment	Postassessment	Preassessment	Postassessment
Observations	$\overline{z}_{11}$	$\overline{z}_{12}$	$\overline{z}_{21}$	$\overline{z}_{22}$
Standard error	$\overline{s}_{11}$	$\overline{s}_{12}$	$\overline{s}_{21}$	$\overline{s}_{22}$
Mean true score	$\overline{\mu}_{11}$	$\overline{\mu}_{12}$	$\overline{\mu}_{21}$	$\overline{\mu}_{22}$
Mean error term	$\overline{e}_{11}$	$\overline{e}_{12}$	$\overline{e}_{21}$	$\overline{e}_{22}$

to administering the treatment to the experimental group. Pretreatment assessment (called the preassessment) indicators are obtained from each member of both groups (treatment and control). The same instrument or an equivalent form of that instrument is used to obtain assessments after the treatment has been administered. The instrument used to obtain the post treatment data is called the post assessment. Post assessment data are also obtained from each member of both groups (treatment and control).

The major inferential question relative to this type of design is whether or not the observed difference over time (preassessment minus post assessment) for the treatment group members is attributable to the treatment, to maturation, to the effect of being exposed to the preassessment, or to some other nontreatment related phenomenon. The issue is addressed by comparing the difference over time for the treatment group with the difference over time for the nontreatment or control group. The question posed is whether or not the observed preassessment-post assessment difference observed for the treatment group is different from the same difference over time for the control group. If the differences over tie for the two groups are not different, it is concluded that the treatment did not have an effect upon the subjects. If the differences over time for the two groups are significantly different, it is concluded that the treatment did have an effect on the experimental subjects.

With this type of design there are two assessment scores for each individual (a preassessment and post assessment indicator). Associated with each assessment indicator is a true score, error term, and standard error of assessment. In order to simplify the notation a particular notational scheme has been employed here.

The fundamental assessment model for group means results in four equations defining the relations between observed scores, true scores, and error components.

$$\left. \begin{array}{c} \overline{z_{ij}} = \overline{\mu_{ij}} + \overline{e_{ij}} \\ where\ \overline{e_{ij}} \sim \mathbb{N}(0, \overline{s_{ij}}) \end{array} \right\} \qquad 6.11$$

The preassessment-post assessment difference (variation over time) for the treatment group, ∇_t, and the control group, ∇_c, can be expressed in terms of true scores and error terms. The expression of these differences is obtained by subtraction and application of the terms in Equation 6.11. These differences are:

$$\nabla_t = \overline{z_{12}} - \overline{z_{11}} = (\overline{\mu_{12}} - \overline{\mu_{11}}) + (\overline{e_{12}} - \overline{e_{11}}) \qquad 6.12$$

$$\nabla_c = \overline{z_{22}} - \overline{z_{21}} = (\overline{\mu_{22}} - \overline{\mu_{21}}) + (\overline{e_{22}} - \overline{e_{21}}) \qquad 6.13$$

Assume that the observed score mean differences for each group over time are not equal ($\nabla_t - \nabla_c \neq 0$). The inferential question is whether or not that nonzero difference implies a differential variation in the true scores over time ($H1$: $\overline{\mu_{12}} - m\overline{\mu_{11}} \neq \overline{\mu_{22}} - \overline{\mu_{21}}$) or attributable to assessment error. The null hypothesis is that the observed nonzero difference ($\nabla_t - \nabla_c \neq 0$) is due to assessment error and does not imply a nonzero differential variation in true scores

$$(H0: \overline{\mu_{12}} - \overline{\mu_{11}} \neq \overline{\mu_{22}} - \overline{\mu_{21}}).$$

The difference between observed variations over time are related to the differential differences between true scores and an error term. Assuming the null hypothesis, the test statistic, ξ, defined to be the quotient of the values of the differential contrast and the associated standard error is normally distributed with a mean of zero and a variance of 1.0.

$$\xi = \frac{\nabla_C - \nabla_T}{S} = \frac{(\overline{z_{22}} - \overline{z_{21}}) - (\overline{z_{12}} - \overline{z_{11}})}{\sqrt{\overline{s_{11}}^2 + \overline{s_{12}}^2 + \overline{s_{21}}^2 + \overline{s_{22}}^2}} \qquad 6.14$$

Therefore, if the value of the test statistic is greater than the expected value of the normal deviate (1.96 at the 95 percent confidence level), the null hypothesis is rejected and it is inferred that a differential variation in true scores exists; the treatment had some impact on the subjects in the treatment group that was not evident in the control group. If the value of the test statistic is less than the expected value of the normal deviate, it is inferred that a differential variation in true scores over time is not evident in the data and the treatment did not exhibit any effect upon the subjects in the treatment group that was not also evident in the control group.

At this point a theoretical discussion of the use of the fundamental assessment model for group data relative to making inferences regarding the preassessment-post assessment, treatment-control design has been presented. The following example describes the numerical details necessary to apply the model.

Table 6.2:
A Pre and Post Assessment Experimental Design

Instrument

Experimental	Preassessment		Post Assessment	
Group	Mean	Std. Error	Mean	Std. Error
Treatment	2.735	0.413	5.707	0.597
Control	2.031	0.356	4.755	0.545

A school district considered adopting an individualized instructional sequence in general mathematics. An issue that concerned the teacher union officials and the district supervisors was whether the increased learning (if any) experienced by students tutored individually over students traditionally tutored would warrant the expenditure of facilitator time. It had not been demonstrated that any difference existed at all between the individualized and traditional curriculum delivery modes. It was decided to conduct an experiment. Four hundred students were randomly assigned to one of two treatment groups. One group with 200 students was to experience the individualized instruction (treatment group), the remaining 200 students were provided traditional experiences (control group). Each of the two groups consisted of 10 classrooms, and facilitators were randomly assigned to classrooms. Each student was administered a comprehensive general mathematics assessments at the beginning and end of the school year. The results are shown below.

The average preassessment and post assessment scores for the subjects assigned to the treatment group were 2.735 and 5.707, respectively. The average preassessment and post assessment indicators for the subjects assigned to the control group were 2.031 and 4.755, respectively. Therefore, the indicator difference, ∇_t, for the treatment group subjects over time was 5.707-2.735, or 2.972. The test score difference, ∇_c, for the subjects assigned to the control group was 5.744-2.031, or 2.724. The value of the differential contrast $\nabla_c - \nabla_t$ is 2.724-2.972, or 0.248 in absolute value. The standard error of the differential contrast is equal to the square root of the sum of the squares of the standard errors of each group,

$$S = \sqrt{(0.413)^2 + (0.356)^2 + (0.597)^2 + (0.545)^2} = \sqrt{0.951},$$

or 0.975.

The value of the test statistic is the quotient of the values of the differential contrast and the standard error of the differential contrast, $\xi = \dfrac{0.248}{0.975}$, or 0.254. This value of the test statistic is not greater than the critical value of a unit normal deviate at the 95 percent confidence level (1.96). It is inferred that no differential variation in true scores was observed for this data set. Therefore, no meaningful improvement was observed for subjects assigned to individualized general mathematics programs that was not also observed for traditionally tutored students.

A procedure for the application of the fundamental assessment model to preassessment-post assessment experimental designs has been presented in this section. An example of the application of the procedure to such a design has also been presented. The remainder of this chapter will discuss procedures for using assessments and the fundamental assessment model for repeated assessments and factorial designs. The next section is concerned with the repeated measurement design. The final section will be attend to the k group factorial design.

Repeated Assessment Designs

Consider a set of k possible treatments. A group of N subjects are exposed to each of the k treatments. Therefore, there exist k assessment indicators for each of the N individuals. Such a design is called a repeated measurement design with k replications.

The j-th assessment score for the i-th individual, z_{ij}, is the sum of the true indicators for that individual, μ_i, a constant component due to the presence of the treatment, t_j, and an error factor, e_{ij}. The standard error of the j-th assessment for the i-th individual is symbolized by s_{ij}. The observed score for the i-th individual obtained during the j-th treatment is an estimate of the sum of the true score component due to the treatment. The observed score for a particular individual is conceptualized as the sum of the individual's true score, a true score component for the treatment, and an error component.

$$z_{ij} = \mu_i + t_j + e_{ij} \text{ where } e_{ij} \sim \mathbb{N}(0, s_{ij}^2) \qquad 6.15$$

The experimenter is often concerned with whether or not treatment p results in scores that are different from the scores obtained for the same subjects in treatment q (that is, $t_p = t_q$ or $t_p \neq t_q$). The null hypothesis is the case where there is no between treatment effect and $t_p = t_q$. Consider the difference between the scores obtained for the same individual when involved with each of the treatments, $z_{ip} - z_{iq}$.

$$
\left.
\begin{aligned}
z_{ip} - z_{iq} &= [\mu_i + t_p + e_{ip}) - [\mu_i + t_q + e_{iq}] \\
&\quad \{t_p - t_q\} + [e_{ip} - e_{iq}]
\end{aligned}
\right\} \qquad 6.16
$$

Under the influence of the null hypothesis, the difference between treatment true scores is exactly zero, $t_p - t_q = 0$. Therefore, the observed score difference can be expressed in terms of random error, $z_{ip} - z_{iq} = e_{ip} - e_{iq}$, [*Equation,* 6.17]. Because the distributions of the error terms are known, it is also known that the distribution of the

variable, $\xi_i = \dfrac{z_{ip} - z_{iq}}{\sqrt{s_{ip}^2 + s_{iq}^2}}$ [*Equation* 6.18] is normally distributed

with zero mean and unit variance and the sum of squares of this statistic over each of the N subjects is distributed as χ^2 with N degrees of freedom (Harris, 1966; Freund, 1962). Define the test statistic ξ_{pq} corresponding to a contrast between treatments p and q by equation 6.18. If that statistic is greater than the critical value of χ^2 with N degrees of freedom, the null hypothesis is rejected and it is inferred that a nonzero between treatment effect exists. If the value of the test statistic is less than the critical value of χ^2 the null hypothesis is not rejected and it is inferred that no significant treatment effect existed.

$$
\xi_{pq} = \sum_{i=1}^{N} \xi_i^2 = \sum_{i=1}^{N} \frac{(z_{ip} - z_{iq})^2}{s_{ip}^2 + s_{iq}^2} \qquad 6.19
$$

The model developed in this section can be extended to multigroup contrasts. The set of all assessment indicators for the i-th individual can be considered to form a matrix, Z_i, with k columns. The set of all standard errors can be considered to form a matrix, S, with N rows and k columns. The standard errors for a particular subject form a particular row of the S matrix. The multigroup contrast can be written in terms of a *1 x k* row vector, Δ. The elements of the row vector sum to zero ($\sum_{i=1}^{N} \Delta_i = 0$) and correspond to the contrast of interest.

For example, in an experiment with three replications, the contrast vector, Δ, contains three elements (a 1 x 3 matrix). To contrast the first treatment with the second treatment, the required contrast vector would be $(1, -1, 0)$. To contrast the second treatment with the mean of the first and third treatments, the required contrast vector would be

$(-\frac{1}{2}, 1, -\frac{1}{2})$. An argument similar to that presented for the two group repeated assessment case results in the observation that the test statistic ξ_Δ is distributed as χ^2 with N degrees of freedom.

$$\left. \begin{array}{c} \xi_\Delta = \sum_{i=1}^{N} \frac{(\Delta Z_i^T)^2}{S_i^2} \\[3mm] where \ S_i = \sum_{j=1}^{N} \Delta_j^2 s_{ij}^2 \end{array} \right\} \qquad 6.20$$

The test statistics for making inferential statements relative to treatment contrasts in the k treatment repeated assessment model have been presented. The remainder of this section will present an example of the application of the model.

Table 6.3:
Repeated Assessment Design Results

	Discipline Condition		
Student	**Harsh**	**Moderate**	**Lax**
1	1.32(0.27)	1.67(0.41)	0.82(0.15)
2	2.71(0.62)	3.51(0.65)	1.21(0.16)
3	1.41(0.20)	2.60(0.60)	0.51(0.10)
4	3.56(0.65)	4.80(0.70)	2.61(0.60)
5	0.85(0.15)	2.30(0.55)	1.30(0.17)

*Standard errors are enclosed in parentheses.

A experimenter wished to determine whether or not the amount of discipline reflected in the climate of a classroom affected the achievement of student in that classroom.

In this hypothetical experiment five students were subjected to three experimentally manipulated discipline conditions: harsh, moderate, and lax. A general achievement assessment was administered after each treatment.

Table 6.4:
Arrangement of Data for a Two Group Repeated Assessment Contrast

	Assessment Results				
	Discipline Treatment				
Student	**Moderate**	**Lax**	z_{12}-z_{13}	$s^2_{12} - s^2_{13}$	ξ^2_1
1	1.67 (0.41)	0.82 (0.15)	0.85	0.191	3.791
2	3.51 (0.65)	1.21 (0.16)	2.30	0.448	11.805
3	2.60 (0.60)	0.51 (0.10)	2.09	0.370	11.806
4	4.80 (0.70)	2.61 (0.60)	2.19	0.850	5.642
5	2.30 (0.50)	1.30 (0.17)	1.00	0.331	3.018

*Standard errors are shown in parentheses.

The experimenter hypothesized that the observed difference between moderate and lax discipline groups was significant based upon the analysis presented in tabular form below (Table 6.4). The value of the test statistic for this contrast was 36.002 with five degrees of freedom. The probability of obtaining a value of χ^2 at least this large due to chance was less than 0.001. The experimenter concluded that the data indicated that students educated in moderately disciplined environments tended to achieve more than students in classrooms that lacked discipline.

The experimenter also wished to contrast the subjects who were enrolled in harshly disciplined classrooms with those enrolled in moderately disciplined or lax classrooms. This was a multitreatment comparison. The required contrast vector was $\Delta = [\, 1\, , \ -\frac{1}{2}\, , \ -\frac{1}{2}\,]$. The assessment indicator, Z, and standard error, S, matrices are shown below.

$$
Z = \begin{bmatrix} 1.32 & 1.67 & 0.82 \\ 2.71 & 3.51 & 1.21 \\ 1.41 & 2.60 & 0.51 \\ 3.56 & 4.80 & 2.61 \\ 0.85 & 2.30 & 1.30 \end{bmatrix} \quad S = \begin{bmatrix} 0.27 & 0.41 & 0.15 \\ 0.62 & 0.65 & 0.16 \\ 0.20 & 0.60 & 0.10 \\ 0.65 & 0.70 & 0.60 \\ 0.15 & 0.55 & 0.17 \end{bmatrix}
$$

The values of the matrices Δz^T and ΔS^T were determined by matrix multiplication and are shown below.

$$
\Delta Z^T = \begin{bmatrix} 0.075 \\ 0.350 \\ -0.145 \\ -0.145 \\ -0.950 \end{bmatrix} \quad \Delta (S^2)^T = \begin{bmatrix} 0.121 \\ 0.496 \\ 0.133 \\ 0.635 \\ 0.105 \end{bmatrix}
$$

The value of the test statistic is the quotient of the square of the i-th entry in ΔZ^T matrix and the i-th entry in the ΔS^T matrix summed over all subjects.

$$
\xi_\Delta = \frac{(0.075)^2}{0.121} + \frac{(0.350)^2}{0.496} + \frac{(-0.145)^2}{0.133} + \frac{(-0.145)^2}{0.635} + \frac{(-0.950)^2}{0.105}
$$

This value of the test statistic was not greater than the critical value of χ^2 with five degrees of freedom at the 0.05 confidence level (11.07). It was concluded that no difference existed between subjects who were subjected to harsh discipline when compared to both moderate and lax discipline treatments.

Factorial Assessment Designs

At this juncture, the analysis of data obtained from two different groups of individuals or the same group of individuals exposed to different treatments has been discussed. The behavioral researcher often uses another type of design, which concerns the comparison of more than two groups with respect to the same attribute. For example, the achievements of five groups of students are compared where each group of students had been exposed to a particular type of instruction. This type of design is called a factorial design with k levels. The number of levels is equal to the number of groups. For the example above, k equals 5. The purpose of this section is to discuss the treatment of the factorial design with k levels.

For the purposes of this presentation, assume that there are k groups, the number of subjects in the j-th group is symbolized by n(j), and the total number of subjects is symbolized by N. The observed indicator and standard error for the i-th subject in the j-th group will be symbolized by z_{ij} and s_{ij}, respectively. The average observed score and the group standard error for all subjects regardless of group assignment will be symbolized by $z_{\bullet\bullet}$ and $s_{\bullet\bullet}$. The aggregate group mean and standard errors can be computed using the following equations.

$$z_{\bullet\bullet} = \frac{1}{N} \sum_{j=1}^{k} \sum_{i=1}^{n(j)} z_{ij} \qquad 6.21$$

$$s_{\bullet\bullet}^2 = \frac{1}{N} \sum_{j=1}^{k} \sum_{i=1}^{n(j)} s_{ij}^2 \qquad 6.22$$

Three major question arise concerning the factorial design.

1. Does there exist nontrivial variation between individuals? That is, do individuals vary nontrivially from the grand mean. If trivial (zero) variation between individuals and the grand mean is found, further analysis would be meaningless.

2. Do the groups, as aggregates, vary nontrivially from the grand mean? If the group means are not different from the grand mean, then the analysis of specific contrasts would not be useful.

3. Do particular groups differ from other groups? Are the first two groups different from the third in a three factorial design? Is textbook A different from all other textbooks? These are the questions the analysis procedures presented in this section address.

VARIATION BETWEEN INDIVIDUALS

The major issue to be addressed in this section is whether or not an observed variation between the assessments obtained for each individual and the grand mean implies that the true scores for the individuals are also meaningfully different from the true score, μ_{ij}, and error term, e_{ij} corresponding to individual i in group j. In addition, consider the true score, $\mu_{\bullet\bullet}$, and error component, $e_{\bullet\bullet}$ corresponding to the grand mean. Using the fundamental assessment model, the following equations can be written between observed indicators, true indicators, and error components.

$$\left.\begin{array}{c} z_{ij} = \mu_{ij} + e_{ij} \\[2mm] z_{\bullet\bullet} = \mu_{\bullet\bullet} + e_{\bullet\bullet} \\[2mm] where \; e_{ij} \sim \mathbb{N}(0, s_{ij}^2) \; and, \\[2mm] e_{\bullet\bullet} \sim \mathbb{N}(0, S_{\bullet\bullet}^2) \end{array}\right\} \qquad 6.23$$

The deviation between the observed score for each individual and the observed mean score can be written, given Equation 6.23, in terms of a true score difference and an error term.

$$z_{ij} - z_{\bullet\bullet} = \{\mu_{ij} - \mu_{\bullet\bullet}\} + (e_{ij} - e_{\bullet\bullet}) \qquad 6.24$$

Under the null hypothesis, true scores for individuals and the group mean true score are not different ($\mu_{ij} - \mu_{\bullet\bullet} = 0$). Therefore, if the null hypothesis is to be accepted, the deviation between observed scores and the grand mean must be attributable to error. Consider the index, d_{ij}, defined by the following equation.

$$d_{ij} \left\{\begin{array}{c} = \dfrac{z_{ij} - z_{\bullet\bullet}}{\sqrt{s_{ij}^2 + s_{\bullet\bullet}^2}} \\[5mm] = \dfrac{e_{ij} - e_{\bullet\bullet}}{\sqrt{s_{ij}^2 + s_{\bullet\bullet}^2}} \end{array}\right. \qquad 6.25$$

If the null hypothesis is to be accepted, the deviation statistic, defined above, is normally distributed with zero mean and unit variance. Given the deviation statistic for a particular individual (that is, a particular set of values for i and j), whether or not the deviation of that particular individual's assessment indicator from the grand mean can be determined by consulting a table of probabilities for the unit normal deviate.

The assessment of the departure from the grand mean for each individual is very laborious. A global statistic summarizing the deviations for all individuals can be easily obtained. Because the individual deviation statistics, d_{ij}, are distributed as $N(0, 1)$ if the null hypothesis is accepted, the sum of the squares of these deviations is distributed as χ_2 with N degrees of freedom. If we define the test statistic, ξ_{total}, as a measure of the overall variation of individual true scores from the grand mean true score, that statistic is distributed as χ^2 with N degrees of freedom.

$$\xi_{total} = \sum_{j=1}^{k} \sum_{i=1}^{n(j)} \frac{(z_{ij} - z_{\bullet\bullet})^2}{s_{ij}^2 + s_{\bullet\bullet}^2} \qquad 6.26$$

If the test statistic, ξ_{total}, defined above is less than the critical value of the χ^2 statistic (df = N), nontrivial individual variation exists and further analysis is suggested.

VARIATION BETWEEN GROUPS

A global statistic by which the nature of true score variation from the grand mean can be assessed has been presented. Once true score variation at the individual level has been determined, one can turn attention to the level of the group. The question of interest is whether or not the observed variations between observed group mean scores and the observed grand mean are sufficient to imply that the group mean true scores are different from the grand mean true score. If the true scores of the groups are not different from the grand mean true score, the analysis of variations between particular sets of groups is not justified. If the true scores corresponding to at least one group is different from the grand mean true score, examination of particular contrasts is justified. The purpose of this section is to describe a procedure by which this issue can be addressed.

Consider the mean of the measurements obtained over all subjects who belong to the j-th group, $z_{\bullet j}$, and the standard error of that mean, $s_{\bullet j}$. If stochastic independence is assumed, the group mean and standard error can be found using the fundamental assessment model for grouped data.

$$\left. \begin{array}{l} z_{\bullet j} = \dfrac{1}{n(j)} \displaystyle\sum_{i=1}^{n(j)} z_{ij} \\[4mm] s_{\bullet j}^2 = \dfrac{1}{n(j)} \displaystyle\sum_{i=1}^{n(j)} s_{ij}^2 \end{array} \right\} \qquad 6.27$$

The fundamental assessment model for groups can be applied to these data and an equation relating the observed group mean with the group mean true scores and error component results.

$$\left.\begin{array}{c} z_{\bullet j} = \mu_{\bullet j} + e_{\bullet j} \\ z_{\bullet \bullet} = \mu_{\bullet \bullet} + e_{\bullet \bullet} \\ \text{where } e_{\bullet j} \sim \mathbb{N}(0, s_{\bullet j}^2) \\ \text{and } e_{\bullet \bullet} \sim \mathbb{N}(0, s_{\bullet \bullet}^2) \end{array}\right\} \qquad 6.28$$

Resulting in an equation where the observed difference between the group mean and the grand mean can be expressed in terms of the true score difference and an error term.

$$z_{\bullet j} - z_{\bullet \bullet} = [\mu_{\bullet j} - \mu_{\bullet \bullet}] + \{e_{\bullet j} - e_{\bullet \bullet}\} \qquad 6.29$$

If the null hypothesis is to be accepted, the group mean and grad mean true scores should not be different,
$[\mu_{\bullet j} - \mu_{\bullet \bullet} = 0] + \{e_{\bullet j} - e_{\bullet \bullet}\}$. The observed difference between group and grand mean should be distributed as a normal deviate with a mean of zero and a variance equal to $s_{\bullet j}^2 - s_{\bullet \bullet}^2 = 0]$. The weighted deviation, $\zeta_{\bullet j}$, should be distributed as a centralized unit normal deviate.

$$\zeta_{\bullet j} = \frac{z_{\bullet j} - z_{\bullet \bullet}}{\sqrt{s_{\bullet j}^2 + s_{\bullet \bullet}^2}} \qquad 6.30$$

The weighted deviation score, $\zeta_{\bullet j}$, indicates a technique for determining the deviation of particular group means from the grand mean. If the observed value of the weighted deviate is greater than 1.96 (the 95 percent confidence level), it can be concluded with 95 percent confidence that the true group mean score is different from the group mean true score. If the observed value of the weighted deviate is less than 1.96 the group mean true score is not different from the grand mean true score at the 95 percent confidence level. Of course, any confidence level can be applied for testing.

In addition to testing each group for departure from the grand mean, a global statistic for making inferences about the set of all groups is available. Because the weighted deviation statistic is distributed as a unit normal deviate, the sum of the squared values of the deviation statistics summed over all groups (values of j) is distributed as χ^2 with k degrees of freedom.

$$\xi_{b.groups} = \sum_{j=1}^{k} \frac{(z_{\bullet j} - z_{\bullet \bullet})^2}{s_{\bullet j}^2 - s_{\bullet \bullet}^2} \qquad 6.31$$

If the value of the global statistic defined by equation 6.31 is greater than the expected value of the χ^2 statistic with k degrees of freedom at the desired confidence level, it can be concluded that the group mean true scores depart nontrivially from the grand mean true score. Otherwise, the null hypothesis is accepted and it is concluded that the group mean true scores do not differ from the global mean true score.

BETWEEN GROUP CONTRASTS

In addition to ascertaining the variation between individuals and globally between groups, it is often desired to assess the magnitude of the variation between the means of particular groups or sets of groups. Procedures by which the variation of particular groups or sets of groups are to be studied will be presented in this section. The procedure is, in practice, not very different from either the two group or k group repeated assessment problems discussed previously.

Consider the situation where there exist k groups as described above. It is desired to contrast a particular set of group means with another particular set of group means. The contrast can be conveniently defined in terms of what are called contrast vectors. Contrast vectors have been discussed previously in this chapter. However, a brief review will be presented at this point.

Contrast Vectors

A contrast vector is a $1xk$ row vector with k columns (where k is the total number of groups). For the purposes of discussion, contrast vectors will be symbolized by ψ . Assume that there are three groups for a particular application (k=3). To contrast the first group with the second group and not consider the third group, the appropriate contrast vector would be (1, -1, 0). To contrast the mean of the first two groups (considered as a conglomerate or as one group) with the third group, the appropriate contrast would be $(\frac{1}{2}, \frac{1}{2}, -1)$. Each contrast can be associated with a particular aggregated mean equal to the sum of the group means weighted by the appropriate entry in the contrast vector. For example, if the means of groups 1, 2, and 3 are 1.25, 6.41, and 2.86, respectively, the value, z_ψ, of the contrast vector $\psi = (\frac{1}{2}, \frac{1}{2}, -1)$ would be

$$\frac{1}{2}(1.25) + \frac{1}{2}(6.41) + (-1)(2.86), \text{ or } 0.97.$$

The standard error of a contrast value, s_ψ, is equal to the square root of the sum of the squares of the standard errors of the group means weighted by the square of the appropriate entry in the contrast vector. For example, if the standard errors of the means of three groups are 0.20, 2.16, and 0.56, respectively, the standard error of the contrast value for the contrast above would be $\sqrt{(\frac{1}{2})^2(0.20) + (\frac{1}{2})^2(2.16) + ((-1))^2(0.66)^2}$, or 1.221.

If the j-th entry of a contrast vector, ψ, is symbolized by ψ_j, the value of the contrasted means and the standard error of that value are expressed by the following equations.

$$z_\psi = \sum_{j=1}^{k} z_{\bullet j \psi} \psi_j \qquad\qquad 6.32$$

$$s_\psi^2 = \sum_{j=1}^{k} s_{\bullet j}^2 \psi_j^2 \qquad\qquad 6.33$$

If the value of a contrast is not different from zero, it is concluded that the man of the two sets of groups that compose the contrast (are contrasted) are not different from each other. If the value of a contrast is nontrivially different from zero, it is concluded that the mean of the two sets of contrasted groups are different. The remainder of this section will concern the problem of assessing the confidence that can be placed in the departure of an observed value of the contrast from zero.

The Test Statistic

Using the fundamental assessment model for groups, the value of a contrast can be expressed in terms of contrasted group true scores and an error term.

$$
\left.\begin{aligned}
z_\psi &= \mu_\psi + e \\
where \ \mu_\psi &= \sum_{j=1}^{k} \psi_j \, \mu_{\bullet j} \\
and \ e_\psi &= \sum_{j=1}^{k} \psi_j \, e_{\bullet j}
\end{aligned}\right\} \qquad 6.34
$$

The null hypothesis for this problem is that there is no difference between groups and that the true score value of the contrasted group mean true scores is zero ($\mu_\psi = 0$). If the null hypothesis is accepted, the observed value of the contrasted group means, z_ψ is due to random assessment fluctuations ($z^\psi = e_\psi$). The value of the weighted contrast defined by the statistic, ξ_ψ, is distributed as a centralized unit normal deviate. If the $1 \times k$ matrix, Z, is the matrix of group means and S^2 is a $k \times k$ matrix with the squared group standard errors on the diagonal and zeros elsewhere, ξ_ψ can be written in closed form and more succinctly using matrix notation.

$$
6.35 \qquad \xi_\psi = \left\{ \begin{aligned}
& \dfrac{\displaystyle\sum_{j=1}^{k} \psi_j \, z_{\bullet j}}{\sqrt{\displaystyle\sum_{j=1}^{k} \psi_j \, s_{\bullet j}^2}} \\[2em]
& \dfrac{\psi \, Z^T}{\sqrt{\psi \, S^2 \, \psi^T}} = \dfrac{\psi \, Z^T}{\| S \, \psi^T \|}
\end{aligned}\right.
$$

If the value of the test statistic is less than 1.96, the groups represented by the contrast weights are not assumed to be different at the appropriate confidence level. If the value of the test statistic is greater than 1.96, the groups represented by the contrast weights are assumed to be different at the 95 percent confidence level.

At this point the details of procedures for analyzing a factorial design have been presented. One issue concerned the assessment of whether observed variation between individuals constituted a departure from the grand mean. A second issue concerned whether or not observed variation between group means constituted a departure from the grand mean.

Table 6.5:
Assessment of Classroom Discipline

| | Experimental Group | | |
	Traditional	Mild	Lax
Individual	1.080 (0.259)	1.203 (0.274)	0.117 (0.086)
	0.119 (0.086)	0.062 (0.062)	1.152 (0.268)
	0.000 (0.080)	1.232 (0.277)	0.523 (0.181)
Data	1.091 (0.261)	0.016 (0.032)	0.044 (0.052)
	0.067 (0.065)	2.069 (0.360)	
	1.081 (0.260)		
	0.045 (0.053)		
Group Mean	0.498 (0.179)	0.916 (0.239)	0.459 (0.169)
Grand Mean		0.6189 (0.1977)	
ξ_j	0.039	-0.129	0.039
Total Statistic	85.7578	(df=16)	
$\xi_{b.group}$	1.4984 (df=2)		

The third issue was whether or not particular contrasts were indicative of nontrivial differences between groups. Examples of the application of these procedures constitute the remainder of this chapter.

An experimenter wished to investigate the relationship between classroom discipline and student achievement. Students were assigned to one of three groups. The groups were designated as traditional, mild, and lax. The students assigned to the traditional group received instruction from a teacher who was rated by her peers as being a strong disciplinarian. Students assigned to the mild or lax groups were taught by teachers who were rated as being mild or lax disciplinarians. Due to the movement of students between classes within the school, the number of students who remained with particular teachers was small. The results of the final achievement testing are shown below.

It appeared upon inspection of the assessment results that there was considerable variation between individuals and that the students assigned to the teacher who was a mild disciplinarian exhibited higher achievement levels than students assigned to other teachers. The hypothesis that there was nontrivial variation between subjects was testing using the ξ_{total} statistic whose value was found to be 85.7578 with 16 degrees of freedom. The probability of obtaining a value of χ^2 as large as this is less than 0.001. The first null hypothesis that there is no variation between individuals was rejected. It was concluded that sufficient variation between subjects existed to warrant further analysis.

The value of χ^2 and the group deviation statistics were calculated.

$$\xi_{b.groups} = \frac{(0.498 - 0.619)^2}{(0.179)^2 + (0.198)^2} + \frac{(0.916 - 0.619)^2}{(0.239)^2 + (0.198)^2} + \frac{(0.459 - 0.619)^2}{(0.169)^2 + (0.198)^2}$$

$$\xi_1 = \frac{(0.498 - 0.619)}{\sqrt{(0.179)^2 + (0.198)^2}}$$

$$\xi_2 = \frac{(0.916 - 0.619)}{\sqrt{(0.239)^2 + (0.198)^2}}$$

$$\xi_3 = \frac{(0.459 - 0.619)}{\sqrt{(0.169)^2 + (0.198)^2}}$$

Each of the individual group deviation statistics was less than the value of 1.96 expected for the normal deviate at the 0.95 confidence level. In addition, the value of the between group test statistic was 1.4984 with two degrees of freedom. The probability of obtaining such a value or larger due to chance was greater than 0.30. The second null hypothesis that the group means were not different fro the grand mean was accepted. The researcher concluded that although considerable variation existed between subjects, the data (as limited as they were) did not indicate that the degree to which a classroom teacher was a disciplinarian had an effect upon student achievement.

Table 6.6:
Factorial Evaluation of Textbooks

	Textbook Used		
Index Reported	**Textbook A**	**Textbook B**	**Textbook C**
Group Mean	0.654 (0.068)	-0.851 (0.151)	-0.364 (0.046)
N of subjects	273	136	68
Deviation statistics	4.845	-5.187	-4.136
Grand Mean		0.080 (0.097)	
ξ_{total}		2218.05 (df=477)	
$\xi_{b.groups}$		67.4934 (df=2)	

*Standard errors are enclosed in parentheses.

An evaluator was assigned the task of determining whether or not one of three possible textbooks had a differential impact upon student achievement. Three groups of students were selected. Each of the students in a particular group was instructed using a particular textbook. Teachers were randomly assigned to textbook groups. The results of an attainment test administered at the end of the school year were tabulated for each of the three groups and are shown below.

The null hypothesis that the students did not exhibit differential behavior was tested using the total deviation statistic. That statistic was 2218.05 (df=477). The probability of obtaining a value of χ^2 that large or larger is less than 0.01. The null hypothesis was rejected and it was concluded that nontrivial variation between students existed. Further analysis was justified.

The values of the between group and deviation statistics were calculated.

$$\xi_{b.groups} = (4.845)^2 + (-5.187)^2 + (-4.136)^2 = 67.4934$$

$$\xi_1 = \frac{0.654 - 0.080}{\sqrt{(0.068)^2 + (0.097)^2}} = 4.845$$

$$\xi_2 = \frac{-0.851 - 0.080}{\sqrt{(0.151)^2 + (0.097)^2}} = -5.187$$

$$\xi_3 = \frac{-0.364 - 0.080}{\sqrt{(0.046)^2 + (0.097)^2}} = -4.136$$

The value of the between group test statistic was 64.4934 with two degrees of freedom. The probability of obtaining a value as larger or larger due to chance was less than 0.001. The absolute value of each deviation statistic was greater than 1.96. The null hypothesis that o between group variation existed was rejected. It was concluded that the group means deviated from the grand mean and that further analysis was indicated.

The department chairperson was concerned with differences that may exist between textbooks A and B and between the combination of textbooks A and B with textbook C. These concerns were translated into contrast vectors. The contrast vector corresponding to a test of the mean difference between textbooks A and B is $\psi_1 = [1, -1, 0]$. The contrast vector corresponding to the contrast of combination of textbook groups A and B with textbook group C is $\psi_2 = [\frac{1}{2}, \frac{1}{2}, -1]$. The values of the contrasts and their associated standard errors were calculated. The setup of each calculation is shown below.

$$z_{\psi_1} = (1)(0.654) + (-1)(-0.851) + (0)(-0.364) = 1.505$$

$$z_{\psi_2} = (\frac{1}{2})(0.654) + (\frac{1}{2})(-0.851) + (-1)(-0.364) = 0.2655$$

$$s^2_{\psi_1} = (1)^2(0.068)^2 + (-1)^2(0.151)^2 + (0)^2(0.046)^2 = 0.0274$$

$$s^2_{\psi_1} = (\frac{1}{2})^2(0.068)^2 + (\frac{1}{2})^2(0.151)^2 + (-1)^2(0.046)^2 = 0.008972$$

$$\xi_{\psi_1} = \frac{1.505}{\sqrt{0.02743}}$$

$$\xi_{\psi_2} = \frac{2.655}{\sqrt{0.0008972}}$$

The values of the normal deviates corresponding to each of the two contrasts were calculated. The value of the normal deviate corresponding to any particular contrast is equal to the magnitude of that contrast divided by standard error of that value. The values of each of the test statistics are greater than the critical value of 1.96 at the 95 percent confidence level. It was concluded that students assigned textbook A exhibited higher achievement assessment scores than students assigned either of the other two textbooks. Also, if a choice was to be hade to purchase quantities of both textbooks A and B or to purchase only textbook C, then textbook C is the better choice-a lesser of two evils. The evaluators recommended that textbook A be adopted.

HIGHER-ORDER FACTORIAL DESIGNS

Many experimenters find themselves attempting to answer questions that cannot be written as a traditional unifactorial design. In many cases more than one factor is required to frame the hypothesis adequately. Using traditional instruments, the researcher may use a two or higher order factorial analysis of variance design. The purpose of this section is to describe how these higher order factorial designs can be examined utilizing latent trait assessment indicators. It will be seen that these higher order designs do not require additional mathematical formulations. The equations generated in the previous sections are, with the aid of contrast vectors, sufficient to estimate all main effects and interactions. Three examples will be presented.

The will begin with a rather simple *2x2* design and proceed to a somewhat more complex *2x3* design with interaction.

A researcher was interested in evaluating the impact of Public Law 94-142 on handicapped students. The law requires, in part, that handicapped children be integrated with nonhandicapped children to the maximum extent possible. The researcher wished to investigate whether or not integration enhanced learning and whether the impact was different for male than female handicapped children. Ninety five handicapped children were selected from a metropolitan high school. The parents of the children were asked to designate whether they wished to have their child assigned to an integrated or segregated classroom. The researcher realized the limitations that this type of assignment procedure imposed on the experimental design. However, the particular school system would not allow random assignment and would only allow one set of achievement assessments to be administered. The results of the end of year assessment are shown in Table 6.7.

Table 6.7
Special Education Evaluation

	Type of Treatment			
	Integrated		Segregated	
	Male	**Female**	**Male**	**Female**
Mean	1.34 (0.40)	0.40 (0.15)	0.50 (0.20)	1.74 (0.62)
Students	40	20	20	15
Grand mean		1.03 (0.38)		

*Standard errors are enclosed in parentheses.

As indicated above this type of design is not different from the one-way designs previously described. In fact, any N-factorial design can be described in terms of a one-way layout. The between group deviation statistics were calculated in the same manner as the previous one-way design.

$$\xi_{b.groups}$$

$$= (0.562)^2 + (-1.542)^2 + (-1.234)^2 + (0.579)^2 = 4.240 \ df = 3$$

$$\xi_1 = \frac{(1.34 - 1.03)}{\sqrt{(0.40)^2 + (0.38)^2}}$$

$$\xi_2 = \frac{(0.40 - 1.03)}{\sqrt{(0.25)^2 + (0.38)^2}}$$

$$\xi_3 = \frac{(0.50 - 1.03)}{\sqrt{(0.20)^2 + (0.38)^2}}$$

$$\xi_4 = \frac{(1.74 - 1.03)}{\sqrt{(0.62)^2 + (0.38)^2}}$$

The value of the between group test statistic was 4.240 with three degrees of freedom. The probability of obtaining a value of χ^2 as large or larger due to chance alone was greater than 0.10. This result was not surprising, as the absolute value of each deviation statistic was less than 1.96. This result tends to indicate that "main effects" were absent.

However, the second and third deviation statistics, although indicating triviality, were rather large. The researcher decided to test for the presence of a sex x treatment interaction. The symbolic contrast vector for that interaction was $\psi = \left[\frac{1}{2}, -\frac{1}{2}, -\frac{1}{2}, \frac{1}{2} \right]$. The value of the contrast and associated standard error were

$$z_\psi = \frac{1}{2}(1.34) - \frac{1}{2}(0.40) - \frac{1}{2}(0.50) + \frac{1}{2}(1.74) = 2.18,$$

and

$$s_\psi^2 = \left(\frac{1}{2} \right)^2 (0.40)^2 - \left(\frac{1}{2} \right)^2 (0.15)^2 - \left(\frac{1}{2} \right)^2 (0.20)^2 +$$

$$\left(\frac{1}{2} \right)^2 (0.62)^2 = 0.152$$

The value of the normal deviate corresponding to the contrast was calculated as the ratio of the value of the contrast and the associated standard error.

$$\psi_1 = \frac{2.18}{\sqrt{0.152}} = 5.597$$

The value of ψ_1 is greater than the critical value of 1.96 at the 95 percent confidence level. It was concluded that a nontrivial interaction was present. Females tended to exhibit greater scores in segregated classes than in integrated classrooms. On the other hand, males tended to exhibit greater test scores in integrated classrooms. The researcher concluded that the evidence indicated that males should be integrated and females should be placed in segregated classrooms. The school board concluded that such a policy could be considered as sufficient evidence for gender discrimination and voted to integrate all handicapped students rather than face a possible Title IX challenge.

A school system has implemented a sequence of computer assisted instruction in mathematics. The program was funded under Title I and designated to assist learning disabled students. An external evaluator was contracted. The evaluator was requested to determine whether or not the amount of time a student spent working with the computer was related to achievement. In addition, the school committee was interested in knowing if students in particular grades exhibited greater achievement than students at other grade levels. Students were allowed to enter the program only if they exhibited achievement test scores within a very narrow range. The students did not substantively differ with respect to entrance behavior. A post assessment was administered after the program was operating for six months.

The overall deviation statistic was calculated.

$$\xi_{b.group} =$$

$$(-4.66)^2 + (-3.33)^2 + (1.72)^2 + (-4.20)^2 + (-0.45)^2$$
$$+ (3.72)^2 + (-0.87)^2 + (5.56)^2 = 107.70$$
$$and \ df = 8$$

The probability of obtaining a value of χ^2 at least as large as 107.70 with eight degrees of freedom due to chance is less than 0.001 and between group variation was evidenced.

Two orthogonal contrasts represent the total variation between grades. Those contrasts are

$$\Psi_1 = \left[1, -\frac{1}{2}, -\frac{1}{2}, 1, -\frac{1}{2}, -\frac{1}{2}, 1, -\frac{1}{2}, -\frac{1}{2} \right] \text{ and}$$

$$\Psi_2 = [0, -1, 1, 0, -1, 1, 0, -1, 1].$$

The first contrast compares sixth grade students with upper class persons. The second contrast compares seventh grade students with eighth grade students. These contrasts together with two additional orthogonal contrasts represent the total variation between categories of time on the computer. The two additional contrasts are:

$$\Psi_3 = \left[-1, \frac{1}{2}, -\frac{1}{2}, \frac{1}{2}, \frac{1}{2}, \frac{1}{2}, \frac{1}{2}, \frac{1}{2}, \frac{1}{2} \right]$$

and $\Psi_4 = [0, 0, 0, -1, -1, -1, 1, -1, 1]$. The first contrast compares the students with less than one hour of instruction with other students with greater exposure to the computer. The last contrast compares students who experienced one to two hours of instruction.

Table 6.8:
Test Statistics for a *3x3* Design

Contrast	Δz_ψ	s_ψ	ξ_ψ
1	-4.0	0.342	-11.70
2	5.0	0.546	-9.16
3	-2.1	0.374	5.48
4	1.1	0.518	2.12

The values of each of the contrasts, the associated standard errors, and deviation test statistics were calculated and shown in Table 6.8. Each of the test statistics were greater in absolute value than the critical value of the normal deviate at the 95 percent confidence level (1.96) and nontrivial variation was observed between grades and between time of instruction groups.

Table 6.9:
Peer Teaching Experiment

	Type of Student					
	Handicapped		**No Special Need**		**Gifted**	
	Nonpeer	**Peer**	**Nonpeer**	**Peer**	**Nonpeer**	**Peer**
Mean	1.41	5.68	8.70	4.93	9.57	6.53
Error	0.14	0.62	0.64	0.55	0.75	0.63
Deviation	-7.82	-0.54	2.95	-1.50	3.60	0.45
Grand	**Mean**		6.14 (0.588)			

The evaluator reported that sixth grade students did not experience as great a level of achievement as upper class persons. Seventh grade students exhibited lower levels of achievement than their eighth grade counterparts. The evaluator also reported that students with less than one hour of instruction did not exhibit achievement levels as high as students who received greater amounts of instruction with the computer. Students who received more than two hours of instruction exhibited greater achievement levels than their counterparts who received one to two hours of instruction.

A researcher wished to study the utility of peer teaching for handicapped children, gifted children, and those with no particular special need. Sixty handicapped, 60 gifted, and 60 students with no particular special need were randomly selected from the population of a large metropolitan school district. Within each group, 30 students were assigned to traditional classrooms and 30 students were assigned to classrooms where peer teaching was frequently employed. The peer and nonpeer teaching groups did not differ in achievement at the beginning of the school year. A post assessment was administered at the end of the school year.

The variation of group means from the grand mean was assessed,

$$\xi_{b.group} = (-7.82)^2 + (-0.54)^2 + (2.95)^2$$
$$+ (-1.5)^2 + (3.6)^2 + (0.45)^2$$
$$= 85.59 \; df = 5 .$$

The probability of obtaining a value of χ^2 with five degrees of freedom at least as large as 85.59 by chance alone is less than 0.05. It was concluded that nontrivial variation existed between groups and that further investigation was warranted.

One contrast represented the variation between teaching styles, between nonpeer teaching groups with peer teaching classrooms, $\psi = [1, -1, 1, -1, 1, -1]$. Two contrasts, $\left[\frac{1}{2}, \frac{1}{2}, -1, -1, \frac{1}{2}, \frac{1}{2} \right]$ comparing nonspecial needs students with special needs students (handicapped and gifted), and $\left[-\frac{1}{2}, -\frac{1}{2}, 0, 0, \frac{1}{2}, \frac{1}{2} \right]$ contrasting handicapped and gifted students were required to represent the variation between the types of students. Two contrasts were required to define the interaction terms.

The contrast $\left[[-\frac{1}{2}, \frac{1}{2}, -\frac{1}{2}, \frac{1}{2}, 0, 0 \right]$ represents the handicapped-nonspecial needs by treatment interaction; and the contrast $\left[-\frac{1}{2}, \frac{1}{2}, 0, 0, \frac{1}{2}, -\frac{1}{2} \right]$ represents the special needs by treatment interaction.

Table 6.10:
Contrasts for a *2x3* Factorial Design

Contrast	Δz_{ψ}	s_{ψ}	ξ_{ψ}
1	2.54	1.44	1.76
2	-2.04	1.03	1.99
3	4.50	0.58	7.72
4	-4.02	0.53	-7.61
5	3.66	0.58	6.26

The values, standard errors, and test statistics were calculated for each contrast vector.

The test statistic corresponding to the first contrast was less than the critical value of 1.96; there was no significant effect associated with teaching style. Students with special needs did perform less well than nonspecial needs students. The latter result was probably due to pretreatment variation. An examination of the test statistic corresponding to the third contrast vector indicates that the gifted students performed better than the handicapped students.

An analysis of the interaction contrasts yields substantively interesting results. The values of both contrasts were found to be nontrivial at the 0.05 confidence level. Handicapped students assigned to peer teaching environments exhibited larger achievement indicator levels than handicapped students assigned to traditional classrooms. Both gifted and nonspecial needs students had lower achievement levels when assigned to peer teaching environments than their counterparts assigned to traditional classrooms. The researcher concluded that the peer teaching strategies were beneficial for handicapped children, but peer teaching may be detrimental to nonhadicapped students.

7

Measurement In Transition

Issues and problems in mental measurement have been described beginning with the theory underlying norm referenced assessment. Norm referenced assessments are constructed to facilitate comparisons among respondents (or groups) in relation to the performance of the norm group (Mills & Hambleton, 1980). Three major problems with norm referenced assessments are apparent. One, a measurement obtained from these types of assessments is dependent upon the particular group of respondent s used to calibrate the events composing the assessment. Two, ability or attainment estimates obtained for a particular respondent from two or more assessments associated with the same content domain are seldom numerically equivalent. Three, the event screening procedures used to obtain events for norm referenced assessments tend to eliminate certain events which subject matter experts consider substantively meaningful.

Item response theory was introduced as an alternative to the norm referenced assessment. Assessments generated according to this model are purported to result in assessment scores that are not a function of the group of respondent s used to calibrate the events. In addition, assessment scores obtained for the same respondent based on two or more substantively equivalent assessments are not significantly different from each other. There are some unresolved issues concerning the methodology employed and results obtained from empirical studies of those assumptions. Furthermore, the event screening procedure used to detect events which fit the requirements of the model also tend to screen out some events that are part of the content domain supposedly sampled by the assessment.

Criterion referenced assessments are thought of as resulting in assessments and assessment events that are very content specific and are constructed to facilitate the interpretation of individual (or group) assessment performance in relation to a set of well defined objectives or competencies (Hambleton & Eignor, 1978; Klein, 1990; Mills & Hambleton, 1980). However, a consensus has not been reached on good procedure for examining the data from either the assessment itself or the events composing the assessment (Ebel & Livingstone, 1981; Mills & Hambleton, 1980; Mills & Simon, 1981).

There are six major uses of assessment results: selection, classification, diagnosis, research, program evaluation, and description (Page, 1977).

Different audiences require different information. For example, school administrators, parents, teachers, and district administrators require different information. Each group may require some common information, but each will requires unique information in carrying out their different role. One of the general problems in assessment is the great gap that exists between the expertise of assessment development and the sophomoric use of assessment scores by the different audiences (Mills & Hambleton, 1980; Page, 1977). When applied to the measurement of achievement, all events have the intent of obtaining the clearest indicator of the presence or absence of the targeted level of achievement, the criterion.

The lack of criterion referenced methodological solidarity is due to definitional ambiguity which has led to multiple applications. Technical points associated with the applications have led to additional methodologies. In my opinion, the state of criterion referenced assessment methodologies is a foundational malaise. This is such an important issue that I will present that ambiguity in some detail.

As Shrock, Mansukhani, Coscarelli, & Palmer (1986) point out the development of criterion referenced assessment has been delayed by an over emphasis on instructional practice and add five types of criterion referenced assessments to the confusion.

Prerequisite assessments: used to ensure that learners have the background knowledge required for the course.

Entry assessments: used to identify skills taught in a course that the entering student may already possess.

Diagnostic assessments: used to assess mastery for a given instructional objective or group of related objectives in an instructional unit.

Postassessments: administered after instruction to assess performance on terminal objectives.

Equivalency assessments: used to determine whether a learner has already mastered the course's terminal objectives before instruction begins.

I wish to add that an over emphasis of instructional vs. curricula issues and the "laboratory derived principles for teaching children" has diverted attention from substantive theory development (Mager, 1962; Popham, 1987; Skinner, 1958). For example, Klauer (1984) confuses mastery and criterion referenced methods by adopting an instructional model.

A grading model is a function that assigns grades to levels of achievement while taking into account the possibility of errors in measurement and decision making. A grading model is norm referenced if the assigned grade reflects the student's position in a group of students; hence, such a grade depends not only on the student's own achievement but also on other students' achievements. A grading model is criterion referenced if the assigned grade is based on the student's achievement level measured by a criterion referenced assessment. In this case, the assigned grade is independent of other students' achievement...A criterion-referenced assessment is a means of classifying students into two classes: those who have mastered the instructional objective and those who have not (Klauer, 1984, p. 237).

Nub, Wienberg, and Schot (1981, 1984) assume that the planning of instruction in terms of "didactic models, proposals, and lists of works" are requirements for teaching. Others have confused inappropriate use of assessment results with a lack of sophistication as opposed to the lack of a theory base or have contributed to the growing spectrum of applications (Hambleton & Eignor, 1978; Mills & Hambleton, 1980; Page, 1977).

CONTENT REFERENCED ASSESSMENTS.

Early in educational history many believed in tangible effects. This is evidenced by certain societal belief structures. A society establishes schools to produce students who can perform certain tasks competently; those tasks require the use of certain knowledges; those knowledges can be assessed; and, the purpose of the system is to certify that a student has learned those knowledges (Caldwell & Courtis, 1923). Mass assessment developed from the failure of schools and colleges to set consistent standards (Wiggins, 1989). Two types of assessments were used for these purposes. A *content mastery* assessment was an inventory of instructional content by which students were promoted or retained depending on whether a criterion score that educators believed would forecast competent performance was attained. The other type of assessment, *task proficiency* assessment, was designed to determine if students could apply knowledge to tasks. These tasks (such as reading the Constitution, translating a passage from Cicero, or operating a lathe) were such that the students either failed or were granted diplomas, depending on whether their scores reached the criterion score. This resulted in promotions and diplomas that meant that students had mastered certain content, could apply their knowledge, and lower grade classrooms burdened and disrupted by a large number of overaged, frustrated students (Billett, 1933). A humanitarian indignation demanded that schools recognize that students were different individuals and that schools study and adapt their curriculum to meet differences in aptitude, ambition, and temperament (Cook, 1941). Educators had no firm evidence that a given score on one of their assessments corresponded to a certain amount of knowledge or proficiency, that their content mastery criterion scores predicted competent task proficiency or represented the most desirable level of task performance (Bormuth, 1978; Congelost, 1984; Glass, 1978; Starch, 1918; Tiegs, 1931, 1939).

The concept of criterion referenced measurement developed by Ebel (1962) and Glaser (1963) has received wide interest and has been described and further developed in Germany as a meaningful new concept for psychological and pedagogical diagnosis (Ingenkamp, 1970; Ingenkamp & Marsolek, 1968; Klauer, Fricke, Herbig, Rupprecht, & Schott, 1972; Klauer, Fricke, Herbig, Rupprecht, & Scott, 1977; Fricke, 1973, 1974b; Herbig, 1976; Pawlik, 1976; Klauer, 1978; Lühmann, 1983). In Germany, criterion referenced assessments are described as scientific instruments or procedures. Fricke (1973, 1974a) considered a criterion referenced assessment as a scientific procedure which tests the question whether and how well a certain curricula goal has been reached. Events employed for this purpose were not identical to the instructional objective, but rather only represented it, serving to compare the individual ability level of a student with a desired level of ability. In order to make these comparisons the following prerequisites are substantial: curriculum of the instructional objective, quantitative, and an assessment of significance for the decision as to whether the curriculum objective has been realized. He continues by stating that a special criterion referenced assessment analysis is necessary in order to compute the assessment criteria (Fricke, 1974a, p. 82). Others think about criterion referenced assessments in other ways.

Shannon (1986) points out that there are three ways people think of criterion referenced assessments: Criterion referenced assessments are used to measure an examinee's status in reference to a well defined behavior domain (Popham, 1978); a criterion referenced assessment is one that is deliberately constructed to yield measurements that are directly interpretable in terms of specified performance standards (Glaser & Nitko, 1971, p. 563); and, finally, diagnostic assessments are constructed to assessment for the presence or absence of specific factors known to impede learning (Simpson & Arnold, 1983). Criterion referenced assessments and diagnostic assessments are often confused (Ebel & Livingstone, 1981; Klein, 1990; Simpson & Arnold, 1983). Criterion referenced (CR) assessments are not uncommonly described as diagnostic assessments. The two terms are often used interchangeably by educationalists (SED, 1977; Brown, 1980; SCRE, 1980). Such assessments should be regarded, more exactly, as defining the subject areas in which pupils fail to attain the criteria levels. The assessments do not reveal the causes underlying nonattainment. Therefore, the claim that they can be used diagnostically rest on certain assumptions as to the nature of pupil failure. The term diagnostic implies that the 'failure to learn' syndrome is due to a defect (in the pupil) which is wholly defined (by the assessment results) and which may perhaps be cured (by a further dose of similar teaching medicine).

Alternative models describe pupil failure to learn as being quantified and defined in terms of subject content (by criterion referenced assessment), shown (by true diagnostic assessments) to be caused by an inappropriateness of the level of instruction, deficiencies in instructional procedures and educational strategies, or by a failure to secure adequate pupil motivation, and to be capable of remediation (which is specific to the cause). With this model, the primary locus of learning pathology is not the pupil, but the teacher's instructional procedures and educational strategies.

Diagnostic assessments differ from criterion referenced assessments in that they assess the presence or absence of specific factors which are known to impede learning. Ideally, the factors which are relevant in particular subject areas have been identified by prior investigation of pupil difficulties, subject content, and teaching practices. For example, in the cognitive domain, poor pupil performance has been associated with inadequately structured prerequisite concepts which is noted by confusion in terminology, the lack of ability to discriminate between concepts or to recognize known processes in a novel context, the lack of key information, or possession of knowledge which competes or conflicts with the material being taught (Simpson & Arnold, 1983). Although diagnostic assessments designed to identify these sources of difficulty may resemble criterion referenced assessments in format, the events will not relate to attainment, but will be asking the question, 'Has the pupil got this misconception, confusion or erroneous reasoning?' (Simpson & Arnold, 1983). The diagnostic assessments ask, 'What do the pupils know?' rather than, 'Do they know what they have been taught?'

The weakness of criterion referenced assessments lies in their intrinsic lack of any true diagnostic capacity. Criterion references assessments are not able to indicate the underlying reasons for poor assessment results or to point to specific remediation (Simpson & Arnold, 1983 p. 39). In this respect, they are not superior to norm referenced assessments.

Hanna and Bennett (1984) and others further suggest that a design criterion for criterion referenced assessments should be instructional sensitivity (Brennan & Stolurow, 1971; Cox & Vargas, 1966; Helmstadter, 1974; Popham, 1971). Haladyna and Roid (1981) defined instructional sensitivity as the tendency of assessment events to vary in difficulty as a result of instruction and argued that ISIs should be considered in building criterion referenced achievement assessments (Also see: Tindal, Fuchs, Fuchs, Shinn, Deno, & Germann, 1985).

Curriculum referenced assessments. Curriculum Referenced Assessments of Mastery are intended to measure achievement, with the emphasis on measuring what a student has learned rather than predicting future success in school (Blankenship, 1985; Deno, 1985; Gallery & Hofmeister, 1977; Knight, 1985). Each assessment event is linked to a specific objective designated as an important learning objective in a school's curriculum. In addition to assessing mastery, the Curriculum Referenced Assessment of Mastery provides a variety of norm referenced scores permitting comparison of schools, class, and individuals to a national sample in the United States.

Domain referenced assessments are based upon the assumption that by identifying the domain through the specific definition of a class of behaviors, skills and information, a set of rules may be created for generating sets of assessment events. It has been argued that where the domain has been sufficiently well defined, a random sample of events can provide a means of achieving an absolute measure of domain proficiency (Kriewall, 1972). Definitional homogeneity is promoted by event generation schemes which involve some logical, systematic and replicable means for constructing events representative of the defined domain. Whether response patterns to such events display homogeneity, however, is one of the main topics of this investigation.

Some authors go further and invent the assessment which *are* not (not, *may* not) be pencil and paper assessments. Criterion referenced performance assessments differ from the popular paper and pencil variety developed to measure knowledge and compare individuals with one another (Campbell & Allender, 1988). While useful, paper and pencil assessments cannot determine whether or not an individual performs a manipulative task with the degree of proficiency required for success on the job. "Requiring each trainee to demonstrate [proficiency in] each task before completing a training program is probably the single most significant difference between the competency based and more conventional approach to training." (Blank, 1982, p. 158). A criterion referenced performance assessment (CRPA) is one which evaluates task proficiency using actual equipment under real or closely simulated work conditions and standards. Performance assessments can be classified a product or process assessments. Campbell and Allender (1988) describe several products of such assessments. The product is the most obvious task output; it is observable and can be physically inspected. Another output of task performance is the completion of procedural steps (process) which can be evaluated by close observation ("Institute of Nuclear," 1985). The key principle to observe in scoring is objectivity. Objectivity is achieved by: (a) setting clear attainment standards, and (b) orienting examiners on how and why to apply them (Campbell & Allender, 1988). Some tasks require the examinee to perform a series of procedural steps in which the examiner unobtrusively observes and records the assessed performances on each performance. Other tasks require the examiner to produce a product. For many of these products, the measurement of task performance is obtained from an inspection of the end product itself. In either case, examinee performance is rated by the examiner as satisfactory or not yet satisfactory (Campbell & Allender, 1988, p. 9).

Product rating: all characteristics that distinguish an acceptable product should be described as accurately and specifically as possible...the characteristics...must be provided to the examiner along with specific instructions for making the measurement.

Process rating: step-by-step description of the process by which the CRPA is performed. The task elements/steps and required standards usually are prepared in checklist form.

Checklists: The "laundry list" approach facilitates the recording of observations and assures consideration of the important aspects of the performance. It eliminates the need to rely on memory when rating the ability to perform a set of procedural steps. (Armijo & Appleby, 1982).

Gable, Hendrickson, and Stowtschek (1986) and others believe that assessment should be integrated with instruction (Jobes & Hawthorne, 1977; Salvia & Ysseldyke, 1985; Wallace & Larsen, 1977; Ysseldyke & Algozzine, 1984). They then go on to say that an assessment is different from instruction only in terms of how the results are used. They state that the major dilemma is how to "bridge the gap" between standardized assessments and the task of planning daily instruction. Often administration of assessments and delivery of instruction are viewed as separate and distinct processes (Stowitschek, Gable, & Hendrickson, 1980). Still, it can be argued that the major difference is how the results are used. When materials are introduced to provide students practice, we call it instruction, whereas the same material applied to determining whether a student can perform a particular task is called assessing. (Gable, Hendrickson, & Stowitchek, 1986, pp. 13-18)..

Skager (1978, p. 1) states that the word "criterion" may be the most overused term in the measurement vocabulary. This situation leads to a lack of clarity in conceptualization, especially in the notion of "criterion referenced" assessment. Probably no concept in measurement is more widely misunderstood by members of the wider educational public.

The confusion began when Glaser (1963) separated assessments into those that are *norm referenced* and those that are *criterion referenced* as a way of emphasizing the distinction between how the assessment scores could be interpreted. Glaser called for assessments whose scores would be *directly* interpretable in terms of some domain necessary for implementing "adaptive" instruction (Glaser & Nitko, 1971), a concept embedded in the much earlier work of Washburn and Morrison, and the idea of direct measurement advanced by Cattell (1944) as "interactive" measurement. There has been a major effort by many to integrate teaching and assessing by developers of various forms of systematic instruction, such as mastery learning (Bloom, 1968, 1976), individually guided education (Klausmeier, Rossmiller, & Sally, 1977), individually prescribed instruction (Hambleton, 1974), and the personalized system of instruction (Keller, 1968). Each of these implies the use of statements of instructional intent, instructional activities that are correlated to these statements, and assessments of the knowledge and skills also reflected in these statements (Haladyna & Roid, 1983). Shoemaker (1975) made one of the most extreme statements in this regard when he said, "An instructional program and its associated item universe are isomorphic" (p.128) (see discussions of the Instructional Quality Inventory, Wulfeck, Ellis, Richards, Wood, & Merrill, 1978, or Roid & Haladyna, 1982). Buros (1977) reminded us that a distinction between assessments designed to "measure" and assessments designed to "differentiate" goes back to the beginning of modern educational measurement. Glaser essentially recycled the notion of assessments directly referenced to what a person can do in defined areas of educational content.

The term "criterion referencing" describes individual achievement as a position on a "continuum" or "progression" of developing competence. Underlying the concept of achievement measurement is the notion of a *continuum of knowledge acquisition* ranging from no proficiency at all to perfect performance. An individual's achievement level falls at some point on this continuum as indicated by the behaviors he displays during assessment. The standard against which a student's performance is compared when measured in (a criterion referenced) manner is the behavior which defines each point along the achievement continuum (Glaser, 1981, pp. 519-520).

The concept of criterion referenced measurement was conceived to encourage the development of procedures whereby assessments of proficiency could be referenced to stages along *progressions of increasing competence* (Glaser, 1981, p. 935).

Ebel's (1962) "content standard" score referred to the percentage of events answered appropriately on an assessment made up of events sampled from a domain. It therefore defined a numerical score referenced to content rather than indirectly to the performance of individuals. Later, Cronbach (1971) saw specified objectives as the foundation of the curriculum and argued that the school curriculum deals with higher levels of achievement for which mastery is not an appropriate concept. Eisner (1968) drew a distinction between instructional and expressive educational objectives.

Jaeger (1987) observed that the term "criterion-referenced measurement" is attributed to Glaser & Klaus (1962); yet, Flanagan (1951) and Ebel (1962) contrasted the value of information based on inferences to a specific domain of content and information based on an examinee's rank within a group. The concept of both "content standard" or "criterion referencing" can be traced to Thorndike (1913). He stated that rivalry with one's own past and with a "bogey," or accepted standard, is entirely feasible, once we have absolute scales for educational achievement comparable to the scales for the speed at which one can run or the height to which one can jump (Thorndike, 1913). Later he proposed methodologies for constructing such scales (Thorndike, 1913).

"Modern" item response theory has its roots in the work of Thurstone and Chave (1929). They stated that the very idea of measurement implies a linear continuum of the same sort as length, price, volume, weight, age. Further, they proported that when the idea of measurement is applied to scholastic achievement, for example, it is necessary to force the qualitative variations into a scholastic linear scale of some kind (Thurstone & Chave, 1929). They used the same sort of reasoning to the whole range of the scale, so that they had at least two, and possibly three, characteristics of each person designated in terms of the scale. These characteristics would be (1) the mean position that an individual occupies on the scale, (2) the range of opinions that the individual is willing to accept, and (3) that one opinion which the individual selects as the one which most nearly represents his/her own attitude on the issue at stake (Thurstone & Chave, 1929, 14-15). The original notion of a continuum of developing competence has been down played or lost; and, criterion referenced assessment is associated instead with long checklists of skills to be taught, assessed, and checked off when mastered (Masters & Evans, 1986). This checklist approach, according to Masters & Evans (1986), fragments a curriculum into bits of knowledge.

In the absence of the framework provided by Glaser's continuum of developing competence, there is often no obvious reason why a teacher should be concerned about one unmastered objective more than any other; every unmastered objective on a checklist looks equally problematic. What is more, a simple checklist rarely provides a useful basis for identifying surprises or for deciding on what aspect of a curriculum a student is ready for next. (Masters & Evans, 1986, p. 260). An example of a checklist, more global than most, can be found in Docking (1976, 1985, 1986) and McGaw (1984).

Student Objectives	Assessment Characteristics Required
1. Perseverance	Continuous, individual, and immediate feedback.
2. Extension	Encouraging
3. Competence	Clearly defined criteria and standards.
4. Independence	Personal "ownership" of learning and assessment.
5. Responsibility	Honest, open, uncompromising.
6. Cooperation with peers	Uncompetitive, noncomparative
7. Cooperation with teacher	Unambiguous, clear requirements.
8. Creativity	Informative and flexible
9. Divergent thought	Detailed knowledge of competencies, adjusts to individual needs.
10. Self esteem	Accurate, fair, noncomparative
11. Enjoyment	Non-threatening, private
12. Self awareness	Develops self assessment skills
13. Challenge	Attainable standards, visible improvement
14. Social belonging	Communality of competencies
15. Social contribution	Uniqueness of competencies

Instead of the checklist approach, Masters and Evans (1986) proposed recognizing the "continuous nature of student learning (p.263)." They purport that a student's achievement is interpreted as a location on a continuum of developing competence. They interpret the purpose of assessment not to be to determine whether some end point has been reached or whether some bit of knowledge or skill has been mastered, but, to mark that student's current level of attainment on an on-going line of development (Masters & Evans, 1986, p. 263).

Wright and Bell (1984) use the term "curriculum mapping." This approach can be contrasted with approaches to assessment which treat subject matter as discrete packages of knowledge or skill to be "mastered." Viewing curriculum as such packages not only encourages a "learn-it-and-forget-it" approach to learning, but also runs the risk of emphasizing easily identifiable bits of knowledge or skill at the expense of more fundamental understandings that run through a curriculum and develop over time (Wright & Bell, 1984). They use the term "continuous" assessment when the purpose of assessment is to estimate a student's current standing on a continuum of developing competence. They state that summing estimates at the end of a course to obtain a "total" would be like adding measures of a child's height made at various times during childhood to obtain a "total" height at adolescence (Wright & Bell, 1984). Under their approach to "criterion referencing" assessment, what is important at any particular time during a course (including the end of the course) is the level of attainment a student has reached, interpreted in terms of the types of behaviors and understandings that characterize that level of attainment.

There are many definitions of criterion referenced assessments (Gray, 1978; Hambleton, 1980, 1981; Nitko, 1980). In 1978, Gray reported the existence of 57 definitions. Hambleton (1980) points out that *criterion* refers to a *domain of content or behavior* to which assessment scores can be referenced.

Glass (1978) argued that the interpretation of *criterion as a standard, mastery level, cut-off score, or pass-fail mark* (p. 243) is a corruption of the intended meaning of the word criterion, and that "criterion referenced" emphasizes assessment design, construction, and links between assessment results and behavioral referents (Linn, 1980, 1982). The research indicates that practitioners score less well than new graduates on the definition of the term criterion (Karni & Lofsness, 1985; Livingston, 1983). Francis and Holmes believe that the differences that result when different criterion referenced methods are used *may be the result of a failure to adequately define the minimally competent candidate.* (Sigmond, 1981). In this study, only 113 items (57%) of the 199 items needed to be answered appropriately to pass the examination. In addition, Alderman, Swinton, and Braswell (1979) has shown that seemingly minor variations in event format can influence performance. Thus, $42 \div 7$, 42 divided by 7, $7\overline{)42}$, 42/7, and $\dfrac{42}{7}$ represent alternative formats that might be used to define the domain. Based on the results reported by Alderman, et al. (1979), the proportion-appropriate score would be expected to differ from one domain to the next. Furthermore, the relative performance of different groups of students on the different domains is apt to depend upon the match between the format of the event domain and the problem format used in instruction. Differential effects due to event format and the match between the format used in instruction and on the assessment are quite consistent with the formulation presented by Harris et al. (1977). It merely emphasizes the fact that event format may be a critical component in the definition of a universe of events. If a student fails to answer appropriately events in one format but could answer them appropriately if they were presented in another format, then the inference that the student cannot divide is invalid. Only a statement about items in the format used can be justified (Linn, 1980, p. 554). Filby and Dishaw (1977) and Berk (1980) have demonstrated that validity is not solely a property of the event or set of events and that achieving an objective is a necessary but not sufficient condition for getting a large proportion of events appropriate. These results provide additional evidence that the mastery/nonmastery criterion is inadequate.

Hambleton (1982), Hambleton, and de Gruijter (1983) and Hambleton and Rogers (1986) point out that the definitional and psychometric problems discussed to this point have impacted professional licensure examinations: Fifteen years ago, the development of many certification and licensure (credentialing) examinations was simple, quick, and painless. Often a small committee of professionals would get together for a few days, rework the previous year's examination, add a modest number of new examination events, and then send the new examination off to the printer. Cutoff (or passing) scores were often set to fail a prespecified number of candidates (e.g. 15%). The amount of psychometric research in examination development usually was limited to producing a correct split-half reliability statistic and to conducting an event analysis. We have also observed over the last 15 years misapplication of measurement theory in preparing credentialing examinations (Hambleton & Rogers, 1986, 210). [For additional examples of misinterpretation see Kempa (1976), Kempa & L' Odiaja (1984), GCE & CSE Joint Council (1983).] Livingston (1980) joined the army of psychometricians that argued that content validity evidence alone can never be sufficient to justify the use of an assessment. Messick (1975, 1979, 1980) took the negative position on this issue. The affirmative is represented by Ebel (1961, 1977) and by the *Uniform Guidelines on Employee Selection Procedures* (Equal Employment Opportunity Commission, 1978). Ebel argues that in many cases the assessment serves to define the characteristic it is intended to measure, and if the assessment events form an adequate sample of the content to be assessed, no additional evidence of the assessment's validity is necessary.

The assumption that reliability indices are not important to criterion referenced assessment originates from an article by Popham and Husek (1969) who argued that "variability is not a necessary condition for a good criterion referenced assessment" and that reliability indices based on score variability are not only irrelevant to "criterion referenced uses, but are actually injurious to their proper development and use" (pp. 3, 4). Kane's (1986) analyses suggested that reliability is an important issue in criterion referenced assessment. Kane suggested that if a criterion referenced assessment had a reliability (defined in terms of internal consistency) below 0.5, a simple a priori procedure would provide better estimates of students' universe scores than would individual observed scores; and, that such coefficients relate to the usefulness of the assessments in estimating universe scores. When the reliability of an assessment is very low, differences in observed scores can be attributed to errors of measurement rather than to differences in individuals' level of mastery of the domain; tests with no variability in scores "give no information and are therefore not useful" (Woodson, 1974, p. 64).

In a discussion of standard setting methods, assessment specialists have distinguished between continuum and state models (Algina & Coulsin, 1978; Brennon & Kane, 1977; Hambleton, Swaminatan, Algina, & Coulsin, 1978; Harris, 1974; Huynh, 1976; Meskauskas, 1976; Shepard, 1976, 1979, 1980; Traub & Crowley, 1980; Wilcox, 1977, 1980). Those models have been used to differentiate norm and criterion referenced assessments as well as latent trait paradigms from mastery assessments. The argument is that the major distinction between continuum and state models is in terms of how the assessment score is to be used.

In essence, no complete solution to the many problems of mental measurement has been found. Partial solutions to some problems currently exist. However, most of the issues related to mental measurement are in need of extensive theoretical and empirical investigation. The measurement specialist, when constructing an assessment, as well as consumers of existing assessments are advised to be cautious. The intended use and purpose of any proposed instrument must be considered in light of the limitations of that model. Each of the three major measurement models and their limitations has been presented. It is hoped that this material will be useful in the decision process.

Assessment specialists, constrained by the focus of their task, have lacked the vision to see that the difference between continuum and state models reflects fundamental philosophical issues. Those issues distinguish developmental education from constructionism as well as curriculum from instruction. Looking at assessment performance from a learning theory perspective provides greater insight into assessment performance and how to interpret assessment results. The examination of assessment results and the construction of assessments predicated upon a developmental curriculum paradigm results in assessments which can be substantively interpreted by educators.

DEVELOPMENTAL EDUCATION

In general, a characteristic of college professors is a lack of knowledge of educational and psychological theory. They believe that developmental education is a relatively new field of study. It has suffered during its emergence for lack of definition relative to its related process, purpose, and philosophy. Early descriptions have limited both the scope and focus of the field (Abraham, 1991; Clowes, 1980, 1982, 1992; Higbee, 1993). Professors' descriptions of developmental education elude to particular subpopulations served or desired outcomes. Additionally, many different labels have been used to identify these subpopulations. These include dispriviledged, disadvantaged, nontraditional, new, and high risk. These labels reflect the focus of developmental education programs as programs which attempted to remediate or compensate for background deficits.

By stepping back and considering a definition of developmental education which encompasses both process and philosophy, we find an emerging field with applications to learning for any stage of development, field of study, and age level. In fact, we find a field which encompasses the ultimate goal of any formal or informal educational (or training) program. The goal of developmental education is to help individuals understand the processes of acquiring knowledge and skills so that the process can be applied throughout the life span as new skills and new knowledge bases are acquired thereby allowing the individual to attain new (higher) levels of proficiency and new goals. The terms comprising developmental education are reflected in this definition. "Developmental," according to Webster's Collegiate Dictionary (1974), is change accompanied by achievement. That is, development or change is a necessary condition for achievement to be realized. Likewise, "education" is defined to be the process whereby less experienced members of society acquire the values (what the society believes to be of worth) and skills (aptitudes) necessary to function as a contributing member of the society. The ultimate aim of any educational program (formal or informal) is development (Astin, 1985; Case, 1985; Claxton, 1990; Clowes, 1980, 1982, 1992; Hashway & Cain, 1993; Havinghurst, 1952; Higbee, 1993; Roberts, 1989).

Viewed together, developmental education is a dynamic approach to learning whose purpose is to foster the development of individuals who are active, critical, and productive societal members. Developmental education is a process which may be applied to all populations and knowledge bases and in any setting. It encompasses a philosophy about humans and learning which sees man as a dynamic, emerging individual with growth potential. The worth of the individual is recognized along with differences in process and purpose of the learning situation. These differences imply that different learning paths will be taken by different individuals in attaining the same goal.

Developmental education recognizes the learner as a bio-psycho-social individual with needs and potentials in each of these areas. Its goal is to enhance strengths and ameliorate weaknesses in order to promote maximization of individual potential (Case, 1985; Cross, 1976; 1987; Hashway, 1988, 1990; Hashway & Cain, 1993; Havinghurst, 1952). The developmental education model brings together all support services and functions necessary in assisting the learner in becoming a fully functioning adult able to make appropriate choices (as defined by the society) current to their developmental stage (Cross, 1976, 1987; Hashway, 1988, 1990; Hashway & Cain, 1993). It seeks to maximize the learning and academic potential of the learner.

Definitions, such as those that define developmental education as a program designed for students entering college with academic or operational skill deficits which place them at a disadvantage, limit the scope and focus of developmental education programs (for examples of such definitions see Abraham, 1991; Boylan, 1986; Claxton, 1990; Clowes, 1980, 1982, 1992; Cross, 1976, 1987; Maxwell, 1979; National Association of Developmental Education, 1992). Using these definitions, only a small group of students benefit from programs which can potentially benefit all learners. Others have tried to remove these limitations by referring to developmental education as a lifelong learning process in which the individual develops and refines the skills necessary to communicate with one's age group, better understand one's sex role, and become a productive member of their society

(Chickering, 1969, 1976; Chickering & Associates, 1981; Clowes, 1992; Hashway, 1988, 1990; Hashway & Cain, 1993; Havinghurst, 1952; Maxwell, 1979).

In sum, developmental education is a philosophy of education in which the learner is viewed as a dynamic individual developing on cognitive, emotional, physical, social, ethical, and moral continua. It is an enabling philosophy which provides the necessary resources and guidance to assist the learning in coming to know and belong in their society. Developmental education as a field of study, therefore, cannot depend upon the constructionist view that learning viewed as a result of something that is done to an inert learner. Developmental learning occurs through dynamic interaction between the learner and the environment, where *the learner, not the environment or the instruction, is the most important element in the equation.* The theory of development becomes the primary focus of study in this emerging field of study. Learning theory, curriculum development theory, and instructional theory are utilized in order to create an environment for individuals who wish to improve their knowledge, abilities, and skills (Clowes, 1992; Hashway, 1988, 1990; Hashway & Cain, 1993).

The developmental approach views successful performance as a process that progresses through a series of stages or learning paths where each step along the learning path is more complex than the preceding one. The learner must be an active participant interacting with materials and resources appropriate to their developmental level. Therefore, any program that has as its purpose the development of the diverse talents of the individual learner can be considered a developmental program (Carter, 1992; Clowes, 1992; Cross, 1976, 1987; Hashway, 1988, 1990; Hashway & Cain, 1993; Havinghurst, 1952; Pruett, 1994). Developmental learning, the axioms of which are described in the next two chapters, is the foundation of any developmental education program. Any academic program purporting to be developmental or train developmental educators must be grounded in the axioms of developmental learning theory.

CURRICULUM VS. INSTRUCTION

Curriculum and instruction are two terms which are intertwined to the point that they are frequently confused. Definitions of both are found in several sources with Fenwick English (1987) giving, perhaps, the most detailed explanations and definitions of curriculum. Therefore, his definitions and explanations will be used liberally. Since other sources have no doubt influenced English, his work is a concise compilation of the work of many curriculum theorists (Bobbitt, 1912, 1913, 1918, 1924, 1926, 1934; Bloom, Englehart, Furst, Hill, & Krathwohl, 1956; Bruner, 1966; Caswell & Campbell, 1937; Dewey, 1900a, 1900b, 1910, 1926, 1964; Thorndike, 1912, 1913, 1932; Tyler, 1930, 1942, 1948, 1949, 1951, 1953, 1959, 1964a, 1964b, 1983).

Curriculum is an internal coding mechanism that guides the work of the organization. The purpose of a curriculum is not to free the organization from its boundaries, but to enable it to function within those boundaries more effectively (that is, the organization reaches more of its objectives with a curriculum) and efficiently (that is, the organization can reach more of its goals at the least possible cost in terms of expenditures of resources). The curriculum becomes effective and efficient according to English (1987) by:

1. Defining the nature of the work to be done
2. Relating all of the tasks to be accomplished one to the other within the total work process or work flow called coordination
3. Defining standards by which work is to be measured or assessed
4. Defining evaluation procedures by which work results can be compared to work performed
5. Formulating changes in the nature of work with feedback from evaluation by revising written work instructions
6. Repeating the above steps until a significantly higher level of work performance is obtained on a consistent basis (p. 6).

The curriculum, therefore, becomes a plan of action, a set of directions whose chief purpose is to guide the work of the institution, whether that work be teaching and instruction in a formal school setting or manufacturing a product in a factory setting.

As a set of directions for the work of schools, curriculum comes in a variety of forms (English, 1987). The textbook is perhaps the most commonly used curriculum guide. Teachers frequently let the textbook form the written set of directions that guides their selection of content (which can be concepts, skills, activities, facts, processes, simulations, or knowledge), determines the time to be spent on that content, and sets the sequencing of the content. The textbook becomes the simplest form of instruction. Anything which makes such determinations fulfills the requirements for a curriculum as a set of directions.

The curriculum is frequently a document aimed at guiding internal operations. It is the tool that ensures that work performed conforms to the purpose for which work is required (English, 1987, p. 11). The curriculum then takes on whatever shape is necessary to impact the work and includes whatever content by which work is designed and delivered (this is instruction). In this manner, curriculum becomes a means to an end and never an end in and of itself. It has become the functional response to the necessity to design, guide, and monitor the work that occurs. It is an absolute requirement for work to be improved, particularly over many years, for many groups of learners or workers, and many teachers, administrators, and leaders. English (1987) states: *Without a curriculum, school people would have to resort to exhortation and good intentions as the major methods for improving learning in schools. Complex operations are rarely improved with such naive and primitive techniques* (p. 11). Curriculum provides the means by which work can be restructured and redone to improve the performance of the institution. It is about structuring the work of any human organization. As a guide to work it should be clear that the curriculum will be ultimately related to the purpose of the organization, the internal authority structure of the organization, and the way the organization divides and subdivides work (that is, work specialization).

One of the reasons why any human organization has a curriculum is to limit the focus and energy of the organization. Organizations require boundaries because of limited resources. Survival of the organization means focusing resources upon certain activities to the exclusion of other activities. This focusing brings about internal consistency and enables the organization to concentrate upon the essential activities and processes of that organization. The curriculum defines and legitimizes some activities and outcomes and declares others out of bounds. A curriculum, according to English (1987) contains all or some of ten elements.

One problem which frequently occurs in organizations, such as established educational institutions, is that the ends of curriculum are nebulous and global. When this occurs it is impossible to know if the means are working. Vagueness in defining a curriculum can propagate the means becoming the end. For a curriculum to be useful to an organization it must be related to specific ends. It is only when this occurs that it can be determined if the curriculum is effective and efficient. Essential information about the work of the organization is contained in a curriculum to guide the organization on a daily operational basis. It also serves to match and reinforce the authority structure and division of labor and provide a record of work to be done and a sequence of events, about the work, to serve as a data base to relate feedback about results and a location to consider interventions in the organization for subsequent work improvements.

ELEMENTS OF A CURRICULUM

1. A rationale or philosophy undergirding the establishing the curriculum,
2. A statement of outcomes or ends, goals, purposes, objectives,
3. A description of methods, processes, or activities,
4. Time requirements or specifications,
5. Specification of relationships,
6. Schedules of actual work tasks or job descriptions,
7. Relationships to supplementary materials or equipment required,
8. Evaluation procedures and references to assessments,
9. Relationships to larger units or work or work standards,
10. Relationships to external agencies and their requirements or specifications (English, 1987, pp. 26-27).

In the final analysis, the curriculum is nothing less than the statement an institution makes about what, out of the totality of man's constantly growing knowledge and experience, is considered useful, appropriate, or relevant to the lives of men and women at a certain point in time. The purpose of curriculum is to guide the teachers or workers in the organization towards common desired outcomes. The genius of curriculum is that across many years and levels of proficiency, the work (which may be teaching) is consistently directed and purposively shaped to promote required and desired learning or production. The fundamental challenge to the implementation of a curriculum is the extent to which it weaves together a coherent system of instruction which is directed toward system goals. If a curriculum promotes such a system within a school and between grades it is said to have continuity. If it does so between schools it is said to promote articulation. The goal of curriculum is articulation. That is, no matter where the student (or worker) goes, experiences have been provided which enable that person to take advantage of the opportunities provided throughout the system and to attain higher levels of proficiency.

Instruction is the curricula delivery mechanism. A curriculum is articulated through institutions. English (1987) refers to their relationship as being "wedded," and states that instruction is always wedded to the curriculum. Learning on the other hand may be and can be a completely separate activity from the function of the school or the approved curriculum. Therefore, the activity of learning is not necessarily the result of instruction. Because of this relationship between instruction and curriculum, English (1987, p. 51) states: "A curriculum not monitored may as well be non-existent. Just as teaching may be thought of as the monitoring of learning, so is supervision the monitoring of teaching." It is well we keep in mind the difference between teaching (the activity which may go on in the classroom), instruction (the delivery of the curriculum), and curriculum (all the decisions made about what, when, where, and how the learner is to work prior to the learner actually beginning work. Otherwise, we are apt to think learning is occurring when a completely separate activity is occurring. And although there may be hidden curriculum (a curriculum not explicitly stated), monitoring of learning is necessary in order to ensure that the goals and purposes of the institution are realized.

Assessment developers and psychometricians can no longer see their craft as different and apart from human development theory. Their art originated in that theory base and has, over the years, become separated in an effort to evolve an "objective science." A science and its' measurement paradigms are integrated with and defined by the theories which define that science. To separate psychometrics from human development theory results in methodologies unrelated to any science or application.

The remainder of this book will focus on psychometric paradigms and program validation techniques based on developmental learning theory. The next chapter will focus on the foundations of developmental learning theory resulting in the *Axioms of Developmental Learning Theory*. The following chapters will examine developmental learning theory from the perspectives of hierarchical interpretations of assessment results and the study of human interaction in the classroom. The methodologies implicit in those theories will be described as the theories evolve. The methodologies and theories are germinal, and, I hope, others will take the challenge and further refine and develop those theories.

8

Principles Of Developmental Learning
Foundations Of A 'Minds on' Curriculum

Curriculum developers make choices about what to emphasize. How much time should be spent on memorization tasks? How much credit to appropriate processes that resulting in an inappropriate answer? Could the time spent in a laboratory be better spent reviewing the basic principles? When and where are manipulatives effective? The answers are dependent upon the philosophy of learning implicit in the curriculum.

Recognizing the need in our society for a citizenry who not only possess a specific set of vocational skills but who are able to visualize a future, we must implement a developmental approach to learning. Manipulatives-"hands on" materials-were introduced into the curriculum on the basis of providing the image behind a "new concept" based upon the "success" of manipulatives in the elementary school setting (Goddard, 1992; Piel and Gretts, 1992). For many learners the concept being introduced will not be a "new concept." If the learner is not new to the concept they can frequently perform operations necessary to arrive at an appropriate answer, they simply have forgotten the set of systematic steps they had used to get the answer. Before introducing new approaches, an acceptable sequence of steps for systematically completing the problem should be provided (Hashway, 1990), and methods should be directly related to the concept since conceptual repetition enhances memory (Hashway, 1990). The use of manipulatives will not in itself increase learner understanding of concepts (Glynn, Yeany, & Burton, 1991).

Assessment construction, analysis, administration, and interpretation must take into account the dynamic nature of the human condition. People are not static but highly dynamic; they change from moment to moment. How they react to the world becomes refined with experience. The very nature of reality is dynamically restructured over time. Individuals are blurry targets for our metrics (Baker & O'Neil, 1985). They not only dynamically change; but, they differ from and influence each other. This is the basis of developmental learning.

To demonstrate the understanding of a concept a learner must be able to state the concept in their own words. The nature of concept formation is of fundamental importance to those concerned with education. In order to educate, teach, or foster learning, one needs to know how concepts are formed. The goal of this Chapter is to provide a new way of looking at developmental learning and curriculum theory. The proposed theory, the developmental model, incorporates information processing theories and neurophysiological evidence. The model has its roots in a classical paper by Newell, Shaw, and Simon (1958) and research described in the *Handbook of Developmental Education,* and elsewhere (Hashway, 1979, 1982, 1983, 1988, 1989, 1990, 1993; Hashway & Hashway, 1993). The developmental model concerns the human processing of information where transformations are applied to the input data. The set of transformations represent logical rules which are applicable to sensory stimuli and result from accumulated knowledge, behavior patterns and experiences. The transformations transform information into particular output behaviors (rationality). Developmental learning starts at the level of the individual and incorporated this individual as the primary component of the learning process. The developmental model does not postulate that individual differences do not exist; it incorporates individual differences as a foundation of the theory, is sufficiently encompassing to include preschool as well as postdoctoral education and everything in between.

McDonald (1964) has pointed out that "Education has needed a science of man." That "science of man" should serve as the foundation of the instructional process. Various theories have attempted to define human behavior. The theories of the stimulus-response (S-R) theorists (Hebb, 1955, 1946; Hull, 1952, 1943, 1933, 1931; Pavlov, 1927; Skinner, 1964, 1949) were the seeds of an educational movement called programmed instruction (Blyth, 1960; Coulson and Silberman, 1960; DeCecco, 1964; Edwards, 1963; Green, 1962; Holland, 1959; Hughes, 1962; Resnick, 1963; Suppes, 1964; Washburne, 1922). The S-R theories did not include dimensions of human personality. Some educational theorists contend that the myopic focus of S-R theories on narrow bands of knowledge is a serious limitation of the theory (Biggs, 1971; Bruner, 1964). Other theories are strongly associated with personality. The theories developed by Freud (1922), Maslow (1965, 1962, 1959, 1950, 1955, 1954, 1942), Maslow and Mittlemann (1951), Rogers (1963, 1955, 1947), Rogers and Dymond (1954), and others (Woodworth, 1918; Woodworth and Scholsberg, 1954) focused upon the impact of emotion on the learning process. Expectations and evidence of hypothesized underlying processes were weak at best. The humanistic models lacked the scientific rigor of the S-R models. The goal of this chapter is to form a symbiosis of these theories and lead to the genesis of a new way of looking at developmental learning and curriculum theory taking into consideration the best points of both the S-R and humanistic models. The proposed theory, the developmental model, goes beyond the predictions and predictive power of both theories and neurophysiological evidence as the processes which take place during learning.

The developmental model concerns the human processing of information. Transformations are applied to the input data. The set of transformations represent logical rules which are applicable to sensory stimuli and result from accumulated knowledge, behavior patterns and experiences. Each person has had different experiences and will behave somewhat differently to the same situation. The allowed transformations are derived from learned behavior. The developmental model predicts individual differences. It is a model which does not start by trying to explain modal behavior. Thinking starts at the level of the individual. The extent to which group behavior is predicted by the model is associated with the extent to which individual behavior is predictable. The thinking model does not postulate that individual differences do not exist (i.e. as the S-R model), it incorporates individual differences as a foundation of the theory. The remainder of this chapter presents an overview of the developmental model and a general theory of knowledge.

DEVELOPMENTAL MODELS

Regardless of whether we are designing programs for remediation or enrichment, those programs must rest upon firm foundations. Foundations of educational programs should have their roots planted in the soil of human learning, always remembering the importance of becoming a self-learner. It is important that all educational programs emphasize human processes for cognitive growth and development. A chapter concerning curriculum would do a disservice to its audience without describing how the curriculum/educational philosophy it purports relates to the process of human learning and development. What is the process of human growth and development? What is the process which separates man from 'lower' life forms? Since the times of the early philosophers man has pondered that question. Only recently have neurologists, psychologists, computer scientists, and educators been able to shed some light on the process of human development.

From the ashes of the theoretical and experimental furnaces of psychological, neurological and cognitive science both old and new, a human information processing model has grown which models human development (Anderson, 1990, 1980; Bartlett, 1932; Hull, 1943, 1952; Humphrey, 1933; Laird, Newell, & Rosenbloom, 1987; Murdock, 1993; Neisser, 1976; Norman, 1970; Posner and McLeod, 1982; Simon, 1979; Spearman, 1904, 1927; Thorndike, 1912, 1913, 1932; Thurstone, 1927, 1938; Tolman, 1936, 1938; Wündt, 1874; Zadek, 1987a, 1987b). Not only does it explain cognitive development it also serves as a basis for intelligent machines, artificial intelligence, and expert systems. The model is more than merely a cognitive psychology or just neurophysiology. Growth and development is more than a mere model of information processing. *Developmental learning* is the discipline which integrates psychology, education, neurology, human physiology, computer and information sciences, embracing learning as an evolutionary process where beliefs (knowledge structures) evolve through experience (Bransford, Nitch, & Franks, 1977; Bryson, 1933; Hall, 1883, 1904; Hart, 1927; Hardin, 1988; Harvis, 1991; Keimig, 1983; Knowles, 1977; Liveright, 1968; Münterberg, 1898; Nist, 1985; Novack & Gowin, 1984; Payne, Krathowoll, & Gordon, 1967; Perkins, 1989; Pines, 1977; President's Commission, 1947; Rouche & Snow, 1977; Sheldon, 1942). *Developmental education* is the application of developmental learning principles to learning situations. An integration of the many disciplines which form the foundation of developmental learning is outlined in this section.

The Activation System. A learner is a system in flux, activated by information and self perpetuated once activated. Learners are systems catalyzed by information. Many psychologists have postulated the existence of drives or motives to define cognitive behavior (Freud, 1922; Hull, 1952; Maslow, 1955; Rogers, 1963). Others have postulated the existence of a complexity program (Biggs, 1971). Neurological and psychological studies have localized the site in the brain for the drive for information or motivation. This area of the brain is called the *Reticular Activation System* (RAS). RAS is the interface between the base of the brain and the spinal column. This area is active when the brain is processing information. It supplies the instruction which tells the cognitive process to GO (Bloom, Lazerson, & Hofstadter, 1985; Hebb, 1955; Hobson and McCarley, 1979; Jouvet, 1969; Ullman, 1973).

The Memory System

There is considerable evidence (Bousfield, & Barclay, 1950; Freedman, & Loftus, 1971; Goss, & Nodine, 1965; Melton, & Martin, 1972; Sternberg, 1969; Winzenz, & Bower, 1970) indicating that human memory consists of three components: short term memory (STM), intermediate term memory (ITM), and long term memory (LTM).

Short Term Memory is an area of the mind used for storing input from sensory processors. Images are stored for short periods of time (less than 1 or 2 seconds). In that time the mind decides whether or not it wishes to deal with the data (Hunter, 1964; Miller, 1966, 1956; Neisser, 1967; Postman, 1955; Treisman, 1966). Short term memory is located in the hippocampus (Alton, 1983; Olton, Becker, & Handelmann, 1983; O'Keefe, & Nadel, 1978; Thompson, Berger, & Madden, 1983; Thompson, Hicks, & Shryrokov, 1980), in the lower portion of the midsection of the central core of the brain (Hunt, 1976; Thompson, et al., 1983, 1980). Most people can store about 7 bits of data in STM which does not seem to be very much. Successive recoding of data lets us store a great deal of information in just 7 bits.

Intermediate Term Memory seems to also be located in the hippocampus (Goss, & Nodine, 1965; Melton, & Martin, 1972; Platt, & MacWhimmey, 1983; Slobin, 1979). Information is stored in the intermediate area for a few minutes or whatever time it takes to make a decision concerning the data. Intermediate memory can be considered to be a temporary working storage area where data is identified, categorized, and modified from sensory STM input and moved into the ITM (Sperling, 1960; Turvey, 1973).

Long Term Memory consists of memory traces which are retained for long periods of time. Long term memory resides in the temporal lobes and in the cerebral cortex (Bousfield, 1953; Freedman and Loftus, 1971; Harlow, 1959). When we first learn something synaptic connections are established between regions in the temporal lobes and areas in the cortex (Pellionisz and Linas, 1980, 1979; Squire, 1984, 1981). For, perhaps, several years, the temporal and contextual areas interact and the memory trace is conceptually integrated with other concepts by a reorganization of the neural circuits (the synaptic network), when complete, the temporal connections are no longer necessary and can be relegated to other tasks. The temporal area contains, primarily, procedural knowledge and the cortex contains the concepts related to experience, our understanding of past experiences and environmental familiarity. The cortex contains those neural structures which define the individual as a unique human being (Cohen and Squire, 1980; Tulvin, 1972).

The complex network of synaptic connections are simultaneously hardware and software. Evidence of the modifiability of neural networks has been shown by Jackson (1958/1869). He demonstrated that if limited damage occurs to a part of the brain, that programming is moved to another part of the cortex.

The Central Processor. The remainder of this Chapter discusses how the different memory organizations interact with each other to produce reality. It will be helpful to use a concept taken from computer science: the central processing unit (CPU), a device which performs all computations and controls the flow of data. Although it is useful to think of a single central processor controlling the actions of the brain, this is not the case. There is no evidence that a single area of the brain acts as the controller of all thoughts and actions. There are many central processing units active at the same time acting on the same or different data. Action takes place when a group of processors, controlling a group of functions and acting on the same data, reach a decision; and, this *distributed information processing model* described above has found some utility in the study of cognitive abilities (Collins and Loftus, 1975; Fahlman, 1979; Hunt, 1976, 1973; Hunt and Poltrack, 1974; Levin, 1976; McClelland, 1981; Mountcastle, 1975; Mountcastle and Edelman, 1978).

Representation of Knowledge and Learning

There seems to be two basic representations of knowledge, imagery and discursive language (Kosslyn, 1980; Neisser, 1967; Paivio, 1971; Tolaas, 1986), supported by unique representation systems. There is a body of research that supports the existence of unique knowledge representations (Benton, 1962; Bogen, 1960; Bogen and Mazzaniga, 1965; Colonna and Faglioni, 1966; Conners and Barata, 1967; De Rezi and Faglioni, 1965; Doehring and Reitan, 1962; Elner and Myers, 1962; Gazzaniza, 1967; Levy, 1969; Sperry, 1968, 1966). Discursive language is supported by a serial processing system and image data by a parallel processing system (Kosslyn, 1980; Neisser, 1967; Paivio, 1971; Tolaas, 1986). Symbolic schemes are shifts from images (parallel) to verbal (serial) representations (Bruner, 1964; Bruner, Olver and Greenfield, 1966; Kosslyn, 1980; Grinder and Bandler, 1976; Piaget and Inheider, 1977 Werner and Kaplan, 1963).

Figure 8.1:
Hyperactivity and Hypoactivity

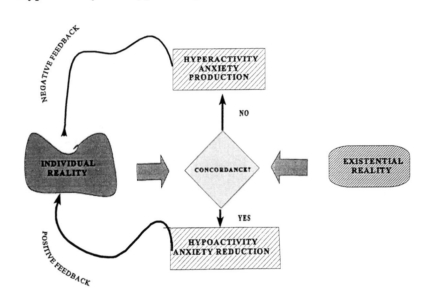

Tolaas (1986) has eloquently presented the position of the transformation theorists as: Presenting the experience of one representational system through language implies transformation. In the typical dreaming state, REM sleep, activity in the visual representational system is aroused internally so that all information drawn from memory, regardless of input channel during the waking state, tends to be given visual representation. Similarly, admitted external and proprioceptive input is generally transformed into visual imagery (Arkin, Artrobus and Ellman, 1978; Tolaas, 1980). What this means is that reporting dreams imposes one mode of being (waking consciousness) and one representational system (language) on another mode of being (dreaming) and another representational system (a sensory mode that is predominantly visual). There is no need for interconceptual controversy. The parallel distributive model provides for both serial and parallel processing of both verbal and image data.

ICONIC THINKING

A study of concept formation and the evolution of thinking from childhood through adulthood yields insight into the developmental learning process. The first stage is the formation of icons (Bruner, 1964). Icons are mental images. They exhibit form and structure. By disengaging interpretive processes we have a pathway into the iconic world (Huxley, 1959). Depth and spatial origination disappears. The iconic world is a world of pure perception which retains extraordinary detail. At the iconic stage, people are able to remember extraordinary amounts of detail.

Thinking at the iconic stage is very rigid. New situations are compared with old situations on the basis of particulars (Piaget, 1932) and precise matches are required to imply equivalence. Developmental learning, at the iconic stage, does not distinguish between reality or perception and is characterized by rule-bound behavior. Situations must be highly consistent with an individual's perception (Piaget, 1950; Vygotsky, 1962).

If information is not in concordance with past experience at the iconic stage, we often require more task relevant information (feedback). There are two kinds of feedback: positive and negative. Positive feedback occurs when new information is as, or more, discordant with the icon as the previous information. This results in more requests for information. Continuing positive feedback results in a state of high anxiety is defined as the search for information in concordance with our world view. Negative feedback releases the level of anxiety. It occurs when we guide our search for knowledge using past knowledge, and new knowledge is sufficiently concordant with our reality constructs that anxiety is reduced (Miller, Galanter and Pribram, 1960).

The learning facilitator needs to know that when a new concept is introduced, it is being encoded at the iconic level. The concept must be presented at the conceptual level, soon followed with as much detail as possible. A new concept is followed by Reticular Activation System excitation and requests for new knowledge. New knowledge should be related to the concept being presented. When new knowledge is related to the defined concept and past knowledge, a state of negative feedback occurs and anxiety is reduced. When new knowledge is not related either to the prior concept or past knowledge, positive feedback and anxiety results. Intense anxiety results from the presentation of uncoordinated information stored in short term or intermediate memory. If integration does not occur in a few minutes, information is lost and learning does not occur.

Information must be conceptually related, and nonredundantly structured to the data that came before. Information should be logically structured to the preceding information. The information that exhibits a high degree of structural similarity is not processed unless it is somewhat different from what came before. Think about driving down a highway when there are no other cars on the road. Soon you will begin to daydream. The road seems to be a never ending stream of the same stimuli. The process of not attending to repetitive stimuli is called the *habituatory decrement*. If material is highly similar to what came before, a high degree of forgetting will take place (Graham, 1973; Groves and Thompson, 1973; Harris, 1943; Humphrey, 1933; Peeke and Herz, 1973; Sokolv, 1963; Syz, 1926; Underwood, 1966). *Conceptual repetition* will enhance memory but identical repetition will reduce retention (Anderson and Bower, 1973; Atkinson and Shiffrin, 1968; Biggs, 1969; Kintsch, Kozminsky, Strely, McKoon and Keenan, 1975; Wanner, 1974).

Habituatory decrements and stimulation supplied by the 'partially known' (Biggs, 1971) is an effective curricular delivery strategy. Successive presentation of the same or extremely similar stimuli results in a decrease in retention (Graham, 1973; Groves and Thompson, 1973; Harris, 1943; Humphrey, 1933; Peeke and Herz, 1973; Sokolv, 1963; Syz, 1926; Underwood, 1966). Conceptual repetition will enhance memory but identical repetition will reduce retention (Anderson and Bower, 1973; Atkinson and Shiffrin, 1968; Biggs, 1969; Kintsch, Kozminsky, Strely, McKoon and Keenan, 1975; Wanner, 1974). The secret seems to be to: *diversify either the material or the methods, means, and mode of presentation sufficiently to make it seem novel and different, and, not to disguise the material so much that it seems unrelated to the topic of the lesson and/or past experience.* The *art of developmental teaching* is to organize and sequence the presentation of material in such a way that it is related to what has come before, and is sufficiently different in either presentation mode or information content to excite the Reticular Activation System (i.e. stimulate the information gathering process).

Conceptual Generalizations

Iconic storage is very detailed. The search of iconic memory, detail for detail, is time consuming. 'Economy of storage' is reached through the generation of concepts, generalized forms of icons. Concepts are not as detail rich as the icon itself. Memory integration is reached at the expense of many details. Once something is learned and placed in the temporal region, dendrites emerge from that region extending into related areas of the cerebral cortex. *Contextual sites* are long columnar structures with thousands of nerve endings terminating on a cortexual column. Thousands of nerves protrude from the cortexual column making their way into temporal areas and the cerebellum. As more information on a topic is accumulated, more neural pathways are 'grown.' Interrelationships emerge between the temporal site and many areas of the cortex. The growth process may span many years. At some magic point, when the learned relationship achieves 'importance' the temporal site is 'reconstructed' in the cortex and a concept is born.

A learned concept has lost much of the original detail of the icon and the rigid concrete rule bound behavior is absent. For example at seventeen, the bright learner associates the word "algebra" with symbolic manipulations. At age forty-seven that same bright learner may associate the word "algebra" with a "branch of mathematics which deals with symbols and numbers which I knew very well (as defined by my learning facilitators) at one time" and/or some basic formula solving skills. When asked how many bolts can be bought at $0.35 each with $176.42, the forty-seven year old former bright algebra learner will solve the associated equation. The learner may not write down the equation or follow all the steps presented in school, but, they will follow a proper process. A cortexual area is activated and related subcortexual networks receive the signal and automatically process the data (Bartlett, 1932; Hamilton, 1859; Kintsch, 1972; Kintsch, Kozminsky, Strely, McKoon, and Keenan, 1975; Minsky, 1975; Selz, 1922; Winograd, 1975).

An implication of the memory consolidation process is that we must provide time for "gestation." In the short term learners can not be expected to understand the implications and ramifications of new information. If discovery learning is expected to result in concept formation, then a long time, perhaps years, must be provided for integration to occur. Time for intellectual gestation must be included in any curriculum system.

As important as gestation time is the structure of the concepts presented. Remembering that iconic images are the first to form, lessons must be structured so that elements of those icons are very similar to concepts and related to past events. Never assume that material recently presented has reached the concept stage. Recently presented materials are temporal with some neural pathways extending into the cerebral cortex. When presenting new information, it should be presented in such a way that it is reflective of relevant iconic elements of related concepts. Neural pathways will be established only within the cortex and temporal areas. A sufficient number of pathways established within the temporal area accelerates the transfer of information into concepts and relocation to sites in the cortex.

When presenting material which is related or dependent upon material taught in the distant past, remember that previously learned material has been conceptualized and many of the details have been forgotten. The relation between the new information and concepts previously learned may not be made by the developmental learner. The details of the prior icons must be reconstructed prior to introducing new information. Therefore, careful attention must be given during curricular development of presenting details of all preconcepts so that these details can be incorporated when the learner is constructing a new concept.

It seems that the cyclical format postulated by Dienes (1967) and later expanded upon by Prendergast (1984) and Hashway (1988, 1990) is correct. Rather than a cycle, it seems that learning may take place in terms of intertwining helical pathways. The linear and/or two dimensional projection of those helical pathways of the mind would appear as optimal to the transfer of learning when different topics are studied in a nonlinear ordering. Learning within a topical area may indeed be linear but given the element of time for concept formation and neural pathway development, that linear organization is representable by a helix. Since different concepts mature at different rates dependent upon prior concept and iconic development, the helixes related to different concepts would overlap in time and curriculum sequencing. What appears to be a hierarchical sequence is the ordering of conceptualization time.

The process of concept formation may be why researchers have obtained results at variance with a linear curriculum design (Hashway, 1991, 1988, 1983, 1982, 1979; Hashway & Hashway, 1992, 1990; Hashway & Gamble, 1990; Prendergast, 1983). Classical linear progressions of topics have been invalidated and a cyclical model of learning optimization discovered. Advanced concepts related to topics, whose basic structure was learned at an early stage, should be introduced much later than classical curriculum designs would suggest. It is necessary to form conceptualizations related to the basic concepts prior to moving on to other more advanced topics in the same area. Other topics seemingly obliquely related to prior topics should be presented in the interim. Cyclical reintroduction of topics using advanced basic skills is appropriate since topics must be temporarily, then contextually, and subsequently conceptually integrated.

CODING
Will reality please stand up!

You may recall that the short term memory span contains approximately 7 'chunks' of information. A 'chunk' is defined as a memory element used to represent a single piece of information or a collection of information. What is a memory element used to represent a single piece or collection of information? Consider the mathematical phrase "3+2". Each symbol of that phrase has relevance. The symbols 3 and 2 correspond to a number of concepts: What is a number?, What is a unit?, factorization of units under the operation of addition (i.e. $2 = 1 + 1$). The "+" symbol represents the concept/process of addition. Each symbol or "chunk" triggers other concepts in memory. Each chunk is insignificant in and of itself. The significance of a chunk is that it is the key to a pathway of the mind.

When presented with the phrase "3+2", most people will replace it in memory with "3+2=5" or merely the symbol "5." When this happens, people are interpreting the information. Think of chunks also as "codes". Codes or chunks can be considered to be links in what computer scientists call a "link list" data set (Harrison, 1973; Flores, 1970). Each piece of information contains an 'arrow' to the next piece of information. Examples of educational materials which make use of a technique of progressively higher coding levels fall into the category called "programmed instruction" (Anderson, 1990; Champagne, Klopfer, DeSena, & Squires, 1981; Chase & Simon, 1973; Chi, Fritovsch, & Glaser, 1981; deGrout, 1966, 1965; Fry, 1963; Green, 1962; Hashway, 1988; Kuipers, 1975; Lysaught and Williams, 1963; Minsky, 1975; Pellegrino & Glaser, 1977; Pellegrino & Lyon, 1979; Prendergast, 1984; Rumelhart & Ortony, 1977; Rumelhart, Lindsy, & Norman, 1972; Randal, 1970; Schank, 1975; Vasniadou & Brewer, 1987).

Information is received by the senses which process that information using relational data kept in long term memory. The senses transmit coded data to the short term memory. This coded data correspond to the icons or concepts associated by past experiences with each piece of information in the sensory data stream. The subtle, yet important, point is that words and numbers are nothing more than representations used for communication. Numbers and words are not representative of human thought processes. Humans do not process symbols. The fact that a learner does not answer a question appropriately is not indicative of a lack of understanding, it is only that the learner has not used a representational system for communication that the evaluator is willing to accept (O'Neil, 1981).

Education is definable as the means by which society standardizes communication. Each person can be an excellent information processor. What discriminated man from animals was the ability to establish the "collective consciousness"- a corpus of common knowledge. That collective consciousness is rooted in the symbolic representation of information in terms of language. Each person is not an animal unto him/herself nor immediate or "real time" processor. Our collective experience, transmitted through language, defines the core of humanity and a commonality of thought. The sharing of information generates the concept of time which adds an additional dimension to the depth and breadth of information; time being defined as the concept of information processed by another person or not currently in our sensory input data stream (Hastings, 1969; Mager and Pipe, 1970).

Look at our example of "3+2." That character string can be considered to be made of three chunks: "3", "+" and "2." The chunks are replaced by areas in memory corresponding to the place where the underlying concepts associated with each chunk resides. Symbols correspond to concept locations. We have been conditioned (formed an associated neural network) to perform the operation of addition when we detect the "+" symbol in an environment consisting of numbers. Dependent upon the sophistication of our conditioning, we will replace the code "3+2" with either "=5", or just "5." In either case, the original problem situation has been replaced with an internal representation of the problem. What we have done is apply a "schema" or plan of attack which corresponds to stimulus symbols.

A person may not apply the same schema if the stimuli are presented separately. Each stimulus activates a particular portion of the cortex. The combined effect of cortexual stimulations results in a particular plan of attack. So extra processes must be invoked to implement generalization in a localist scheme. One commonly used teaching method is to allow activation to spread from a local unit to other units that represent similar concepts (Collins and Luftus, 1975). When one concept unit is activated, it will partially, activate its neighbors and so any knowledge stored in the connections emanating from these neighbors will be partially effective (Hinton, McClelland and Rumelhart, 1987).

Figure 8.2:
Conditional Concordance

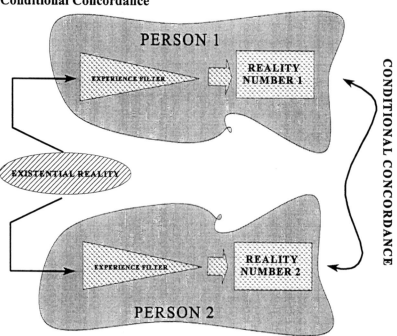

Information about a complex concept is stored in memory and becomes available when the concept is activated. Furthermore, an element that is part of a knowledge frame is able to activate the whole frame. This process is one of pattern completion: a partial stimulus pattern is matched with its representation in memory and activates the total knowledge unit. A person could say "so what" when presented with the sensory strand "3+2." Prior predisposition is the foundation through which our responses are generated. The "so what" response is an example of how attitudes are formed from the use of schema and preconditioned neural patterns. Attitudes are not mysterious metaphysical entities they are the direct result of neural networks.

The term schema was first introduced by Bartlett (1932). Schema have been described as data structures which represent broad concepts, objects, elements and actions (Rumelhart and Ortony, 1977), active organizations of past reactions (Bartlett, 1932), a set of propositions and images (Anderson, 1980), patterns of encoding (Johnson, 1978), higher level descriptions of chunks (Smolensky, 1987), and a representation of a situation or event

(Kintsch, 1978). Regardless of the definition used, it is commonly agreed that schema are filters. They serve as a means of internally organizing reality and filtering essential from nonessential information. Consider our "3+2" example. We applied a schema and replaced the input with the single chunk "5". It became no longer necessary to remember the original stimuli; only the result was necessary.

When we are given materials to learn, reproductions in memory are different from the original materials (Bartlett, 1932; Hunter, 1964). Sensory and motor systems use different representation systems (Pellionisz and Llinas, 1980, 1979). Words are interpreted contextually and sequences of words are interpreted based upon experience (Anderson and Bower, 1973; Filmore, 1968; Kintsch, 1978; Kintsch, Kozminsky, Strely, McKoon and Keenan, 1975).

Humans see the world through schema. The schema correspond to ganglia networks formed through experience via the temporal cortexual assimilation process. Although there is a commonality of knowledge, if formal education was the only way of conveying knowledge, we would all be identical. By processing experiences, we modify our schematic structure. It is the diversity of experience and the resulting schemata that explain the rich diversity of human spirit.

The universe appears external to the observer (Beer, 1966) and is

Figure 8.3:
Relativistic Reality

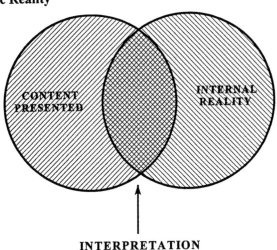

INTERPRETATION

interpreted in terms of the neural network or accumulated knowledge. The details of existential reality are lost in our conceptions and cognitive mappings, and reality exits in each learner's mind. Do not assume the existence of an existential reality separated from the observer (Norwich, 1983). A distinct reality exists in each consciousness. Consciousness involves the process of association, recollection and knowledge modification. The modification of knowledge occurs through recognition, and confirms or alters our concept of self and hence reality (Edelman and Mountcastle, 1978). What is perceived as reality is relative to our expectations.

The intent of any lesson is irrelevant. What is important is how the learner perceives the lesson (Bestor, 1954; Harvey, Hunt and Schroder, 1961; Koerner, 1968). Learning facilitators need to identity the reality constructs of the learners. Learning can not occur until the learners can associate and interpret what is to be learned. Each learner perceives different stimuli most effectively using different sensory modalities. Learning facilitators must be aware of the preferable learning modes of their learners and provide lessons using the greatest number of learning modes possible.

Learners try to emulate accepted behavior patterns. Educators must continuously provide structured feedback not only indicating that something is inappropriate; but, constructive feedback informing the learner when something is appropriate. In the event of an inappropriate response, feedback must be framed in terms of what the appropriate response should be. *Feedback to an inappropriate response serves no useful purpose,* does not contribute to growth and is a deterrent to progress since it does not help the learner make new memory associations that can enhance the process of concept formations.

Neuropsychology and the most recent studies in learning theory offer sound basis for not introducing concepts to adult learners with manipulatives or other "hands on" approaches. The trendy emphasis on "hands on" will not, in itself, increase learners' understanding. To test an understanding of concept we need to make sure that learners can give clear explanations of the concept. We need to understand how the learner is thinking so that instruction can be given directly addressing the misunderstanding, not providing another instructional process which may not be conceptually related to the concept being introduced, as might occur with the use of manipulatives. Learning does not take place until the learner can associate and interpret what is to be learned and the process must allow time for concept development to occur. Manipulatives can confuse this process since they assume broad generalizations of newly introduced concepts. Manipulatives, used in a "hands on" and not developmental fashion creates the need for learners to emulate behaviors without an understanding of the underlying concepts.

The theory of developmentalism yields new and unique ways of looking at measurements, their interpretation, their analysis, and their use. The next three chapters describe some of these unique approaches and interpretation schemes.

9

Qualitative Knowledge Structures
An Application of the Unified Field Theory of Developmentalism to the Theory of Knowledge and Hierarchy Validation

This chapter discusses the theory, method, and results of the application of developmentalism to the validation of behavioral grammars. The differential metric of psychological space is combined with the energy-entropy relations of The Unified Field Theory to develop the methodology. An overview of developmentalism and the Unified Field Theory, with specific focus on the interaction of energy and entropy principles, demonstrating that a learning system selforganizes into local grammars from specific lexicons are presented. A discussion of topological spaces and the methodological foundations of the formulae for extracting grammars from existing data sets and outlines the steps for the extraction of grammars are also discussed. Segment four contains the implications of these findings to the development of individual psychological spaces.

These results invalidate classical hierarchy (network-grammar-learning) theory and methodologies. Previous educational hierarchal (learning) theories and validation paradigms were based upon sophomoric (deterministic) heuristics, and insufficient theories of knowledge and knowledge structures. The developmental theories, reflecting neuro-psychological (qualitative) paradigms, represent sufficiently sophisticated theories of knowledge and result in valid heuristics.

Since the time of Eve humans have attempted to impose an order on the universe. Since the Age of Enlightenment the physical and phenomen-ological models of the universe have been considered distinct. The physical, presumed Cartesian, and phenomenological universes led to different philosophies of the universe and humanism (cf. Broudy, 1977 for a discussion of the Platonic, Aristilean, and Socratic positions). Early psychophysicists knew that perceptions of the physical world were determined by the state of the phenomenological world (Helmholtz, 1996, 1896, 1866; Wündt, 1890, 1874). It is only recently that neurophysicists and neuropsychologists have identified a nonCartesian world of the senses (symbols) and a phenomenalogical world of perceptions of sensory data.[1] Sensory data are modified, not only by the external world, but also phenomenalogical processor action.

Toward developing a "scientific" basis for the study of human behavior, theorists have posited topological models underlying perceptual and phenomenalogical thinking since the beginning of formal psychological theory (Freud, 1922; James, 1890; Köhler, 1920; Lewin, 1935). Psychometrists applied elementary topological theory to data reduction methodologies.[2] The result has been the application of qualitative methodologies such as multidimensional scaling, factor analysis, structural equation modeling, quantal analysis, etc.. Due to mathematical and computational constraints the formulation of these methodologies upon a Riemannian or flat manifold and in certain cases the more restrictive Euclidean metric is unrealistic (Attneave, 1950; Berthet, Feytmans, Stevens, & Genette, 1976; Carlton & Shepard, 1990a, 1990b; Hashway, 1976a, 1976b; Mahalanobis, 1936).

Recent physiological evidence and psychological theory indicates that human sensory, perceptual, and inferential spaces are not only multidimensional, but are also nonRiemannian (Cramer & Shepard, 1990a, 1990b; Hashway, 1988/89; Hashway & Hashway, 1990; Kosslyn, Thompson, Klm, & Alpat, 1995; Shepard & Cooper, 1982; Wilson & McNaughton 1994). Enhancements in computing and mathematical power have allowed psychophysicists to explore human behavior on a differential manifold. We now have both the computing and mathematical power to escape from the limitations of the Riemannian space and least squares algorithms. We have the capability to build qualitative and deterministic models of behavioral systems which are theoretically realistic and in concordance with evidence from other fields; and, move back toward an eclectic merger of physical and psychological worlds resulting in a grand unified theory.

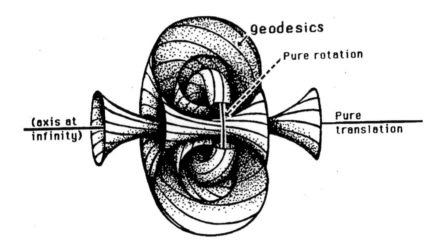

Figure 9.1: **Geodesic Hyperspace Of The Perception Of Solid Objects From Cramer & Shepard (1990a).**

here results invalidate classical hierarchy (network-grammar-learning) theory and methodologies. Previous educational hierarchal (learning) theories and validation paradigms were based upon sophomoric (deterministic) heuristics,[3] and insufficient theories of knowledge and knowledge structures.[4]

The purpose of this section is to synthesize a theory of knowledge structures (beliefs) from diverse research and theory bases.[5] The developmental theories, reflecting neuropsychological (qualitative) paradigms, represent sufficiently sophisticated theories of knowledge and result in valid heuristics. This chapter discusses the theory, method, and results of the application of developmentalism to the validation of behavioral grammars. The differential metric of psychological space is combined with the energy-entropy relations of The Unified Field Theory to develop the methodology with specific focus on the interaction of energy and entropy principles, demonstrating that a developmental system selforganizes into local grammars from specific lexicons. The third segment describes the methodological foundations of the formulae for extracting grammars from existing data sets and outlines the steps for the extraction of grammars. Segment four contains a description of the implications of these findings to the development of individual psychological spaces.

DEVELOPMENTALISM

Developmentalism posits that humans are dynamic organisms interacting within a psychological environment, influenced by and influencing a local environment where internal reality structures are changed as a result of that influence and collective local realities are also changed as a result of the interaction. A person is represented by a vector of state, X, in a local psychological space. The state vector represents the position and extent of belief in a psychological space. Individuals are dynamic whose positions can not be determined with certainty. Any change of state requires either expenditure (work) or absorption (exhilaration) of energy. A person is conceptualized as interacting with others. Influence is characterized by a work function which represented the influence of all people at all states. The concept matrix of the psychological space defines the geometry of the space and motion is constrained by the geodesics of that space. Individuals are identified with a particular geodesic only in probability. Not only can a person' position not be determined with certainty; s/he can be moving along different geodesics at the same time.

The 'spirit' or 'free will' is a manifestation of actions predicated upon unique individual experiences (James, 1890; Köhler, 1920; Lewin, 1935). The 'spirit' or 'free will' is observed when the result of the inferences derived from the projection of the characteristics of a situation on an individual' conceptual hyperspace varies from the mean projection taken over the members of that individual' social group.

People are characterized by common (shared) and unique experiences. This is manifest in the study of the behavior of individuals in a group by common (modal) tendencies and variations from those central tendencies. In the past, individual variation has been quantified by the 'total sum of squared deviations from the mean.' This conceptualization assumes that the space is unidimensional with a rectilinear metric that is uniform over the entire range of values of that attribute. The index was not based upon a theory of behavior.

The concept of *Entropy* ($\mathcal{H}$) is a direct measure of disorder. Entropy is the tendency of a population to move toward total disorder. The lower the entropy the greater the disorder and the larger the entropy the less the disorder. If **X** is a state vector in some psychological hyperspace and p(**X**) is the probability density function in that hyperspace, then

$$\mathcal{H} = - N \int \cdots \int p(X) \ln \{ p(X) \} \, dV,$$

where dV is an element of volume in that space. Theoretically, equilibrium is reached when $\mathcal{H}$ is minimized. The probability density function is parameterized in terms of some set of unknown parameters,

$$\{ \alpha_1, \cdots, \alpha_k \},$$

defining ∇^α as the gradient operator in the k-dimensional space of parameters, the entropy is minimized when $\nabla^\alpha \mathcal{H} = 0$ or

$$\nabla^\alpha \int \cdots \int p(X) \ln \{ p(X) \} \, dV = 0 .$$

The astute reader will immediately recognize this as the maximal likelihood solution to the paramaterization problem. What statisticians have thought to be a purely mathematical problem in behavioral statistics turns out to be a characteristic of human behavior. This formulation of the field equations allows for the determination of the structural parameters (network) of the common conceptual hyperspace or, 'local reality.' The probability function, p(**X**), or more specifically the associated parameters define the relational and metric properties of the conceptual hyperspace (conceptual and social structure)

A social ordering or equilibrium is reached at the point that the entropy resulting from the 'conflict' between 'free will' and the imposed ordering is minimized. For any program, the group will move toward the point where $\nabla^\alpha \mathcal{H} = 0$ and the resulting geometry reflects the will of the individual. The final parameter space is the social or conceptual ordering acceptable to that group of learners. The concordance between the geometry of the equilibrium hyperspace and that intended by the developers measures the extent to which the developers have achieved their objectives.

Dynamics in psychological space

It takes work for a learner to move from one place to another. Individuals remain stagnant and not expend energy. The influence of other individuals as well as any social program causes individuals to feel more or less uncomfortable—expend energy to maintain position. That is called the *Law Of Least Action;* a person moves along the path which minimizes the energy expended. The influence of a program and other individuals can be thought of as a potential energy function, ϕ , where the change in ϕ between two points represents the amount of work required to move between the two points. If $\mathscr{L}$ is a path in a psychological hyperspace and ∇ Is the gradient operator over that hyperspace, the work required to move along $\mathscr{L}$ is $\mathscr{E}_{\mathscr{L}} = -\oint_{\mathscr{L}} \nabla \phi \, \delta s$, where δs is an element of arc length along $\mathscr{L}$

The law of least action implies that between any two points in hyperspace there exists a unique parametric form (line) where $\nabla \mathscr{E}_{\mathscr{L}} = 0$ everywhere on $\mathscr{L}$. That means that there exists a unique path, $\mathscr{L}$, the geodesic between two points that minimizes the work required to transcend that path. The set of geodesics between all paths define the geometry of the psychological hyperspace.

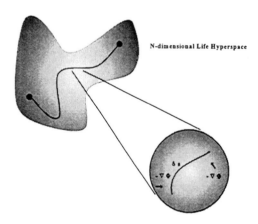

Figure 9.2: **Motion In Psychological Space**

THE UNIFIED FIELD THEORY

Human dynamics follows two relations. First, in the hyperspace of parameters, the entropy is minimized. Secondly, between any two points in psychological hyperspace, there exists at least one line where the divergence of the energy function is zero. Symbolically, these two dynamic relations are;

$$\nabla^{\alpha}\, \mathcal{H} = 0 \quad \text{and} \quad \nabla\, \mathcal{E}_{\mathcal{L}} = 0$$

or, in expanded notation:

$$\forall_{X,\,Y\,\in\,\mathcal{K}}\; \exists_{\mathcal{L}\,\in\,\mathcal{K}^n}\; \nabla\, \mathcal{E} = -\nabla \oint_{\mathcal{L}} \nabla\, \phi\, \delta\, s$$

$$and,\ in\ \alpha^{\,n}$$

$$\exists!_{\,\alpha_1\,\cdots\,\alpha_n}\; \nabla^{\alpha}\, \mathcal{H} = -\nabla^{\alpha} \int \cdots \int p(x)\, Ln\, \{\, p(X)\, \}\, d\,V = 0$$

In any developmental situation the second equation provides a solution in terms of the structural parameters of the equilibrium space which resulted from entropy minimization. The first equation provides a means for determining the geometry of the resulting space as well as the influence of a program and other learners upon all learners who occupy all states in the hyperspace.

The dynamic nature of The Unified Field Theory equations imply that as order is imposed upon a system the entropy of that system is increased. The increased entropy is derived from the energy required by people for stabilization of their positions. Systems which have a very loose ordering have less entropy resulting in more movement (more kinetic energy). A concrete example is a comparison of the amount of work required on the part of the leader in a highly disciplined and structured learning situation versus a democratic situation where, within constraints, the learner can define their unique path towards goals if not the goals themselves.

This system is a form of 'ordered chaos.' Each person is moving along their unique geodesic in psychological space experiencing the reward and frustrations of 'selfdirection'. On the whole it appears chaotic because each person or subgroup are engaged in different activities, on different development paths (curves, geodesics) at the same time. The fundamental principle is that a social program should not 'fight mother nature.' *Individuals evolve individually. Any attempt to circumvent individuality results in an expenditure of a large amount of energy with the same or lessor results as a developmental system which honors 'freedom with structure.'* Structure implies a well organized program which allows the individual to exercise the freedom to, and responsibility for, selecting their own paths toward societal goals.

The perception of a reality is a local phenomenon caused through a dynamic equilibrium between energy and entropy minimization. Local organizations, Babbles, form and evaporate. Local realities are modified through exercise of the 'spirit' or 'free will' as well as interactions with other local realities. The desire and perceived need to change is imparted to a person' spirit or free will. Local realities are isolated singularities in a particular subspace of the psychological hyperspace. People may form groups along certain conceptual dimensions; but, that group may dissolve in other subspace. *Humans may simultaneously be a group (in one subspace) and adversaries (in another subspace) at the same time!*

GEODESICS & TOPOLOGICAL MODELING

All modeling procedures as well as measurement paradigms assume a relationship between a set of dependent variables $\{ y_i \mid i = 1 \cdots M_Y \}$ and independent variables $\{ x_i \mid i = 1 \cdots M_X \}$. Each of these sets define a hyperspace with a geometry (Guggenheimer, 1997; Levi-Civita, 1977; McCullagh, 1987; Smith, 1963; Synge & Schild, 1949). The geometry of a hyperspace is depictable in terms of the distance formula, $ds^2 = \sum_{\mu, \nu = 1} g_{\mu, \nu} dx_\mu dx_\nu$, where the coefficients, $g_{\mu, \nu}$, are components of an $M_X \times M_X$ (or, $M_Y \times M_Y$) matrix called the *metric tensor* G^X (or, G^Y). If the relations between X and Y are defined by $\begin{cases} f : X \Rightarrow Y \\ f^{-1} : Y \Rightarrow x \end{cases}$, where $y_I = f_I(x_1, \cdots, x_M)$ and $x_I = f_I^{-1}(y_1, \cdots, y_M)$, the Jacobean of each transformation is defined as the matrix of derivatives of the metric tensor, $\begin{cases} J_Y = \left\{ \dfrac{\partial f_i}{\partial x_j} \right\} \\ \\ J_X = \left\{ \dfrac{\partial f_i^{-1}}{\partial y_j} \right\} \end{cases}$,

and in the case where $M_X = M_Y$
$$\begin{cases} G^X = J_Y^T \, G^Y \, J_Y \\ G^Y = J_X^T \, G^X \, J_X \end{cases}.$$

The metric tensor can be calculated easily by substituting

$$y_\mu = \left. \frac{1}{\left. \dfrac{\partial y_\alpha}{\partial y_\mu} \right|_{y_\alpha = 0}} \left[\int^{y_\alpha} e^{\int_0^{y_\alpha} \sum_{i,j} \left[\Gamma_{i,j}^\alpha \frac{\partial y_i}{\partial y_\mu} \frac{\partial y_j}{\partial y_\mu} \right] dy_\alpha} \, dy_\alpha \right] \right|_{y_\alpha = y_\alpha(0)}$$

$$dx_i^2 = \sum_{\mu,v} \frac{\partial x_i}{\partial y_\mu} \frac{\partial x_i}{\partial y_v} \, dy_\mu \, dy_v \text{ into the formula for } ds^2 \text{ and combining}$$

like terms $g_{\mu,v}^Y = \displaystyle\sum_{i,j=1} g_{i,j}^X \frac{\partial x_i}{\partial y_\mu} \frac{\partial x_j}{\partial y_v}$.

A space is flat, or Riemannian, if all the g's are constant. A special flat space is the Euclidian space where
$$ds^2 = \sum dy_\mu^2 \left[where \; g_{\mu,v}^{X,Y} = \delta_\mu^v \right]. \text{ The flatness of a space is}$$
determined in terms of the equations of the geodesics and the radius of curvature. Each of these elements are determined by calculating the Christoffel symbols of the first,

$$\Gamma_{i,j,k} = \frac{1}{2} \left\{ \frac{\partial g_{i,k}}{\partial y_j} + \frac{\partial g_{k,j}}{\partial y_i} + \frac{\partial g_{i,j}}{\partial y_k} \right\}, \text{ and second,}$$

$$\Gamma_{i,j}^\alpha = \sum_k g^{\alpha,k} \, \Gamma_{i,j,k}, \text{kinds where } G^{-1} = \left\{ g^{i,j} \right\}.[6]$$

The radius of curvature is expressed

$$\text{as } R = \frac{1}{\sqrt{\sum\limits_{i,j,k,l} g^{i,j} g^{k,l} R_{i,j,k,l}}}$$

where the Ricci tensors, $R_{I,j,k,l}$, are expressible in terms of derivatives of the Christoffel symbols of the first kind

$$R_{i,j,k,l} = \left[\frac{\partial \Gamma_{i,k}}{\partial y_j} - \frac{\partial \Gamma_{k,j}}{\partial y_i} \right] + \sum_\alpha \left[\Gamma^\alpha_{j,k} \Gamma_{i,l,\alpha} - \Gamma^\alpha_{j,l} \Gamma_{i,k,\alpha} \right].$$

The geodesics are solutions of the Laplacian equation,

$$\frac{\partial^2 y_\alpha}{\partial y_\mu^2} + \sum_{i,j} \left[\Gamma^\alpha_{i,j} \frac{\partial y_i}{\partial y_\mu} \frac{\partial y_j}{\partial y_\mu} \right] = 0 \text{ , or}$$

Expressing that the difference between observed and hypothesized values of a variable is $d s^2 = \sum\limits_{obs} \sum\limits_\mu [y_\mu^{obs} - \hat{y}_\mu]^2$ assumes that the Y hyperspace is Euclidean; a hypothesis {assumption} which we will see is not valid. The Euclidean distance formula is a valid measure of distance if and only if we assume that $y_1 = x_1$ and $g^{X,Y}_{\mu,v} = \delta^v_\mu = \begin{cases} 1 \text{ } if \text{ } \mu = v \\ 0 \text{ } if \text{ } \mu \neq v \end{cases}$ a trivial solution. If the solution of the equations $y_\mu = f_\mu (x_1 , \cdots , x_M)$ is nontrivial and defined in terms of undetermined

parameters, $\left\{ \alpha^v_\mu \mid \mu = 1 , \cdots , M_Y \text{ and } v = 1 , \cdots , M_X \right\}$, the sum

f squared distances between observed and predicted values is

$$\varphi = \sum\limits_{obs} \sum\limits_{\mu,v} [y_\mu^{obs} - \hat{y}_\mu] [y_v^{obs} - \hat{y}_v] . \text{ Parameters are estimated}$$

by either the exact solution of $\dfrac{\partial \varphi}{\partial \alpha^v_\mu} = 0$, if it exists, or, iteratively estimated from the first and second derivatives, $\dfrac{\partial \varphi}{\partial \alpha_{\mu}^{v}}$ and $\dfrac{\partial^2 \varphi}{\partial \alpha_{\mu}^{v} \partial \alpha_{\mu}^{v}}$

More details will be described in the next chapter.

DEVELOPMENTAL LEXICAL STRUCTURE

Social imperatives as well as recent interest in developmentalism require a solution to the problems previously outlined concerning network formation.[7] Developmentalism, when applied to social or content learning, assumes that development is a latent (not directly observed) construct which only manifests itself in terms of observable outcomes. The validity of a learning theory is predicated upon correspondence with observation. The knowledge base is a language with a corpus of terms and a grammar. The corpus is a collection of linguistic objects which represent desired outcomes. The needs of the theorist determine the specificity of the elements. At certain points the theorist may have an interest in entire gestalts, or very specific objectives (entrance, enabling, or terminal). A corpus is a finite set of terms, called nodes, corresponding to concepts which theorists agree are irreducible for some particular purpose. There is an isomorphism between any corpus of N nodes and the set of N positive integers. Using the theory of knowledge as a model, *psychological space* is an N-dimensional subspace of the psychological space which is composed of vectors,

$$\psi^{i} = \{x_j^i \mid j = 1, \dots, N\},$$

representing the *developmental state* of any individual, i, relative to the corpicular elements, x_j^i.[8] Any particular state may be mastery, proficiency, or a nonevaluative assessment of the individual. The learning space is the family of all possible, 2^N, state vectors.[9]

Particular, "allowed," orderings, called prerequisite relations, discriminate knowledge bases pertaining to the same set of nodes. The i-th. node is *subordinate* to the j-th. node if attainment of x_i is assumed prior to attaining x_j. If x_i is subordinate to x_j, and their are no intermediary nodes, the subordinate relationship is represented as a directed digraph, $x_i \rightarrow x_j$, x_i is *subordinate* to x_j, and x_j is *superordinate* to x_i. If $x_1 \rightarrow x_2$, of all possible diadic pairs, (x_1, x_2), the only allowable states are $(1,0)$ and $(1,1)$, representable in terms of a matrix $\begin{bmatrix} 1 & 0 \\ 1 & 1 \end{bmatrix}$. This is where developmental

learning grammars depart from their counterparts in cognitive science which assume that $x_i \rightarrow x_j$ results in , implies that if
$$\{x_1 \rightarrow x_2 \rightarrow x_3 \mid x_1 \rightarrow x_4,\} \text{ and } x_1 = 1,$$
$x_2 = x_3 = x_4 = 1$. Developmentalism provides for alternative paths to the same goal by utilizing the third postulate called the *Principle of Compensating Strengths* (Hashway, 1997).

The Principle of Compensating Strengths

If two knowledge bases are prerequisite to a third, proficiency in one may compensate for a lack of proficiency in the other so that the learner can gain proficiency in the third.

From a developmental perspective the digraph 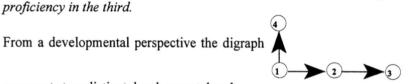 represents two distinct developmental paths,
$$x_1 \rightarrow x_2 \rightarrow x_3, \text{ and } x_1 \rightarrow x_4..$$

The first contains four allowed $\{[0000], [1000], [1100], \text{ and } [1110]\}$, and not allowed $\{[1010], [0100], [0110], [0101], \text{ and } [0010]\}$ developmental states. The second path implies three allowed developmental stages $\{[0000], [1000], \text{ and } [1001]\}$ and one unanticipated stage, $[0001]$. both paths imply other unanticipated stages $\{[0101], [0111], \text{ and } [0011]\}$. The *developmental learning space* corresponding to the previous digraph is

characterized by either $\mathfrak{C}_1 = \begin{bmatrix} 1 & 0 & 0 & 0 \\ 1 & 1 & 0 & 0 \\ 1 & 1 & 1 & 0 \\ 1 & 0 & 0 & 1 \end{bmatrix}$ or $\mathfrak{C}_2 = \begin{bmatrix} 1 & 0 & 0 & 0 \\ \frac{1}{2} & \frac{1}{2} & 0 & 0 \\ \frac{1}{3} & \frac{1}{3} & \frac{1}{3} & 0 \\ \frac{1}{2} & 0 & 0 & \frac{1}{2} \end{bmatrix}$. Either

matrix can be interpreted as a collection of all row vectors corresponding to particular developmental stages. The product of $\mathfrak{C}_1$ and any state vector results in a vector whose elements correspond to the number of skills acquired along each developmental chain including the terminal skill. The product of $\mathfrak{C}_2$ and any state vector results in a vector whose components correspond to the proportion of elements acquired along each developmental path (Cate, Huton, & Nesselroade, 1986; Fredricksen, 1974; McCall, Applebaum, & Hogerty, 1973; Meredith, & Tisak, 1988; Rao, 1958; Surra, 1988; Tucker, 1966; Wood, 1992). In either case, the product of either $\mathfrak{C}_1$ or $\mathfrak{C}_2$ and any state vector is a vector representing progress along each developmental path. This is where developmental grammarians depart from using the grammars of cognitive or information scientists. The developmental grammarian is concerned with progress toward final developmental stages not only the final state of the entire system. A developmental grammar is represented by a matrix whose rows are the vectors corresponding to all developmental paths.

The Error of Binary Trees

Previous methodologies have focused upon discovering binary relations between two variables ($x_i \rightarrow x_j$), and using those binary relations to build decision trees (Cybenko, 1989; Dahl, 1987; Jacobs, 1988; Lippmann, 1987). The prior example serves as a counter example to the theorem that developmental grammars can be identified from binary trees. It appears that *a developmental grammar is determined by the longest chains and subsidiary developmental stages determined by successive elimination.* Consider the long chains $\psi_1 = [1110]$ and $\psi_2 = [1001]$ corresponding to:
$$\{ x_1 \rightarrow x_2 \rightarrow x_3 \mid x_1 \rightarrow x_4 \}.$$
Decompositions of ψ_1 and ψ_2 into developmental stages results in sets of allowed developmental state vectors $\{[1110], [1100], [1000], [0000]\}$, and $\{[1001], [1000], [0000]\}$ respectively. If ψ_1 is expected with probability Ψ_1, and each associated developmental state, ψ_j^i, with probability $p(\psi_j^i)$, then the probability of occurrence of the ψ-th state is

$$p(\psi) = \sum_{j=1} \Psi_j \, p_j(\psi) \, u(\psi \mid \psi_j).$$ Certain sequences may de-

compose to the same state along different developmental paths and proceed identically from that point. Consider the sequences $\begin{cases} \psi_1 : x_1 \to x_2 \to x_3, \\ \qquad and \\ \psi_2 : x_1 \to x_2 \to x_4 \end{cases}$,

developmentally decomposing into $\{[1110], [1100], [1000], [0000]\}$, and $\{[1101], [1100], [1000], [0000]\}$; $\psi_1 \ne \psi_2$; but, $\{\psi_1{}^i\} \cap \{\psi_2{}^i\} = \{[1100], [1000], [0000]\}$. Consequently, $[1100]$, $[1000]$, and $[0000]$ are expected to occur with frequencies

$$p([1100]) = \Psi_{[1110]}\, p_{[1110]}([1100]) + \Psi_{[1101]}\, p_{[1101]}([1100]),$$
$$p([1000]) = \Psi_{[1110]}\, p_{[1110]}([1000]) + \Psi_{[1101]}\, p_{[1101]}([1000]),$$
$$and$$
$$p([0000]) = \Psi_{[1110]}\, p_{[1110]}([0000]) + \Psi_{[1101]}\, p_{[1101]}([0000]),$$

respectively and each probability is greater than the probability of a developmental stage evolving from a single developmental path. i.e.

$$\forall_{i \ne j} \ if \ \psi \in \{\psi^i\} \cap \{\psi^j\}, then \ p(\psi) > \Psi_i\, p_i(\psi),$$
$$and \ p(\psi) > \Psi_j\, p_j(\psi).$$

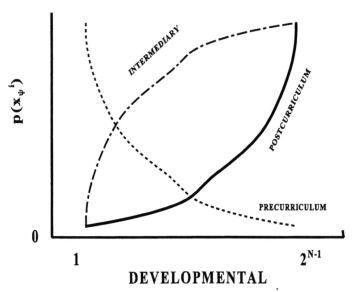

Figure 9.3: Developmental Decompositions

Given N corpicular elements, any vector, ψ, is an N digit binary number, $\{\psi_i\}$. Hence, any vector, ψ, is representable as the decimal equivalent of the binary sequence, $x_\psi = 1 + \sum_{i=1}^{N} \psi_i 2^{i-1}$ (Claverie, Sauvejet, &

Bovjueleret, 1990; Dumas, & Nino, 1982). Furthermore, if x_ψ is a known decimal representation of some binary sequence, ψ then:

$$\psi_x^N = x_\psi - 2^{N-1} [\, (x_\psi - 1) 2^{1-N} \,] \text{, and}$$

$$\underset{i<N}{\forall} \; let \; x_\psi^i = x_\psi^{i+1} - \sum_{j=1}^{N} \psi_j^x 2^{j-1} \text{, and}$$

$$\psi_i^x = x_\psi^{i-1} - 2^{i-1} [\, (x_\psi^i - 1) 2^{1-i} \,] .^{10}$$

Consequently, there is an isomorphism between the set of all decompositions of the j-th. developmental chain and the set of integers

$$\{\, x_{i,j}^\psi = 1 + \sum_{k=1^N} \psi_k^{i,j} 2^{k-1} \,|\, \psi^{i,j} \in \{ \psi^i \} \,\}. \text{ This procedure is a binary}$$

analogy to a general N-decimal sequence from a corpicular alphabet of size Q.[11]

Any developmental path, ψ, is representative of a set of state vectors $\{\psi^i\}$ generated by developmental decomposition of ψ, and $\psi \in \{\psi^i\}$. Any decomposition is isomorphic to the set of integers

$$X_\psi = \{\, x_\psi \,|\, x_\psi^i = 1 + \sum_{j=1}^{N} \psi_j^i 2^{j-1} \,\}, \text{ and it is sufficient to consider}$$

properties of X_ψ, since $p(x^j)=p(x_\psi^i)$ where $\psi^i \in \{\psi\}$ and $x^i \in X_\psi$. Since the ψ^i can be ordered in terms of developmental stages, X_ψ can also be so ordered. Consider $\psi=[1101]$, an ordered set of developmental stages may be $\{[0000], [1000], [1100], [1101]\}$ isomorphic to $\{1, 2, 4, 12\}$. In general, without prior knowledge of the corpicular vocabulary, it is not necessarily true that if ψ^i is a developmental decomposition of ψ^j then $x_\psi^i < x_\psi^j$, and if ψ^i is a developmental decomposition of ψ^j, then $x_\psi^i < x_\psi^j$, however, if $\{\psi^i\}$ can be ordered, X_ψ can also be ordered in such a way that the cardinal ordering of X_ψ corresponds to the $\{\psi^i\}$ in terms of increasing developmental complexity and for the purposes of this paper $\{\psi^i\}$ and X_ψ will be considered so ordered where $\psi^1 = [0, \dots, 0]$ and $x_\psi^1 = 1$.

The probability of observing a developmental stage, ψ^i, is a function of the particular point that an observation is made in the developmental learning process. After curriculum delivery a greater frequency of large x_ψ s are expected than at intermediary or precurricula stages. Initially, a greater proportion of 1s and low x_ψ s are expected than at intermediary or post developmental learning system stages. At intermediary delivery levels it is expected that a greater frequency of intermediary x_ψ s will be observed than at the extreme points of the developmental learning process. A similar argument can be developed for populations with different experience levels. Regardless of the delivery stage or population, the distribution of x_ψ^i is expressible in terms of an exponential distribution,

$$p(x_\psi^i) = \sum_\psi \Psi_\psi e^{\beta_\psi x_\psi^i} u(x_\psi^i | X_\psi).^{12}$$

Assessment and learning relies on perceptions of reality. Assessment results as well as the rate at which learning progresses is a function of the degrees of concordance between different knowledge spaces. The most fundamental as well as important curriculum development, assessment, evaluation or measurement act is the precise definition of the *form and structure* of the desired knowledge space or belief system.

STRUCTURAL ANALYSIS

For k nodes, the 2^k possible sequences can become large for moderate k. Prior to estimating sequence parameters it is necessary to eliminate sequences which may be due to chance. The problem of parameter estimation involves estimation of marginal node as well a sequence probabilities. This discussion will present a method for identifying sequences whose appearance may be chance expectations, a two stage process of obtaining model parameter estimates corresponding to marginal node frequencies which, subsequently, are starting parameters for a maximal likelihood estimation of model parameters corresponding to sequence frequencies.

Certain sequences may appear due to chance and should be eliminated before analysis. Fortunately, classical test theory provides some direction. Given the chance probability of a node, φ, the probability of observing a sequence, ψ, due to chance is $\mu_{\psi,1} = \varphi^{\tau_\psi}(1-\varphi)^{\tau_\psi}$ with a 95 percent confidence interval of $\pm 1.96\sqrt{\dfrac{\mu_{\psi,1}(1-\mu_{\psi,1})}{N}}\,x$ where τ_ψ is the total score corresponding to the sequence. Furthermore, for any sequence, ψ, corresponding to a total score, τ_ψ, the probability of obtaining τ_ψ due to chance is $\mu_{\psi,2} = \begin{pmatrix} k \\ \tau_\psi \end{pmatrix} \varphi^{\tau_\psi}\,\varphi^{k-\tau_\psi}$ with a standard error of $\sigma_{\psi,2} = \sqrt{\dfrac{\mu_{\psi,2}(1-\mu_{\psi,2})}{N}}$. It is suggested that sequences with observed proportions within the 95 percent confidence intervals of $\mu_{\psi,1}$, or $\mu_{\psi,2}$ not be included in subsequent analysis.

PARAMETER ESTIMATION

Given an hypothesized set of developmental sequences $\{\psi\}$ the difficulty of item ρ is the sum over all sequences for which ρ is a member of the probability of obtaining that sequence,

$$\acute{\varepsilon}_\rho = \sum_\psi \Psi_\psi\, e^{\beta_\psi x}\, u\,(1 + 2^{\rho-1} \mid X^\psi).$$ This results in a non-traditional view of nodal (item) difficulty as a composite of difficulty and complexity. A node (item) may be difficult (easy) if it requires a greater (lesser) amount of ability for a correct response, or there are fewer (a greater) number of developmental paths (ways of mastering) the nodal (item) skill.

From a random start, the least squares solution would lead to a set of initial estimates for a maximal likelihood solution. The iterative process would continue until either $\kappa = \sum_\rho (\varepsilon_\rho - \acute{\varepsilon}_\rho)^2$, or the parameter estimates converge. The iteration equations are:

$$\Psi_\psi^{k+1} = \Psi_\psi^k + \frac{\sum_\rho (\varepsilon - \acute{\varepsilon}) e^{\beta_\psi x_\rho} u(x_\rho | X_\psi)}{\sum_\rho e^{2\beta_\psi x_\rho} u(x_\rho | X_\psi)}, \text{ and}$$

$$\beta_\psi^{k+1} = \beta_\psi^k - \frac{\sum_\rho (\varepsilon_\rho - \acute{\varepsilon}_\rho) \Psi_\psi x_\psi e^{\beta_\psi x^\rho} u(x_\rho | X^\psi)}{\sum_\rho \Psi_\psi x_\rho^2 e^{\beta_\psi x_\rho} [\varepsilon - \acute{\varepsilon} - \Psi_\psi e^{\beta_\psi x_\rho}] u(x_\rho | X_\psi)} 1^{13}$$

The least squares solution could be the starting values for a maximal likelihood solution where the loglikelihood function is

$$N \sum_\rho [\varepsilon_\rho Ln(\varepsilon_\rho) - \varepsilon_\rho) - Ln(\acute{\varepsilon}_\rho)] \text{ and the parameter estimation}$$

equations are $\Psi_\psi^{k+1} = \Psi_\psi^k + \dfrac{\sum_\rho \dfrac{e^{\beta_\psi x_\rho} u(x_\rho | X_\psi)}{\acute{\varepsilon}_\rho}}{\sum_\rho \dfrac{e^{2\beta_\psi x_\rho} u(x_\rho | X_\psi)}{\acute{\varepsilon}_\rho^2}}$, and

$$\beta_\psi^{k+1} = \beta_\psi^k - \frac{\sum_\rho \dfrac{\Psi_\psi x_\rho e^{\beta_\psi x_\rho}}{\acute{\varepsilon}} u(x_\rho | X_\psi)}{\sum_\rho \dfrac{\Psi_\psi x_\rho^2 e^{\beta_\psi x_\rho}}{\acute{\varepsilon}_\rho^2} [\acute{\varepsilon} - \Psi_\psi e^{\beta_\psi x_\rho}] u(x_\rho | X_\psi)}.$$

As discussed above, the number of times x is observed, n(x), is a sum over all developmental histories decomposing to x of products of mixture parameters, Ψ_ψ, and an exponential function of x and a population parameter, β_ψ. Let X_ψ represent the set of all decimal equivalents of $\{\psi^i\}$, the number of times x is expected in a population of size N is

$\hat{\eta}_x = N \sum_\psi \Psi_\psi e^{\beta_\psi x} u_\psi(x | X_\psi).^{14}$ This type of estimation problem require maximum likelihood solutions. The loglikelihood function,

$$\mathcal{L} = [\sum_x o_x Ln(o_x) - Ln(N)] - \sum Ln[\sum_\psi \Psi_\psi e^{\beta_\psi x} u_\psi(x | X_\psi)$$

is[15] extrimized when $\dfrac{\partial \mathcal{L}}{\partial \Psi_\psi} = 0$ and $\dfrac{\partial \mathcal{L}}{\partial \beta_\psi} = 0$. Successive values of Ψ_ψ, and β_ψ are calculated until either they, or $\mathcal{L}$, converge. Those successive values are $\Psi_\psi^{k+1} = \Psi_\psi^k + \dfrac{\sum\limits_x e^{\beta_\psi x} \mathscr{F}_x^{-1} u_\psi(x|X_\psi)}{\sum\limits_x e^{2\beta_\psi x} \mathscr{F}_x^{-1} u_\psi(x|X_\psi)}$, and

$\beta_\psi^{k+1} = \beta_\psi^k + \dfrac{\sum\limits_x x e^{\beta_\psi x} \mathscr{F}_x^{-1} u_\psi(x|X_\psi)}{\sum\limits_x \dfrac{x^2 \mathscr{F}_x^{-2} e^{\beta_\psi x} u_\psi(x|X_\psi)}{\Psi_\psi e^{\beta_\psi x} - \mathscr{F}_x}}$, where

$$\mathscr{F}_x = \frac{\hat{\eta}(x)}{N} = \sum_\psi \Psi_\psi e^{\beta_\psi x} u_\psi(x|X_\psi).$$

NonEuclidean Solution

Given the starting values obtained from the equations above, the non-Euclidean solution to the generalized three parameter model is obtained. The general three parameter latent trait model specifies probability relations between two

variables $\begin{cases} P(y = 1|x) = c + \dfrac{1-c}{1+e^{\alpha(x-\beta)}} \\ P(y = 0|x) = \dfrac{1-c}{1+e^{-\alpha(x-\beta)}} \end{cases}$ the ratio of these two

probabilities is $z = \dfrac{c + e^{\alpha(x-\beta)}}{1-c}$. The metric tensor is

$g_{11} = \dfrac{(1-c)^2}{\alpha^2[(1-c)z-c]^2}$ and the corresponding differential metric is

$$ds^2 = \sum \frac{(1-c)^2}{\alpha^2[(1-c)z-c]^2} (z-\hat{z})^2.$$

The values of the three parameters α, β, and c are determined iteratively using the appropriate differentials of the distance metric.

$$\nabla_\alpha d s^2 = - \frac{2(1-c)^2}{\alpha^3} \sum \frac{(z - \hat{z})(z - \hat{z} + \alpha^2)}{[(1-c)z - c]^2}$$

$$\nabla_\beta d s^2 = - 2 \sum \frac{(z - \hat{z})(1 - c)}{\alpha[(1-c)z - c]}$$

$$\nabla_c d s^2 = - \frac{2}{\alpha^2} \sum \left\{ \frac{\{(1-c)[(1-c)z - c] - (1-c)^2(z+1)\}(z - \hat{z}) + 2[z(1-c) - c + 1]}{[(1-c)z - c]^3} \right.$$

Iterations are continued until either the differential metric is sufficiently near zero in absolute value, or the values of all three gradients are sufficiently close to zero.

Endnotes

1.   Anderson & Bower, 1973; Beer, 1966; Caramazza, 1996; Edelman & Mountcastle, 1978; Filmore, 1968; Gobel, 1990; Just & Carpenter, 1985; Kintsch, 1978; Kintsch, Kozminsky, Strely, McKoon & Keenan, 1975; Knight, 1996; Pellionisz & Llinas, 1980, 1979; Vanderberghe, Price, Wise, Josephs, & Frackowiak, 1996).

2.   Bollen, 1989; Goldberger, 1973; Harman, 1967; Kerlinger, 1986; Larzafeld & Henry, 1968; Lingoes, 1973; Mulaik, 1972; Pedhazur, 1982; Rummel, 1970; Shepard, 1966; Shepard, Romney & Nerlove, 1972.

3.   Airasian, 1971a, 1971b, 1971c, 1970, 1975; Baker & Hubert, 1977; Bart, 1981; Bart & Krus, 1975; Baker & Hubert, 1977; Bergen, 1980; Dayton & Macready, 1976; DiSessa, 1982; Embretson, 1984; Gagné, 1965, 1963a, 1963b; Gagné, Mayer, Garsten & Paradise, 1962; Gagné & Paradise, 1961; Gagné & Bassler, 1963; Hashway, 1976a, 1976b, 1979, 1982a, 1982b, 1983; Hill, 1987; Krus, 1975; Krus, Bart & Airsian, 1975; Mort & Furno, 1960; Preece, 1976; Resnick & Wang, 1969; Shavelson & Stanton, 1975; Trembath & White, 1979; Walbesser & Eisenberg, 1972a,

1972b; White, 1974, 1979a, 1979b, 1981; White & Gunstone, 1980; Whitely, 1980, 1981; Whitely & Barnes, 1979; Whitely & Schneider, 1981.

4. Capie & Jones, 1971; Dayton & Macready, 1976; Embretson, 1984; Walbesser & Eisenberg, 1972a, 1972b

5. Barron, 1989; Barron & Barron, 1989; Baum, Bennett, Frye & Soloway, 1990; Choi & Huberman, 1983; Claverie, Sauvaget & Bougueleret, 1990; Eigen & Winkler-Oswatitsch, 1990; Falmagne, 1989; Hackett, 1968, 1970; Hall & Robinson, 1945; Hill, 1984; Hutchinson, 1989; Pellionisz & Llinas, 1979, 1980; Reutzel & Hollingsworth, 1990; Saccone, Lanave, Pesole & Preparata, 1990; Staden, 1990.

6. The number of calculations is reduced by using the symmetry relations $\Gamma_{ijk} = \Gamma_{jIk}$ and $\Gamma_{Ij}^{\ \alpha} = \Gamma_{jI}^{\ \alpha}$.

7. Carlson, Khoo & Elliot, 1990; Glynn, Yeany & Britton, 1991; Silver & Marshall, 1990; Stensvold & Wilson, 1990; White & Glynn, 1990.

8. Carlson, Khoo & Elliot, 1990; Glynn, Yeany & Britton, 1991; Silver & Marshall, 1990; Stensvold & Wilson, 1990; White & Glynn, 1990.

9. Although the x_j^i are, most generally, continuous, the arguments which follow lose no generality by the assumption that they are binary.

10. Where [ ] represents the greatest integer function.

11. If ψ is an N-array it corresponds to a sequence of N elements from an alphabet of size Q where: $Q = \text{Max}_{\psi, i}\{\psi_i\}$ and $\forall_\psi \exists !_x x = 1 + \sum_{i=1}^{N} \psi_i Q^{i-1}$ and $\forall_x x \le 1 + (Q^N - 1)(Q-1) \exists !_\psi \psi_N = (x-1)\text{MOD } Q^{N-1}$ and $\forall_{k<N} \psi_k = (x - 1 - \sum_{i=k+1}^{N} \psi_i Q^{i-1})\text{MOD } Q^{k-1}$

12. Where $u(x_\psi^i | X_\psi)$ is the Heaviside unit step function on the set X_ψ.

13. Where $x_\rho = 1 + 2^{\rho-1}$.

14. Where $u_\psi(x | X_\psi)$ is the Heaviside unit step function on X_ψ.

15. Where o is the number of times x is observed in the sample.

10

Geometrix
Developmental Qualitative and Deterministic Modeling Methodology

In this chapter it is posited that recent psychometric and neurophysiological evidence point to the nonEuclidean nature of the psychological space which is the fundamental premise of developmentalism. The topological nature of the psychological space is applied to qualitative and deterministic data analysis. Application of differential geometry results in new formulae for estimating parameters for common procedures such as multiple regression and factor analysis thru polynomial and probabilistic models. It is shown that classical parameter estimation formulae evolve in limit from general topological models as the geometry becomes Euclidean. The methodology for examining the geometries of psychological space is presented. The application of that strategy to behavioral data yield a rich understanding of the nature and structure of psychological space.

Since the time of Job humans have attempted to impose an order on the universe. Since the Age of Enlightenment the physical and phenomenological models of the universe have been considered distinct. The physical, presumed cartesian, and phenomenological universes led to different philosophies of humanism, the universe, and educational delivery (cf. Broudy, 1977 for a discussion of the Platonic, Aristilean, and Socratic positions). Early psychophysicists knew that perceptions of the physical world were determined by the state of the phenomenological world (Helmholtz, 1996, 1896, 1866; Wündt, 1890, 1874). It is only recently that neurophysicists and neuropsychologists have identified a Cartesian world of the senses (symbols) and a phenomenalogical world of perceptions of sensory data (Anderson and Bower, 1973; Beer, 1966; Caramazza, 1996; Edelman and Mountcastle, 1978; Filmore, 1968; Gobel, 1990; Just & Carpenter, 1985; Kintsch, 1978; Kintsch, Kozminsky, Strely, McKoon and Keenan, 1975; Knight, 1996; Pellionisz and Llinas, 1980, 1979; Vandenberghe, Price, Wise, Josephs, & Frackowiak, 1996). Sensory data are modified by not only changes in the external world; but, they are modified by the action of phenomenalagical processors.

Toward developing a "scientific" basis for the study of human behavior, theorists have posited topological models underlying perceptual and phenomenalogical thinking since the beginning of formal psychological theory (Freud, 1922; James, 1890; Köhler, 1920; Lewin, 1935). Psychometrists applied elementary topological theory to data reduction methodologies (Bollen, 1989; Goldberger, 1973; Harman, 1967; Jöreskog, 1970; Kerlinger, 1986; Larzafeld & Henry, 1968; Lingoes, 1973; Mulaik, 1972; Pedhazur, 1982; Rummel, 1970; Shepard, 1966; Shepard, Romney & Nerlove, 1972). The result has been the application of qualitative methodologies such as multidimensional scaling, factor analysis, structural equation modeling, quantal analysis, etc.. Due to mathematical and computational constraints the formulation of these methodologies upon a Riemannian or flat manifold and in certain cases the more restrictive Euclidean metric is unrealistic (Attneave, 1950; Berthet, Feytmans, Stevens, & Genette, 1976; Carlton & Shepard, 1990a, 1990b; Hashway, 1976a, 1976b; Mahalanobis, 1936).

Recent physiological evidence and psychological theory indicates that human sensory, perceptual, and inferential spaces are not only multidimensional, but are also nonRiemannian manifolds (Hashway, 1988/89; Hashway & Hashway, 1990; Kosslyn, Thompson, Klm, & Alpat, 1995; Shepard & Cooper, 1982; Wilson & McNaughton 1994). Enhancements in computing and mathematical power have allowed psychophysicists and behavioral statisticians to explore human behavior on a differential manifold. We now have both the computing and mathematical power to escape from the limitations of the Riemannian space and least squares algorithms. We have the capability to build qualitative and deterministic models of behavioral systems which are theoretically realistic and in concordance with evidence from other fields and move back toward an eclectic merger of physical and psychological worlds and a grand unified theory.

The purpose of this chapter is to present the methods of topological modeling and applications to different situations. This paper is organized into four segments. The first will contain an overview of developmentalism; the theory of humanism upon which this work is based. Then the topological methodology will be described. The third and forth segments will present applications of the topological model to deterministic and qualitative scenarios.

Developmentalism posits that humans are dynamic organisms interacting within a psychological environment, influenced by and influencing a local environment where internal reality structures are changed as a result of that influence and collective local realities are also changed as a result of the interaction. A person is represented by a vector of state, X, in a local psychological space. The state vector represents the position and extent of belief in a psychological space. Individuals are dynamic whose positions can not be determined with certainty. Any change of state requires either expenditure (work) or absorption (exhilaration) of energy. A person is conceptualized as interacting with others and that influence could be characterized by a work function which represented the influence of all people at all states. The concept matrix of the psychological space defines the geometry of the space and motion is constrained by the geodesics of that space. Individuals are identified with a particular geodesic only in probability. Not only can a person' position not be determined with certainty; s/he can be moving along different geodesics at the same time.

The 'spirit' or 'free will' is a manifestation of actions predicated upon unique individual experiences (James, 1890; Köhler, 1920; Lewin, 1935). The 'spirit' or 'free will' is observed when the result of the inferences derived from the projection of the characteristics of a situation on an individual' conceptual hyperspace varies from the mean projection taken over the members of that individual' social group. People are characterized by common (shared) and unique experiences. This is manifest in the study of the behavior of individuals in a group by common (modal) tendencies and variations from those central tendencies. In the past, individual variation has been quantified by the 'total sum of squared deviations from the mean.' This conceptualization assumes that the space is unidimensional with a rectilinear metric which is uniform over the entire range of values of that attribute. The index was not based upon a theory of behavior.

TOPOLOGICAL MODELING OF DYNAMICS IN PSYCHOLOGICAL SPACE

All modeling procedures as well as measurement paradigms assume a relationship between a set of dependent variables $\{ y_i \mid i = 1 \cdots M_Y \}$ and independent variables $\{ x_i \mid i = 1 \cdots M_X \}$. Each of these sets define a hyperspace with a geometry. The geometry of a hyperspace is depictable in terms of the distance formula, $d s^2 = \sum_{\mu, \nu = 1} g_{\mu, \nu} d x_\mu d x_\nu$, where the coefficients, $g_{\mu, \nu}$, are components of an $M_X \times M_X$ (or, $M_Y \times M_Y$) matrix called the *metric tensor* G^X (or, G^Y). If the relations between X and Y are defined by

$$\begin{cases} f & : X \Rightarrow Y \\ f^{-1} & : Y \Rightarrow x \end{cases}, \text{ where } y_I = f_I(x_1, \cdots, x_M) \text{ and } x_I = f_I^{-1}(y_1, \cdots, y_M), \text{ the}$$

Jacobean of each transformation is defined as the matrix of derivatives of the

metric tensor, $\begin{cases} J_Y = \left\{ \dfrac{\partial f_i}{\partial x_j} \right\} \\ \\ J_X = \left\{ \dfrac{\partial f_i^{-1}}{\partial y_j} \right\} \end{cases}$, and in the case where $M_X = M_Y$

$$\begin{cases} G^X = J_Y^T G^Y J_Y \\ G^Y = J_X^T G^X J_X \end{cases}. \text{ The metric tensor can be calculated easily by}$$

substituting $d x_i^2 = \displaystyle\sum_{\mu,\nu} \frac{\partial x_i}{\partial y_\mu} \frac{\partial x_i}{\partial y_\nu} d y_\mu d y_\nu$ into the formula for ds^2 and

combining like terms

$$g_{\mu,\nu}^Y = \sum_{i,j=1} g_{i,j}^X \frac{\partial x_i}{\partial y_\mu} \frac{\partial x_j}{\partial y_\nu}.$$

A space is flat, or Riemannian, if all the g's are constant. A special flat space is the Euclidian space where

$$d s^2 = \sum d y_\mu^2 \left[where \ g_{\mu,\nu}^{X,Y} = \delta_\mu^\nu \right]. \text{ The flatness of a space is}$$

determined in terms of the equations of the geodesics and the radius of curvature. Each of these elements are determined by calculating the Christoffel symbols of the first,

$$\Gamma_{i,j,k} = \frac{1}{2} \left\{ \frac{\partial g_{i,k}}{\partial y_j} + \frac{\partial g_{k,j}}{\partial y_i} + \frac{\partial g_{i,j}}{\partial y_k} \right\}, \text{ and second,}$$

$$\Gamma_{i,j}^\alpha = \sum_k g^{\alpha,k} \Gamma_{i,j,k}, \text{ kinds where } G^{-1} = \left\{ g^{i,j} \right\}.[1] \text{ The radius}$$

of curvature is expressed as $R = \dfrac{1}{\sqrt{\displaystyle\sum_{i,j,k,l} g^{i,j} g^{k,l} R_{i,j,k,l}}}$ where the Ricci tensors, $R_{i,j,k,l}$, are expressible in terms of derivatives of the Christoffel symbols of the first kind

$$R_{i,j,k,l} = \left[\frac{\partial \Gamma_{i,k}}{\partial y_j} - \frac{\partial \Gamma_{k,j}}{\partial y_i} \right] + \sum_\alpha \left[\Gamma^\alpha_{j,k} \Gamma_{i,l,\alpha} - \Gamma^\alpha_{j,l} \Gamma_{i,k,\alpha} \right]$$

The geodesics are solutions of the Laplacian equation,

$$\frac{\partial^2 y_\alpha}{\partial y_\mu^2} + \sum_{i,j} \left[\Gamma^\alpha_{i,j} \frac{\partial y_i}{\partial y_\mu} \frac{\partial y_j}{\partial y_\mu} \right] = 0 \text{ , or}$$

$$y_\mu = \frac{1}{\frac{\partial y_\alpha}{\partial y_\mu}\bigg|_{y_\alpha = 0}} \left[\int^{y_\alpha} e^{\int_0^{y_\alpha} \sum_{i,j} \left[\Gamma^\alpha_{i,j} \frac{\partial y_i}{\partial y_\mu} \frac{\partial y_j}{\partial y_\mu} \right] dy_\alpha} \, dy_\alpha \Bigg|_{y_\alpha = y_\alpha(0)} + \int_0^{y_\alpha} e^{\int_0^{y_\alpha} \sum_{i,j} \left[\Gamma^\alpha_{i,j} \frac{\partial y_i}{\partial y_\mu} \frac{\partial y_j}{\partial y_\mu} \right] dy_\alpha} \, dy_\alpha \right]$$

Examples of the geometries generated by elementary transformations are presented in the next two sections.

Expressing that the difference between observed and hypothesized values of a variable is $ds^2 = \sum_{obs} \sum_\mu [y_\mu^{obs} - \hat{y}_\mu]^2$ assumes that the Y hyperspace is Euclidean; a hypothesis {assumption} which we will see is not valid. The Euclidean distance formula is a valid measure of distance if and only if we assume that $y_I = x_I$ and $g^{X,Y}_{\mu,v} = \delta^v_\mu = \begin{cases} 1 & if \ \mu = v \\ 0 & if \ \mu \neq v \end{cases}$, a trivial solution. If the solution of the equations $y_\mu = f_\mu(x_1, \cdots, x_M)$ is nontrivial and defined in terms of undetermined parameters, $\left\{ \alpha^v_\mu \mid \mu = 1, \cdots, M_Y \ and \ v = 1, \cdots, M_X \right\}$, the sum of squared distances between observed and predicted values is

$$\varphi = \sum_{obs} \sum_{\mu, \nu} [y_{\mu}^{obs} - \hat{y}_{\mu}] \ [y_{\nu}^{obs} - \hat{y}_{\nu}]$$. Parameters are estimated

by either the exact solution of $\dfrac{\partial \varphi}{\partial \alpha_{\mu}^{\nu}} = 0$, if it exists, or, iteratively

estimated from the first and second derivatives, $\dfrac{\partial \varphi}{\partial \alpha_{\mu}^{\nu}}$ and $\dfrac{\partial^2 \varphi}{\partial \alpha_{\mu}^{\nu} \partial \alpha_{\mu}^{\nu}}$

THE LEAST SQUARES PARADOX

Let X be a space of independent variables with metric G^X such that $d s_X^2 = \sum_{i,j} g_{i,j}^X d x_i d x_j$. Let Y be a space of dependent variables; where f is a set of general functionals such that:

$\mathcal{F} : (X, G^X) \rightarrow (Y, G^Y)$. The Jacobian of this set of transformations

is $J = \left[J_{ij}^{\mathcal{F}} \right] = \left[\dfrac{d y_i}{d x_j} \right]$. With a little algebra, the metric in Y, G^Y, is:

$$G^Y = \left[J J^T \right]^{-1} J G^X J^T \left[J J^T \right]^{-1}$$

Therfore, $d s_Y^2$, the distance between the observed values of the dependent variables, y, and their estimated values, $\hat{y}$, is expressed by the equation $d s_Y^2 = \sum_{\mu, \nu} g_{\mu, \nu}^Y (y_{\mu} - \hat{y}_{\mu})(y_{\nu} - \hat{y}_{\nu})$. This means that

$d s_Y^2$ is the least squares metric only when Y is Euclidean

$g_{\mu, \nu}^Y = \delta_{\nu}^{\mu} = \begin{cases} 1 \ if \ \mu = \nu \\ 0 \ if \ \mu \neq \nu \end{cases}$. The metric tensor, $g_{\mu, \nu}^Y$, is a function

of the unknown parameters in the transformation equation $\mathcal{F} : (X, G^X) \rightarrow (Y, G^Y)$. The Euclidean assumption (the least squres solution) means we have prior knowledge of the functional form of $g_{\mu, \nu}^Y$ and, hence, the parameters of the function which we are trying to estimate before we estimate them!

The methodology described above eliminates this paradox. Applications to specific deterministic and qualitative solutions are described below.

DETERMINISTIC SOLUTIONS

In this section common relationships such as multiple regression, factor analysis, polynomial regression, and functional transformations will be considered.

The two variable regression model corresponds to the transformation
$\begin{cases} y_1 = x_1 \\ y_2 = a x_1 + b x_2 \end{cases}$. Assuming the Mahalanobis metric in the domain space, $G_X = R^{-1}$, the distance between an estimated and observed values of y_2 is:

$$ds^2 = \frac{1 + \dfrac{2ra}{b} + \left[\dfrac{a}{b}\right]^2}{1 - r^2} \, dy_1^2 - \frac{2\,[b\,r - a]}{b^2(1 - r^2)} dy_1 \, dy_2 + \frac{dy_2^2}{b^2(1 - r^2)}$$

and since the metric of Y^2

$$\left\{ \frac{1}{1 - r^2} \begin{bmatrix} 1 + \dfrac{2\,r\,a}{b} + \left[\dfrac{a}{b}\right]^2 & -\dfrac{2\,(r\,b - a)}{b^2} \\ 0 & \dfrac{1}{b^2} \end{bmatrix} \right\}, \text{ all Ricci}$$

tensors are zero; the flat nature of X^2 is imposed upon Y^2. Making classical deterministic assumptions,[2] then $\dfrac{\partial}{\partial(a \vee b)}\left[\displaystyle\sum_o ds^2\right] = 0$ results in exact solutions to the regression problem.

$$\begin{cases} a = r_{x_1, y_1} - b\, r_{x_1, x_2} \\ \\ b = \dfrac{1 - r_{x_1, y_1}^2}{r_{x_2, y_2}^2 - r_{x_1, x_2} r_{x_1, y_1}} \end{cases}$$
.[3] By taking the limit, $G_X \to I$, as the domain space X^2 becomes Euclidean, the

solution $\displaystyle\lim_{R^{-1} \to I} [\,a, b\,] = \left[r_{x_1, y_2}, \ \dfrac{1 - r_{x_1, y_2}^2}{r_{x_1, y_2}^2} \right]$, the classical

regression solution. For the case of two variable regression, classical parameter estimation techniques apply only when the domain space is Euclidean. The domain space is Cartesian if and only if the domain space is Riemannian (with a Mahalanobis like metric). These assumptions do not apply to psychological space and the application of classical methods are not applicable for the study of human behavior.

Multiple Regression

The multiple regression problem is a mapping from X^M to Y^M such that

$$
\begin{cases}
y_1 = x_1 \\
\quad \vdots \\
y_{M-1} = x_{M-1}, \text{ assuming the Mahalanobis metric in the domain} \\
y_M = \displaystyle\sum_{i=1}^{M} a_i x_i
\end{cases}
$$

space, $G_{X^{M-1}} = R_{M-1}^{-1}$, the equation of the metric in the space of Y^M is calculated using

$$
ds^2 = \sum_{i=1}^{M-1} \left[\left[\frac{a_M r_{i,M-1}^2 - 2a_i}{a_M^2} \right] + \sum_{j=1}^{M-1} \left\{ r_{i,j}^{-1} - \frac{a_j r_{iM}^{-1}}{a_M} + \frac{a_i a_j}{a_M^2} \right\} \, dy_i \right] dy_j + \frac{dy_M^2}{a_M^2} .
$$

Adopting classical assumptions the distance between observed and predicted values of Y_M, summed over all observations, is

$$
ds^2 = \sum_o \left[\frac{y_o}{a_M} + \sum_{i=1} \frac{a_i}{a_M} x_i \right]^2 .
$$
Taking derivatives of ds^2 with respect to a_j $\left(\dfrac{\partial}{\partial a_j} ds^2 \right)$ for all $j \neq M$, an exact solution exists and it is the classical solution,

$$
A_{M-1} = R^{-1} R_{X y_M} .
$$
For $j = M$, the equation $\dfrac{\partial}{\partial a_j} ds^2 = 0$

results in the quadratic equation

$$a_M^2 + 2 a_M \left[\sum_{i=1}^{M-1} a_i r_{iM} - 1 \right] +$$

$$\left[\sum_{i,j}^{M-1} a_i a_j r_{i,j} - 2 \sum_{i=1}^{M-1} a_i r_{iM} + 1 \right] = 0$$

with two roots,

$$a_M = 1 - \sum_{i=1}^{M-1} a_i r_{iM} + \frac{1}{2} \sqrt{ \sum_{i,j}^{M-1} a_i a_j [r_{iM} r_{jM} - r_{ij}] } .$$

Assuming a relatively trivial Riemannian structure to the domain space (Mahalanobis, $G_X = R^{-1}$), unless

$$\sum_{i,j}^{M-1} a_i a_j [r_{iM} r_{jM} - r_{ij}] < 0 \qquad \text{there are two solutions to the}$$

multiple regression problem! Only by taking the limiting condition where X $^{M-1}$ becomes increasingly Euclidean, $R_{M-1}^{-1} \to I_{M-1}$, , the quadratic equation yields an extraneous solution ($a_M = 1$) and the classical solution, $\lim_{R \to I} a_M \to 1 - \sum r_{iM}^2$. Classical multiple regression procedures apply only in the limited case where the behavior domain is Euclidean. It does not apply in the case where the behavior space is Riemannian. These results call into questions all results predicated upon classical regression paradigms.

Polynomial Regression

The polynomial mapping function is $y = \sum a_j x^j$ where the metric tensor on the y-line has one solution, $g = \dfrac{1}{\sum_{j,k} j k a_j a_k x^{j+k-2}}$. The distance between observed and predicted values, summed over all observations, is

$$\sum_o \frac{(y - \hat{y})^2}{\sum_{j,k} j\,k\,a_j\,a_k\,x^{j+k-2}}. \text{ For each coefficient, } \frac{\partial}{\partial a_j}\,d s^2 = 0$$

does not have a closed form solution, and requires the calculation of first and second derivatives to estimate parameters iteratively.

$$\frac{\partial}{\partial a_\mu} \odot d s^2 =$$

$$-\sum \left\{ \frac{2\mu x^{\mu-2}(y - \hat{y})^2 \sum_k k a_k x^k}{\left[\sum jk a_j a_k x^{k+j-2}\right]^2} + \frac{2(y - \hat{y})x^\mu}{\sum jk a_j a_k x^{k+j-2}} \right\} = 0$$

$$\frac{\partial^2}{\partial a_\mu^2} \odot d s^2 =$$

$$\left\{ \frac{\sum 8\mu^2 x^{2\mu+2}}{\left[\sum jk a_j a_k x^{k+j-2}\right]^2} \left[2x^{\mu-2}\left[-\mu^2(y - \hat{y})(1 - 41y + y\hat{y}) + 2\mu(y - \hat{y})\sum k a_k x^k + \sum jk a_j a_k x^{k+j}\right]\right] \right\}$$

The radius of curvature of Y-space is

$$\frac{1}{\sqrt{\frac{5}{4}\left[\sum_{j,k} jk(k+j-2)a_j a_k x^{k+j-3}\right] - \sum jk(k+j-2)(k+j-3)a_k a_j x^{k+j-3}}},$$

indicating that, depending upon the particular values of the parameters, the Y-space is highly distorted. For the simple case where $a_0 = 1$, $a_1 = 2$, and $a_2 = 1$. Even the simplest polynomial spaces are highly distorted resembling laminar flows. Distances between observed and predicted values vary considerably with the observed values. Large differences at extreme values on the right do not represent small departures from prediction. Small deviations at low values correspond to much larger distances. It seems that the geometry of the polynomial space attempts to compensate for differences in scale.

Factor Analysis

This is most often used to calculate the values of variables, used in other subsequent analyses, between spaces of observations, X^K, and latent structures, Y^M. Since the spaces are often of different dimensions a little matrix algebra is needed to show that, if Y^M is Euclidian, the distance metric is $d s^2 = \sum_{\mu\nu}\left[\sum_l b_{l\mu} b_{l\nu}\right] dx_\mu dx_\nu$, where B = $(A^T A)^{-1} A^T$ and A is the factor structure matrix. If X^K is Mahalanobis we have K^2 simultaneous nonlinear equations $\sum_i b_{i\mu} b_{i\nu} = r_{\mu\nu}^{-1}$. Assuming that the simplest classical model applies, we have $R^{-1} = A A^T$ or $r_{\mu\nu}^{-1} = \sum_i a_{\mu i} a_{\nu i}$. Each equation, $r_{\mu\nu}^{-1}$, can be used to calculate the factor patterns $\{ a_{\mu j} \mid j = 1, \cdots, M \}$ by noting that

$$\frac{\partial r_{\mu\nu}^{-1}}{\partial a_{\mu j}} = a_{\nu j} + a_{\mu j} \delta_{\nu\cdot}^{\mu}, \text{ that } \Psi_{\mu\nu} = r_{\mu\nu}^{-1} - \sum_i a_{\mu i} a_{\nu i} \text{ and estimating}$$

parameters so that $\Psi_{\mu\nu} \approx 0$ iteratively where the $k+1^{st}$ solution is

$$a_{\mu j}^{k+1} = a_{\mu j}^{k} + \frac{\Psi_{\mu\nu}}{a_{\mu j} + a_{\mu j} \delta_{\nu}^{\mu}}.$$ An alternative is to identify the $a_{\mu\nu}$

where $\Psi_{\mu\nu}^{*} = \| r_{\mu\nu}^{-1} - \sum_i a_{\mu i} a_{\nu i} \|$, where:

$$a_{\mu j}^{k+1} =$$

$$a_{\mu j}^{k} + \frac{\Psi_{\mu\nu}^{*}}{(a_{\mu j} + a_{\mu j} \delta_{\nu}^{\mu}) \mathcal{H}_{\Psi_{\mu\nu}^{*}} - (a_{\mu j} + a_{\mu j} \delta_{\nu}^{\mu}) \mathcal{H}_{-\Psi_{\mu\nu}^{*}}}$$

and $\mathcal{H}_{\Psi}$ is the Heavyside unit step function.

Nonlinear Solutions With Euclidean Metrics On X^M

Nonlinear multiple regression is a mapping from $X \rightarrow Y$ where the homomorphisms may contain powers and products of the independent variables. Each functional form presents a unique situation which requires a particular solution. A number of elementary cases will be presented as models.

Multiple Quadratic Regression

This represents a mapping where $\begin{cases} y_1 = a x_1^2 + b x_2^2 \\ y_2 = c x_1 + d x_2 \end{cases}$. The metric in the

Y space, assuming X is Euclidean, is,

$$\frac{1}{4}\left[\begin{array}{cc} \dfrac{\bar{a}^2}{\bar{a}y_1+\bar{b}y_2}+\dfrac{\bar{c}^2}{\bar{c}y_1+\bar{d}y_2} & 2\left[\dfrac{\bar{a}\,\bar{b}}{\bar{a}y_1+\bar{b}y_2}+\dfrac{\bar{c}\,\bar{d}}{\bar{c}y_1+\bar{d}y_2}\right] \\[4mm] 0 & \dfrac{\bar{b}^2}{\bar{a}y_1+\bar{b}y_2}+\dfrac{\bar{d}^2}{\bar{c}y_1+\bar{d}y_2} \end{array}\right]$$

where $\bar{A}=A^{-1}$. The metric equation has an exact minimum solution.

$$\begin{bmatrix} a & b \\ c & d \end{bmatrix}=\frac{4}{DN}$$

$$\left[\begin{array}{cc} \dfrac{\overline{y_2}}{D_2}\sum\left[\dfrac{y_1}{x_2}\right]^2-\dfrac{\overline{y_1}}{D_2}\sum\dfrac{y_1y_2}{x_2^2} & -\dfrac{\overline{y_1}}{D_1}\sum\left[\dfrac{y_1}{x_1}\right]^2+\dfrac{\overline{y_1}}{D_1}\sum\dfrac{y_1y_2}{x_1^2} \\[6mm] -\dfrac{\overline{y_1}}{D_2}\sum\left[\dfrac{y_2}{x_2}\right]^2+\dfrac{\overline{y_2}}{D_2}\sum\dfrac{y_1y_2}{x_2^2} & -\dfrac{\overline{y_1}}{D_1}\sum\left[\dfrac{y_1}{x_1}\right]^2+\dfrac{\overline{y_2}}{D_1}\sum\dfrac{y_1y_2}{x_1^2} \end{array}\right]$$

Where:
$$\begin{cases} D_1=\sum\left(\dfrac{y_1}{x_1}\right)^2\sum\left(\dfrac{y_2}{x_1}\right)^2-\left[\dfrac{y_1y_2}{x_2}\right]^2 \\[5mm] D_2=\sum\left(\dfrac{y_1}{x_2}\right)^2\sum\left(\dfrac{y_2}{x_2}\right)^2-\left[\dfrac{y_1y_2}{x_2}\right]^2 \end{cases}\quad\text{and}$$

$$\begin{aligned} D =\; & \frac{\overline{y_1}\,\overline{y_2}}{D_1D_2}\left[\sum\left(\dfrac{y_2}{x_1}\right)^2\sum\left(\dfrac{y_1}{x_2}\right)^2-\sum\left(\dfrac{y_1}{x_1}\right)^2\sum\left(\dfrac{y_2}{x_2}\right)^2\right] \\[3mm] & -\frac{\overline{y_1}2}{D_1D_2}\left[\sum\left(\dfrac{y_2}{x_2}\right)^2\sum\dfrac{y_1y_2}{x_1^2}-\sum\left(\dfrac{y_1}{x_1}\right)^2\sum\dfrac{y_1y_2}{x_2^2}\right] \\[3mm] & +\frac{\overline{y_2}^2}{D_1D_2}\sum y_1^2\left(\dfrac{1}{x_1^2}-\dfrac{1}{x_2^2}\right)\sum\dfrac{y_1y_2}{x_1^2} \end{aligned}$$

All summations are taken over all observations. Although an exact solution exists, it is, perhaps, more useful to examine the geometry of the resulting spaces. Depending upon the values of the parameters, the geodesics of Y^2 can represent a double hyperbolic, double ellipsoidal, or ellipsoidal-hyperbolic space.

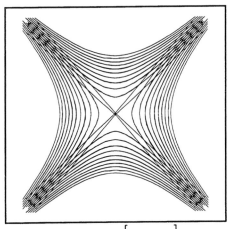

Case 1: $A = \begin{bmatrix} -2 & 1 \\ 1 & -2 \end{bmatrix}$

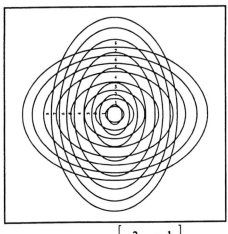

Case 2: $A = \begin{bmatrix} 2 & -1 \\ -1 & 2 \end{bmatrix}$

The geometry of the spaces resulted from the application of a Euclidean metric in X^2 to a relatively elementary set of simultaneous equations. The Riemannian (and, trivial, Euclidean) geometries do not appear to reflect human behavior. The application of a nonRiemannian X^2 will result in a more complex structure.

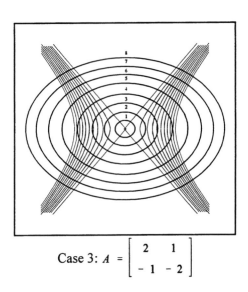

Case 3: $A = \begin{bmatrix} 2 & 1 \\ -1 & -2 \end{bmatrix}$

Triple Exponential Transformation

Consider the mapping from X^3 to U^3 where $\begin{cases} u_1 = x \\ u_2 = e^{ax+by} \\ u_3 = e^{cz} \end{cases}$. Assuming that X^3 is Euclidean, the metric tensor in U^3 is

$$
\begin{bmatrix}
1 + \dfrac{a^2}{b^2} - \dfrac{2a}{b^2 u_2} & 0 & \\[2em]
0 & \dfrac{1}{b^2 u_2^2} & 0 \\[2em]
0 & 0 & \dfrac{1}{c^2 u_3^2}
\end{bmatrix}
\quad \text{and the nonzero Christoffel symbols of}
$$

the first andsecond kinds are

$$
\Gamma_{222} = \frac{1}{b^2 u_2^2}, \ \Gamma_{122} = \Gamma_{212} = \frac{a}{b^2 u_2^2},
$$

$$
\Gamma^2_{12} = \Gamma^2_{21} = \frac{a^2 c^2 u_3^2}{a^2 u_2^2}, \ \text{ and } \ \Gamma^2_{22} = -\frac{1}{u_2}.
$$

U^3

is a convoluted simply connected space. The   distance between observed and estimated vectors in U^3 is:

$$
ds^2 = \sum \left(1 + \frac{a^2}{b^2} \right) du_1^2 =
$$

$$
- \frac{2a}{b^2 e^{ax+by}} du_1 du_2 + \frac{du_2^2}{b^2 e^{2ax+2by}} + \frac{du_3^2}{c^2 e^{2cz}}.
$$

The determination of the parameters (a, b, c) requires minimization of the distance function.

Parameter a

Function (ϕ, $\phi = 0$)

$$\sum (u_3 - e^{-cz}) (u_3 - e^{-cz} + z u_3)$$

First Derivative

$$- \sum z^2 u_3 e^{-cz}$$

Parameter b

Function (ϕ, $\phi = 0$)

$$- \frac{N}{b^2}$$

$$- 2 \sum y u_2 e^{-ax-bx} [1 - u_2 e^{-ax-by}]$$

First Derivative

$$2 \frac{N}{b^3}$$

$$- 2 \sum y^2 u_2 e^{-ax-bx} [2 u_2 e^{-ax-by} - 1]$$

Parameter c

Function (ϕ, $\phi = 0$)

$$\sum \frac{2 u_2 x}{b} e^{-ax-by} [1 - u_2 e^{-ax-by}]$$

First Derivative

$$\sum \frac{-2 u_2 x^2}{b} e^{-ax-by} [1 - 2 u_2 e^{-ax-by}]$$

Logarithmic Regression

Consider the case where $\begin{cases} y_1 = x_1 \\ y_2 = \alpha^{-1} \ln \{x_2\} \end{cases}$. where the, is metric

tensor, assuming that X^2 is Euclidian, is $\begin{bmatrix} 1 & 0 \\ 0 & \alpha_2 \, e^{2 \alpha y_2} \end{bmatrix}$. The distance

between observed and predicted values, assuming $\alpha \neq 0$, is

$$\alpha^2 \sum x_2^2 y_2^2 - 2 \alpha \sum x_2^2 y_2 \ln [x_2] + \sum x_2^2 (\ln [x_2])^2$$

where the exact solution of $ds^2 = 0$ is

$$\alpha = \frac{\sum x_2^2 y_2 \pm \sqrt{(\sum x_2^2 y_2 \ln [x_2])^2 - (\sum x_2^2 y_2^2)^2 \sum x_2^2 (\ln [x_2])^2}}{\sum x_2^2 y_2^2}$$

and the minimization solution $\left[\dfrac{\delta}{\delta \alpha} \, ds^2 = 0 \right]$ is

$$\alpha = \frac{\sum x_2^2 y_2 \ln [x_2]}{\sum x_2^2 y_2^2}$$. Both of these solutions depart from the exact

solution

$$\alpha = \frac{\sum y_2 \ln [x_1] \pm \sqrt{(\sum y_2 \ln [x_1])^2 - \sum y_2^2 \sum (\ln [x_1])^2}}{2 \sum y_2^2}$$

or the minimization solution $\alpha = \dfrac{\sum y_2 \ln [x_1]}{\sum y_2^2}$ assuming that Y^2 is

Riemannian.

Inverse Sine Transformation

The transformation $y = a \sin^{-1}(bx)$ results in the metric

$$g_{22} = a^{-2}b^{-2}Cos^2\left\{\frac{y}{a}\right\}, \text{ and } \Gamma_{22}^2 = -\frac{1}{a}Tan\left[\frac{y}{a}\right].$$

The solution to the minimization of the distance equation with respect to parameters has two solutions: an exact solution for a,

$$\frac{\sum y^2}{(y-b^2)\sum \sin^{-1}(bx)}$$ when b is known, and a iterative solution of

$\psi = 0$ where:

$$\psi = \sum\left\{\frac{y}{ab}\right\}^2 - \frac{2y\sin^{-1}(bx)}{ab^2} + \frac{\left[\sin^{-1}(bx)\right]^2}{b^2} - y^2 - \left[\sin^{-1}(bx)\right]^2$$

and

$$\frac{\partial\psi}{\partial b} = \sum \frac{-2y^2}{a^2b^2} - \frac{4y\sin^{-1}(bx)}{ab^3} - \frac{2y}{ab\cos\left[\sin^{-1}(bx)\right]} - \frac{\left[\sin^{-1}(bx)\right]^2}{b^3}$$
$$\frac{2\sin^{-1}(bx)}{b\cos\left[\sin^{-1}(bx)\right]} + \frac{2b}{a^2\cos\left[\sin^{-1}(bx)\right]} - \frac{2b\sin^{-1}(bx)}{a^2\cos\left[\sin^{-1}(bx)\right]}$$

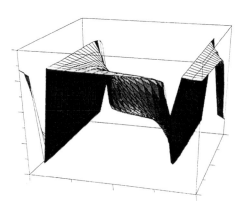

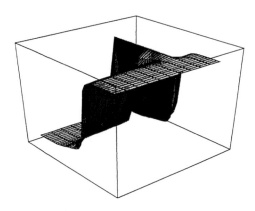

The one cup of one geodesic manifold from two different perspectives are shown above. The geodesic of this space is extremely convoluted with geodesic lines merging at infinity and returning.

Conclusions

The relaxation of the Euclidean fifth postulate resulted in new geometries (Sakai, 1996; Stillwell, 1996). The relaxation of the general Euclidean nature of space-time resulted in general relativity and the "new cosmology" (Gribbin, 1988; Hawking, 1996; Heisenberg, 1959, 1970, 1971). The relaxations of notions of cause and effect resulted in new quantum or probalistic forms of reality where all that was, is, and ever will be are simultaneously present and absent at the same time. The studies reported here have shown that the relaxation of the Euclidean postulate results in rich methodologies and results concerning the nature of psychological space.

As expected, the geometries of the data spaces approach Euclidean geometries; these formulae result in classical formulae. The nonEuclidean metric spaces indicate that psychological space is nonlinear and cooberate the findings in the neurosciences (Caramazza, 1996; Knight, 1996; Vandenberghe, Price, Wise, Josephs, & Frackowiak, 1996). The elementary form of a Rieanian space, the Malhalanobis metric, reults in nonclassical manifolds. Flat spaces under particular transformations result in complex differential manifolds. This strategy provides the behavioral researcher with the power to examine more powerful models of human development, thinking, and learning.

Constrained by the developmental stages of mathematics and computing power at the time, although human scientists knew better (Köhler, 1920; Lewin, 1935), they were limited to Euclidean and linear models. The same constraints do not exist today. Human scientists have at their disposal the mathematics and computing power to develop new models which examine human behavior in ways reflective of the nature of psychological space.

This opens the question of the training of behavioral scholars and whether scholars are trained similarly to practitioners or technicians. There is a need to examine the mathematical training of all professionals and all children. The global society needs to retrofit our schools in such a way that computational skills are sufficiently acquired in the first few years of schooling to an extent reflective of the real needs of an expanding technological capacity releasing time for the study of the mathematics needed for the next millenium. The future of technological societies depend upon retooling their educational delivery systems and social structures away from the pedantics of antiquated needs of an industrial society toward the conceptualistics of a modern world. Or, does the future of humana lie in the third world nations where change can occur more easily and the philosophies are less pedantic and crystalized into the social fabric?

Endnotes

1.   The number of calculations is reduced by using the symmetry relations $\Gamma_{ijk} = \Gamma_{jik}$ and $\Gamma_{ij}{}^{\alpha} = \Gamma_{ji}{}^{\alpha}$.

2. $d y_1{}^2 = d x_1{}^2 = 0$

3.   Assuming that all variables are normalized. Otherwise, the correlations are replaced by the corresponding covariances.

11

Developmental Dynamics

The relatively new *developmental* approach to learning embraces learning as an evolutionary process where beliefs (knowledge structures) evolve through experience (Bryson, 1933; Cross, 1971, 1976; Hall, 1883, 1904; Hart, 1927; Hashway, 1989a, 1990; Keimig, 1983; Knowles, 1977; Liveright, 1968; Maxwell, 1971, 1979; Münrterberg, 1898; Nist, 1985; Novack & Gowin, 1984; President's Commission, 1947; Rokeach, 1973; Rouche & Snow, 1977; Sheldon, 1942; Thorndike, 1901; Wolff, 1740). A well developed curriculum system must include a provision for monitoring skill acquisition (Glaser, 1963, 1968, 1971a, 1971b; Glaser & Cox, 1968; Glaser & Klaus, 1962; Nitko, 1968, 1970) and beliefs (probalistic knowledge structures) (Bransford, Nitsch & Franks, 1977; Hashway, 1979, 1986, 1991; Payne, Krathowohl & Gordon, 1967; Pines, 1977; Perkins, 1989; Scandura, 1966, 1973, 1977, 1976; Suppes & Atkinson, 1960; Suppes & Morningstar, 1972). The monitoring of concept development is not enough. The assumption implicit in these theories is that belief acquistion occurs, either because of instruction or as a result of instruction, by the individual in isolation of his/her environment, not taking into account the interaction of individuals as dynamic parts of the development process.

Developmental curriculum theories need a theory of the development of belief structures. The thesis of this section, predicated upon organizational development theory (Goodman, Jennings & Associates, 1977; Kast & Rosenzweig, 1974; Katz & Kahn, 1966; Pelz & Andrews, 1966; Thibault & Kelley, 1967; Thompson, 1966; Williams, 1978), is that belief structures evolve not only from the individual action but, also, from the interaction of individuals. It is important to model the interaction of individuals in group situations with the goal of identifying and studying the dynamics via which the group and individuals within a group contribute to development of belief structures. A theory of human interaction as the dynamic interaction between individuals in a psychological space will be posited and the mathematical modeling of this theory results in a mechanism for deriving the energy function from an attribute distribution function. A process for determining the functional form of the attribute distribution function from a hypothesized energy model will also be developed.

Theory Development

The fundamental assumption is that every individual has an influence upon all other individuals and that influence is expressible in terms of a work function, $\phi(\chi, \tau)$, which represents the work required for a person at position χ to maintain their position on some attribute subject to the influence of an individual located at τ on the same attribute dimension. Given that individuals are distributed on any attribute dimension, the total work, or "energy," required to maintain the position χ, $\mathfrak{Z}(\chi)$, is

$$-N \int_{-\infty}^{\infty} \phi(\chi,\tau)\psi(\tau)d\,\tau \quad \text{where } \psi(\tau) \text{ represents the distribution of individ-}$$

uals on the attribute dimension and N is the total number of individuals in the influence group. Expanding the energy function in a Taylor series about μ_1, the mean of the attribute distribution, we have:

$$\mathfrak{Z}(\chi) = -N \sum_{n=0}^{\infty} \frac{1}{n!} \frac{\partial^n \phi(\chi, \mu_1)}{\partial \mu_1^n} \int_{-\infty}^{+\infty} (\tau - \mu_1)^n \, \psi(\tau)\, d\tau$$

$$= -N \sum_{n=0}^{\infty} \frac{\mu_n}{n!} \phi_n(\chi, \mu_1)$$

, where μ_n is the

n-th. central moment of the attribute distribution, and

$$\phi_n(\chi, \mu_1) = \frac{\partial^n \phi(\chi, \tau)}{\partial \tau^n} \Big|_{\tau = \mu_1} \quad . \text{ Without loss of generality,}$$

centralized coordinates, $u = \tau - \mu_1$, can be used and

$$\mathfrak{Z}_u = -N \sum_{n=0}^{\infty} \frac{\mu_n}{n!} \phi_n(\chi, u) \quad where \quad \phi_n(\chi, u) = \frac{\partial^n \phi(\chi, u)}{\partial u^n} \Big|_{u=0} \quad .$$

The Schrödinger equation becomes

$$\frac{\partial^2 \psi(u)}{\partial u^2} - N \psi \sum_{n=0}^{\infty} \frac{\mu_n}{n!} \phi_n(u) = 0 \,, \quad \text{implying that the energy function}$$

is a function of the attribute distribution,

$$\mathfrak{Z}_u = \frac{1}{\psi(u)} \frac{\partial^2 \psi(u)}{\partial u^2}$$. Typically, the attribute distribution as well as

all its' central moments are known, and the potential energy function can be determined by solving the differential equation,

$$\sum_{n=0}^{\infty} \left[\frac{\mu_n}{n!} \right] \frac{\partial^n \phi}{\partial u^n} = \frac{1}{N \psi} \frac{\partial^2 \psi}{\partial u^2} \ .$$

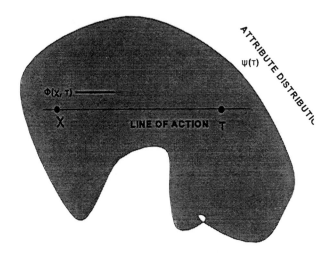

Action At A Distance Model

The Multivariate Case

The position of the "influencing" individual is represented in a space of M-dimensions by a vector **T**, and the position of the "influenced" individual in the same M-space by the vector **X**, and the energy exerted by **T** on **X** by the vector function $\psi(\mathbf{X,T}) = \{\psi_{i,j} (\mathbf{X,T}) \mid i, j \in ZM\}$. The M-space is a geodesic space with metric $\mathbf{G} = [g_{i,j}]$. Any of the elements of the metric tensor may be a nonconstant function of M-space coordinates. i.e. $g_{i,j} = g_{i,j}(\tau_1, \tau_2, \cdots, \tau_M)$. In a Remanian (flat) space, **G** is a constant matrix. In a Euclidean space, a special case of a Remanian space,

$g_{i,j} = \delta_{i,j}$, *the Dirac delta~function,* $\begin{cases} 1, & \textit{if } i=j \\ 0, & \textit{otherwise} \end{cases}$.

For the general case, the energy function is

$\mathfrak{Z}(X) = -N \int \psi(T) < \Psi(X,T) \mid dS >$, where $\psi(T)$ is a scaler multivariate

probability density function, $<A|B>$ is the Dirac product of two vectors, and dS is the differential of the geodesic. Therefore,

$$\mathfrak{Z}(X) = -N \sum_{i,j} \int_{-\infty}^{+\infty} \int_{-\infty}^{+\infty} g_{i,j}(X,\,T)\; \psi_{i,j}(X,\,T)\; \phi(\,\tau_i,\,\tau_j)d\,\tau_i\,d\,\tau_j \; ,$$

where the Schrödinger equation is

$$\nabla^2 \psi + \psi\,\mathfrak{Z}(X) = 0,\; \textit{where } \mathfrak{Z}(X) = \frac{\nabla^2 \psi}{\psi} \;.$$ The multivariate

case reduces to solving the equation

$$\sum_{i,j=1}^{M} \int_{-\infty}^{\infty} \int_{-\infty}^{\infty} g_{i,j}(X,T)\; \phi_{i,j}(X,T)\; \psi(\tau_i,\tau_j)\,d\,\tau_i\,d\,\tau_j = -\frac{\nabla^2 \psi}{N\,\psi}$$

for the multivariate potential energy function when the metric properties of the space are known, or for the potential energy and metric tensors when the metric properties of the space are not known.

Total System Energy

Any population can be considered to be a closed system where all individuals interact with each other resulting in a particular configuration at any point in time. The total energy in the system is the weighted sum over all states of the work required to maintain that state. The total energy of a univariate system is

$$\overline{\mathfrak{Z}} = \int_{-\infty}^{\infty} \mathfrak{Z}_x \psi(x)dx = -N \sum_{n,m=0}^{\infty} \frac{\mu_n \mu_m}{n!\,m!} \frac{\partial^{n+m} \phi(\chi,\,\tau)}{\partial \chi^m \partial \tau^n} \Big|_{\chi,\,\tau=0} \; ,$$

and in the multivariate case,

$$-N \sum_{p,\, q,\, i,\, j\, =\, 0}^{\infty} \int_{-\infty}^{\infty} \int_{-\infty}^{\infty} \int_{-\infty}^{\infty} \int_{-\infty}^{\infty} g_{i,\, j}(\chi,\, \tau)\, \phi_{i,\, j}(\chi,\, \tau)\, \psi(\tau)\, g_{p,\, q}(\chi,\, \tau)$$

$$\psi(\chi)\, d\tau_i\, d\tau_j\, d\chi_q\, d\chi_q$$

Knowing the total system energy function allows for predictions of system behavior under changes of distributional constraints.

For notational convenience, where appropriate, $f_{n,\, m}$ will symbolize

$\dfrac{\partial^{n+m} f}{\partial \chi^n \partial \tau^m}$, and $D_p{}^n$ will symbolize the differential operator $\dfrac{\partial^n}{\partial \rho^n}$ for

some particular variable or parameter, ρ.

Group Dynamics

Consider two groups with variances $\sigma_1{}^2$ and $\sigma_2{}^2$ respectively, where the first group is centered at 0 and the second centered at $\mu_1{}^2$. Of the total number of individuals in both groups, let A symbolize the proportion in the first group. Then, $\psi(\tau) = A\psi_1(\tau) + (1-A)\psi_2(\tau)$, and the energy required to maintain a position at χ is

$$\mathbf{3}_\chi = \phi(\chi,\, (1-A)\, \mu_1{}^2) + \tfrac{1}{2}\, \phi_{0,\, 2}(\chi,\, (1-A)\, \mu_1{}^2)\, [A\, \sigma_1{}^2 + (1-A)\, \sigma_2{}^2 + A\, (1-A)(\mu_1{}^2)^2\,].$$

The influence of groups 1 and 2, individually and respectively, are

$\phi(\chi,\, 0) + \tfrac{1}{2}\, \phi_{0,\, 2}(\chi,\, 0)\, \sigma_1{}^2$ and $\phi(\chi,\, (1-A)\, \mu_1{}^2) + \tfrac{1}{2}$

$\phi_{0,\, 2}(\chi,\, (1-A)\, \mu_1{}^2)\, \sigma_2{}^2$. Therefore, $\mathbf{3}_\chi$ is not equal to $\mathbf{3}_\chi{}^1 + \mathbf{3}_\chi{}^2$;

the principle of conservation of energy does not apply! The work required to maintain a position in a multigroup population is greater than the sum of the work required to maintain a position relative to each group in the population.

In the case of M groups,

$$\psi(\chi) = \Sigma_i A_i \psi_i (\chi \mid \mu_i^2, \sigma_i^2),$$

$$\mathbf{3}_\chi = \sum_{i=1}^{M} A_i \int_{-\infty}^{\infty} \phi(\chi, \tau) \psi_i (\tau \mid \mu_1^i, \sigma_i^2) \, d\tau$$

$$= \frac{1}{2} \sum_{i=1}^{M} A_i (D_\tau^2 + 2) \phi(\chi, \tau)|_{\tau = \mu_1^i} \sigma_i^2,$$

and the total energy is

$$\frac{1}{4} \sum_{i=1}^{M} A_i (\sigma_i^2 D_\chi^2 + 2)(\sigma_i^2 D_\tau^2 + 2) \phi(\chi, \tau)|_{\chi, \tau = \mu_1^i}, \qquad \text{noting that}$$

$$\forall_\chi \quad \frac{\mathbf{3}_\chi^i - \phi(\chi, \mu_1^i)}{\phi_{0,2}(\chi, \mu_1^i)} = \frac{\sigma_i^2}{2}, \qquad \text{a constant.}$$

SOLUTION OF THE SHRÖDINGER EQUATION

Solution of the Shrödinger equation requires the solution of a differential equation of countably infinite degree. The properties of centralized moments of commonly encountered distributions yields practical constraints which may be imposed upon the differential equation resulting in an equation of finite degree whose method of solution is well known.

The n-th coefficient of equation, $\displaystyle\sum_{n=0}^{\infty} \left[\frac{\mu_n}{n!} \right] \frac{\partial^n \phi}{\partial u^n} = \frac{1}{N \psi} \frac{\partial^2 \psi}{\partial u^2}$. is the

quotient of the μ_n, the n-th central moment of the probability distribution, and n factorial. For the *uniform distribution*, $\psi(x)=1$ when $0<x<1$, and the

n-th. coefficient is 1 if n=0, 0 if n is odd, and $\displaystyle\frac{1}{n \, 2^{n-1} \, n!}$ if n is even. For the *normal distribution*, $\psi(x) = \dfrac{1}{\sigma\sqrt{2\pi}}\ e^{-\frac{x^2}{2\sigma^2}}$, and the n-th. coefficient

is 1 if n=0, 0 if n is odd, and

$$\frac{\sigma^n\,2^{-\frac{n}{2}}}{[n/2]!\,[(n-2)/2]!} \quad \text{when n is even, and [x] is the least integer}$$

function of x. For the *exponential distribution* $\psi(x)=\lambda^{-1}\,e^{-\lambda x}$, where $0<x<\infty$, and the n-th. coefficient is

$$\frac{1}{(-\lambda)^n\,n!}\sum_{j=0}^{n} j!\binom{n}{j}(-1)^j = \frac{1}{(-\lambda)n\,n!} + \frac{\mu_{n-1}}{\lambda\,(n-1)!} \ . \text{ For the}$$

gamma distribution

$n,\ \psi(x)=\dfrac{\alpha^k\,e^{-\alpha k}\,x^{k-1}}{\Gamma(k)}$ *where* $\Gamma(x)$ *is the gamma function of*

$0<x<1$, and the n-th. coefficient is

$$\frac{\alpha^{k-n-1}(-n)^n}{\Gamma(k)}\sum_{j=0}^{n}\frac{1}{k^j\,(n-j)!}. \quad \text{For the } \textit{beta distribution, } 0<x<1,$$

$$\frac{x^{\alpha-1}(1-x)^{\beta-1}}{B(\alpha,\ \beta)}, \textit{ where } B(\alpha,\ \beta) = \int_0^1 x^{\alpha-1}(1-x)^{\beta-1}\,dx \ ,$$

and the n-th. coefficient is

$$\frac{(-1)^n}{B(\alpha+1,\ \beta)}\sum_{j=0}^{n}\frac{B^j(\alpha,\ \beta)\,B(\alpha+j,\ \beta)}{B^j(\alpha+1,\ \beta)} \ .$$

In each of these cases, the coefficients of the differential equation decrease rapidly with increasing n. Assuming that n=2 is sufficient to approximate the energy function, the differential equation, where $\lambda^2 = \sigma^2/2$, and σ^2 is the second central moment (variance) of the distribution, becomes

$$\lambda^2 \frac{\partial^2 \phi}{\partial \tau^2} + \phi = g(\chi), \ and \ g(\chi) = -\frac{1}{N\psi} \frac{d^2\psi}{d\chi^2}.$$

The solution of this equation with the boundary conditions

$\phi(\chi, \chi) = 0$, and $\dfrac{\partial \phi}{\partial \tau} = 0 \ at \ \tau = \chi$ is

$$\phi(\chi, \tau) = -g(\chi)[1 - \cos\{(\chi - \tau)\sqrt{2}/\sigma\}] \ .$$

The energy functions for the normal, exponential, gamma, beta, and uniform distributions, respectively, are:

$$-\frac{\chi^2 - \sigma^2}{N\sigma^4}\left[1 - \cos\left\{\frac{\chi - \tau}{\sigma/\sqrt{2}}\right\}\right], \ -\frac{\lambda^2}{N}\left[1 - \cos\{(\chi - \tau)\lambda^{-1}\sqrt{2}\}\right], \ x$$

$$-\frac{(k-1)(k-2)}{N\chi^2}\left[1 - \cos\left[\frac{(\chi - \tau)\sqrt{2\Gamma(k)}}{\sqrt{\alpha^{k-3}(k^2 + 2k + 2)}}\right]\right],$$

$$-\frac{(\alpha-1)(\alpha-2)(1-\chi)^2 - 2(\alpha-1)(\beta-1)\chi(1-\chi) + (\beta-1)(\beta-2)\chi^2}{N\chi^4}$$
$$\left[1 - \cos\left[\frac{(\chi - \tau)\sqrt{2B^3(\alpha+1, \beta)}}{\sqrt{B(\alpha, \beta)}\sqrt{B(\alpha+2, \beta)\,B(\alpha, \beta) + 2B^2(\alpha+1, \beta)}}\right]\right] \quad ,$$

and 0 where the mean system energy becomes $-N[(\sigma^2/2)g''(\mu_1) + g(\mu_1)]$. For symmetric distributions centered at zero, $\mu_1 = 0$, the total system energy is zero. For uniform distributions, the energy at all points as well as the total system energy is zero.

In the case of the normal distribution, with its second degree attributional energy term, individuals at positions one standard deviation, or greater, to the left, or right of the mean of the attribute distribution experience a need to exert energy to maintain their positions against the influences of others in the group. However, individuals who have positions within the one standard deviation barrier, *derive energy from the group*. In the case of the negative exponential distribution ($\lambda = 1$), the work function is essentially sinusoidal with a period of approximately 4.7 where everyone must exert some work to maintain their position.

When the Energy Function is Hypothesized

Assume that $\phi(\chi, \tau)$ is known. Then, given

$$\frac{\sigma^2}{2} \frac{\partial^2 \phi}{\partial \tau^2} + \phi = -\frac{1}{N \psi} \frac{\partial^2 \psi}{\partial \chi^2},$$ solve for the probability density

function, ψ. Since ψ is exclusively a function of χ we note that

$$h(\chi) = N\left[\frac{\sigma^2}{2} \frac{\partial^2 \phi}{\partial t^2} + \phi\right]$$ must, exclusively, be a function of χ only,

and, $\dfrac{\sigma^2}{2} \dfrac{\partial^3 \phi}{\partial \tau^3} + \dfrac{\partial \phi}{\partial \tau} = 0 \;\; \forall_{\chi}$ constrains the functional forms of

allowed energy functions to the family of solutions described above. If $\phi(\chi, \tau) = -g(\chi)[1 - \cos\{\lambda(\chi - \tau)\}]$ then $\lambda = \sigma^{-\frac{1}{2}}\sqrt{2}$, and $h(\chi) = -g(\chi)$. Starting with the functional form $\psi(\chi) = A\,e^{\lambda(x)} + B\,e^{-\lambda(x)}$, and knowing that $\psi(\tau)$ is a probability density function in defined in terms of centralized coordinates the solution is

$$\psi(\tau) = A\,e^{\int^{\tau} \sqrt{-h(\xi)}d\xi} + B\,e^{-\int^{\tau} \sqrt{-h(\xi)}d\xi}, \text{ where}$$

$$A = \rho B \; ; \; B = \left[\rho \int_{-\infty}^{\infty} e^{\int^{\chi} \sqrt{-h(\xi)}\, d\xi} \, d\chi + \int_{-\infty}^{\infty} e^{-\int^{\chi} \sqrt{-h(\xi)}\, d\xi} \, d\chi \right]^{-1} \; ;$$

$$and, \; \rho = e^{-2\int^{\chi} \sqrt{-h(\xi)}\, d\xi} \Big|_{\chi = \chi_0} ,$$

$$where \quad \frac{\partial \psi}{\partial \chi} = 0 \; at \; \chi = \chi_0$$

For example, if $g(x) = - k\, x^2$ the resulting distribution is normal with a standard deviation of $\sigma = k^{-\frac{1}{4}}$, if $g(x)$ is a constant the resultant distribution is uniform with probability zero everywhere, and if $g(x) = -k\, x^{-2}$, the resultant distribution when $k > 1$ and $x > 1$ is th Cauchy distribution, $(1 - k)\, x^{-k}$.

A theory of human interaction as dynamic interaction between individuals in attribute space has been posited. The mathematical modeling of this theory has resulted in a mechanism for deriving the energy function from he attribute distribution function. A process for determining the functional form of the attribute distribution function from a hypothesized energy model has also been developed. The remainder of this document will describe a process for conducting *a qualitative study* to validate this theory as well as provide for extending the theory. A proposed instrument is contained in the Appendix A of this proposal.

Data Collection Technique

Osgood, Succi & Tannenbaum (1971) and others (Mosier, 1941; Noble, 1952; Ogden & Richards, 1923; Osgood, 1941, 1946, 1948, 1952, 1953, 1956; Osgood & Luria, 1954; Osgood & Sebeok, 1952; Osgood & Tannenbaum, 1955; Reaves, 1954; Remmers, 1954; Remmers & Silence, 1934; Riess, 1940, 1946; Rowon, 1954; Stagner & Osgood, 1946; Succi, 1952; Tannenbaum, 1953, 1955, 1956) have determined that structure of belief system (attitudes) space is three dimensional (Evaluation, Potency, and Activity). Attitudes on each dimension is assessed using a *Semantic Differential Scale* where subjects are asked to indicate their feelings on a seven point scale for each of a set of bipolar adjective pairs associated with each dimension. A proposed instrument is contained in Appendix B. In each dimension. A proposed instrument is contained in Appendix B. In addition to assessing student attitudes toward a particular subject, each student should be asked to indicate their strength of belief which will be interpreted as an energy index as well as the extent to which they feel influenced by others in their class as an alternative energy index. These indicators are obtained for each of three semantic dimensions.

Students should be asked to rate the influence that each individual in a class may have upon them as well as their seating position in the classroom. This data will allow for detailed study of the impact of individuals at various affective positions upon others at other affective locations. The data will also provide a means for studying migration patterns of individuals within groups in terms of seating patterns and attribute positions of individuals in neighborhoods about the migrating students' physical and affective position.

The instrument should be administered at the beginning and end of each class session, taking no more than five minutes at the beginning and five minutes at the end of each period. For each individual let x^i, E^i be the attitude scale and energy scores on occasion i and let t^i be the time of the i-th. occasion from the beginning of this research in hours. The velocity, time rate of change, for a particular individual, at time $t^{k,i} = \frac{1}{2}(t^k + t^i)$, can be calculated by $v^{k,j} = (x^k - x^i)/(t^k - t^i)$, and the position and energies at that time by $x^{k,i} = \frac{1}{2}[x^k + x^i]$, and $E^{k,i} = \frac{1}{2}[E^k + E^i]$. Over one semester at least thirty observations can be made over time intervals ranging between one class period, an interclass session interval, and the entire semester, approximately, $\frac{1}{2}(30)(29)$, or 435, velocity, speed, energy, and position values will be calculated for each individual.

Appendix A

Constructing a Preliminary Item Bank

CONSTRUCTING A PRELIMINARY
ITEM BANK

Three assessment paradigms were outlined in the previous chapter: norm referenced, criterion referenced, and item response theories. Although each type of test is based on different psychometric models, the tests themselves appear the same. One will not be able to decide from looking at an assessment, which kind it is. All three types are composed of assessment events that are functionally the same. Each psychometric model assumes that there exists a preliminary set of assessment events, constructed according to specified guidelines. Once a preliminary item bank is generated, the items are administered to a representative sample of learners. The data obtained from the preliminary sample is then analyzed to find those events for which students respond according to the desired psychometric model. The final event bank consists of those events that correspond to the desired psychometric model.

This chapter describes a procedure for constructing the preliminary item bank. The chapter is composed of four main sections. A measure-men philosophy underlies the event bank construction (Chi, Glaser & Rees, 1982; Frederiksen, 1980, 1986; Greeno, 1973; Hunt, Lunneborg, & Lewis, 1975; Hunt, Frost, & Lunneborg, 1973; Pellegreno, & Glaser, 1979, 1980; Sternberg, 1977). The nature of that philosophy will be outlined in the first section, *Nature of Measurement.* That philosophy implies the existence of a well defined behavior domain. The nature of developmental objectives is described in the second section. Event banks are defined by a set of specifications. The structure of those specifications will be described. The fourth and final section presents guidelines for constructing events.

THE NATURE OF MEASUREMENT

The first problem in designing any measurement instrument or event bank is specifying what is to be measured. A clear definition of the attribute that is to be measured must exist. The definition makes the subtle assumption that the attribute exists somewhere other than in the mind of the person constructing the instrument. The word "exist" is used to mean that there is agreement among content experts that particular events are indicative of what they are willing to call a particular behavior. Remember, the sciences of psychology, physics, mathematics, and zoology as well as all arts and humanities are only constructs (languages) used by people in their fields to define themselves.

Consider the following set of measurements. The measurements were obtained from ten individuals relative to two variables (x, y) over a three month period.

SUBJECT	X	Y	SUBJECT	X	Y
1	3	6	6	31	29
2	1	3	7	43	41
3	4	5	8	57	53
4	9	10	9	73	68
5	16	15	10	91	85

By blind application of statistical formulae, the mean and standard deviation for each variable (X=32.8, S_x=30.5, Y=31.5, S_y=27.5) and the correlation coefficient between the two variables (0.98) can be calculated. These results suggest that the two averages are not different (t=0.04; df=1; p>0.99) and that the variables are linearly related (r=0.98; p<0.05). Although the data conveys a great deal of information about the two variables, it yields no substantive information.

Observations that are not related to a substantive domain are merely numbers; and, despite what statistical treatment is applied to those numbers, the results apply only to those particular numbers and have no extrinsic nor intrinsic value. The first task of the measurement specialist, when constructing an assessment, is to precisely define the domain for which measurements are to be obtained. A technique by which the specification of an educational domain can be derived will be discussed later in this chapter.

Any assessment is a means by which information is gathered for making some inference. *Any measurement, assessment, or evaluation is a relation between one or more qualitative observations and a set of numbers.* The numbers are equivalent to verbal representations of the qualitative events.

Assessments need not be dichotomous (correct/incorrect). They can be a judgement of proficiency. A judgement (test, assessment, or otherwise), to have value, must be credible. To be credible, a judgement should be similar regardless of the process used to obtain that judgement as well as the individuals who perform the assessment. The process of attaining credible assessments involve the use of assessment paradigms which include precise specification of the elements upon which the assessment and, ultimately, the judgement is based. These paradigms are often checklists related to the behavior specification of interest. Process or product assessment is decomposable into dichotomous events whose evaluation, through some algorithm, results in an index on a continuum of proficiency.

MEASUREMENTS AS OBSERVATIONS

What occurs when an assessment is administered? Despite the nature of the assessment (performance, multiple choice, etc.), the subject is presented with a situation. That situation may ask for a written solution to a problem, a selection of one of a set of alternative solutions, or the performance of a particular task. Action by the respondent is required. For the purpose of this volume, an assessment event is considered a stimulus to action. The nature of that action may be recall, the application of a given technique (e.g., solution of a mathematical equation), the application of some higher order skill, or a combination. An event is selected if it is decided that it will elicit the particular behavioral processes that the investigator is interested in observing.

The response of a subject to an event is considered either correct or incorrect. The decision of whether a given response is correct is decided based on a decision rule established a priori by the person who constructed that event. If the response to the stimulus event corresponds to what has been predetermined to be "correct," it is inferred that the behavioral process of interest was successfully executed. If the response is not "correct," it is inferred that the behavioral process of interest was not successfully executed.

In summary, when a subject is introduced to a particular assessment event it is assumed that the response is an indication of the degree to which the subject can successfully execute a particular set of behavioral processes. The cognitive process assumed to be elicited may be prerequisite to some learning task in which the subject may be involved in the future (i.e., aptitude test item); previously learned (i.e., achievement test item); or, involve forming a summative belief or value concerning a particular event or object (i.e., an attitude item).

MEASUREMENTS AS CONSTRUCT
MANIFESTATIONS

Have you ever seen love, hate, fear, gravity, speed, heat, electrons, efficiency, organizational loyalty, or a good job? Each of these words represent a particular notational scheme used to communicate what is called a *latent construct*. A construct is a global term that can be used for any category of events that we wish to believe are, in some way, related. A construct is an organizational scheme by which a particular set of events are classified as being associated with each other to a greater extent than they are individually and collectively related to events classified as belonging to another construct. In the literature, the concept of a construct is related to a factor (Harman, 1970; Mulaik, 1972; Pedhazur & Schmelkin, 1991; Rummel, 1970), cluster (Anderberg, 1973; Hartigan, 1975; Van Ryzin, 1977), or, more recently, a latent construct (Hambleton, Swaminathan, & Rogers, 1991; Hambleton & Zaal, 1991; Lord, 1980; Lord, & Novick, 1977; Rasch, 1988).

Why is a construct latent? A construct is considered to be an entity which can not be directly observed. The existence of a construct is inferred from what is called its manifestations. Manifestations are observable events which occur simultaneously so frequently that it is inferred that there exists some unobserved "cause." That "cause" is the latent construct and the observed events are the manifestations assumed to be "caused" by the existence of that latent construct. Any construct is a term, category, or heading by which we choose to organize a particular set of events. A construct is a label for a class of events. The construct is a invention of the mind. Whether it is directly observable has no consequence to its applicability in developing a theory (mental construct) about events. Humans are unique in that they define reality more in terms of mental objects than sensory objects.

Two objects, in vacuum, tend to move toward each other. A pedantic individual would say that all that can be said about the situation is that there are two objects that have changed their positions relative to some observer. The scholar attempts to explain observations by formulating a generalized theory which extends beyond the immediate (observed) events. The existence of a gravitational field acting between and on the objects is formulated, the logical consequences determined, and tested.

A latent construct is a part of a theory of event spaces. Latent trait theory is a method of developing and testing a theory about the relationships between and among attributes (human or otherwise) which may or may not be observable but explain what man is willing to observe at the time.

Our eyes can not see, nor our ears hear, what our mind can not fathom. Latent trait theory is a methodology for developing a theory of events and relationships which occur in *psychological space*. Whether or not these theories are "real" is indeterminable. Whether or not events in psychological or knowledge spaces actually "cause" events to occur in existential, manifest, observational, or perceptual space is also neither determinable nor relevant. What is relevant, is that man lives in a psychological space, interpreting existential events in terms of the lexicon and language of that space, and a theory of "reality" is a theory of man and his psychological space. A theory of "reality" is a theory of human knowledge structure and what theorists are is willing to believe about that structure.

The responses to assessment events are interpreted to be manifestations of certain psychological processes. The psychological processes are not observable and reside in a psychological or *knowledge space*. The presence and strength of entities in the psychological or knowledge space is reflected through the strengths or existence of certain events which are agreed upon to be manifestations of the space of latent constructs.

Figure A.1:
The Assessment Scenario

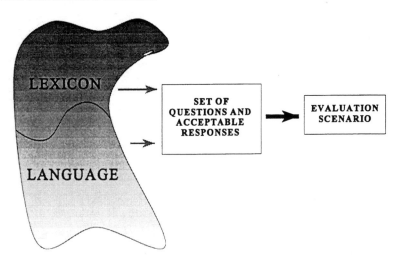

Measurements as Estimates

There are many possible qualitative events associated with a particular behavioral process. For example, assume that the particular behavioral process of interest is that when presented with *two* single digit numbers, the subject will correctly recall their sum. There are only 100 possible events associated with that process. On the other hand, if the process of interest is that when presented with two or more single digit numbers, the subject will correctly generate their sum, there are an infinite number of possible events. Most behavioral processes that are of substantive interest are associated with very large or infinite numbers of qualitative events.

The response of a particular subject to a specific event is an indicator of how that subject will respond to the other events in the behavior range. However, the response to only one event from the domain is a crude estimate of how a subject would respond to all events in the domain. Responses to two, three, or more events sampled from a domain result in successively better approximations. Frequently, an investigator cannot present the subject with every event associated with a particular behavioral process. A subject is presented with a finite set of events sampled from, and representative of the set of all events associated with the behavioral process of interest. In this sense, the result obtained from the use of any behavioral measurement device is at best an *estimate*.

Measurements are always with respect to a particular range of content. Measurements map a domain of qualitative events onto a set of numbers. Measurements are infallible mappings from a range of events to a domain of numbers. Measurements are infallible because they are definitions-operationalizations including a subset of all events in the domain and a particular algorithm for mapping events on to the domain of numbers. The *validity* of a measurement is the extent to which the subset of events represent the entire range of events, and the extent to which the results of the application of a particular scoring algorithm reflect relationships between events in the domain. The *reliability* of a measurement is the extent to which a particular number (assessment score) reflects an individual's position in the space of qualitative events.

Any knowledge base is composed of two parts. One part is the lexicon, corpus, or set of terms used by that knowledge base. For example, biology uses a particular vocabulary which is distinct and different from Syrian literature and Hispanic culture. The lexicon is a dictionary, a set of terms or objects, which, in part, defines the content. The elements of the lexicon are called "atoms" of knowledge. Their definitions are whatever the content specialists are willing to accept. The mind does not represent knowledge as words. The knowledge base of icons are representable as words only for communication.

Figure A.2:
The Learning/assessment Event

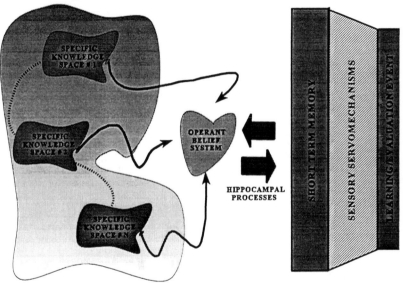

The observation that "atoms" of knowledge are icons, not words, has significant educational as well as assessment implications. A subject that can not communicate in the vocabulary of a particular knowledge base may be well aware of the content. That subject may be conversant in the use of a different set of terms (language); Arabic and Hindu speaking mathematicians at the same conference. Therefore, an incorrect response is only an implication, not an inference, of the lack of knowledge. Likewise, a correct response is necessary but not sufficient for inferring competence. Words are only a communication vehicle by which competence is communicated, not a direct affirmation of competence (see figure A.1).

Figure A.3:
The Thematic Interface

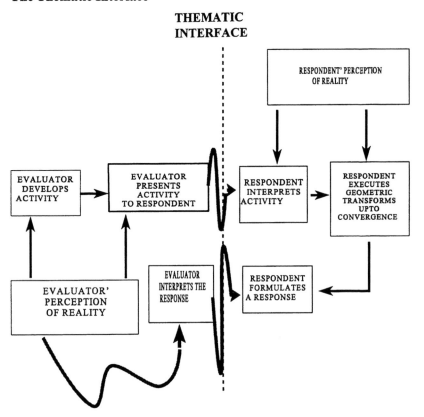

The second element of a knowledge system is the language itself. The language, distinct from the vocabulary, defines the set of allowed relations between lexical elements. The language is the mechanism by which the content expert ascertains "truth" or "fact." If it is posited that two elements, or a chain of lexical elements, are true and no allowed linguistic transformation of the atoms results in that chain, the expert concludes that the proposition is false. The lexicon is useful for determining whether a particular knowledge space is applicable to a particular situation. It is via the language that accepted reality or "truth" is determined. We should recognize that "truth" varies between individuals, groups, geographies, and times. For lexical clarity, we will no longer use the word "truth." We will define a fact as an event that, after knowledge base transformations, an individual is willing to assume exists. Later, we will see that a fact can be represented as a covariant or contravariant tensor of the knowledge space.

A *knowledge space* is an individual's perception of reality with respect to a particular range of content. There are different microworlds (Minsky, 1975), or "realities," which have important assessment implications. First, there is the individual's perception of reality. There is a perception of reality, *local reality,* held by a group defined by associational or geographic boundaries. There is the *event dependent reality* held by content area "experts" or societies at a particular time. There is an individual perception of reality held by the evaluator or a local reality held by a group of assessors, or curriculum developers. A knowledge space is an event dependent entity whose lexicon and language are organic (growing) and dynamic (changing) entities.

Furthermore, most events are not unitary in that they require the use of many different knowledge spaces. "Many test questions require that a person have some level of ability in more than one skill area in order to answer the questions correctly. Mathematics story problems are a common example of this type of question. Reading, problem solving, and computational abilities may be required to solve such problems." (Rechase & McKinley, 1991, p. 25). The learning/assessment/evaluation event requires the learner/assessee to identify the applicable knowledge spaces, construct an operant belief system consisting of applicable lexicons and languages, apply appropriate lexical transformations to the characteristics of the learning/assessment event until a stable conclusion is reached (Bobrow & Norman, 1975; Chi, Feltovich, & Glaser, 1981; Greeno, 1977; Heller & Greeno, 1979; Larkin, McDermott, Simon, & Simon, 1980).

It is the function of the curriculum developer to insure that the local reality in his/her content area or region is reflected in the curriculum. The functions of the assessor are to insure that his/her individual reality reflects the collective reality of the curriculum, and that the assessment paradigm reflects that collective reality. The assessment act is the event by which the assessor reports the extent to which a particular individual's reality space reflects the expectations defined by the collective reality. i.e. the extent to which an individual's knowledge space is isomorphic to the collective knowledge space in terms of both form and content.

It is important to identify events which occur in the act of assessment (see figure A.3). The evaluator establishes an individual perception of the knowledge base of interest. That perception consists of precise definitions of the knowledge space in terms of both vocabulary and lexical relationships. Based upon the evaluator's knowledge space, s/he develops an activity which s/he believes reflects the knowledge space and presents that activity to the respondent. Based upon elements which are in common between the activity and the individual's perception of reality the learner/assessee interprets the assessment/learning activity by constructing an operant reality (knowledge) space consisting of lexical atoms and a language related to atoms in common between the activity and the individual's collective knowledge. By applying transformations in the operant knowledge base on the corpus of the operant knowledge base, the operant reality space is expanded and contracted by the addition of related atoms and lexical transformations related to the operant atoms and eliminating those atoms and transformations inconsistent with atoms in common between the assessment/learning activity and the individual's collective knowledge space. This process continues until geometric and algebraic convergence occurs. If convergence does not occur, anxiety results, search algorithms executed, and after some amount of time frustration results and the learner/assessee "gives up."

When conceptual convergence occurs, the assessee/learner translates that convergence into the language of the assessor. The assessor, using his/her perception of reality, following a predefined algorithmic process, interprets the response. The assessor infers the structure of the assessee-learner's knowledge space from the assessee/learner's response and develops a model in the assessor's mind of what he/she perceives as the structure of the assessee/learner's knowledge space. The assessor compares the perceived structure of the assessee/learner's knowledge space with the structure and form of the collective knowledge space and reports the degree of concordance.

Assessment and learning relies on perceptions of reality. Assessment results as well as the rate at which learning progresses is a function of the degrees of concordance between different knowledge spaces. The most fundamental as well as important curriculum development, assessment, evaluation or measurement act is the precise definition of the *form and structure* of the desired knowledge space or belief system.

The Behavioral Continuum

If a diverse group of subjects react to a representative sample of events sampled from a behavior range, an equally diverse set of responses is expected. Different subjects possess varying degrees of proficiency. The response of a particular subject to all events associated with a particular behavioral process is not dichotomous (yes/no, success/failure, etc.). Responses to a set of events reflect a *degree of proficiency or extent of belief.* The response is assessed on a continuum of proficiency or attitude. In this sense, a behavioral process is representable in one dimension and called "unidimensional." No scale is assumed to underlie the continuum. A subject may receive a score of 0 or 1 or any possible intermediate score, e.g., .87, .72, $1/\pi$, -1.32 or 279.3. Many score reporting schemes are possible.

What is assumed, however, is that there is *one and only one* continuum underlying the behavioral process. Otherwise, a single index representative of a complex set of mutually exclusive behavioral continua will confound the interpretation of that index. For example, a single index designed to estimate a person's arithmetic *and* dancing ability is, of itself, not meaningful and is not an indication of *either* arithmetic or dancing abilities. Colloquially, a single index designed to address a multitude of talents is very similar to comparing apples and reindeer.

In summary, it was pointed out that assessment events elicit a particular behavioral response. The response is an indication of the degree to which the assessor is willing to believe that the underlying behavioral process was successfully executed. An assessment protocol is composed of a finite sample of events representative of the entire range of possible events associated with a particular behavioral process. The assessment result is an estimate of how well a subject can execute the language of the knowledge space over the entire domain of atomic sequences (events). The estimated performance is assumed to reflect proficiency on a unique continuum underlying the behavioral process.

This interpretation of an assessment score places restrictions and constraints on the events composing that assessment. The quality of any estimate is only as good as the sampling of items used to obtain that estimate. The remainder of this chapter presents a technique for constructing the specifications for an initial event bank and for constructing assessment events.

DEVELOPMENTAL OBJECTIVES

As previously stated, the first step of the mental measurement process is to define the behavioral process (Bloom, 1968, 1976; Haladyna & Roid, 1983; Hambleton, 1974; Keller, 1968; Klaosmeier, Rossmiller, & Sally, 1977). The definition of behavior is not unique to measurement (Roid & Haladyna, 1982; Shoemaker, 1975; Wolfeck, Ellis, Richards, Wood, & Merrill, 1978). Historically, the specification and definition of behavior is the first step in curriculum development (Bloom, Englehart, Furst, Hill & Krathwohl, 1956; Bobbit, 1912, 1918, 1922, 1924, 1926, 1934, 1937, 1948; Bransford, Nitsche & Franks, 1977; Broudy, 1977; Courtis, 1916a, 1916b; Morrison, 1938; Payette, 1969; Rist, 1990; Scandura, 1966; 1973, 1976, 1977; Suppes, 1964; Tyler, 1930, 1942, 1948, 1949, 1950, 1951, 1953, 1959, 1964a, 1964b; Thorndike, 1911, 1912). Skinner (1958) capitalized on the industrial psychology in education movement prevalent since the 1880s by espousing the careful sequencing of instructional materials in very small steps, frequent positive reinforcement, and the old concept of self paced learning. To educators unfamiliar with the literature and history of their field, this was, as Popham (1987) observed, "revolutionary and exciting." An important factor in the behavioral objective movement was Mager's (1962) workbook *Preparing Objectives for Programmed Instruction.* The process has found a great deal of success in the realm of programmed instruction (Flanagan, 1967, 1969; Glaser, 1968; Glaser & Nitko, 1970, 1971; Lindvall & Cox, 1969; Nitko, 1968; Roudabush & Ross, 1971; Suppes, 1964). The goal of instructional design is to understand and improve methods of instruction by deciding which methods of instruction should be used under given conditions to bring about the desired curricula goal (Van Patten, Chao, & Reigeluth, 1986).

Many texts are devoted to the specification of objectives (Baker & Popham, 1973; Popham & Baker, 1970a, 1970b; Krathwohl & Payne, 1971; Mager, 1962). The distinction between curriculum and instruction is described in Chapter 8. The purpose of this section is not to describe the process of formulating educational objectives. The intent of this section is to present an overview of the large range of specificity which educational objectives can assume and the use of objectives in constructing assessments.

Curriculum objectives are designed to satisfy at least three goals:

1. Assist curriculum developers in planning for effective attainment of organizational goals;

2. Provide a clear basis for determining whether the organizational goal has been achieved; and,

3. Provide information in sufficient detail as to permit for the revision of curricula and paradigms.

In essence, instructional objectives should specifically delineate the end products of the instructional process. Curricula objectives, on the other hand, specify how attainment of organizational goals will be achieved and evaluated. An instructional objective can take on various degrees of specificity. The highest degree of specificity is at the individual problem level. For example, the student will be able to solve the problem "3 + 5 = ?" and obtain the correct sum "8". An instructional objective of less specificity is: the student will calculate the sum of any two positive integers less than ten, where carrying is not an issue, with 80% accuracy. An objective with considerably less precision would be: a student will be able to perform one digit addition of integers with 80% accuracy.

If educational objectives are defined for each assessment event, an infinite number of objectives are possible. Curriculum scholars often suggest organizing objectives into modules or curriculum units (Flanagan, 1967, 1969; Glazer & Nitko, 1970, 1971; Nitko, 1968; Hashway, 1988, 1990). Each unit or module represents a collection of learning objectives. The educational objectives of a module define the behavioral domain of the module. For example, within the domain of operations with whole numbers, a module could be defined by the objective: given two or more positive integers, the student will correctly form the sum, difference, and quotient. This module could then be further subdivided into subsidiary modules such as given any two one digit positive integers, the student will correctly form the sum.

Once the objectives for a module are defined, the assessment developer should specify exemplary events for each objective. These exemplary events help define the range of events from which assessment events will be sampled to assess modular proficiency.

We have seen that curriculum units may be effectively established in terms of collections of behavioral objectives closely associated with the same learning domain. Certain objectives may be associated with more than one curriculum module. In addition, more than one module may compose a curriculum sequence. One event bank may be required to serve many programs or a single program with many modules. The objective and module associations are described by a list of specifications that define the characteristics of an event bank. The process by which such a list of specifications is generated is described below.

Objective

Module	1	2	3	4	5	6	7	8	9	10	Total
1	5	0	2	4	8	2	0	0	2	2	25
2	0	6	10	0	2	0	0	5	4	4	31
3	3	3	2	1	1	6	6	10	6	6	49
Total	8	9	14	5	11	8	6	15	12	12	105

Specifying the event domain. The specifications for an event bank involve a module by objectives matrix. The modules are listed on the vertical stem of the matrix. The objectives spanned by the events in the bank are listed on the horizontal stem of the matrix. For example, if an event bank is to span three modules and ten objectives, the specification matrix might be:
The numbers in the matrix are the relative proportion of the total number of events in the bank assigned to each module. For example, 2% of the events are assigned to objective 3 and module 1 while 10% are assigned to a combination of objective 3 and module 2. Objective 3 is considered more important for the mastery of module 2 than mastery of module 1. The purpose of a specification matrix is to define the relationships between events, objectives and modules. The matrix informs the assessment protocol developers of the number of events that must be generated for each objective. For example, in the situation described above, 14% of the events in the bank must correspond to objective 3 and 5% of the events must correspond to objective 4.

Although, perhaps, not ideally, many educational events are defined in terms of test items. The remainder of this chapter discusses the construction of those items.

GUIDELINES FOR CONSTRUCTING
TEST ITEMS

It has been pointed out that the psychometric procedures for screening test items and test scores were developed slowly. The techniques for item writing were developed at an even slower rate.

An item bank constructed in this manner allows a great deal of flexibility in assessment construction. For any particular module, the constructor can estimate the student's level of proficiency relative to a particular objective by choosing at random from the items corresponding to that objective. Proficiency in an entire module can be estimated by first deciding, from the matrix, the relative importance of each objective. Then, a number of test items, determined by the number in the matrix, is sampled at random from the bank of items corresponding to the objective. To estimate proficiency in an entire sequence of modules and for all objectives, the test constructor can generate a sampling of all items in the bank using the relative proportions in the matrix. For example, referring to the matrix, the test constructor may wish to estimate proficiency for objective 2 in module 3. S/he can randomly sample three of the items from the total of nine related to objective 2.

The most significant advance in item writing has been called "item forms" (Bormuth, 1970). Item forms are essentially item formats with certain missing elements, such as the particular numbers of an arithmetic problem. Those missing elements are supplied (i.e., computer generated) by a selection algorithm.

Although some enhancements to item writing have emerged, the general "do's and don'ts" have not changed since Ruch proposed them in 1929 (cf. Adkins & Preinoff, 1947; Durost & Prescott, 1962; Ebel, 1965; Geberich, 1956; Hawkes, Lindquest & Mann, 1936; Travers, 1950; Wesman, 1971; Womer, 1966; Wood, 1960). Those readers who are interested in a more comprehensive treatment of test item writing are referred to the previously cited volumes and articles. A particularly comprehensive synopsis can be found in Wesman (1971).

From this review of the nature of assessment, two major points emerge which are of special value to the developmental measurement specialist.

First, specifying educational objectives is fundamental to assessment event and curriculum development. Second, the use of a module by objective matrix can be very helpful in specifying the characteristics of a assessment event bank.

The assessment specialist, following this outline, can pretest events with a sample of students. The purpose of pretesting is to determine possible sources of ambiguity, poor distractors, and events which are responded to in an unusual fashion. Pretesting also serves to decide which events correspond to the psychometric properties of the desired model. The next section will describe various item formats and the remaining chapters will be devoted to a study of how event data can be used to improve event quality and determining which events satisfy a particular psychometric model.

Do's and Don't of Item Writing

1. Use correct forms of expression, grammar, spelling, punctuation, and capitalization. Otherwise, the reader will be distracted from the original problem situation. Use words which have precise meanings. Imprecise words confuse the reader and open the item to degrees of generality beyond that intended by the item writer.
2. Avoid the use of double negatives. The double negative results in confusion with the original intent of the question.
3. Avoid "trick," or puzzle questions. These questions tap the ability of the student to second guess the examiner, rather than test specific knowledge.
4. Avoid items that are partly true and partly false. Provide an item for which competent critics can agree on a best answer.
5. Avoid long sentences with many dependent or modifying clauses. Such sentences obscure the intent of the item.
6. Avoid words that prejudice replies. For example, if a key word in the stimulus is singular the possible responses should also be singular.
7. Test items are independent. The answer to one test item should not suggest the answer to another item.
8. For tests other than general ability types, avoid general intelligence or general knowledge items. Items should tap specific instructional objectives. A student should not be able to reason the correct response to the item without prior instruction.
9. Each item should elicit a single behavioral process and call for a

single idea.
10. Each of the possible responses should have equal plausibility. If one or more possible responses have less credibility than the others, the probability of correct response due to chance guessing is increased.

Some Item Formats

Writing Good Items. As with all types of writing and other work, an understanding of the subject is prerequisite to writing good events or items. The value system of the event writer must be grounded in a well developed theory of learning including the physiological, educational, and developmental characteristics of the learner. The writer needs to have good communication skills as well as be a technician with imagination, ingenuity, inventiveness, and judgement. Writers also tend to have skills focused on items at a particular taxonomic level; proficiency in writing at the knowledge level does not imply proficiency at other levels.

The nature of event concepts stem from the assessment plan. An assessment plan outlines the areas to be covered indicators of the relative emphasis each area should receive, but does not specify the content and purpose of each individual assessment event. Events must be appropriate for the assessment plan and those who will be assessed. The event must be important (Will it discriminate between attainment levels?) and useful (Can it be administered in an appropriate space/time?).

Form and Applicability of Events

There are several forms of items and within each form there are several varieties. The arrangement of words, phrases, sentences, or symbols determine the form. There are pitfalls with each form of assessment item. The writer must understand what each form can and can not assess, as well as the situations in which that form can and cannot be profitably used.

Short answer form. The short answer is commonly called "fill in the blank". It has been suggested that the short answer format is superior to the multiple response format; the ability to produce a correct response as opposed to selecting a response may represent a higher level of attainment. This argument is often accepted at face value as being unchallengeable and unassailable. It is reasonable to believe that a student who knows a fact and can produce it without clues should also be able to recognize the fact when presented in a multiple choice form, and the opposite may not be true. Other conditions are not equal. The nature of the function being measured and the skill with which the events are constructed in practice usually moderate the format decision.

It is more difficult to write a free response item than a multiple response item for skills above the recall level. Single response events are useful for assessing events where the assessee can identify *exactly* what response is expected and format that response in terms of a single word, name, symbol, or sign. When either the attribute to be assessed is not at the knowledge level or the appropriate response is not merely a single character or phrase, the multiple response format is the appropriate assessment format.

There are three varieties of the short answer format, the question, completion, and identification (association) variety.

The Question Variety

Who edited the 2nd edition of *Educational Measurement?*
   (Robert L. Thorndike)

In what year did Columbus discover America?
   (1492)

The Completion Variety

(Eli Whitney) invented the cotton gin.

Type I diabetes is characterized by catabolism and the development of ketosis in the absence of insulin replacement therapy.

The Identification or Association Variety

After each state, write its capital and largest city.

State	Capitol	Largest City
Texas	Austin	Houston
Oklahoma	Oklahoma City	Oklahoma City
Louisiana	Baton Rouge	New Orleans

Being able to develop a test item in free response form so that a student knows exactly what response is expected is difficult because the expected response should be a single word, a name, a symbol, a sign, etc. Do not lift statements verbatim from context and attempt to use them as short answer items. Ambiguity in the item and variations in the answers are almost certain to result from this procedure. Make the question, or the directions, explicit and avoid indefinite questions. If you want to elicit a response that *Abraham Lincoln was the 16th President of the United States,* then ask the question in a manner that will result in the appropriate response. Do not build ambiguity into the stem by asking *Who was Abraham Lincoln?* The responses to this question could vary greatly (President of the United States, great orator, lawyer from Illinois, etc.). All are correct responses, but not if you wanted the response, *16th President.*

Alternate Choice Forms. Alternate choice forms are choice items in which only one of the possible alternatives is explicitly stated. A true/false item consists of a statement that is to be judged as being either true or false. A popular variant is the *alternate choice variety.* The right/wrong, yes/no, cluster, and correction varieties are conceptually equivalent.

True/False variety. Declarative statements that are either true or false compose this variety.

> The gravitational pull of the moon is one of the causes of rising and ebbing of the tides: (T)   F

The Wrong/Right variety. A sentence, equation, or expression that is to be marked right/wrong depending on whether it is correctly or incorrectly written compose this variety.

> Hoping to make a difference, many went with their children to the school board to protest the dress code.   (R)   W

The Yes/No variety. Direct questions that are to be answered by a yes/no response compose this variety.

> Did the Financial Accounting Standards Board precede the Accounting Principles Board?   Yes   (No)

The Cluster variety. This variety is composed of an incomplete stem with several suggested completions, each is to be judged true/false.

To increase owner's equity:
a.	debit cash and credit accounts receivable.	T	(F)
b.	debit cash and credit sales.	(T)	F
c.	debit cash and credit owner's investment.	(T)	F
d.	credit cash and debit owner's drawing.	T	(F)

The Correction variety. The examinee is directed to make every false statement a true statement by suggesting a substitute for the underlined word. This variety is composed of a selection of responses and the supplying of responses.

The invention of the automatic cotton picker drastically affected migrant farm workers in the South during the 19th century. (20th)

or

Manifestations of hyperglycemia include slurred speech.
A. increased thirst.   A.
B. shaky feeling and dizziness.
C. hunger.

Good true/false items are difficult to prepare. Statements presented out of context lose meaning and can be ambiguous, and those that do not lose meaning are likely to measure trivia. Most true/false items assess memory for facts. The requirement that a response be absolute tends to limit applicability and validity of this event format.

Multiple response formats. This format has often been used to assess verbal association and simple facts. It can be used to assess complex abilities and fundamental understandings. The rules for writing good multiple response events are basic in concept but require experienced writers for implementation. Events should be expressed as clearly as possible using words that have precise meaning while avoiding complex or awkward word arrangements. All qualifications that are needed to provide a reasonable basis for option selection should be included in the stem. Neither non-functional words nor nonessential specifications should be included in either the stem or the responses. An event and the responses should be as accurate as possible. The level of difficulty of the event should be appropriate for the group and purpose for which it is intended.

There are eight different types of multiple choice forms. The item stem and two or more responses.

Correct answer variety. This type of multiple choice is composed of an item stem followed by several responses, one of which is absolutely correct while the others are incorrect.

The cotton gin was invented by:
a.   Singer
(b.)   Whitney
c.   Howe
d.   Stephenson
e.   Fulton

Best answer variety. The examinee is supposed to select the best answer. The stem will be presented with two or more responses, one being the best response.

What is the basic purpose of closing temporary accounts at the end of an accounting cycle.
a.   To prepare the income statement.
(b.)   To prepare the general ledger for the next accounting cycle.
c.   To condense the general ledger.
d.   To prepare the cash flow statement.

Multiple response variety. This type of item calls for more than one correct response. The examinee is instructed to select all the correct responses.
Which of the following are cardinal symptoms of diabetes mellitus?
(a.) Excessive thirst   (b.)   Excessive hunger
(c.) polyuria   (d.)   weight gain

Incomplete statement variety. The item stem consists of a portion of a statement rather than a direct question. The examinee is instructed to complete the statement.

The most widely accepted etiologic theory related to juvenile diabetes states that:

a   the process is poorly understood and no predictions can be made.

(b.)   there is multi factor causation.

c   both parents have a defective gene which is passed on to the child.

d   the disease can be prevented by healthful living habits.

Negative variety. In this type item, the responses include several correct answers and one that is not correct. The examinee is asked to mark the incorrect response. For example:

Which of the following is *not* a cardinal symptom of diabetes mellitus?

a.   Excessive thirst

b.   Excessive hunger

c.   polyuria

(d.)   weight gain

Substitution variety. Well written prose is systematically altered to include errors in spelling, punctuation, word usage, etc. The altered phrases, words, etc. (both the correct and the incorrect), are underlined and numbered. The examinee is instructed to select the phrase (original or altered) that provides the best expression. For example:

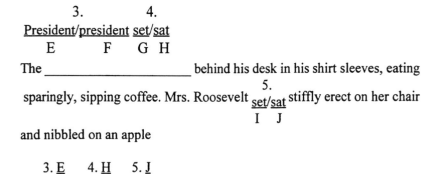

Incomplete alternatives variety. Incomplete or coded alternatives can be used by an item writer if the writer feels that the suggestion of a correct response would make the answer obvious and the item would not function appropriately. The following example would have the examinee think of a one word response to the question and indicate that response on the basis of its first letter.

The name of Roy Roger's horse began with the letter:
a.   A to E
b.   F to J
c.   K to O
(d.)   P to T
e.   U to Z

Combined response variety. First, an item stem is followed by several responses, one or more correct, and second a set of code letters indicating various possible set of codes that designates the correct responses.

In the etiology of juvenile diabetes
(a.)   increased genetic susceptibility is a factor.
b.   excessive dietary sugar intake is a factor.
(c.)   autoimmune response is a factor.
(d.)   there is multi-factor causation.

The Matching Format. This item type consist of a list of premises and a list of responses. There are three types of matching forms: perfect matching, imperfect matching, and statement classification.

If one and only response is to match, it is "perfect matching." There are directions for the examinee to match one of the premises with one of the responses.

B   1. Current Asset   A. withdrawal
C   2. Current Liability   B. cash
D   3. Long Term Asset   C. accounts payable
E   4. Long Term Liab.   D. land
A   5. Owner's Equity   E. mortgage payable

If one response may match more than one stem, it is called "imperfect matching" and the examinee will be given instructions to match the appropriate response with the stem.

A	1. Cash	A.	Current Asset
E	2. Withdrawals	B.	Long Term Asset
B	3. Land	C.	Current Liability
D	4. Mortgage Payable	D.	Long Term Liability
A	5. Accounts Receivable	E.	Owner's Equity
C	6. Accounts Payable	F.	Revenues
G	7. Salary Expense	G.	Expenses
B	8. Copyrights		
E	9. Owner's Investments		
F	10.Sales		

In the form of statement classification, the examinee would receive instructions to determine the instructions on insulin replacement therapy for a person with diabetes mellitus and match the stem to the appropriate response.

B 1. Kevin, an eight year old, is diagnosed with Type I diabetes, the nurse explains to his parents:

C 2. Marcus, a newly diagnosed diabetic, is on a 2600 ADA exchange diet:

A 3. Marcus, should have a goal of:

A. achieving good metabolic control as evidenced by daily blood sugars and period Hgb A1C's.

B. lifelong insulin replacement therapy is required.

C. dividing food and calorie requirements among starch, meat, and fat.

Decisions of which attributes are to be assessed as well as the psychometric paradigm are made in advance based upon curricula paradigms and organizational goals. The events should be constructed to focus on those attributes. If both reasoning and computational attributes are to be assessed, different events or different assessments should be prepared to assess each attribute. After preparing a draft assessment device, the draft is field tested. Predicated upon psychometric analysis of the field test data, events are either eliminated or modified. Event modifications are predicated upon the field test data. There are often two to three times more events in the draft assessment than considered necessary in the final assessment instrument. It is very important that the field test sample represents the population for which the assessment is to be applied. Otherwise, events may be unnecessarily modified or eliminated and other events may not be appropriately modified or retained. The remainder of this volume describes methods for psychometric evaluation of events, reporting of results, use of assessments for individual and program assessment, and approaches to assessment interpretation which incorporate developmental learning theory and results in interpretations relevant to the structure of the psychological space.

Appendix B

Academic Attitude Questionnaire
An Instrument for Studying Developmental Dynamics

ACADEMIC ATTITUDE QUESTIONNAIRE

Professor Robert M. Hashway, Ph.D.
Grambling State University

*The purpose of this study is to assess your feelings concerning **the subject** of this course in terms of three areas: Evaluation, Potency, and Activity. Please make your judgments in terms of **this subject** (not the professor, textbook, assignments, etc.) on the basis of what **this subject** means to you. On each page of this instrument you will find a set of scales upon which you are to rate **this subject** in terms of your feelings toward this subject.   **Here is how you are to use the scales.** If you feel that this subject is very closely related to one end of the scale, place your mark (X) as: FAIR X : : : : : UNFAIR, or FAIR : : : : : X UNFAIR. If your feel that this subject is quite closely related to one or the other end of the scale, place your mark (X) as: FAIR : X : : : : UNFAIR, or FAIR : : : : X : UNFAIR. If you feel that this subject is only slightly related to one side as opposed to the other side (but not neutral), then place your mark (X) as: FAIR : : X : : : UNFAIR, or FAIR : : : X : : UNFAIR. The direction toward which you check depends upon which of the two ends of the scale seem most characteristic of your feelings. If you consider this subject to be neutral, both sides of the scale equally associated with this subject, or if the scale is completely irrelevant, unrelated to this subject, then you should place your mark (X) in the middle space as: FAIR : : : X : : : UNFAIR.*

Sometimes you may feel as though you've seen the same item before. This will not be the case, so do not look back and forth through the items or try to remember how you checked similar items earlier. Make each item a separate and independent judgement.

Work at fairly high speed and do not worry or puzzle over individual items. It is your first impressions, the immediate feelings that we want. On the other hand, please do not be careless, because we want your true impressions.

I. Please indicate your feelings toward this subject on this EVALUATION scale.

GOOD	:_:_:_:_:_:	BAD	MEANINGFUL	:_:_:_:_:_:	MEANINGLESS
KIND	:_:_:_:_:_:	CRUEL	OPTIMISTIC	:_:_:_:_:_:	PESSIMISTIC
SAFE	:_:_:_:_:_:	DANGEROUS	IMPORTANT	:_:_:_:_:_:	UNIMPORTANT
SUPERIOR	:_:_:_:_:_:	INFERIOR	PLEASURABLE	:_:_:_:_:_:	PAINFUL
POSITIVE	:_:_:_:_:_:	NEGATIVE	PERFECT	:_:_:_:_:_:	IMPERFECT

How strong are your EVALUATIVE feelings toward this subject?   Very Weak_:_:_:_:_:_: Very Strong
How strongly do you believe that your EVALUATIVE feelings toward this subject are influenced by others in this class?
                    Very Weakly_:_:_:_:_:_: Very Strongly

II. Please indicate your feelings toward this subject on this POTENCY scale.

HARD	:_:_:_:_:_:	SOFT	SEVERE	:_:_:_:_:_:	LENIENT
STRONG	:_:_:_:_:_:	WEAK	CONSTRAINED	:_:_:_:_:_:	FREE
HEAVY	:_:_:_:_:_:	LIGHT	MASCULINE	:_:_:_:_:_:	FEMININE
LARGE	:_:_:_:_:_:	SMALL	DOMINEERING	:_:_:_:_:_:	LAX
DEEP	:_:_:_:_:_:	SHALLOW	WIDE	:_:_:_:_:_:	NARROW

How strong are your POTENCY feelings toward this subject? Very Weak_:_:_:_:_:_: Very Strong
How strongly do you believe that your POTENCY feelings toward this subject are influenced by others in this class?
                    Very Weakly_:_:_:_:_:_: Very Strongly

III. Please indicate your feelings toward this subject on this ACTIVITY scale.

ACTIVE	:_:_:_:_:_:	PASSIVE	IMPULSIVE	:_:_:_:_:_:	DELIBERATE
HOT	:_:_:_:_:_:	COLD	ENERGETIC	:_:_:_:_:_:	INERT
FAST	:_:_:_:_:_:	SLOW	EMOTIONAL	:_:_:_:_:_:	UNEMOTIONAL
ALIVE	:_:_:_:_:_:	DEAD	MOTIVATED	:_:_:_:_:_:	AIMLESS
VIOLENT	:_:_:_:_:_:	MODERATE	LABORIOUS	:_:_:_:_:_:	EFFORTLESS

How strong are your ACTIVITY feelings toward this subject? Very Weak_:_:_:_:_:_: Very Strong
How strongly do you believe that your ACTIVITY SCALE feelings toward this subject are influenced by others in this class?
                    Very Weakly_:_:_:_:_:_: Very Strongly

IV. The diagram to the right is of the seats in this classroom.

CIRCLE the seat that you are currently occupying.

ROW 4	1 3 5 7 / 2 4 6 8
ROW 3	1 3 5 7 / 2 4 6 8
ROW 2	1 3 5 7 / 2 4 6 8
ROW 1	1 3 5 7 / 2 4 6 8

FRONT OF THE ROOM

V.   Below is a list of

the students in this class. **PLACE AN X TO THE LEFT OF YOUR NAME.** *Then, indicate the extent to which you feel each student may influence your feelings toward this subject.*

xxxxxxxxx *Very Weak* _: : : : : :_ *Very Strong*   xxxxxxxxx *Very Weak* _: : : : : :_ *Very Strong*
xxxxxxxxx *Very Weak* _: : : : : :_ *Very Strong*   xxxxxxxxx *Very Weak* _: : : : : :_ *Very Strong*
xxxxxxxxx *Very Weak* _: : : : : :_ *Very Strong*   xxxxxxxxx *Very Weak* _: : : : : :_ *Very Strong*
xxxxxxxxx *Very Weak* _: : : : : :_ *Very Strong*   xxxxxxxxx *Very Weak* _: : : : : :_ *Very Strong*
xxxxxxxxx *Very Weak* _: : : : : :_ *Very Strong*   xxxxxxxxx *Very Weak* _: : : : : :_ *Very Strong*
xxxxxxxxx *Very Weak* _: : : : : :_ *Very Strong*   xxxxxxxxx *Very Weak* _: : : : : :_ *Very Strong*
xxxxxxxxx *Very Weak* _: : : : : :_ *Very Strong*   xxxxxxxxx *Very Weak* _: : : : : :_ *Very Strong*
xxxxxxxxx *Very Weak* _: : : : : :_ *Very Strong*   xxxxxxxxx *Very Weak* _: : : : : :_ *Very Strong*
xxxxxxxxx *Very Weak* _: : : : : :_ *Very Strong*   xxxxxxxxx *Very Weak* _: : : : : :_ *Very Strong*
xxxxxxxxx *Very Weak* _: : : : : :_ *Very Strong*   xxxxxxxxx *Very Weak* _: : : : : :_ *Very Strong*

Bibliography

Abraham, A. A. (1991). *They came to college? A remedial/developmental profile of first-time freshmen in SREB states. Issues in Higher Education.* Atlanta, GA: Southern Regional Education Board.

Ackerman, T. A. (1991). The use of unidimensional parameter estimates of multidimensional items in adaptive testing. *Applied Psychological Measurement, 15,* 1, 13-24.

Adkins, D.C., & Primoff, E.S. (1947). *Construction and analysis of achievement tests.* Washington, DC: U.S. Government Printing Office, 1947.

Adler, M. J. (1982). *The paideia proposal: An educational Manifesto.* New York: Macmillan.

Ahmann, J.S., & Glock, M.D. (1967). *Evaluating pupil growth* (3rd ed.). Boston: Allyn and Bacon.

Ahmavaara, Y. (1954). The mathematical theory of factorial invariance under selection, *Psychometrika, 19,* 27-38.

Ahmavaara, Y. (1957). On the unified factor theory of mind, *Annales Akademiae Scientiarum Fennicae, 106,* p. 176.

Airasian, P. W. (1971a). The role of evaluation in mastery learning. In J.H. Block (Ed.), *Mastery learning theory and practice* (pp. 77-87). New York: Holt, Rinehart, and Winston.

Airasian, P. W. (1971b). The use off hierarchies in curriculum analysis and instructional planning. *California Journal of Educational Research, 22*(1), 34-41.

Airasian, P. W. (1971c). A study of behaviorally dependent, classroom taught task hierarchies. *Educational Technology Research, 3*(1), 3-12.

Airasian, P. W. (1970). The use of hierarchies in the analysis and planning of chemistry instruction. *Science Education, 54*(1), 91-95.

Airasian, P. W., Kellaghan, T., & Madaus, G.F. (1975, October). *The consequences of introducing educational testing: A societal experiment: Site visit report to the funding agencies.* Dublin, Ireland: St. Patrick's College. Unpublished manuscript.

Airasian, P. W., & Madaus, G. F. (1976, July). *A study of the sensitivity of school and program effectiveness measures.* Report submitted to the Carnegie Corporation of New York.

Airasian, P. W., & Madaus, G. F. (1973). *Proposal to investigate the sensitivity of criterion variables used in program evaluation and policy research and a proposed replication of the Coleman Study in Ireland and England.* Funded by the Carnegie Corporation of New York.

Airasian, P. W., & Madaus, G. F. (1972). Criterion-referenced testing in the classroom. *Measurement in Education, 4*(3), 1-8.

Alderman, D. L., Swinton, S. S., & Braswell, J. S. (1979). Assessing basic arithmetic skills and understanding across curricula: Computer-assisted instruction and compensatory education, *The journal of children's mathematical behavior, 2,* 3-28.

Alexander, H. W. (1947). The estimation of reliability when several trials are available. *Psychometrika, 12,* 79-99.

Algina, J., & Noe, M. J. (1978). A Study of the accuracy of Subkoviak's single-administration estimate of the coefficient of agreement using two true-score estimates. *Journal of Educational Measurement, 15*(2), 101-110.

Alton, D. L. (1983). Learning in a marine snail. *Scientific American, 249,* 70-84.

Anastasi, A. (1976). *Psychological testing* (4th ed.). New York: MacMillan Publishing.

Anderberg, M. J. (1973). *Cluster analysis for applications.* New York: Academic Press.

Anderson, E. B. (1973a). A goodness of fit test for the Rasch Model. *Psychometrika, 38,* 123-139.

Andersen, E. B. (1973b). *Conditional inference and models for measuring.* Copenhagen: Danish Institute for Mental Health.

Anderson, J. R. (1980). *Cognitive psychology and its implications.* San Francisco: W. H. Freeman.

Anderson, J. R. (1990). *Cognitive Psychology and Its Implications.* New York: W. H. Freeman and Company.

Anderson, J. R., & Bower, G. H. (1973). *Human associative memory.* Washington, DC: Winston.

Anderson, J., Kearney, G. E., & Everett, A. V. (1968). An evaluation of Rasch's structural model for test items. *British Journal of Mathematical and Statistical Psychology,* 231-238.

Anderson, R. C. (1972). How to construct achievement tests to assess comprehension. *Review of Educational Research, 42,* 2.

Anderson, R. C., Reynolds, R. E., Schallert, D. L. & Goetz, E. T. (1977). Frameworks for comprehending discourse. *American Educational Research Journal, 14(4),* 367-381.

Andrews, B. J., & Hecht, J. T. (1976). A preliminary investigation of two procedures for setting examination standards. *Educational and Psychological Measurement, 36,* 45-50.

Angoff, W. H. (1984). Scales, norms, and equaivalent scores. Princeton, NJ: Educational Testing Service.

Angoff, W. H. (1982). Summary and derivation of equating methods used at ETS. In P. W. Holland & D. B. Rubin (Eds.), *Test equating.* New York: Academic Press.

Angoff, W. H. (1971). Scales, norms, and equivalent scores. In R. L. Thorndike (Ed.), *Educational Measurement (2nd ed.),* Washington DC: American Council on Education.

Arbib, M. A. (1964). *Brains, machines, and mathematics.* New York: McGraw.

Arbib, M. A. (1972). *The metaphorical brain.* New York: Wiley-Interscience.

Archer, E. L., & Leverette, H. (1985). *Development and administration of an employee competence test.* Paper presented at the annual meeting of the American Educational Research Association ED 262 058.

Aring, M. K. (1993). What the 'V' work is costing America's Economy, *Phi Delta Kappan, 74,* 396-404.

Arkin, A. M., Artrobus, J. S., & Ellman, S. L. (1978). *The mind in sleep: Psychology and psychophysiology.* Hillsdale, NJ: Lawrence Erlbaum Associates.

Armijo, L. A., & Appleby, J. A. (1982). *Vocational education curriculum specialist (Test Module 19).* Palo Alto, CA: American Institute for Research in the Behavioral Sciences.

Armor, D. J., & Couch, A. S. (1972). *Data-text primer.* New York: The Free Press.

Arneklev, B., Gee, D., & Ingebo, G. (1976, April). *Optimum range of difficulty for linking items.* Paper presented at the annual meeting of the American Educational Research Association, San Francisco.

Association of American Colleges (1985). *Integrity in the college curriculum: A report to the academic community. The findings and recommendations of the project on redefining the meaning and purpose of baccalaureate degrees.* Washington, DC: Author.

Astin, A. (1985). *Achieving educational excellence.* San Francisco: Jossey-Bass.

Astin, A. W. (1964). Criterion-centered research. *Educational and Psychological Measurement, 24*(2), 807-822.

Atkinson, R. C., & Shiffrin, R. (1968). Human memory: A proposed system and its control processes. In K. W. Spence & J. A. Spence (Eds.), *The psychology of learning and motivation: Volume 2.* New York: Academic Press.

Attneave, F. (1950). Dimensions of similarity, *American Journal of Psychology, 63,* 516-556.

Ault, L. H. (1972). *Multiple-choice versus created-response test results.* New York: Teachers College, Columbia University. (ED 091 426).

Ausubel, D. P. (1968). *Educational psychology: A cognitive view.* New York: Holt, Rinehart & Winston.

Ayres, L. P. (1912). Measuring educational processes through educational results. *School Review, 20,* 300-309.

Ayres, L. P. (1909). *Laggards in Our Schools: A Study of Retardation and Elimination in City School Systems.* New York: Charities Publication Committee.

Bach, E., & Hams, R. (Eds.). (1968). *Universals in linguistic theory.* New York: Holt, Rinehart, and Winston.

Baker, E. L. & O'Neil, H. F. (1985). *Assessing instructional outcomes.* Los Angeles, California: California State University, Center for the Study of Evaluation ED 266 175.

Baker, E. L. (1964). Beyond objectives: Domain-referenced tests for evaluation and instructional improvement. *Educational Technology, 14,* 10-16.

Baker, F. B. & Hubert, L. F. (1977). Inference procedures for ordering theory, *Journal of educational statistics, 3,* 217-233.

Bargh, J. A. (1984). Automatic and conscious processing of social information. In R. S. Wyer & T. K. Srull (Eds.), *Handbook of social cognition, 3.* Hillsdale, NJ: Erlbaum, 1-43.

Baker, E. L., & Popham, W. J. (1973). *Expanding dimensions of instructional objectives.* Englewood Cliffs, NJ: Prentice Hall.

Barlow, J. A. & Burt, C. (1954). The identification of factors from different experiments, *British Journal of statistical psychology, 7,* 52-56.

Barron, A. R. (1989). Statistical properties of artificial neural networks. In *Proceedings of the 28th. Institute of Electronic and Electrical Engineers Conference on Decision and Control,* 280-285.

Barron, A. R. & Barron, R. (1989). Statistical learning networks: A unifying view. In E. J. Wegman, D. J. Gantz & J. J. Miller (Eds.), *Computing science and statistics: Proceedings of the 20th symposium on the interface,* 193-202.

Bart, W. M. (1981). The ordering analytic approach to hierarchical analysis. In *Advances in hierarchical analysis: methods, applications and critique.* symposium conducted at the American Educational Research Association meeting, Los Angeles.

Bart, W. M. & Krus, D. J. (1975). An ordering-theoretic method to determine hierarchies among items. In Kraus, D. J., Bart, w. M. & Airasian, P. W. (Eds.) *Ordering theory and methods.* Los Angeles: Theta Press, 47-53.

Bartlett, F. C. (1932). *Remembering*. Cambridge, England: University Press.

Barton, A. R. (1980). A simple technique for improving the quality of parameter estimates in learning hierarchy validation studies. *Psychometrika, 45*, 2, 269-271.

Baum, H. I., Bennett, R. E., Frye, D. & Soloway, E. (1990). Scoring constructed responses using expert systems, *Journal of Educational Measurement, 27*, 93-108.

Beard, J. G., Fletcher, G., & Richards, L. (1984). *Domain-referenced tests: Achieving equivalence through Rasch pre-equating*. Paper presented at the Annual Meeting of the American Educational Research Association, New Orleans, Louisiana, April 23-27, ED 247 294.

Becker, J. D. (1975). Reflections on the formal description of behavior. In D. G. Bobrow & A. Collins (Eds.), *Representation and understanding*. New York: Academic Press, 35-82.

Becker, J. D. (1973). A model for the encoding of experiential information. In R. C. Schank & K. M. Colby (eds.), *Computer models of thought and language*. San Francisco, Ca.: Freeman.

Becker, s. & le Cun, Y. (1988). Improving the convergence of back-propagation learning with second order methods. In *Proceedings of the 1988 Connectionist models summer school*, 29-37.

Beer, S. (1966). *Information and human learning*. Glenview, IL: Scott, Foresman, and Company.

Beeson, G. W. (1977). Hierarchical learning in electrical science. *Journal of research in science teaching, 14*, 117-127.

Bell-Gredler, M. E. (1986). *Learning and instruction: Theory into practice*. New York: Macmillan Publishing Company.

Benton, A. L. (1962). Clinical symptomatology in right and left hemisphere lesions. In V. Mountcastle (Ed.), *Interhemispheric relations and cerebral dominance*. Baltimore: John Hopkins Press.

Bergen, J. R. (1980). The structural analysis of behavior: An alternative to the learning-hierarchy model, *Review of educational research, 50*, 4, 625-646.

Berk, R. A. (1984). Selecting the index of reliability. In R. A. Berk (Ed.), *A guide to criterion-referenced test construction*. Baltimore: Johns Hopkins University Press, 231-266.

Berk, R. A. (1980). Item analysis. In R. A. Berk (Ed.), *Criterion-referenced measurement: The state of the art*. Baltimore, MD: John Hopkins University Press.

Berk, R. A. (1978). A consumers' guide to criterion-referenced test item statistics. Paper presented at the National Council on Measurement in Education, Toronto, Ontario, March 1978. ED 159 214.

Berthet, P., Feytmans, E., Stevens, D. & Genette, A. (1976). A new divisive method of classification illustrated by its application to ecological problems, *Proceedings of the 9th. International Biometric Conference, 2*, 366-382.

Besel, R. (1973, February). *Using group performance to interpret individual responses to criterion-referenced tests*. Paper presented at the annual meeting of the American Educational Research Association, New Orleans. (ED 076 658).

Besel, R. R. (1973a). *Program for computing least squares estimates of item parameters for the Mastery Learning Test Model: Fixed GMP*. Los Alamitos, CA: Southwest Regional Laboratory for Educational Research and Development.

Besel, R. R. (1973b). *Program for computing least squares estimates of item parameters* for the Mastery Learning Test Model: VARIABLE GMP Version. Los Alamitos, CA: Southwest Regional Laboratory for Eduational Research and Development.

Besel, R. (1973c). Estimating mastery learning parameters via the two-group method. Los Alamitos, CA: Southwest Regional Laboratory for Educational Research and Development, No. TN-3-73-24.

Bhatnager, R. K. & Kanal, L. N. (1986), Handling uncertain information: a review of numeric and nonnumeric methods. In Kanal, L. N. & Lemmer, J. F. (Eds.), Uncertainty in artificial intelligence. New York: North-Holland, 3-26.

Bollen, K. A. (1989). Structural equations with latent variables. New York: John Wiley & Sons.

Broudy, H. S. (1977). Types of knowledge and purposes of education. In R. C. Anderson, R. J. Spiro & Wm. E. Montague (Eds.), Schooling and the acquisition of knowledge, Hillsdale, NJ: Lawrence Erlbaum Associates, Publishers, 2-17.

Biggs, J. B. (1971). Information and human learning. Glenview, IL: Scott, Foresman, and Company.

Biggs, J. B. (1969). Coding and cognitive processes. British Journal of Psychology, 60, 287 - 305.

Billett, R. O. (1933). Provision for individual differences, marking and promotion. National Survey of Secondary Education, Monograph No. 13. Washington, DC: U. S. Office of Education.

Binet, A., & Simon, T. (1916). The development of intelligence in children (the Binet-Simon Scale). Translated by K. S. Kite. Baltimore: Williams & Wilkins.

Birenbaum, M., & Shaw, D. J. (1985). Task specification chart: A key to a better understanding of test results. Journal of Educational Measurement, 22(3), 219-230.

Birenbaum, M., & Tatsuoka, K. K. (1982). On the dimensionality of achievement test data. Journal of Educational Measurement, 19, 259-266.

Birnbaum, R. (1988). How colleges work: The cybernetics of academic organization and leadership. San Francisco, California: Jossey-Bass Publishers.

Bishop, J. (1992). Workforce preparedness. Working Paper No. 92-04. Ithaca, NY: Cornell University.

Bitterman, M. E. (1967). Learning in animals. In H. Helson and W. Bevan (Eds.), Contemporary approaches to psychology. New York: Van Nostrand.

Bitterman, M. E., Fedderson, W. F., & Tyler, D. W. (1953). Secondary reinforcement and the discrimination hypothesis. American Journal of Psychology, 66, 456-464.

Black, M. (1937). Vagueness: An exercise in logical analysis, Philosophy of science, 4, 427-455.

Blalock, H. M. (1969). Theory construction. N.J.: Prentice-Hall.

Blank, W. E. (1982). Handbook for developing competency-based training programs. Englewood Cliffs, NJ: Prentice-Hall.

Blankenship, C. (1985). Using curriculum-based data to make instructional decisions. Exceptional Children, 52, 233-238.

Blischke, W. R. (1964). Estimating the parameters of mixtures of binomial distributions. Journal of the American Statistical Association, 59, 510-528.

Blischke, W. R. (1962). Moment estimators for the parameters of a mixture of two binomial distributions. Annals of Mathematical Statistics, 33, 444-454.

Block, J. H. (1971a). Criterion-referenced measurement: Potential. School Review, 79, 289-298.

Block, J. H. (1971b). Introduction to mastery learning: Theory and practice. In James H. Block (Ed.), *Mastery learning theory and practice* (pp. 2-13). New York: Holt, Rinehart, and Winston.

Block, N. J., & Dworkin, G. (Eds.). (1976). *The IQ controversy.* New York: Pantheorn Books.

Bloom, B. S. (1976). *Human characteristics and school learning.* New York: McGraw-Hill.

Bloom, B. S. (1968). Learning for Mastery, *Evaluation comment, 1,* 1-12.

Bloom, B. S., Engelhart, M. D., Furst, E. J., Hill, W. H., & Krathwohl, D. R. (1956). *Taxonomy of educational objectives. Handbook I: Cognitive domain.* New York: Longman.

Bloom, F. E., Lazerson, A., & Hofstadter L. (1985). *Brain, mind and behavior.* New York: W. H. Freeman and Company.

Blyth, J. W. (1960). Teaching machines and human beings. In A. A. Lumsdaine and R. Glaser (Eds.), *Teaching machines and programmed learning* (pp. 643-647). Washington, DC: National Education Association, Department of Audio-Visual Instruction.

Bobbitt, F. (1948). Harvard reaffirms the academic tradition, *The School Review, 54,* 326-333.

Bobbitt, F. (1937). A correlated curriculum evaluated [Book review]. *The English Journal, 26,* 418-420.

Bobbitt, F. (1934). Questionable recommendations of the Commission on the Social Studies, *School and Society, 40,* 201-208.

Bobbitt, F. (1926). The orientation of the curriculum-maker. In G. M. Whipple (ed.), *The Foundations and Technique of Curriculum-Construction, Part II. The Foundations of Curriculum-Making. The Twenty-sixth Yearbook of the National Society for the Study of Education.* Bloomington, Il: Public School Publishing, 41-55.

Bobbitt, F. (1924). *How to make a curriculum.* New York: Houghton Mifflin.

Bobbitt, F. (1922). *Curriculum-Making in Los Angeles.* Chicago: University of Chicago.

Bobbitt, F. (1918). *The curriculum.* New York: Houghton Mifflin.

Bobbitt, F. (1913). Some general principles of management applied to the problems of city-school systems. In *Twelfth yearbook of the National Society for the Study of Education, Part 1.* Chicago: University of Chicago Press.

Bobbitt, F. (1912). The elimination of waste in education, *The Elementary School Instructor, 12,* 259-271.

Bobrow, D. G. (1985). *Qualitative reasoning about physical systems.* Cambridge, MA: Massachusetts Institute of Technology Press.

Bobrow, D. G. (1975). Dimensions of representation. In D. G. Bobrow & A. Collins, *Representation and understanding.* New York: Academic Press, 2-34.

Bobrow, R. J., & Brown, J. S. (1975). Stematic understanding: Synthesis, analysis, and contingent knowledge in specialized understanding systems. In D. G. Bobrow and A. Collins (Eds.), *Representation and understanding.* New York: Academic Press, 103-129.

Bobrow, D. G., & Norman, D. A. (1975). Some principles of memory schemata. In D. G. Bobrow and A. M. Collins (Eds.), *Representation and understanding: Studies in cognitive science.* New York: Academic Press.

Bock, R. D. (1975). *Multivariate statistical methods in behavioral research.* New York:

McGraw-Hill.

Bock, R. D. & Aitkin, M. (1981). Marginal maximum likelihood estimation of item parameters: An application of an EM algorithm. *Psychometrika, 46,* 443-459.

Bodner, G. (1983). Analyzing faculty salaries in class action sex discrimination cases, *Journal of College and University Law, 10,* 305-323.

Bog, W. R. & Gall, M. D. (1983). *Educational Research,* NY: Longman.

Bogen, J. E. (1960). The other side of the brain, Volume I: Dysgraphia and dyscopia following cerebral commissurotomy. *Bulletin of the Los Angeles Neurological Society,* 39, 73-105.

Bogen, J. E., & Mazzaniga, M. S. (1965). Cerebral commissurotomy in man. Minor hemisphere dominance for certain visuspatial functions. *Journal of Neurosurgery,* 23, 391-399.

Bog, W. R. & Gall, M. D. (1983). *Educational Research,* NY: Longman.

Bok, C. C. (1985). The quality of education in America universities, *Education and the welfare of the republic.* Boston, MA: New England Association of Schools and Colleges.

Boldt, R. F. (1972). An estimation procedure for the Rasch Model allowing for missing data. *Research Memorandum 72-5.* Princeton, NJ: Educational Testing Service.

Bollen, K. A. (1989). *Structural equations with latent variables.* New York: John Wiley & Sons.

Bombay, S. & Saltzman, B. (1982). The role of statistics in employment discrimination litigation-A university perspective, *Journal of College and University Law, 9,* 263-278.

Bormuth, J. H. (1978). *Feasibility of criterion-referenced testing and evaluation.* Paper presented at the annual meeting of the American Educational Research Association, Toronto, Ontario, Canada, March 27-31, ED 159 225.

Bormuth, J. R. (1970). *On the theory of achievement test items.* Chicago: University of Chicago Press.

Bousfield, W. A. (1953). The occurrence of clustering in the recall of randomly arranged associates. *Journal of General Psychology,* 49, 229-240.

Bousfield, W. A., & Barclay, W. D. (1950). The relationship between order and frequency of occurrence of restrictive associative responses. *Journal of Experimental Psychology,* 40, 643-647.

Bower, G. H. (1961). Application of a model to paired-associate learning. *Psychometrika,* 26, 255-280.

Bower, G. H., & Winzenz, D. (1969). Group structure, coding, and memory for digit series. *Journal of Experimental Psychology Monograph, 80,* 1-17.

Boyer, E. L. (1985). Reflections on the great debate. In P. G. Altbach, G. P. Kelly & L. Weis (eds.), *Excellence in education.* New York: Prometheus Press.

Boyer, E. L. (1983). *High School: A report on secondary education in America.* New York: Harper & Row.

Boylan, H. (1986, October 19). Developmental education: A hundred years of promise . . . a decade of crisis. National Conference on Exemplary Programs in Developmental Education, *Journal of Developmental Education.*

Bradley, J. F. (1968). *Distribution-free statistical tests.* Englewood Cliffs, NJ: Prentice-Hall.

Bransford, J. D., & Franks, J. J. (1976). Toward a framework for understanding learning.

In G. Bower (ed.), *Psychology of learning and motivation,* Volume 10. New York: Academic Press.

Bransford, J. D., Nitsch, K. E. & Franks, J. J. (1977). Schooling and the facilitation of knowing. In R. C. Anderson, R. J. Spiro & W. E. Montague (Eds.), *Schooling and the acquisition of knowledge.* Hillsdale, New Jersey: Lawrence Erlbaum Associates, 31-55.

Braun, H. I. & Holland, P. W. (1982). Observed-score equating: A mathematical analysis of some ETS equating procedures. In P. W. Holland and D. B. Rubin (Eds.), *Test equating.* New York: Academic Press.

Brecht, H., Hopkins, S., & Stanley, B. (1972). *Perspectives in educational and psychological measurement.* Englewood Cliffs, NJ: Prentice-Hall.

Breddock, W., Lloyd-Jones, S., & Schoer, W. (1963). *Research in written composition.* Champaign, IL: National Council of Teachers of English.

Brennan, R. L. (1981). Some statistical procedures for domain-referenced testing: A handbook for practitioners. Iowa City: American College Testing. (ED 205 601).

Brennan, R. L. (1974, January). *The evaluation of mastery test items, Final report, Project No. 2B118, Grant No. OEG-2-2-2B118.* Washington, DC: United States Department of Health, Education, and Welfare, National Center for Educational Research and Development. (ED 092 593).

Brennan, R. L. (1972). A generalized upper-lower item discrimination index. *Educational and Psychological Measurement, 32,* 289-303.

Brennan, R. L. & Kane, M. T. (1979). Generalizability theory: A review. In R. Traub (Ed.), *Methodological developments: New directons for testing and measurement* (No. 4). San Francisco: Jossey-Bass.

Brennan, R. L. & Prediger, D. J. (1981). Coefficient kappa: Some uses, misuses, and alternatives, *Educatinal and psychological measurement, 41,* 687-689.

Brennan, R. L., & Stolurow, L. M. (1971, February). *An empirical decision process for formative evaluation.* Paper presented at the annual meeting of the American Educational Research Association. (ED 048 343).

Brink, N. E. (1972). Rasch's logistic model vs. the Guttman method. *Educational and Psychological Measurement, 32,* 921-927.

Britton, J. (1975). *The development of writing abilities.* New York: Macmillan.

Brodinsky, B. (1977). Back to the basics: The movement and its meaning. *Phi Delta Kappan, 58,* 7, 522-526.

Broudy, H. S. (1977). Types of knowledge and purposes of education. In R. C. Anderson, R. J. Spiro & Wm. E. Montague (Eds.), *Schooling and the acquisition of knowledge,* Hillsdale, NJ: Lawrence Erlbaum Associates, Publishers, 2-17.

Broudy, H. S. (1970) On knowing with. *Proceedings of the 26th Annual Meeting of the Philosophy of Education Society.*

Brown, J. S. & Burton, R. R. (1978). Diagnostic models for procedural bugs in basic mathematical skills, *Cognitive Science, 2,* 155-192.

Brown, J. S., Collins, A. & Harris, G. (1978). Artificial intelligence and learning strategies. In H. F. O'Neil, Jr. (ed.), *Learning strategies.* New York: Academic Press, 107-152.

Bruner, J. S. (1966). *Toward a theory of instruction.* New York: Norton.

Bruner, J. S. (1964a). The course of cognitive growth. *American Psychologist, 19,* 1-15.

Bruner, J. S. (1964b). Some theorems on instruction. In E. R. Hilgard (Ed.), *Theories of learning and instruction. The sixty-third yearbook of the National Society for the*

Study of Education. Chicago: University of Chicago Press.

Bruner, J. S. (1960). *The process of education*. Cambridge, MA: Harvard University Press.

Bruner, J. S., Olver, R. R., & Greenfield, P. M. (1966). *Studies in cognitive growth*. New York: Wiley.

Bruno, J. E. (1982). On staffing inner-city schools, *Phi Delta Kappan, 63*, 534-535.

Bryson, L. (1936). *Adult education*. New York: American Book Company.

Buch, T. B. (1916, April). Standard tests and scales of measurements. *Psychological Clinic, 10*, 49-57.

Buckingham, B. R. (1916). Notes on the derivation of scales in school subjects: With special application to arithmetic. In G. M. Whipple (Ed.), *Standards and tests for the measurement of the efficiency of schools and school systems. The 15th Yearbook of the National Society for the Study of Education* (pp. 23-40). Bloomington, IL: Public School Publishing.

Bullard, E. P. (1909). Industrial training through the apprenticeship system. In *Bulletin No. 9 of the National Society for the Promotion of Industrial Education*. New York: National Society for the Promotion of Industrial Education, 51-63.

Buros, O. K. (Ed.). (1978). *The mental measurements yearbook: An index to tests, test reviews, and the literature on specific tests*. Highland Park, NJ: Gryphon Press.

Buros, O. K. (1977). Fifty years in testing: Some reminiscences, criticisms, and suggestions. *Educational Researcher, 6*, 9-15.

Buros, O. K. (1974). *Tests in Print II: An index to tests, test reviews, and the literature on specific tests*. Highland Park, NJ: Gryphon Press.

Burt, C. (1938). The unit hierarchy and its properties, *Psychometrika, 3*, 151-168.

Burt, C. (1941). *The factors of the mind: An introduction to factor analysis in psychology*. New York: MacMillan.

Burt, C. (1948). The factorial study of tempermental traits, *British Journal of statistical psychology, 1*, 178-203.

Burt, C. (1949). Alternative methods of factor analysis and their relations to Pearson's method of ``Principal axes.", *British journal of psychological statistics, 2*, 98-121.

Burton, R. R. (1981). *Diagnosing bugs in a simple procedural skill*. Palo Alto, CA: XEROX Palo Alto Research Center.

Bush, G. (1991). Remarks by the President at the Presentation of the National Education Strategy, In *America 2000 An Education Strategy SOURCEBOOK*. Washington, D. C.: U.S. Government Printing Office, 1-9.

Bush, R. R., & Mosteller, F. (1955). *Stochastic models for learning*. New York: Wiley.

Buxton, R. (1989). Modeling uncertainty in expert systems, *International journal of man-machine studies, 31*, 415-476.

Bylander, R. (1988). A critique of qualitative simulation from a consolidation viewpoint. *IEEE Transactions on Man, and Cybernetics, 18(2)*, 252-263.

Caldwell, O. W., & Courtis, S. A. (1923). *Then and now in education, 1845-1923*. Yonkers, N.Y.: World Book Co..

Campbell, C. P., & Allender, W. R. (1988). Procedures for constructing and using criterion-referenced performance tests. *Canadian Vocational Journal, 23(3)*, 2-9.

Campbell, D. S. (1935). *Curriculum development*. New York: American Book Company.

Campbell, D. T. (1969). Reforms as experiments, *American psychologist, 24*, 409-429.

Campbell, D. T. (1975). Assessing the impact of planned social change. In G. M. Lyons (ed.), *Social research and public policies*. Hanover, N.H.: The public affairs center,

Dartmouth College.

Campbell, D.T. & Stanley, J. C. (1963). Experimental and quasi-experimental designs for research on teaching. In N. L. Gage (ed.), *Handbook of research on teaching*. Skokie, Illinois: Rand McNally.

Campbell, N. R., *Measurement and calculation.* p. 131.

Cancelli, A. A., Bergan, J. R., & Jones, S. (1982). Psychometric and instructional validatin approaches in the hierarchical sequencing of learning tasks, *Journal of school psychology, 20*, 3, 232-243.

Cancelli, A. & Kratochwill, T. R. (1981). Advances in criterion-referenced assessment. In T. R. Kratochwill (Ed.), *Advances in school psychology*. Hillsdale, N.J.: Lawrence Erlbaum Associates.

Cangelost, J. S. (1984). Another answer to the cut-off score question. *Educational Measurement, Issues and Practice, 3(*4), 23-25.

Capie, W. & H. L. Jones (1971). An assessment of hierarchy validation techniques, *Journal of Research in Science Teaching, 8*, 137-147.

Caramazza, A. (1996) Pictures, words and the brain, *Nature, 383*, 6597,216-217.

Carbonell, J. R. & Collins, A. M. (1974). Natural semantics in artificial intelligence. *American Journal of Computational Linguistics, 1*, 3-10.

Carey, S. (1985). *Conceptual change in childhood*. Cambridge, Ma: MIT Press.

Carey, S. (1986). Cognitive science and science education, *American Psychologist, 41*, 1123-1130.

Carlson, R. A., B. Khoo & R. G. Elliot (1990). Component practice and exposure to a problem solving context, *Human Factors, 32*, 3, 267-286.

Carlson, R. A., B. Khoo & R. G. Elliot (1990). Component practice and exposure to a problem solving context, *Human Factors, 32*, 3, 267-286.

Carlson, R. A., M. A. Sulliban & W. Schneider (1989). Practice and working memory effects in building procedural skill, *Journal of Expe*

Carlton, E. H. & Shepard, R. N. (1990a). Psychologically simple motions as geodesic paths. I. Asymmetric Objects, *Journal of mathematical psychology, 34*, 2, 127-188.

Carlton, E. H. & Shepard, R. N. (1990b). Psychologically simple motions as geodesic paths. II. Symmetric Objects, *Journal of mathematical psychology, 34*, 2, 189-228.

Carroll, J. M (1990). The Copernican plan: Restructuring the American high school, *Phi Delta Kappan, 71*, 5, 358-365.

Carroll, J. B. (1971). Problems of measurement related to the concept of learning for mastery. In J.H. Block (Ed.), *Mastery learning theory and practice* (pp. 29-46). New York: Holt, Rinehart, and Winston.

Carroll, J. B. (1970). Problems of measurement related to the concept of learning for mastery. *Education Horizons, 48*, 71-80.

Carroll, J. B. (1963). Problems of school learning. *Teachers College Record, 64*, 723-733.

Carroll, J. B. (1950). Problems in the factor analysis of tests of varying difficulty. *American Psychologist, 5*, 369.

Carroll, J. B., & Freedle, R. O. (Eds.). (1972). *Language comprehension and the acquisition of knowledge*. Washington, DC: Winston.

Carroll, R. M. (1976). An empirical comparison of metric and nonmetric analyses of correlation coefficients. *Educational and Psychological Measurement, 36*, 283-296.

Carter, J. (1992). *Factors impacting the core curriculum performance of college freshmen*. Doctoral dissertation. Grambling, LA: Grambling State University.

Carver, R. P. (1975). The Coleman Report: Using inappropriately designed achievement tests. *American Educational Research Journal, 12*(1), 77-86.

Carver, R. P. (1970, December). *The criterion-referenced aspects of the Carver-Dachy Chunked Reading Test.* Paper presented at the meeting of the National Reading Conference, St. Petersburg, FL. (ED 047 911).

Case, R. (1985). *Intellectual development: Birth to adulthood.* New York: Academic Press.

Caswell, H. L., & Campbell, D. S. (1937). *Readings in curriculum development.* New York: American Book Company.

Cate, R. M. , Huton, T. L. & Nesselroade, J. R. (1986). Premarital relationships: Toward identification of alternative pathways to marriage. *Journal of social and clinical psychology, 4,* 1, 3-22.

Cattell, R. B. (1949). A note on factor invariance and the identification of factors. *British Journal of Statitical Psychology, 2,* 134-139.

Cattell, R. M. (1944). Psychological measurement; Normative, positive, interactive, *Psychological Review, 51,* 292-303.

Champagne, A. B., Hoz, R. & Klopfer, L. E. (1987). *Construct validation of the cognitive structure of physics concepts.* Unpublished manuscript, Learning Research & Develoopment Center, University of Pittsburgh.

Cattell, R. B. & Cattell, A. K. S. (1955). Factor rotation for proportioning profiles: Analytical solution and an example, *British journal of statistical psychology, 8,* 83-91.

Champagne, A. B., Klopfer, L. E.,DeSena, A. T. & Squires, D. A. (1981). Structural representations of students' knowledge before and after science instruction. *Journal of research in science teaching, 18,* 97-111.

Chandler, J. W. (1987). The why, what, and who of assessment: The college perspective. In *Assessing the outcomes of higher educaton, Proceedings of the 1986 ETS invitational conference.* Princeton, N.J.: Educational Testing Service, 11-18.

Charters, W. W. (1925) Curriculum for Women, in *Procedings of the High School conference.* Urbana, IL.: University of Illinois.

Charters, W. W. (1923). Minimal essentials in elementary language and grammar. In G. M. Whipple (Ed.), *The 16th Yearbook of the National Society for the Study of Education* (pp. 85-110). Bloomington, IL: Public School Publishing.

Charters, W. W. (1923). *Curriculum construction.* New York: MacMillan.

Charters, W. W. (1921). "The reorganization of Women's Education." *Educational Review, 62,* 224-231.

Chase, F. & Bell, Wm. E. (1980). Introduction: The urban education studies, 1977-1980. In F. S. Chase (ed.), *Educational quandaries and opportunities.* Dallas: Urban Education Studies.

Chase, W. G. & Simon, H. A. (1973). The ming's eye in chess. In W. G. Chase (Ed.), *Visual informatin processing.* New York: Academic Press, 215-281.

Chate, W. (1970). *Meaning and structure of language.* Chicago: University of Chicago Press.

Chi, M. T. H., Feltovich, P. J. & Glaser, R. (1981). Categorization and representation of physics problems by experts and novices, *Cognitive Science, 5,* 121-152.

Chi, M. T. H., Glaser, R. & Rees, E. (1982). Expertise in problem solving. In R. Sternberg (Ed.), *Advances in the psychology of human intelligence* (Vol. I). Hillsdale, N.J.: Erlbaum.

Chickering, A. (1976). Developmental change as a major outcome. In M. T. Keeton and
    Associates, *Experimental Learning: Rationale, characteristics, and assessment*. San
    Francisco: Jossey-Bass.
Chickering, A. (1969). *Education and identity*. San Francisco: Jossey-Bass.
Chickering, A. & Associates. (1981). *The modern American college*. San Francisco:
    Jossey-Bass.
Choi, M. Y. & Huberman, B. A. (1983). Dynamic behavior of nonlinear neural networks,
    Physical Review, A, 28, 1204-1206.
Chomsky, N. (1968). *Language and mind*. New York: Harcourt.
Chomsky, N. (1965). *Aspects of the theory of syntax*. Cambridge, MA: MIT Press.
Chomsky, N. (1957). *Syntactic structures*. The Hague: Mouton.
Christensen, J. (1990). A hierarchical planner that generates its own hierarchies.
    Proceedings of the Conference of the American Association for Artificial Intelligence,
    1004-1009.
Cicirelli, V. G. (1969). *The impact of Headstart: An evaluation of the effects of Headstart
    on children's cognitive and affective development*. Study by the Westinghouse
    Learning Corporation and Ohio University. Washington, DC: Office of Economic
    Opportunity.
Claverie, J-M, Sauvaget, I. & Bougueleret, L. (1990). k-Tuple frequency analysis: From
    intron/exon discrimination to T-cell epitope mapping. In R. F. Doolittle (ed.),
    *Methods in enzymology, Volume 183: Molecular evolution: Computer analysis of
    protein and nucleic acid sequences*. New York: Academic Press, Harcourt Brace
    Jovanovich, Publishers, 237-252.
Claxton, J. (1990). Fostering student learning and development through effective teaching.
    R. M. Hashway (Ed.), *Handbook of developmental education*. New York: Praeger.
Clayton, C. (1989). We can educate all our children, *The Nation, 249*, 132-135.
Clowes, D. A. (1992). Remediation in higher education. In J. C. Smart (Ed.), *Higher
    education: Handbook of theory and research, Vol III*. (pp. 460-493). New York:
    Agathon Press.
Clowes, D. A. (1982). More than a definitional problem. *Current Issues in Higher
    Education, 1*, 4-6.
Clowes, D.A. (1980). More than a definitional problem: Remedial, compensatory, and
    developmental education. *Journal of Developmental and Remedial Education, 4*(1),
    8-10.
Cobean, N., Airasian, P., & Rakow, E. (1975, May). *A comparison of discriminant
    analysis and intraclass correlation for selecting items which maximaly discriminate
    between groups*. Paper presented at the annual meeting of the New England
    Educational Research Organization, Provincetown, Massachusetts.
Cohen, B. H. (1970). Some or none characteristics of coding. *Teaching Machines and
    Programmed Learning* (pp. 452-468). Washington, DC: National Education
    Association, Department of Audio-Visual Instruction.
Cohen, D. (March, 1990). More voices in Babel? Educational research and the politics of
    curriculum. *Phi Delta Kappan, 71*, 518-522.
Cohen, J. (1960). Coefficient of agreement for nominal scales, *Educatinal and
    psychological measurement, 20*, 37-46.
Cohen, J. (1968). Weighted kappa: Nominal scale agreement with provision for scaled
    disagreement or partial credit, *Psychological Bulletin, 70*, 213-220.

Cohen, M., & Narens, L. (1979). Fundamental unit structures: A theory of ratio scalability. *Journal of Mathematical Psychology, 20*, 193-232.

Cohen, N. J., & Squire, L. R. (1980). Preserved learning and retention of pattern analyzing skill in amnesia: Dissociation of knowing how and knowing that. *Science, 210*, 207-209.

Coleman, J., Campbell, E., Hobson, C. J., McParland, J., Mood, A., Weinfeld, F. D. and York, R. L. (1966). *Equality for Educational Opportunity*. U.S. Department of Health, Education and Wealfare, Office of Education. Washington, D.C.: U.S. Government Printing Office.

Coleman, J., Campbell, E., Hobson, C. J., McParland, J., Mood, A., Weinfeld, F. D. and York, R. L. (1966). *Equality for Educational Opportunity*. U.S. Department of Health, Education and Welfare, Office of Education. Washington, D.C.: U.S. Government Printing Office.

Coleman, J. S., Hoffer, T. & Kilgore, S. (1982). *High school achievement - Public, Catholic and private schools compared.* New York: Basic Books.

Collins, A. M., & Loftus, E. F. (1975). A spreading-activation theory of semantic processing. *Psychological Review, 82*, 407-425.

Collins, A. M. & Quillian, M. R. (1972). How to make a language user. In E. Tulving & W. Donaldson (eds.), *Organization of memory*. New York: Academic Press.

Collis, G. M. (1985). Kappa, measures of marginal symmetry and intraclass correlation, *Educational and psychological measurement, 45*, 55-62.

Colonna, A., & Faglioni, P. (1966). The performance of hemisphere-damaged patients on spatial intelligence tests. *Cortex, 2*, 293-307.

Conners, C. K., & Barata, F. (1967). Transfer of information from touch to vision in brain-injured and emotionally disturbed children. *The Journal of Nervous and Mental Disease, 145*(2), 139-141.

Conover, W. J. (1971). *Practical nonparametric statistics.* New York: Wiley.

Cook, A. (1974, November 10). Say students ill-prepared for life. Lowell, MA: *The Sun*, 44.

Cook, W. W. (1941). *Grouping and promotion.* Series on individualization of instruction, No. 2, Minneapolis: University of Minnesota Press.

Cooper, C. R., & Odell, L. (Eds.). (1977). *Evaluating writing: Describing, measuring, judging*. Urbana, IL: National Council of Teachers of English.

Cooper, L. A. (1975). Mental rotation of random two-dimensional shapes, *Cognitive Psychology, 1*, 20-43.

Coulson, J. E., & Cogswell, J. F. (1965). Effects of individualized instruction on teaching. *Journal of Educational Measurement, 2*(4), 59-64.

Coulson, J. E., & Silberman, H. F. (1960). Results of an initial experiment in automated teaching. In A. A. Lumsdaine & R. Glaser (Eds.), *Teaching machines and programmed learning* (pp. 452-468). Washington, DC: National Education Association, Department of Audio-Visual Instruction.

Courtis, S. A. (1916, December). Measuring the child's capacity. *Normal Instructor and Primary Plans*, 45-46.

Courtis, S. A. (1916, November). Measuring the child's capacity. *Normal Instructor and Primary Plans*, 53-54.

Courtis, S. A. (1913). The reliability of single measurements with standard tests. *Elementary School Teacher, 14*(7), 486-504.

Cox, R. C. (1971). Evaluative aspects of criterion-referenced measures. In W. J. Popham (Ed.), *Criterion-referenced measurement*. Englewood Cliffs, NJ: Educational Technology Publications, 55-66.

Cox, R. C. (1970, March). *Evaluative aspects of criterion-referenced measures*. Paper presented at the annual conference of the American Educational Research Association, Minneapolis. (ED 038 679).

Cox, R. C., & Graham, G. T. (1966). The development of a sequentially scaled achievement test. *Journal of Educational Measurement, 3*, 147-150.

Cox, R. C., & Sterrett, B. G. (1970). A model for increasing the meaning of standardized scores. *Journal of Educational Measurement, 7*, 227-228.

Cox, R. C., & Vargas, J. S. (1966, February). *A comparison of item selection techniques for norm-referenced and criterion-referenced tests. Report No. BR-S-0253-REPRINT-7*. Pittsburgh, PA: Learning Research and Development Center, University of Pittsburgh. (ED 010 517).

Craik, K. (1943). *The nature of explaination*. Cambridge: Cambridge University Press

Crehan, K. D. (1974). Item analysis for teacher-made mastery tests. *Journal of Educational Measurement, 11*(4), 255-262.

Cremin, L. A. (1957). *The republic and the school: Horace Mann on the education of freeman*. New York: Bureau of Publications, Teachers College, Columbia University.

Cressie, N. & Holland, P. W. (1983). Characterizing the manifest probabilities of latent trait models, *Psychometrika, 48*, 129-141.

Cronbach, L. J. (1991). Functional evaluation design. In M. W. McLaughlin and D. C. Phillips (Eds.), *Evaluation and Education: At Quarter Century*. Chicago: University of Chicago Press, 323-376.

Cronbach, L. J. (1971a). Comments on mastery learniing and its implications for curriculum development. In Eisner, E. W. (Ed.), *Confronting curriculum reform*. Boston: Little, Brown, 49-55.

Cronbach, L. J. (1971b). Test validation. In R. L. Thorndike (Ed.), *Educational measurement*. Washington, D.C.: American Council on Education.

Cronbach, L. J. (1970). *Essentials of psychological testing*. (3rd. ed.). New York: Harper & Row.

Cronbach, L. J. (1969). Validation of educational measures. *Proceedings of the 1969 invitational conference on testing problems* (pp. 35-52). Princeton, NJ: Educational Testing Service.

Cronbach, L. J. (1963). Course improvement through evaluation, *Teachers College Record, 64*, 672-683.

Cronbach, L. J. (1951). Coefficient alpha and the internal structure of tests. *Psychometrika, 16*, 297-334.

Cross, K. P. (1987). *Adults as learners*. San Francisco: Jossey-Bass.

Cross, K. P. (1976). *Accent on learning*. San Francisco: Jossey-Bass.

Cross, K. P. (1971). *Beyond the open door*. San Francisco: Jossey-Bass.

Cross, L., Impara, J., Frary, R. (1984). A comparison of three methods for establishing minimum standards on the national teacher examination, *Journal of Educational Measurement, 21*, 113-129.

Cybenko, G. (1989). Approximation by superpositions of a sigmoidal function, *Mathematics of control, signals, and systems, 2*, 4, 303-314.

Dahl, E. D. (1987). Accelerated learning using the generalized delta rule. In *Proceedings of the Institute of Electronic and Electrical Engineers 1st International Conference on Neural Networks, 2*, 523-530.

D'Agostino, R. B., & Tietjen, G. L. (1973). Approaches to the null distribution of b1. *Biometrika 60*, 169-173.

D'Agostino, R. B., & Tietjen, G. L. (1971). Simulation probability points of b2 in small samples. *Biometrika, 58*, 669-672.

David, H. A. (1969). *The method of paired comparisons.* London, England: Charles Griffin & Company.

David, H. A., Hartley, H. O., & Pearson, E. S. (1954). The distribution of the ratio in a single normal sample of range to standard deviation. *Biometrika, 41*, 482-493.

Davis, F. B. (1971, February). *Criterion-referenced tests.* Paper presented at the Annual Meeting of the American Educational Research Association, New York. (ED 050 154).

Davis, F. B. (1951). Item selection techniques. In E.F. Lindquist (Ed.), *Educational Measurement* (pp. 266-328). Washington, DC: American Council on Education.

Davis, F. B., & Diamond, J. J. (1974). The preparation of criterion referenced tests. *CSE Monograph No. 3* (pp. 116-138). Los Angeles: University of Southern California, Graduate School of Education, Center for the Study of Evaluation.

Davison, M. L. (1983). *Multidimensional scaling.* New York: John Wiley and Sons.

Dayton, C. M., & Macready, G. B. (1976). A probabilistic model for validation of behavioral hierarchies. *Psychometrika, 41*(2), 189-204.

Dean, A. D. (1908). Education of workers in the shoe industry, *Bulletin No. 8 of the National Society for the Promotion of Industrial Education.* New York: National Society for the Promotion of Industrial Education, 7-110.

DeCecco, J. P. (1964). *Educational technology.* New York: Holt, Rinehart, and Winston.

Deese, J. (1962). On the structure of associative meaning, *Psychological review, 69*, 161-175.

de Groot, A. B. (1966). Perception and memory versus thought. In B. Kleinmutz (ed.), *Problem solving: Research, method and theory.* New York: Wiley.

de Groot, A. B. (1965). *Thought and choice in chess* The Hague: Mouton.

de Kleer, J., & Brown, J. S. (1986). A qualitative physics based on confluences. In D. G. Bobrow (Ed.), *Qualitative reasoning about physical systems.* Amsterdam: Elsvier Science.

Deno, S. (1985). Curriculum-based measurement: The emerging alternative, *Exceptional children, 52*, 219-232.

Détienne, F. (1991). A schema-based model of program understanding, *Mental models and human-computer interaction, 2*, 225-239.

De Rezi, E., & Faglioni, P. (1965). The comparative efficiency of intelligence and vigilance tests in detectinmission of tactual learning. *Journal of Neurophysiology, 25*, 380-391.

Détienne, F. (1991). A schema-based model of program understanding, *Mental models and human-computer interaction, 2*, 225-239.

Dewey, J. (1976). *The school and society.* Jo Ann Boydston (Ed.). Carbondale, Ill.: Southern Illinois University Press

Dewey, J. (1939). *Freedom and culture.* New York: G. P. Putnam's Sons.

Dewey, J. (1927). *The public and its problems.* New York: Henry Holt.

Dewey, J. (1926). Individuality and experience. Journal of the Barnes Foundation.

Dewey, J. (1916). The need of an industrial education in an industrial democracy, *Manual Training and Vocational Education, 17*, 409-414.

Dewey, J. (1910). *How we think*. Boston, MA: D. C. Heath.

Dewey, J. (1909). *Moral Principles in Education*. Boston: Houghton Mifflin.

Dewey, J. (1900a). *The child and the curriculum*. Chicago: University of Chicago Press.

Dewey, J. (1900b). *The school and society*. Chicago: University of Chicago Press.

Dewey, J. (1900c). The aim of history in elementary education. *The Elementary School Record, 1*, 199-203.

Dewey, J. (1899). *Lectures in the Philosophy of Education*. R. D. Archambault (Ed.). New York: Random House.

Dewey, J. (1898). The primary-education fetish. *The Forum, 25*, 315-328.

Dewey, J. (1897). Criticisms wise and otherwise on modern child study. *Journal of Proceedings and Addresses of the Thirty-Sixth Annual Meeting of the National Education Association*, 867-868.

Dewey, J. (1896). Interest in relation to training of the will. In *Second supplement to the Herbart Yearbook for 1895*. Bloomington, Il.: National Herbart Society, 209-246.

Dienes, Z. P. (1967). Some basic processes involved in mathematics learning. *Journal of Research in Mathematics Education*, 21-28.

diSessa, A. A. (1982). Unlearning Aristotelian physics: A study of knowledge-based learning, *Cognitive science, 6*, 37-75.

Divgi, D. R. (1981a). *Does the Rasch model relly work? Not if you look closely.* Paper presented at the annual meeting of the American Educational Research Association, Los Angeles.

Divgi, D. R. (1981b). Model-free evaluation of equating and scaling, *Applied psychological measurement, 5*, 203-208.

Divgi, D. R. (1980). *Evaluation of scales for multi-level test batteries.* Paper presented at the annual meeting of the American Educational Research Association, Boston, April.

Docking, R. A. (1986). Criterion-referenced grading techniques, *Studies in educational evaluation, 12*, 281-296.

Docking, R. A. (1985). *Profile based decision-making techniques for grading and certification.* Paper presented at the International Association for Educational Assessment conference, Oxford, England.

Docking, R. A. (1976). Sum problems in assessment, *Unicorn, 2*, 2, 59-64.

Doehring, D. G., & Reitan, R. M. (1962). Concept attainment of human adults with lateralized cerebral lesions. *Perceptual and Motor Skills*, 14, 27-33.

Doss, D. A. (1983). *Mother got tired of taking care of my baby.* Austin, Texas: Office of research and evaluation, Austin Independent School District, Publication Number 82.44.

Dougherty, K. J. & Hammack, F. M. (1990). *Education and society.* New York: Harcourt, Brace & Jovanovich.

Dubois, D. (1986). Belief structures, possibility theory and decomposable confidence measures on finite sets, *Computation and artificial intelligence, 5*, 403-416.

Dubois, P. H. (1970). *A History of Psychological Testing.* Boston: Allyn and Bacon.

Dubois, P. H. (1965). A test-dominated society: China 1115 B.C. - 1905 A.D. In C. W. Harris (Ed.), *Proceedings of the 1964 Invitational Conference on Testing Problems* (pp. 3-11). Princeton, NJ: Educational Testing Service.

Dumas, J. P. & Ninio, J. (1982). *Neucleic Acids Research, 10*, 197.

Duncan, V. (1980). *Oregon early school leavers study*. Salem: Oregon Department of Education.

Durkheim, E. (1971). Elementary forms of religious life. In: Cosin, B. R., Dale, I. R., Esland, G. M. & Swift, D. F. (Eds.), *School and Society*. London: Routledge & Kegan Paul.

Durost, W. N., & Prescott, G. A. (1962). *Essentials of measurement for teachers*. New York: Harcourt, Brace, G World.

Dyer, H. S. (1960). A psychometrician views human ability. *Teachers College Record, 61,* 394-403.

Eaton, E. A. (1983). *Multvariate statistics: A vector space approach*. New York: McGraw-Hill.

Ebel, R. L. (1981). Issues in testing for competency. Washington, DC: National Council on Measurement in Education.

Ebel, R. L. (1977). Comments on some problems of employment testing, *Personnel Psychology, 30,* 55-63.

Ebel, R. L. (1970, March). *Some limitations of criterion-referenced measurement*. Paper presented at the annual conference of the American Educational Research Association. Minneapolis. (ED 038 670).

Ebel, R. L. (1969). Knowledge vs. ability in achievement testing. *Proceedings of the 1969 invitational conference on testing problems* (pp. 66-76). Princeton, NJ: Educational Testing Service.

Ebel, R. L. (1968). The value of internal consistency in classroom examinations. *Journal of Educational Measurement, 5,* 71-73.

Ebel, R. L. (1965). *Measuring educational achievement*. Englewood Cliffs, NJ: Prentice-Hall.

Ebel, R. L. (1962). Content standard test scores. *Educational and Psychological Measurement, 22,* 15-25.

Ebel, R. L. (1961). Must all tests be valid? *American Psychologist, 16*(10), 640-647.

Ebel, R. L. (1954). Procedures for the analysis of classroom tests. *Educational and Psychological Measurement, 14,* 352-364.

Ebel, R. L. & Livingston, S. A. (1981). Issues in testing for competency. *Measurement in education, 12,* 2, 2-7. ED 208 001.

Eckstein, S. G., & Shemesha, M. (1992). Mathematical models of cognitive development. *British Journal of Mathematical and Statistical Psychology, 45,* 1-18.

Edelman, G., & Mountcastle, V. B. (1978). *The mindful brain*. Cambridge: Massachusetts Institute of Technology Press.

Edmonds, R. (1979). Effective schools for the urban poor. *Educational Leadership*, October, 15-24.

Edmonston, L. P., & Randall, R. S. (1972, April). *A model for estimating the reliability and validity of criterion-referenced measures*. Paper presented at the annual meeting of the American Educational Research Association, Chicago. (ED 065 591).

Educational Testing Service (1977, September). *Basic skills assessment around the nation*. Princeton, NJ: Educational Testing Service.

Educational Testing Service. (1968, March). *State testing programs: A survey of functions, tests, materials, and services*. Princeton, NJ: Educational Testing Service, Evaluation and Advisory Service.

Edwards, A. L. (1957). *Techniques of attitude scale construction*. New York: Appleton,

Century, Crofts.

Edwards, A. L., & Kenney, K. F. P. (1965). A comparison of the Thurstone and Likert techniques of attitude scale construction. *Journal of Applied Psychology, 30,* 72-83.

Edwards, A. L., & Kilpatrick, F. B. (1974). A technique for construction of attitude scales. In G. M. Maranell (Ed.), *SCALING: A sourcebook for behavioral scientists* (pp. 336-347). Chicago: Aldine Publishing.

Edwards, R. (1963). Teaching machines and programmed instruction. *Canadian Education and Research Digest, 3*(4), 265.

Eigen, M., & Winkler-Oswatitsch, R. (1990). Statistical geometry on sequence space. In R. F. Doolittle (ed.), *Methods in enzymology, Volume 183: Molecular evolution: Computer analysis of protein and nucleic acid sequences.* New York: Academic Press, Harcourt Brace Jovanovich, 505-529.

Eisner, E. W. (March, 1990). Who decides what schools teach (Curriculum Reform). *Phi Delta Kappan,* 71, 523-525

Embretson, S. (1984). A general latent trait model for response processes, *Psychometrika, 49, 2,* 175-186.

Emrick, J. A. (1971). An evaluation model for mastery testing, *Journal of educational measurement, 8,* 321-326.

Emrick, J. A., & Adams, E. N. (October, 1969). *An evaluation model for individualized instruction* (Report RC 2674). Yorktown Heights, NY: Interatioal Business Machines Corporation, Thomas J. Watson Research Center.

Eisner, E. W. (March, 1990). Who decides what schools teach (Curriculum Reform). *Phi Delta Kappan,* 71, 523-525.

Eliot, C. W. (1908). Industrial education as an essential factor in our national prosperity. In *Bulletin No. 5 of the National Society for the Promotion of Industrial Education.* New York: National Society for the Promotion of Industrial Education, 9-14.

Eliot, C. W. (1905). The fundamental assumptions in the report of the Committee of Ten (1893), *Educational Review, 30,* 325-342.

Eliot, C. W. (1892a). Shortening and enriching the grammar school course. *Journal of Proceedings and Addresses of the National Education Association, Session of the Year 1892,* 617-625.

Eliot, C. W. (1892b). Where popular education has failed. *The Forum, 14,* 411-428.

Ellwod, C. A. (1914). Our compulsory education laws, and retardation and elimination in our public schools, *Education, 34,* 572-576.

Elner, F. F., & Myers, R. E. (1962). Corpus callosum and the interhemispheric transmission of tactual learning. *Journal of Neurophysiology, 25,* 380-391.

Emrick, J. A. (1971, November). *The experimental validation of an evaluation model for mastery testing.* Washington, DC: U.S. Department of Health, Education, and Welfare, Office of Education, Bureau of Research, OEG-1-71-0002. (ED 069 202).

Emrick, J. A. (1971). An evaluation model for mastery testing. *Journal of Educational Measurement, 8,* 321-326.

Englehart, M. D. (1965). A comparison of several item discrimination indices. *Journal of Educational Measurement, 2,* 69-76.

English, F.W. (1988). *Curriculum auditing.* Lancaster, PA: Technomic Publishing Company, Incorporated.

English, F. W. (1987). *Curriculum management for schools, colleges, business.* Springfield, IL: Charles C. Thomas.

Ennis, R. H. (1989). Critical thinking and subject specificity: Clarification and needed research. *Educational Researcher, 18*, 4-10.

Entin, J. (1986). Sweatt v. Painter, the End of Segregations, and the Transformation of Education Law, *The Review of Litigation, 5*, 3-71.

Equal Employment Opportunity Commission. (1978). Uniform guidelines on employee selection procedures, *Federal Register, 43*, 38290-38309.

Estes, W. K. (1960). Learning theory and the new memtal chemistry. *Psychological Review, 67*, 207-223.

Estes, W. K., Hopkins, B. L., Hopkins, M., & Crothers, E. J. (1960). All-or-none conservation effects in the learning and retention of paired associates. *Journal of Experimental Psychology, 60*, 329-339.

Estes, W. K., & Suppes, P. (1959). Foundations of linear models. In R. R. Bush & W. K. Estes (Eds.), Studies in mathematical learning theory. Stanford: Stanford University Press, 137-179.

Everitt, B. S. (1968). Moments of the statistics kappa and weighted kappa, *The British journal of mathematical and statistical psychology, 21*, 97-103.

Ewell, P. T. (1985). *Levers for change: The role of state government in improving the quality of postsecondary education.* Denver, CO: National Center for Higher Education Management Systems.

Fahlman, S. E. (1979). *NETL: A system for representing and using real-world knowledge.* Cambridge, MA: Massachusetts Institute of Technology Press.

Falmagne, J. C. (1989). A latent trait theory via a stochastic learning theory for a knowledge space. *Pychometrika, 54(2)*, 283-303.

Fantini, M. D. (1986). *Regaining excellence in education.* Columbia: Merrill.

Fauconnier, G. (1994). *Mental Spaces: Aspects of meaning construction in natural language.* New York: Cambridge University Press.

Ferguson, G. A. (1971). *Statistical analysis in psychology and education.* New York: McGraw Hill.

Ferguson, G. A. (1949). On the theory of test discrimination. *Psychometrika, 14*, 61-68.

Ferguson, R. L. (1970, March). *Computer-assisted criterion-referenced testing.* Pittsburgh, PA: University of Pittsburgh Learning Research and Development Center, Working Paper No. 49.

Fernandez, E. (1977). New Mexico assesses its educational system. *Phi Delta Kappan, 59(1)*, 57-58.

Fhanér, S. (1974) Item sampling and decision making in achievement testing. *British Journal of Mathematical and Statistical Psychology, 27*, 172-175.

Filby, N. N. & Dishaw, M. M. (1977). *Construct validation of group-administered achievement tests through individual testing (Beginning Teacher Education Study Technical Note BTES III-A).* San Francisco: Far West Laboratory.

Fillbrandt, J. R., & Merz, W. R. (1977). The assessment of competency in reading and mathematics using community based standards. *Educational Research Quarterly, 2(1)*, 3-11.

Filmore, C. J. (1968). The case for case. In E. Bach & R. T. Harms (Eds.), *Universals in linguistic theory (pp. 1-90).* New York: Holt, Rinehart, and Winston.

Findley, W. G. (1956). A rationale for evaluation of item discrimination statistics. *Educational and Psychological Measurement, 19*, 175-180.

Fine, T. L. (1973). *Theories of probability: An examination of foundation.* New York:

Academic Press, 1973.

Finn, J. D. (1974). *A general model for multivariate analysis.* New York: Holt, Rinehart, and Winston.

Finney, R. L. (1928). *A sociological philosophy of education.* New York: Macmillan.

Firestone, Wm. A. (1989). Beyond order and expectations in high schools serving at-risk youth, *Educational Leadership*, 46, 41-45.

Fishburn, P. C. (1970). *Utility theory for decision making.* New York: Wiley.

Fisher, D. (1986). A proposed method of conceptual clustering for structured and decomposable objects. In T. M. Mitchell, J. G. Carbonell, & R. S. Michalski (Eds.), *Machine learning: A guide to current research (67-70).* Boston, MA.: Kluwer Academic Publishers.

Flanagan, J. C. (1982). Discussion of "Some issues in test equating." In P. W. Holland & D. B. Rubin (Eds.), *Test equating.* New York: Academic Press.

Flanagan, J. C. (1969). Program for learning in accordance with needs. *Psychology in the Schools*, 6, 133-136.

Flanagan, J. C. (1967). Functional education for the seventies. *Phi Delta Kappan*, 49, 27-32.

Flanagan, J. C. (1951). Units, scores, and norms. In E. F. Lindquist (Ed.), *Educational Measurement.* Washington, DC: American Council on Education, 695-763.

Fleiss, J. L. & Cicchetti, D. V. (1978). Inference about weighted kappa in the non-null case, *Applied psychological measurement, 2,* 113-117.

Fleiss, J. L., Cohen, J. & Everitt, B. S. (1969). Large sample standard errors of kappa and weighted kappa, *Psychological Bulletin, 72,* 323-327.

Flores, I. (1970). *Data structure and management.* Englewood Cliffs, NJ: Prentice Hall.

Forbes, D. W. (1976, April). *The use of Rasch logistic scaling procedures in the development of short multi-level arithmetic achievement tests for public school measurement.* Paper presented at the annual conference of the American Educational Research Association, San Francisco.

Forbes, D. W., & Ingebo, G. S. (1975, April). *An empirical test of the content homogeneity assumption involved in Rasch item calibration.* Paper presented at the annual conference of the American Educational Research Association, Washington, DC.

Forster, F. (1976, April). *Sample size and stable calibrations.* Paper presented at the annual conference of the American Educational Research Association.

Foshay, A. W. (1991). Functions and purposes for campus laboratory school. *National Association of Laboratory Schools Journal, 15*(3), 3-16.

Fox, J. N. (1991). University laboratory schools. *National Association of Laboratory Schools Journal, 15*(2), 1-9.

Frazier, B. W., & Armentrout, W. D. (1927). *An introduction to education.* New York: Scott Foresman.

Fredricksen, C. H. (1974). Models for the analysis of alternative sources of growth in correlated stochastic variables. *Psychometrika, 39*(2), 223-245.

Frederiksen, J. R. (1980). Component skills in reading: Measurement of individual differences through chronometric analysis. In R. F. Snow, P.A. Federico, & W. E. Montague (Eds.), *Aptitude, learning, and instruction. Volume 1, Cognitive process analysis of aptitutde.* Hillsdale, NJ: Erlbaum.

Frederiksen, N. (1986). Construct validity and construct similarity: Methods foruse in test development and test validation. *Multivariate Behavioral Research, 21*(1), 3-38.

Freedman, J. L., & Loftus, E. F. (1971). Retrieval of words from long-term memory. *Journal of Verbal Learning and Verbal Behavior, 10*(2), 107-115.

Fremer, J. (1974). *Developing tests for assessment programs: Issues and suggested procedures.* Princeton, NJ: Center for Statewide Educational Assessment, Educational Testing Service. (ED 093 990).

French, J. W. (1951). The description of aptitude and achievement factors in terms of rotated factors, *Psychometric monographs, 5.* Chicago: University of Chicago Press.

Freund, J. E. (1962). *Mathematical statistics.* Englewood Cliffs, NJ: Prentice Hall.

Freud, S. (1922). *Beyond the pleasure principle.* London, England: International Psychoanalytical Library.

Fricke, R. (1974a). Zur theorie lehrzielorientierter tests. *Lernzielorientierter Unterricht, 2,* 18-28.

Fricke, R. (1974b). *Kriteriumsorientierte leistungmsessung.* Stuttgart: Kohlhammer.

Fricke, R. (1972). Lehrzielorientierte messung mit hilfe stochastischer meßmodelle. In K.J. Klauer, R. Fricke, M. Herbig, H. Rupprecht, & F. Schot, *Lehrzielorientierte tests.* Düsseldorf: Schwann, 126-160.

Fricke, R., & Lühmann, R. (1983). Criterion-referenced tests-theory and application. *Studies in Educational Evaluation, 9,* 195-207.

Fry, E. B. (1963). *Teaching machines and programmed instruction: An introduction.* New York: McGraw-Hill.

Gable, R. A., Hendrickson, J. M., & Stowitschek, J. J. (1986). ''How can I get there from here?'' Making standardized test results useful for instructional decisionmmaking. *The Pointer, 30(2),* 13-18.

Gagné, R. M. (1974) *Essentials of learning for instruction.* Hildale, IL: Dryden Press.

Gagné, R. M. (1970). *The conditions of learning.* N.Y.: Holt, Rinehart & Winston.

Gagné, R. M. (1965). *The conditions of learning.* New York: Holt, Rinehart, and Winston.

Gagné, R. M. (1963, December). Learning and proficiency in mathematics. *Mathematics Teacher, 56,* 620-626.

Gagné, R. M., & Bassler, O. C. (1963). Study of retention of some topics of elementary nonmetric geometry. *Journal of Educational Psychology, 54*(3), 123 -131.

Gagné, R. M., Mayer, J. R., Garsten, H. L., & Paradise, N. E. (1962). Factors in acquiring knowledge of a mathematical task. *Psychological Monographs: General and applied,* 76, No. 526.

Gagné, R. M., & Paradise, N. E. (1961). Abilities and learning sets in knowledge acquisition. *Psychological Monographs,* Whole No. 518, 75, 14, 1-23.

Gaines, W. G. (1972, November). *Measuring social studies achievement: Criterion-referenced versus norm-referenced tests for the classroom teacher.* Paper presented at the annual meeting of the Mid-South Educational Research Association, New Orleans. (ED 078 072).

Gallery, M., & Hofmeister, D. (1977). A method for assessing the treatment valididty of tests in special education. *Exceptional Children, 25,* 100-113.

Galton, F. (1883). *Inquiries into human faculty and its development.* London: Macmillan.

Galton, F. (1969). *Hereditary genius: An inquiry into its laws and consequences.* London: Macmillan.

Gazzaniza, M. S. (1967, August). The split brain in man. *Scientific American,* 24-29.

GCE and CSE Board's Joint Council for 16+ National Criteria (1983). *Recommended statement of 16+ National criteria for chemistry.* 15-16. London, England: Author.

Geary, R. C. (1947). Testing for normality, *Biometrika, 34,* 209-242.

Gerberick, J. R. (1956). *Specimen objective test items: A guide to achievement test construction.* New York: Longmans Green.

Geschwind, N. (1970). The organization of language and the brain. *Science, 170,* 940-944.

Gibson, J. J., & Gibson, E. J. (1955). Perceptual learning: Differentiation or enrichment? *Psychological Review, 62,* 32-41.

Gick, M. L., & Holyoak, K. J. (1980). Analogical problem solving. *Cognitive Psychology, 12,* 306-355.

Gilman, D. A. (1977a). Minimum competency testing: An insurance policy for survival skills. *National Association of Secondary School Principals Bulletin,* 61, 77-84.

Gilman, D. A. (1977b). Minimal competency testing. *American School Board Journal, 164,* 41-43.

Ginsberg, A. L. (1989). Revitalizing program evaluation: The U.S. Department of Education experience, *Evaluation Review, 13,* 579-597.

Giovanni, A., & Agostino, P. (1991). Actions representation in a 4-D space. *International Journal of Man-Machine Studies, 35,* 825-841.

Glaser, R. (1981). The furture of testing: A research agenda for cognitive psychology and psychometrics. *American Psychologist, 36,* 923-936.

Glaser, R. (1972). Individuals and learning: The new aptitudes. *Educational Researcher, 1,* 5-13.

Glaser, R. (1971a). Instructional technology and the measurement of learning outcomes: Some questions. In W. J. Popham (Ed.), *Criterion-referenced measurement* (pp. 5-16). Englewood Cliffs, NJ: Educational Technology Publications.

Glaser, R. (1971b). A criterion-referenced test. *Criterion-referenced Measurement.* W. J. Popham (ed.). Englewood Cliffs, N.J.: Educational Technology Publications, 41-54.

Glaser, R. (1968). Adapting the elementary school curriculum to individual performance. In *Proceedings of the 1967 Invitational Conference on Testing Problems* (pp. 3-36). Princeton, NJ: Educational Testing Service.

Glaser, R. (1963). Instructional technology and the measurement of learning outcomes: Some questions. *American Psychologist, 18,* 519-521.

Glaser, R. & Cox, R. C. (1968). Criterion-referenced testing for the measurement of educational outcomes. In *Instructional process and medical innovations.* R. A. Weisgerber (ed.). Chicago, Illinois: Rand McNally and Co., 545-550.

Glaser, R. & Klaus, D. J. (1962). Proficiency measurement: Assessing human performance. *Psychological principles in systems development.* R. M. Gagne (ed.). New York: Holt, Rinehart, and Winston, 419-474.

Glaser, R., & Nitko, A. J. (1971). Measurement in learning and instruction. In R. L. Thorndike (Ed.), *Educational Measurement.* Washington, DC: American Council on Education, 625-670.

Glass, G. V. (1978). Standards and criteria. *Journal of Educational Measurement, 15,* 237-261.

Glenn, N. D. (1977). *Cohort Analysis,* Sage Univeristy paper series on quantitative applications in the social sciences, 07-005. Beverly Hills and London: Sage Publications.

Glennon, V. J. (1976). Mathematics: How firm the foundations?, *Phi Delta Kappan, 61,* 77-84.

Glynn, S. M., R. H. Yeany & B. K. Britton (1991). A constructive view of learning science. In *S. M. Glynn, R. H. Yeany, & B. K. Britton (Eds.), The Psychology of Learning Science.* Hillsdale, NJ: Lawrence Erlbaum Associates, Publishers.

Gobel, R. P. (1990). The mathematics of mental rotations, *Journal of Mathematical Psychology, 34.*

Goldberger, A. S. (1973). Structural equation models: An overview. In A. S. Goldberger & O. D. Duncan (Eds.), *Structural equation models in the social sciences.* New York: Seminar Press, 1-18.

Godshalk, F. I., Swineford, F., & Coffman, W. E. (1966). *The measurement of writing ability.* New York: College Entrance Examination Board.

Goldchmid, B., & Goldchmid, M.L. (1976). Peer teaching in higher education: A review. *Higher Education, 5,* 9-33.

Goldchmid, B., & Goldchmid, M.L. (1974). Individualizing instruction in higher education: A review, *Higher Education, 3,* 1-24.

Goldchmid, B., & Goldchmid, M.L. (1973). Modular instruction in higher education, *Higher Education, 2,* 15-32.

Goodman, P. S., Pennings, J. M. & Associates (1977). *New Perspectives on Organizational Effectiveness.* San Francisco: Jossey-Bass Publishers.

Goss, A. E., & Nodine, C. F. (1965). *Paired-associates learning: The role of meaningfulness, similarity, and familiarization.* New York: Academic Press.

Govindaraj, T. (1987). Qualitative approximation methodology for modeling and simulation of large dynamic systems: Applications to a marine steam power plant. *IEEE Transactions on Systems, Man, and Cybernetics, 17,* 6, 937-955.

Graham, N. (1973). Spatial frequency channels in human vision: Detecting edges without edge detectors. In C. S. Harris (Ed.), *Visual coding and adaptability* (pp. 163-218). Hillsdale, NJ: Academic Press.

Grant, C. A. (1989). Urban teachers: Their new colleges & curriculum, *Phi Delta Kappan,* 70, 10, 764-776.

Gray, W. M. (1978). A comparison of Piagetian theory and criterion-referenced measurement, *Review of Educational Research, 48,* 223-249.

Green, E. J. (1962). *The learning process and programmed instruction.* New York: Holt, Rinehart, and Winston.

Greeno, J. G. (1977). Proces of understanding in problem solving. In N. J. Castellan, D. B. Pisoni & G. R. Potts (Eds.), *Cognitive theory* (Vol. 2). Hillsdale, N. J.: Erlbaum.

Greeno, J. G. (1973). The structure of memory and the process of solving problems. In R. Solso (Ed.), *Contemporary issues in cognitive psychology: The Loyola symposium.* Washington, DC: Winston.

Greiner, R. (1986). Learning by understanding analogies. In T. M. Mitchell, J. G. Carbonell, & R. Michalski, (Eds.), *Machine learning: A guide to current research.* Boston, MA.: Kluwer Academic Publishers, 81-84.

Gregson, R. (1975). *Psychometrics of similarity.* New York: Academic Press.

Gribbin, J. (1984). *In search of Schrödinger's cat.* New York: Bantam Books.

Grimes, J. E. (1975). *The thread of discourse.* The Hague: Mouton.

Grinder, J., & Bandler, R. (1976). *The structure of magic.* Palo Alto, CA: Science and Behavior Books.

Grossberg, S. A. (1980). How does a brain buid a cognitive code? *Psychological Review,* 87(1), 1-51.

Grossberg, S. A. (1978). A theory of human memory: Self-organization and performance of sensory-motor codes, maps, and plans. *Progress in Theoretical Biology, 55,* 235-371.

Groves, P. M., & Thompson, R. F. (1973). A dual-process theory of habitation: Neural mechanisms. In H. V. S. Peeke & M. J. Herz (Eds.), *Habitation* (pp. 175-205). New York: Academic Press.

Guggenheimer, H. W. (1977). *Differential Geometry.* NY: Dover Publications.

Guilford, J. P. (1956). The structure of intellect, *Psychological Bulletin, 53,* 267-293.

Guilford, J. P. (1954). *Psychometric methods.* New York: McGraw-Hill.

Guilford, J. P. (1948). Factor analysis in a test-development program. *Psychological Records, 55,* 79-94.

Gulliksen, H. (1950). *Theory of Mental tests.* NY: John Wiley & Sons.

Gunstone, R. F. & White, R. T. (1981). Understanding gravity, *Science education, 65,* 91-299.

Gussarsky, E. & Gorodetsky, M. (1988). On the equilibrium concept: Constrained word associations and conception. *Journal of Research in Science Teaching, 25,* 5, 319-333.

Gutkin, R. (Ed.) *Handbook of school psychology.* New York: John Wiley, 351-379.

Guttman, L. (1944). A basis for scaling qualitative data. *American Sociological Review, 9,* 139-1150.

Hackett, M. G. (1968). *A hierarchy of skills in listening comprehension and reading comprehension,* Doctoral dissertation, University of California, Berkeley.

Hackett, M. G. (1970). *A hierarchy of skills in listening comprehension and reading comprehension.* Tallahasse, Fl.: Florida State University. (ERIC Document Reproduction Service No. ED 041 701).

Haladyna, T. M. (1974). *An investigation of full- and subscale reliabilities of criterion-referenced tests.* Paper presented at the annual meeting of the American Educational Research Association, Chicago. (ED 091 435).

Haladyna, T. M., & Roid, G. H. (1983). Reviewing criterion-referenced test items. *Educational Technology, 17,* 35-38.

Haladyna, T. M., & Roid, G. H. (1981). The role of instructional sensitivity in the empirical review of criterion-referenced test items. *Journal of Educational Measurement, 18,* 1, 39-53.

Hall, G. S. (1883). The contents of children's mind, *Princeton review, 2,* 249-272.

Hall, G. S. (1904). *Adolescence.* New York: Appleton.

Hall, J. W. (1911). To what extent are children of the fifth grade in this city being taught genuine composition? Research within the field of education, its organization, and encouragement. *The School Review Monographs, 1,* 61-62.

Hall, M. (1975, April). *Statewide assessment of student performance: Comparative study.* Paper presented at the annual meeting of the American Educational Research Association, Washington, DC.

Hall, W. E. & Robinson, F. P. (1945). An analytical approach to the study of reading skills, *Psychological Review, 36,* 429-442.

Halliday, M. A. K., & Rugaiya, H. (1976). *Cohesion in English.* New York: Longman.

Hambleton, R. K. (1986). Determining optimal test lengths with a fixed total testing time. ERIC document: ED 270 482.

Hambleton, R. K. (1982). Advances in criterion-referenced testing technology, In C. Reynolds & T.

Hambleton, R. K. (1980). Contributions to criterion-referenced testing technology: An introduction, *Applied psychological measurement, 4,* 4, 421-424.

Hambleton, R. K. (1981). Advances in criterion-referenced testing technology. In C. R. Reynolds & T. B. Gutkin (Eds.), *Handbook of school psychology.* New York: Wiley.

Hambleton, R. K. (1974). Testing and decision-making procedures for selecting individualized instructional programs. *Review of Educational Research, 44,* 371-400.

Hambleton, R. K., & Cook, L. L. (1977). Latent trait models and their use in the analysis of educational test data. *Journal of Educational Measurement, 14*(2), 75-97.

Hambleton, R. K., & de Gruijter, D. N. M. (1983). Application of item response models to criterion-referenced test item selection. *Journal of Educational Measurement, 20,* 355-367.

Hambleton, R. K. & Eignor, D. R. (1978). Guidelines for evaluating criterion-referenced tests and test manuals. *Journal of Educational Measurement, 15,* 321-327.

Hambleton, R. K., & Gorth, W. P. (1970). *Criterion-referenced testing: Issues and applications.* Paper presented at the annual meeting of the Northeastern Educational Research Association, Liberty, NY. (ED 060 025).

Hambleton, R. K., & Novick, Melvin R. (1973). Toward an integration of theory and method for criterion-referenced tests. *Journal of Educational Measurement, 10,* 159-170.

Hambleton, R. K., & Rogers, H. J. (1986). Technical advances in credentialing examinations. *Evaluation and the Health Professions, 9,* 2, 205-229.

Hambleton, R. K., Swaminathan, H., Algina, J., & Coulson, D. B. (1978). Criterion-referenced testing and measurement: A review of technical issues and developments. *Review of Educational Research, 48*(1), 1-48.

Hambleton, R. K., Swaminathan, H., & Rogers, H. J. (1991). *Fundamentals of item response theory.* Newbury Park, CA: SAGE Publications, Inc.

Hambleton, R. K., & Zaal, J. N. (1991). *Advances in educational & psychological testing.* Boston: Kluwer Academic Publishing.

Hamilton, W. (1859). *Lectures on metaphysics and logic: Volume 1.* Boston: Gould and Lincoln.

Handrick, F. A. (1975, November). *Delaware educational assessment program 1974-75.* Report of the Spring 1975 testing program. Dover: Delaware State Department of Public Instruction, Division of Research, Planning, and Evaluation.

Hanna, G. S., & Bennett, J. A. (1984). Instructional sensitivity expanded. *Educational and Psychological Measurement, 44,* 3, 583-596.

Hanson, N. R. (1970). A picture theory of theory meaning. In R. G. Colodny (Ed.), *The nature and function of scientific theories.* Pittsburgh, PA: University of Pittsburgh Press, 233-274.

Haratunian, H. (1973). *Validation of a learning hierarchy using classroom interaction.* Unpublished doctoral dissertation, Boston University.

Hardin, C. J. (1988). Access to higher education: Who belongs? *Journal of Developmental Education, 12,* 2-6.

Harlow, H. F. (1949). The formation of learning sets. *Psychological Review, 56,* 61-65.

Harman, H. H. (1970). *Modern factor analysis.* Chicago: University of Chicago Press.

Harnisch, D. L. (1981). Analysis of item response patterns: Consistency indices and their application to criterion-referenced tests. Paper presented at the Annual meeting of the American Educational Research Association. Los Angeles, April. (ED 209 335).

Harris, B. (1966). *Theory of probability.* Reading, MA: Addison Wesley.

Harris, C. W. (1974). Some technical characteristics of mastery tests. In C. W. Harris, M. C. Aiken, and W. J. Popham (Eds.), *Problems in criterion-referenced measurement* (Center for the Study of Evaluation Monograph No. 3). Los Angeles: Center for the Study of Evaluation.

Harris, C. W. (1972). *An index of efficiency for fixed-length mastery tests.* Paper presented at the annual meeting of the American Educational Research Association, Chicago.

Harris, C. W. (1971, March). *An interpretation of Livingston's reliability coefficient for criterion-referenced tests.* Santa Barbara: University of California at Santa Barbara. (ED 058 312).

Harris, C. W., Pearlman, A. P. & Wilcox, R. R. (1977). *Achievement test items-Methods of study* (CSE Monograph Series in Evaluation, No. 6). Los Angeles: University of California, Center for the Study of Evaluation.

Harris, J. D. (1943). Habituatory response decrement in the intact organism. *Psychological Bulletin, 40,* 385-422.

Harris, W. T. (1896a). How the will combines with the intellect in the higher orders of knowing, *Journal of Proceedings and Addresses of the Thirty-Fifth Annual Meeting of the National Education Association,* 440-446.

Harris, W. T. (1896b). *Psychologic Foundations of Education: An Attempt to Show the Genesis of the Higher Faculties of the Mind.* New York: D. Appleton.

Harris, W. T. (1889). The intellectual value of tool-work. *Journal of Proceedings and Addresses of the National Education Association, Session of the Year 1889,* 92-98.

Harris, W. T. (1888). What shall the public schools teach? *The Forum, 4,* 573-581.

Harris, W. T. (1886). Psychological inquiry, *Journal of Proceedings and Addresses of the National Education Association, Session of the Year, 1885,* 91-101.

Harris, W. T. (1880). Equivalents in a liberal course of study: Formal and substantial studies. *Journal of Proceedings and Addresses of the National Education Association, Session of the Year 1880,* 167-175.

Harris, Z. (1968). *Mathematical structures of language.* New York: John Wiley.

Harrison, M. C. (1973). *Data structures and programming.* Glenview, IL: Scott, Foresman and Company.

Hart, J. (1927). *Adult education.* San Francisco: Jossey-Bass.

Hartigan, J. A. (1975). Clustering algorithms. New York: John Wiley and Sons.

Harvey, O., Hunt, D., & Schroder, H. (1961). *Conceptual systems and personality organization.* New York: Wiley.

Harvey, T. J. (1975, May). Some thoughts on norm-referenced and criterion-referenced measures. *Research in Education, 13,* 79-86.

Hashway, R. M. (1990). *Handbook of developmental education.* New York: Praeger.

Hashway, R. M. (1989a). Learning center designs. *Teaching and Research in Developmental Education, 5(*2), 25-38.

Hashway, R. M. (1989b). Computer education-What is it?. *Interface: The Computer Education Quarterly,* 10(1), 7-9.

Hashway, R. M. (1989c). Does money make a difference? An econometric analysis of school outcomes. *National Forum for Educational Research Journal,* 2, 2, 59-71.

Hashway, R. M. (1988/1989). Expected difficulty of Rasch items, *Louisiana educational research journal,* 14, 3, 91-95.

Hashway, R. M. (1988). *Foundations of developmental education.* New York: Praeger

Publishers.

Hashway, R. M. (1986). From text processing to communications: The evolution of computer training. *Technological Horizons in Education*, 14(3), 88-89.

Hashway, R. M. (1983). Sequencing the learning of reading and study skills. *Journal of Instructional Psychology*, 1(10), 41-50.

Hashway, R. M. (1982a). Extending mastery learning systems-The sequencing of mathematics content. *Illinois School Research and Development Journal*, 18(2), 25-31.

Hashway, R. M. (1982b). Extending mastery learning systems-The sequencing of mathematics content. *Journal of the Association for Supervision and Curriculum Development*, 18(2), 25-31.

Hashway, R. M. (1979). The expanded individualized instruction system (EIPI). *Educational Technology*, 19, 33-38.

Hashway, R. M. (1978a). *Objective mental measurement: Individual and program evaluation using the Rasch Model*. New York: Praeger Special Studies, Praeger Publishers.

Hashway, R. M. (1978b). New software for courses in test construction. *Educational and Psychological Measurement*, 38, 159-166.

Hashway, R. M. (1977a). *ANALYSIS: A comprehensive computer program for the analysis of achievement test data*. Chestnut Hill, MA: Laboratory for Statistical and Policy Research, Boston College.

Hashway, R. M. (1977b, May). *New software for courses in multivariate statistics and test construction*. Paper presented at the annual conference of the New England Educational Research Organization, Manchester, NH.

Hashway, R. M. (1977c). *A comparison of tests derived using Rasch and traditional psychometric paradigms*. (Doctoral dissertation, Boston College, 1977). University Microfilms.

Hashway, R. M. (1976a). *Distance functions in functional data spaces*. Paper presented at the Ninth Annual Mathematical Psychology Meeting, New York University, August 30 to September 1.

Hashway, R. M. (1976b). *The geometry of multivariate data spaces after linear and nonlinear homeomorphic transformation*. Paper presented at the meeting of the American Statistical Association, Boston, Massachusetts.

Hashway, R. M. (1976c, June). *Can tests which maximally discrmininate between individuals also detect between treatment differences?* Paper presented at the Symposium on Application of Statistics, Dayton, OH.

Hashway, R. M., & Cain, K. S. (1993). *Curriculum directions for the next millennium*. Grambling, LA: Educational Research Quarterly.

Hashway, R. M., Harutunian, H., Lambiase, F., Prendergast, J., & Schoen, K. (1979). *Competiencies in mathematics*. Wellesley, MA: The Massachusetts State College System.

Hashway, R. M. & Hashway, S. E. (1992). Solving mathematical word problems-Integrating two different world models. In T. L. Ballock & A. M. Scales (eds.), *Innovative learning strategies, Tenth Yearbook of the International Reading Association*, 3-8.

Hashway, R. M., & McDermot, A. (1980). *The diagnostic prescriptive achievement monitoring system*. Wellesley, MA: The Commonwealth Career Center.

Hashway, R. M., Rogers, P. H. & Gamble, S. T. (1990). The impact of public vs. private high school preparation upon the performance of freshmen enrolled in two Louisiana public universities. *Louisiana Education Research Journal, 15,* 2, 42-46.

Hashway, R. M., Rogers, P. H., Jackson, L. G., & Barham, W. (1993). Similarities and Differences Between College Persistence and Achievement Indices, *Louisiana Educational Research Journal,* in press.

Hawkes, H. E., & Lindquist, E. F. (1936). In C. R. Mann (Ed.), *The construction and use of achievement examinations.* Boston: Houghton Mifflin.

Hawking, S. W. (1996). *The Cambridge lectures.* West Hollywood, CA: Cover.

Havinghurst, R. J. (1952). *Developmental tasks and education (2nd ed.).* New York: McKay.

Hays, W. L. (1973). *Statistics for the social sciences* (2nd ed.). New York: Holt, Rinehart, and Winston.

Head, J. O. & Sutton, C. R. (1981). *Structures of understanding and the ontogenesis of commitment.* Paper presented at the meeting of the American Educational Research Association, Los Angeles.

Heald, M. A. (1969, June). Least squares made easy. *American Journal of Physics, 37*(6), 655-662.

Hebb, D. O. (1955). Drives and the C.N.S. (conceptual nervous system). *Psychological Review, 62,* 243-254.

Hebb, D. O. (1946). On the nature of fear. *Psychological Review, 53,* 259-276.

Heisenberg, W. (1959). *Physics and philosophy.* New York: Harper & Row.

Heisenberg, W. (1970). *The physicist's conception of nature.* Westport, Connecticut: Grenwood Press.

Heisenberg, W. (1971). *Physics and beyond.* New York: Harper & Row.

Heller, W. (1964). *The problem of poverty in America. The annual report of the council of economic advisors.* Washington, DC: Government Printing Office.

Heller, J. I., & Greeno, J. G. (1979). Information processing analyes of mathematical problem solving. In R. W. Tyler & S. H. White (Eds.), *Testing, teaching, and learning: Report of a conference on research on testing.* Washington, D. C.: U. S. Department of Health, Education, and Welfare, National Institute of Education.

Helm, J. (Ed.). (1967). *Essays on the verbal and visual arts.* Seattle: University of Washington Press.

Helmholtz, H. von. (1962). *Physiological optics.* New York: Dover.

Helmholtz, H. von. (1896). *Handbuch der physiologischen optik.* Leipzig: Zweite Auflage.

Helmholtz, H. von. (1866). *Handuch der physiologischen optik.* Hamberg: Voss.

Helmstadter, G. C. (1974). *A comparison of Bayesian and traditional indexes of test item effectiveness.* Paper presented at the convention of the National Council on Measurement in Education, Chicago. (ED 087 821).

Helper, J. (1973). *Materials and procedures for assessing learner needs in Colorado.* Denver, DO.: Colorado State Deparment of Education, Division of Elementary and Secondary Education.

Henryssen, S. (1971). Gathering, analyzing, and using data on test items. In R. L. Thorndike (Ed.), *Educational Measurement* (2nd ed.) (pp. 130-159). Washington, DC: American Council on Education.

Herbig, M. (1974). Ein lehrzielorientiertes zensierungsmodell. *Zeitschrift für er Ziehungswissenchaftliche for Schung,8,* 129-142.

Heron, W. (1966). The pathology of boredom (1957). In S. Coopersmith (Ed.), *Frontiers of psychological research*, San Francisco: Freeman.

Hess, R. A. (1987). A qualitative model of human interaction with complex dynamic systems. *Transactions of the International Association of Electrical and Electronic Engineers, Systems, Man, Cybernetics, 17*, 33-51.

Higbee, J. L. (1993). Developmental versus remedial: More than semantics. *Research and Teaching in Developmental Education, 9*(2), 99-107.

Higgins, E. T., & Bargh, J. A. (1987). Social cognition and social percetion, *Annual review of psychology, 38*, 364-426.

Hill, P. W. (1984). Testing hierarchy in educational taxonomies: A theoretical and empirical investigation, *Evaluation in education: An international review series, 8, 3*, 181-279.

Hinton, G. (1979). Some demonstrations of the effects of structural descriptions in mental imagery, *Cognitive science, 3*, 231-250.

Hinton, G. E., McClelland, J. L., & Rumelhart, D. E. (1987). Distributed representations. In D. E. Rumelhart & J. L. McClelland (Eds.), *Parallel distributed processing. Explorations in the microstructure of cognition: Vol. 1: Foundations* (pp. 77-109). Cambridge: The Massachusetts Institute of Technology Press.

Hinton, G. E., & Sejnowski, T. J. (1987). Learning and relearning in Boltzmann Machines. In J. L. McClelland & D. F. Rumelhart, *Parallel distributed processing, Explorations in the microstructure of cognition, Volume 2: Psychological and biological models*. Cambridge, MA: The Massachusetts Institute of Technology Press (282-317).

Hively, W., Patterson, H. L., & Page, S. H. (1968). A "universe-defined" system of arithmetic achievement tests. *Journal of Educational Measurement, 5*, 275-290.

Hobson, A., & McCarley, R. (1979). The forms of dreams and the biology of sleep. In B. Wolman (Ed.), *Handbook of dreams*. New York: Van Nostrand Reinhold.

Hoffman, C. M., Snyder, T. D. and Sonnenberg, Wm. (1992). *Historically black colleges and universities*. Washington, D.C.: U.S. Department of Education, Office of Educational Research and Improvement.

Holland, J. (1959). A teaching machine program in psychology. In E. Galanter (Ed.), *Automatic teaching: The state of the art* (pp. 69-82). New York: John Wiley.

Hollander, M., & Wolfe, D. (1973). *Non-parametric statistical methods*. New York: John Wiley and Sons.

Holte, R. C. (1986). A conceptual framework for concept identification. In T. M. Mitchell, J. G. Carbonell, & R. S. Michalski (Eds.), *Machine learning: A guide to current research*. Boston, MA.: Kluwer Academic, 99-102.

Holtzman, W. H. (Ed.). (1970). *Computer-assisted insstruction, testing, and guidance*. New York: Harper and Row.

Holzinger, K. J. (1936). *Preliminary reports on Spearman-Holzinger unitary trait study*. Chicago: University of Chicago, Statistical Laboratory, Department of Education.

Holzinger, K. J. & Harman, H. H. (1937). Relationships between factors obtained from certain analyses, *Journal of educational psychology, 28*, 321-345.

Horn, D. & Usher, M. (1991). Parallel activation of memories in an oscillatory neural network, *Neural Computation, 3*, 31-43.

Hoyt, C. J. (1941). Test reliability estimated by analysis of variance. *Psychometrika, 6*, 153-160.

Hsu, Tse-Chi. (1971, February). *Empirical data on criterion-referenced tests*. Paper presented at the annual meeting of the American Educational Research Association, New York. (ED 050 139).

Hughes, J. E. (1962). *Programmed instruction for schools and industry.* Chicago: Science Research Associates.

Hull, C. L. (1952). *A behavior of intelligence.* Hillsdale, NJ: Lawrence Erlbaum Associates, 237-260.

Hull, C. L. (1943). *Principles of behavior.* New York: Appleton-Century-Crofts.

Hull, C. L. (1933a). Differentiation habitation to internal stimuli in the albino rat. *Journal of Comparative Psychology,* 16, 255-273.

Hull, C. L. (1933b). *Hypnosis and suggestibility: An experimental approach.* New York: Appleton, Century,Crofts.

Hull, C. L. (1931). Goal attraction and directing ideas conceived as habit phenomena. *Psychological Review,* 38, 487-506.

Hull, C. L., Honland, C. I., Ross, R. T., Hall, M., Perkins, D. T., & Fitch, F. B. (1940). *Mathematico-deductive theory of rote learning.* New Haven, CN: Yale University Press.

Humphrey, G. (1933). *The nature of learning.* New York: Harcourt.

Hunt, E. (1976). Varieties of cognitive power. In L. B. Resnick (Ed.), *The nature of intelligence* (pp. 237-260). Hillsdale, NJ: Lawrence Erlbaum Associates.

Hunt, E. (1973). The memory we must have. In R. Schark and K. Colby (Eds.), *Computer models of thought and language.* San Francisco: Freeman.

Hunt, E., Lunneborg, C., & Lewis, J. (1975). What does it mean to be high verbal? *Cognitive Psychology,* 7, 194-227.

Hunt, E. B., Frost, N., & Lunneborg, C. L. (1973). Individual differences in cognition: A new approach to intelligence. In G. Bower (Ed.), *Advances in learning and motivation (Volume 7).* New York: Academic Press.

Hunt, E., & Poltrock, S. (1974). The mechanics of thought. In B. Kantowitz (Ed.), *Human information processing: Tutorials in performance and cognition.* Hillsdale, NJ: Lawrence Erlbaum Associates.

Hunter, I. M. L. (1964). *Memory: facts and fallacies.* London, England: Penguin Books.

Hush, D. R. & Horne, B. G. (1991). Progress in supervised neural networks, *IEEE signal processing magazine,* 10, 1, 8-27.

Hutchinson, J. W. (1989). Netscal: A network scaling algorithm for nonsymmetric proximity data. *Psychometrika,* 54, 1, 25-51.

Huxley, A. (1959). *The doors of perception and heaven and hell.* London, England: Penguin Books.

Huynh, H. (1977). Two simple classes of mastery scores based on the beta-binomial model. *Psychometrika,* 42(4), 601-608.

Huynh, H. (1976). On the reliabiity of decisions in domain-referenced testing, *Journal of educational measurement,* 13, 253-264.

Huynh, H. & Mandeville, G. K. (1978). *An approximation to the true abiity distribution in the binomial error model and applications.* Paper presented at the annual meeting of the American Educational Research Association, March 27-31.

Ingebo, G. S. (1987). *Riding the Rasch tiger. Part 2: Implications for district testing programs (Where the rubber meets the road).* Paper presented at the annual meeting of the National Council on Measurement in Education, Washington, D.C. ED 286 922.

Ingenkamp. K. (1970). Normbezogene und kriterienorientierte tests. *Didacta Medica, 3,* 65-70.

Ingenkamp, K. & Marsolek, T. (1968). *Mölichkeiten und grenzen der testanwendung in der schule.* Weinheim: Beltz.

Institute of Nuclear Power Operations. (1985). *Principles of training systems development. (Manual, INPO 85-006).* Atlanta, GA: Nuclear Power Institute.

Irvine, D. J. (1976, December). How good is our school district?, *Journal of the New York State School Boards Association,* 27-30.

Ivens, S. H. (1972, April). *A pragmatic approach to criterion-referenced measures.* Paper presented at the annual meeting of the American Educational Research Association, Chicago. (ED 064 406).

Ivens, S. H. (1970). *An investigation of item analysis, reliability, and validity in relation to criterion-referenced tests.* Unpublished doctoral dissertation, Florida State University.

Jackson, J. H. (1958). On localization. In J. H. Jackson (Ed.), *Selected readings: Volume 2.* New York: Basic Books (Originally Published in 1869).

Jackson, P. A. (1973). After apple picking. *Harvard Educational Review, 4*(1), 51-60.

Jacobs, R. A. (1988). Increased rate of convergence through learning rate adaptation, *Neural networks, 1,* 4, 295-308.

Jaeger, R. M. (1987). Two decates of revolution in educational measurement!? *Educational Measurement-Issues and Practice, 6,* 4, 6-14.

Jaeger, R. M. (1976). *Measurement consequences of selected standard-setting models.* Paper presented at the annual meeting of the National Council on Measurement in Education. San Francisco, April

James, W. (1890). *Principles of psychology.* New York: Holt.

Jarvis, P. (1992). *Paradoxes of Learning: On becoming an individual in society.* San Francisco: Jossey-Bass.

Jaspen, N. (1946). Serial correlation. *Psychometrika, 11,* 23-30.

Jencks, C. (1972). *Inequality: A reassessment of the effects of family and schooling in America.* New York: Basic Books.

Jenkins, W. L. (1956). Triserial r: A neglected statistic. *Journal of Applied Psychology, 40,* 63-64.

Jennings, W., & Nathan, J. (1976). Startling/disturbing research on school program effectiveness. *Phi Delta Kappan, 58,* 568-572.

Jobs, N. & Hawthone, L. (1977). Informal assessment for the classroom. *Focus on Exceptional Children, 9,* 1-13.

Johnson, J. M. & Pennypacker, H. S. (1980). *Stratigies & TActics of Human Behavioral Research,* Englewood Cliffs, NJ: Lawrence Erlbaum and Associates.

Johnson-Laird, P. N. (1983). *Mental Models.* Cambridge, Ma.: Harvard University Press.

Johnson-Laird, P. N. (1975). Models of Deduction. In R. J. Falmagne (ed.) *Representation and Process in Children and Adults.* Hillsdale, N.J.: Lawrence Erlbaum.

Johnson, N. F. (1978). Coding processes in memory. *Canadian Journal of Psychology, 15,* 165-171.

Johnson, N. F., & Migdoll, D. M. (1971). Transfer and retroaction under conditions of changed organization. *Cognitive Psychology, 2,* 229-237.

Johnson, N. F. (1978). Coding processes in memory. *Canadian Journal of Psychology, 15,* 165-171.

Johnson, P. E. (1964). Associative meaning of concepts in physics, *Journal of educational psychology, 55,* 84-88.

Johnson, P. O. & Jackson, R. W. B. (1959). *Modern statistical methods: Descriptive & inferential.* Skokie, Illinois: Rand Mc Nally.

Johnson, P. O. & Neyman, J. (1936). Tests of certain linear hypotheses and their application to some educational problems, *Statistical reserch memoirs, 1,* 57-93.

Johnson-Laird, P. N. (1985). Logical thinking does it occur in daily life? In B. F. Chipman, J. W. Segal & R. Glaser, *Thinking and Learning Skills, Volume 2: Research and Open Questions.* Hillsdale, N.J.: Lawrence Erlbaum.

Johnson-Laird, P. N. (1983). *Mental Models.* Cambridge, Ma.: Harvard University Press.

Johnson-Laird, P. N. (1975). Models of Deduction. In R. J. Falmagne (ed.) *Representation and Process in Children and Adults.* Hillsdale, N.J.: Lawrence Erlbaum.

Jöreskog, K. & Sorbom, D. (1989). *Lisrel 7: A guide to the program and applications.* Chicago: SPSS Inc.

Jouvet, M. (1969). Biogenic amines and the states of sleep. *Science, 163,* 32-41.

Just, M. A. & Carpenter, P. A. (1985). Cognitive coordinate systems: Accounts of mental rotation and individual differences in spatial abilities, *Psychological Review, 92,* 137-192.

Kaitz, H. B. (1945). A note on reliability. *Psychometrika, 10,* 127-131.

Kane, M. T. (1986). The role of reliability in criterion-referenced tests, *Journal of educational measurement, 23,* 3, 221-224.

Kaplan, R. S. (1982). *Advanced management accounting.* Englewood Cliffs, NJ: Printice-Hall, Inc.

Karni, K. R. & Lofsness, K. G. (1985). Determination of passing scores on certificatin examinations: An unresolved issue, *Journal of allied health, 14,* 4, 415-426.

Kast, F. E. & Rosenzweig, J. E. (1974). *Organization and Management-A Systems Approach.* New York: McGraw-Hill Book Company.

Katz, D. & Kahn, R. L. (1966). *The Social Psychology of Organizations.* New York: John Wiley & Sons, Inc..

Kaufman, R. & Herman, J. (1991). *Strategic planning in education.* Lancaster, Penn: Technomic Publishing Co.

Keimig, R. L. (1983). *Raising academic standards: A guide to learning improvement: Association for the Study of Higher Education-ERIC higher education research report No. 4.* Washington, D.C.: Association for the Study of Higher Education.

Kellaghan, T., Airasian, P. W., Madaus, G. F., & Fontes, P. (1975). *The mathematical attainments of post-primary school entrants.* Dublin, Ireland: Educational Research Centre, St. Patrick's College. Unpublished manuscript.

Keller, F. S. (1968). Goodbye, Teacher ... *Journal of applied behavior analysis, 1,* 79-89.

Kelly, G. A. (1955). *The psychology of personal constructs.* New York: Norton.

Kempa, R. F., & L'Odiaga (1984). Criterion-referenced interpretation of examination grades. *Educational Research, 26,* 56-64.

Kempa, R. F. (1976). *A criterion-referenced grading scheme for advanced level GCE chemistry examinations.* London, England: Examinations report prepared for the School Examinations Department, University of London.

Kendall, M. G. (1970). *Rank correlation methods* (4th ed.). London: Charles Griffin.

Kenney, T. J. (1969). Permutation transformations on phase structures in letter sequences. *Journal of Experimental Psychology, 82,* 28-33.

Kerlinger, F. N. (1986). *Foundations of behavioral research.* New York: Holt, Rinehart and Winston.

Kerlinger, F. M., & Pedhauzer, E. J. (1973). *Multiple regression in behavioral research.* New York: Holt, Rinehart, and Winston.

Kestin, J. & Dorfman, J. R. (1971). *A course in statistical thermodynamics.* NY: Academic Press.

Kifer, E. W., & Bramble, W. (1974, April). *The calibration of a criterion-referenced test.* Paper presented at the annual meeting of the American Educational Research Association, Chicago. (ED 091 434).

Kifer, E. W., Mattson, L., & Carlid, M. (1975, June). *Item analysis using the Rasch model.* Sweden: Institute for the Study of International Problems in Education, Stockholm University.

Kihlstrom, J. (1987). The cognitive unconscious, *cience, 237,* 1445-1452.

Kilpatrick, W. H. (1926). Statement of position. In G. M. Whipple (ed.). *The foundations and technique of curriculum-construction. Part II. The foundations of curriculum-making. The twenty-Sixth Yearbook of the National Society for the study of education* (pp. 229-246). Bloomington, Illinois: Public School Publishing.

Kinneavy, J. L. (1971). *A theory of discourse.* Englewood Cliffs, NJ: Prentice Hall.

Kintsch, W. (1978). Comprehension and memory of text. In W. K. Estes (Ed.), *Handbook of learning and cognitive processes: Volume 6. Linguistic functions in cognitive theory* (pp. 57-86). Hillsdale, NJ: John Wiley and Sons.

Kintsch, W. (1972). Notes on the structure of semantic memory. In E. Tulvin and W. Donaldson (Eds.), *Organization of memory* (pp. 249-308). New York: Academic Press.

Kintsch, W., Kozminsky, E., Strely, W. J., McKoon, G., & Keenan, J. M. (1975). Comprehension and recall of text as a function of content variables. *Journal of Verbal Learning and Verbal Behavior, 14,* 196-214.

Klauer, K. J. (1984). On criterion-referenced grading models. *Journal of Educational Statistics, 9,* 3, 237-251.

Klauer, K. J. (1974). *Methodik der lehrzieldefinition und lehrstoffanalyse.* Düsseldorf: Schwann.

Klauer, K. J. (1978). *Handbuch der Pädagogischen diagnostik.* Düsseldorf: Schwann.

Klauer, K. J., Fricke, R., Herbig, R., Rupprecht, H. & Schott, F. (1972). *Lehrzielorientierte tests.* Düsseldorf: Schwann.

Klauer, K. J., Fricke, R., Herbig, M., Rupprecht, H., & Schott, F. (1977). *Lehrzielorientierte leistungsmessung..* Düsseldorf: Schwann.

Klausmeier, H. J., Rossmiller, R. A., & Saily, M. (Eds.) (1977). *Indiviudally guided elementary education: Concepts and practices.* New York: Academic Press.

Klein, J. W. (1990). *Characteristics which differentiate criterion referenced from norm referenced tests.* Carson City, Nevada: Nevada State Department of Education, Planning, Research and Evaluation Branch . ED 324 327.

Kleinbaum, D. G., & Kupper, L. L. (1978). *Applied regression analysis and other multivariable methods.* North Scituate, MA: Duxbury Press.

Kliebard, H. M. (1987). *The struggle for the American curriculum 1893-1958.* New York: Routlege.

Klien, M. F. (1991). Curriculum myths and the role of the laboratory school. *National Association of Laboratory Schools Journal, 15*(4), 1-23.

Knight, F. D. (1985). The curriculum referenced tests of mastery, *Journal of Reading, 29,*

2, 144-147.

Knight, R. R. (1996). Contribution of human hippocampal region to novelty detection, *Nature, 383,* 6597, 256-259.

Knowles, M. (1977). *A history of the adult education movement in the United States.* New York: Robert E. Kreiger.

Koffa, K. (1929). *The growth of the mind (2nd ed.).* New York: Harcourt.

Köhler, W. (1920). *Die physischen Gestalten.* Erlangen: Weltkreisverlag.

Kolb, J. R. (1968). Effects of relating mathematics to science instruction on the acquisition of quantitative science behaviors. *Journal of Research in Science Teaching, 5,* 174-182.

Kolb, J. R. (1967). Effects of relating mathematics to science insruction on the acquisition of quantitative science behaviors. *Journal of Research in Science Teaching, 5,* 174-182.

Kolen, M. J. (1981). Comparison of traditional and item response theory methods for equating tests. *Journal of Educational Measurement, 18,* 1-11.

Kolmogorov, A. (1941). Confidence limits for an unknown distribution function. *Annals of Mathematical Statistics, 12,* 461-463.

Kosecoff, J., & Fink. A. (1976, December). *A system for describing and evaluating criterion-referenced tests.* Princeton, NJ: ERIC Clearinghouse on Tests, Measurements and Evaluation. (ED 135 840).

Kosslyn, S. M., Thompson, Wm. L., Klm, I. J. & Alpert, N. M. (1995). Topographical representations of mental images in primary visual cortex, *Nature, 378,* 496-498.

Kosslyn, S. M. (1980). *Image and mind.* Cambridge: Harvard University Press.

Kraemer, H. C. (1964). Point estimation in learning models. *Journal of Mathematical Psychology, 1,* 28-53.

Krathwohl, D. R., & Payne, D. A. (1971). Defining and assessing educational objectives. In R. L. Thorndike (Ed.), *Educational Measurement* (pp. 17-45). Washington, DC: American Council on Education.

Kraus, D. J., Bart, w. M. & Airasian, P. W. (Eds.) *Ordering theory and methods.* Los Angeles: Theta Press, 47-53.

Kriewall, T. E. (1972, April). *Aspects and applications of criterion-referenced tests.* Paper presented at the annual meeting of the American Educational Research Association, Chicago. (ED 063 333).

Kriewell, T. E. (1969). *Applications of information theory and acceptance sampling principles to the management of mathematics instruction.* Unpublished doctoral dissertation, University of Wisconsin.

Kriewall, T. E., & Hirsch, E. (1969, February). *The development and interpretation of criterion-referenced tests.* Paper presented at the annual meeting of the American Educational Research Association, Los Angeles. (ED 042 815).

Krug, E. A. (1962). Graduates of secondary schools in and around 1900: Did most of them go to college?, *School Review, 70,* 266-272.

Krus, D. (1975). *Order analysis of binary data matrices.* Los Angeles: Theta Press.

Krus, D. J., Bart, W. M., & Airasian, P. W. (1975). *Ordering theory and methods.* Los Angeles: Theta Press.

Kruskal, J. B. (1964a). Multidimensional scaling by optimizing goodness-of-fit to a nonmetric hypothesis. *Psychometrika, 29,* 1-28.

Kruskal, J. B. (1964b). Nonmetric multidimensional scaling: A numerical method.

Psychometrika, 29, 29-52.

Kruskal, J. B., & Wish, M. (1978). *Multidimensional scaling.* Sage University paper series on Quantitative Applications in the Social Sciences, Series No. 07-011. Beverly Hills: Sage Publications.

Kuipers, B. J. (1975). A frame for frames: Representing knowledge for recognition. In D. B. Bobrow & A. Collins (eds.) *Representation and Understanding-Studies in Cognitive Science.* New York: Academic Press, Inc. 151-184

Kujovich, G. (1987). Equal opportunity in higher education and the black public college: The era of separate but equal. *Minnesota Law Review, 72,* 29-172.

Lachman, R., Lachman, J., & Butterfield, E. C. (1979). *Cognitive psychology and information processing.* Hillsdale, NJ: Lawrence Erlbaum.

Laird, J. E., A. Newell & P. Rosenbloom (1987). SOAR: An architecture for general intelligence, *Artificial Intelligence, 33,* 1-64.

Lampert, M. (1988). *Instructor's think about students' thing about geometry: The effects of new teaching tools.* Cambridge, Ma: Educational Technology Center.

Langley, P. (1988). Machine learning as an experimental science. *Machine Learning, 3,* 5-8.

Langley, P., Kibler, D., & Granger, R. (1986). Components of learning in a reactive environment. In T. M. Mitchell, J. G. Carbonell, & R. S. Michalski (Eds.), *Machine learning: A guide to current research.* Boston, MA.: Kluwer Academic Publishers, 167-172.

Larkin, J. H., McDermott, J., Simon, D. P., & Simon, H. A. (1980). Expret and novice performance in solving physics problems. *Science, 208,* 1335-1342.

Larzarsfeld, P. F. & Henry, N. W. (1968). *Latent structure analysis.* Boston: Houghton Mifflin.

Law, A. I. (1974, April). *Major changes in the California State Assessment Program.* Paper presented at the annual meeting of the American Educational Research Association, Chicago.

Lawler, R. W. (1986). The development of structures through interaction. In T. M. Mitchell, J. G. Carbonell, & R. S. Michalski, (Eds.), *Machine learning: A guide to current research.* Boston, MA.: Kluwer Academic Publishers, 173-177.

Levi-Civita, T. (1977). *The absolute differential calculus.* NY: Dover publications.

Levin, J. A. (1976). *Proteus: An activation framework for cognitive process models (Technical Report Number ISI/WP-2).* Marina del Rey, CA: University of Southern California, Information Sciences Institute.

Levine, D. U. (1982). Successful approaches for improving academic achievement in inner-city elementary schools, *Phi Delta Kappan,* 63, 523-529.

Levy, J. (1969). Possible basis for the evolution of lateral specialization of the human brain. *Nature, 224,* 614-615.

Lewicki, P. (1986). *Nonconscious social information processing.* San Diego, CA: Academic Press.

Lewin, K. (1935). *A dynamic theory of personality.* New York: McGraw-Hill.

Lewis, A. C. (1985). Washington report: Young and poor in America, *Phi Delta Kappan,* 67, 252-253.

Leyden, T. (1953). The identification and invariance of factors, *British jorunal of statistical psychology, 6,* p. 119.

Lien, A. J. (1976). *Measurement and evaluation of learning* (3rd ed.). Dubuque, IA:

William C. Brown.

Likert, R. A. (1932). A technique for the measurement of attitudes, *Archives of Psyhcology, No. 140*.

Lindquist, E. F. (1951). *Educational Measurement.* Washington, D.C.: American Council on Education.

Lindvall, C. M., & Cox, R. C. (1969). The role of evaluation in programs for individualized instruction. In R. W.Tyler (Ed.), *Educational evaluation: New roles, new measures. The sixty-eighth yearbook of the National Society for the Study of Education.* Chicago: The National Society for the Study of Education.

Lindvall, C. M., & Nitko, A. J. (1969, February). *Criterion-referenced testing and the individualization of instruction.* Paper presented at the annual meeting of the National Council on Measurement in Education, Los Angeles. (ED 036 167).

Lingoes, J. C. (1973). *The Guttman-Lingoes nonmetric program series.* Michigan: Mathesis Press.

Linke, R. (1974). Influence of cultural background on hierarchical learning. *Journal of Educational Psychology, 66,* 911-918.

Linn, R. L. (1982). Two weak spots in the practice of criterion-referenced measurement, *Educational measurement: Issues & Practice, 1,* 1, 12-13, 25.

Linn, R. L. (1980). Issues of validity for criterion-referenced measures, *Applied psychological measurement, 4,* 547-561.

Lippmann, R. P. (1987). An introduction to computing with neural nets, *Institute of Electronics and Electrical Engineers: Acoustics, Speech & Signal Processing Magazine, 4,* 2, 4-22.

Liveright, A. A. (1968). *A study of adult education in the United States.* Boston: Center for the Study of Liberal Education for Adults.

Livingston, S. A. (1980). Comments on criterion-referenced testing, *Applied psychological measurement, 4,* 4, 575-581.

Livingston, S. A. (1973). A note on the interpretation of the criterion-referenced reliability coefficient. *Journal of Educational Measurement, 10*(4), 311.

Livingston, S. A. (1972a). Criterion-referenced applications of classical test theory. *Journal of Educational Measurement, 9,* 13-26.

Livingston, S. A. (1972b). A reply to Harris' "An interpretation of Livingston's reliability coefficient for criterion-referenced tests." *Journal of Educational Measurement, 9*(1), 31.

Livingston, S. A. (1972c). Reply to Shavelson, Block, and Ravitch's "Criterion-referenced testing: Comments on reliability." *Journal of Educational Measurement, 9*(2), 139-140.

Livingston, S. A. (1970). *The reliability of criterion-referenced measures.* Baltimore, MD: Center for Social Organization of Schools, Technical Report #73, John Hopkins University. (ED 042 082).

Livingston, S. A., & Wingersky, (1979). Assessing the reliability of tests used to make pass/fail decisions, *Journal of Educational Measurement, 16,* 247-260.

Livingston, S. A. & Zieky, M. (1983). *A comparative study of standard setting methods.* Princeton, NJ: Educational Testing Service.

Locke, J. ([1690] 1977). *An Essay Concerning Human Understanding.* London: Dent.

Loevinger, J. (1965). Person and population as psychometric concepts. *Psychological Review, 72,* 143-155.

Loevinger, J. (1947). A systematic approach to the construction and evaluation of tests of ability. *Psychological Monagraphs, 61*, 285.

Looney, M. A. (1987). Threshold loss agreement indices for criterion-referenced measures: A review of applications and interpretations, *Research Quarterly for Exercise & Sport, 58*, 3, 360-368.

Lord, F. M. (1980). *Applications of item response theory to practical testing problems.* Hillsdale, N. J.: Lawrence Erlbaum Associates.

Lord, F. M. (1977). Practical applications of item characteristic curve theory, *Journal of Educational Measurement, 14*, 117-138.

Lord, F. M. (1957). Do tests of the same length have the same standard error of measurement? *Educational Psychological Measurement, 17*, 510-521.

Lord, F. M. (1952). A theory of test scores. *Psychometric Monographs, No. 7.*

Lord, F., & Novick, M. (1974). *Statistical theories of mental test scores* (2nd ed.). Reading, MA: Addison-Wesley.

Lott, J. R. & Lemming, G. M. (1980). *Juvenile delinquency and education: An economic study.* Los Angeles: International Institute for Economic Research, Westwood Center.

Lowes, J. L. (1927). *The road to Xandu: A study of the ways of the imagination.* Boston: Houghton Mifflin.

Luce, W., Bush, P., & Galanter (Eds.). (1963). *Handbook of mathematical psychology, Vol. II.* New York: Wiley.

Lumsdaine, A. A., & Glaser, R. (Eds.) (1969). *Teaching machines and programmed learning.* Washington, DC: National Education Association.

Lyons, J. (1968). *Introduction to theoretical linguistics.* London: Cambridge University Press.

Lysaught, J., & Williams, C. M. (1963). *A guide to programmed instruction.* New York: John Wiley.

Mackenzier, D. E. (1983). Research for school improvement: An appraisal of some recent trends, *Educational researcher, 12*, 4, 5-17.

Madaus, G. F. & Stufflebeam, D. L. (1989). *Educational evaluation: Classic works of Ralph W. Tyler.* Ohio State University: Bureau of Educational Research.

Mager, R. R. (1962). *Preparing objectives for programmed instruction.* San Francisco: Fearon Press.

Mahalanobis, P. C. (1936) On the generalized distance in statistics, *Proceedings of the National Institute of Science, Calcutta, 12*, 49-55.

Mahmoud, M. S., & Singh, M. G. (1981). *Large scale systems modeling.* New York: Pergamon.

Mandler, G. (1967). Organization and memory. In K. Spence and J. Spence (Eds.), *The psychology of learning and motivation: Volume 1* (pp. 328-372). New York: Academic Press.

Mandler, G. & Nakamura, Y. (1987). Aspects of consciousness. *Personality and social psychology bulletin, 13*, 299-313.

Manning, R. E. (1987). The why, what and who of assessment: The accrediting association perspective. In *Assessing the outcomes of higher education, Proceedings of the 1986 ETS invitational conference.* Princeton, N.J.: Educatoinal Testing Service, 31-38.

Markus, G. B. (1979). *Analyzing panel data.* Sage university paper series on quantitative applications in the social scienes, 07-018, Beverly Hills and London: Sage Publications.

Marr, D. (1978). Representing visual information. In A. R. Hanson and E. M. Riseman (Eds.), *Computer vision systems*. New York: Academic Press.

Marr, D., & Nishihara, H. K. (1978). Representation and recognition of the spatial organization of three-dimensional shapes. *Proceedings of the Royal Society, Series B, 200*, 269-294.

Marshall, J. L. (1973, February). *Reliability indices for criterion-referenced tests: A study based on simulated data.* Paper presented at the annual meeting of the National Council for Measurement in Education, New Orleans.

Marzano, R. J. (1991). *Cultivating Thinking in English and the Language Arts.* Urbana, Ill.: National Council of Teachers of English.

Maslow, A. H. (1965). Some basic propositions of a growth and self-actualization psychology. In G. Lindzey & C. Hall (Eds.), *Theories of personality: Primary sources and research* (pp. 307-316). New York: Wiley.

Maslow, A. H. (1962). *Toward a psychology of being.* Princeton, NJ: Van Nostrand.

Maslow, A. H. (1959). Psychological data and value theory. In A. H. Maslow (Ed.), *New knowledge in human values.* New York: Harper.

Maslow, A. H. (1955). Deficiency motivation and growth motivation. In M. R. Jones (Ed.), *Nebraska symposium on motivation.* Lincoln: University of Nebraska Press.

Maslow, A. H. (1954). *Motivation and personality.* New York: Harper.

Maslow, A. H. (1950). Self-actualizing principle: A study of psychological health. In W. Wolf (Ed.), *Personality symposium.* New York: Grune and Stratton.

Maslow, A. H. (1942). Self-esteem (dominance feeling) and sexuality in women. *Journal of Social Psychology, 16*, 259-294.

Maslow, A. H., & Mittelmann, B. (1951). *Principles of abnormal psychology: The dynamics of psychic illness.* New York: Harper.

Massachusetts Commission on Industrial and Technical Education (1906). *Report of the Commission on Industrial and Technical Education.* Boston: Wright & Potter Printing.

Massey, F. J. (1951). The Kolmogorov-Smirnov test for goodness of fit. *Journal of the American Statistical Association, 51.*

Masters, G. N., & Evans, J. (1986). A sense of direction in criterion-referenced assessment. *Studies in Educational Evaluation, 12*, 3, 257-265.

Matarazzo, J. D. (1972). *Wechsler's measurement and appraisal of adult intelligence* (5th ed.). Baltimore: Williams & Wilkins.

Maxwell, M. J. (1979). *Improving student learning skills.* San Francisco: Jossey-Bass.

Maxwell, M. J. (1971). Evaluating college reading and study skills programs, *Journal of Reading, 14*, 214-221.

Mayer, R. E. (1983). Can you repeat that? Qualitative effects of repetition and advance organizers on learning from science prose. *Journal of Educational Psychology, 75*, 40-49.

Mayeske, G. W., Wisler, C. E., Beaton, A. F., Weinfeld, F. D., Cohen, W., Proshek, J. M., & Tabler, K. A. (1969). A study of our nation's schools. Washington, DC: U.S. Department of Health, Education, and Welfare.

McCall, R. B., Applebaum, M. I., & Hogarty, P. S. (1973). Developmental changes in mental performance. *Monographs of the Society for Research in Child Development, 38*, 3, Seral 150.

McClelland, J. L. (1981). Retrieving general and specific information from stored knowledge of specifics. *Proceedings of the Third Annual Meeting of the Cognitive Science Society* (pp. 170-172).

McClelland, D. C., Atkinson, J. W., Clark, R. A., & Lowell, E. L. (1953). *The achievement motive.* New York: Appleton-Century-Crofts.

McClurkin, J. W., Optican, L. M., Richmond, B. J., & Gawne, T. J. (1991). Concurrent processing and complexity of temporally encoded neuronal messages in visual perception. *Science, 253,* 675-676.

McCullagh, P. (1987). *Tensor methods in statistics.* NY: Chapman & Hall

McDermott, J. J. (1973). *The philosophy of John Dewey, Volume 1: The structure of experience.* New York: G. P. Putnam's Sons.

McDonald, F. J. (1964). The influence of learning theories on education (1900 - 1950). In E. R. Hilgard (Ed.), *Theories of learning and instruction. The sixty-third yearbook of the National Society for the Study of Education.* Chicago: University of Chicago Press.

McGaw, B. (1984). *Assessment in the upper secondary school in Western Australia.* Report of the Ministerial Working Party on School Certification and Tertiary Admissions Procedures.

McKinley, R. L., & Reckase, M. D. (1983). MAXLOG: A computer program for the estimation of the parameters of a multidimensional logistic model. *Behavior Research Methods and Instrumentation, 15*(3), 389-390.

McLuhan, M. (1967). *The medium is the message.* Westminister, Md.: Random House.

McNeil, J.D. (1977). *Curriculum: A comprehensive introduction.* Boston, MA: Little, Brown, and Company.

McNemar, Q. (1962). *Psychological statistics* (3rd ed.). New York: John Wiley & Sons.

Mead, R. J. (1974, August). *Evaluation of instruction using the Rasch latent trait model.* Chicago: University of Chicago, MESA. Unpublished manuscript.

Mead, R., Wright, B., Ginther, & Haberman. (1974, October). *Analysis of fit of data to the Rasch latent trait model.* Chicago: University of Chicago, MESA. Unpublished manuscript.

Mellon, J. (1969). *Transformational sentence-combing.* Urbana, IL: National Council of Teachers of English.

Melton, A. W., & Martin, E. (1972). *Coding processes in human memory.* Washington, DC: Winston.

Meredith, W., & Tisak, J. (1988). *"Tuckerizing" curves.* Unpublished manuscript.

Merrill, M. D. (1965). Correction and review on successive parts in learning a hierarchical task. *Journal of Educational Psychology, 56*(5), 225-234.

Merrill, M. D., & Stolurow, L. M. (1966). Hierarchical preview vs. problem oriented review in learning and imaginery science. *American Educational Research Journal, 3,* 251-261.

Meskauskas, J. A. (1976). Evaluation models for criterion-referenced testing: Views regarding mastery and standard-setting. *Review of Educational Research, 46*(1), 133-158.

Messick, S. (1979). *Constructs and their vicissitudes in educational and psychological measurement* (Research Report RR 79-11). Princeton, NJ: Educational Testing Service.

Messick, S. (1975). The standard problem: Meaning and values in measurement and evaluation, *American Psychologist, 30,* 955-966.

Metfessel, N. S. & Michael, Wm. B. (1967). A paradigm involving multiple criterion measures for the evaluation of the effectiveness of school programs, *Educational and Psychological Measurement, 27,* 931-943.

Meyers, B. (1975). *The organization of prose and its effects on memory.* North Holland.

Michalski, R. (1974). Variable valued logic system VI, *Procedings of the 1974 international symposium on multiple-valued logic.* Morgantown, WV: West Virginia University, 321-346.

Michell, T. M., Carbonell, J. G., & Michalski, R. S. (1986). *Machine learning: A guide to current research.* Boston: Kluwer-Academic.

Miller, D. C. (1991). *Handbook of research design and social measurement.* Newbury Park, Ca.: Sage Publications, Inc..

Miller, G. A. (1966). Information and memory. In Coopersmith, S. (Ed.), *Frontiers of psychological research.* San Francisco: Freeman.

Miller, G. A. (1956). The magical number 3 + 2. *Psychological Review, 63,* 81-97.

Miller, G. A., Galanter, E., & Pribram, K. (1960). *Plans and the structure of behavior.* New York: Holt.

Millenson, J. R. (1967). An isomorphism between stimulus - response notation and information processing flow diagrams. *The Psychological Record, 17,* 305-319.

Millman, J. (1973). Passing scores and test lengths for domain-referenced measures. *Review of Educational Research, 43,* 205-216.

Millman, J. (1972, April). *Passing scores and test lengths for domain-referenced measures.* Paper presented at the annual meeting of the American Educational Research Association, Chicago. (ED 065 555).

Millman, J. (1970). Reporting student progress: A case for a criterion-referenced marking system. *Phi Delta Kappan, 52,* 226-230.

Millman, J., & Popham, W. J. (1974). The issue of item and test variance for criterion-referenced tests: A clarification. *Journal of Educational Measurement, 11,* 137-138.

Mills, C. N. & Hambleton, R. K. (1980). *Guidelines for reporting criterion-referenced test score information.* Paper presented at the annual meeting of the American Educational Research Association, Boston, MA, April 7-11, ED 189 130.

Mills, C. N., & Simon, R. (1981). A method for determining the length of criterion-referenced tests using reliability and validity indices. Amherst, MA: Massachusetts University, Amherst, School of Education. (ED 205 594).

Minsky, M. (1975). A framework for representing knowledge. In P. Winston (Ed.), *The psychology of computer vision* (pp. 211-277). New York: McGraw-Hill.

Mislevy, R. J. (1987). *Exploiting auxiliary information about items in the estimation of Rasch item difficulty parameters.* Princeton, NJ: Educational Testing Service ED 288 914.

Moffett, J. (1972). *Language in the inner city: Studies in black English vernacular.* Philadelphia: University of Pennsylvania Press.

Moffett, J. (1968). *Teaching the universe of discourse.* New York: Houghton Mifflin.

Mood, A. M. (1971). Partitioning variance in multiple regression analysis as a tood for developing learning models. *American Educational Research Journal, 8*(4), 191-202.

Mood, A. M. (1969). Macro-analysis of the American educational system. *Operations Research, 17,* 770-784.

Monroe, W. S. (1923). A preliminary report of an investigation of the economy of time in arithmetic. *The 16th Yearbook of the National Society for the Study of Education* 9PP. 111-127). Bloomington, IL: Public School Publishing.

Monroe, W. S., De Voss, J. C., & Kelly, F. J. (1917). *Educational tests and measurements.* Boston: Houghton Mifflin.

Morris, C. N. (1982). On the foundations of test equating. In P. W. Holland and D. B. Rubin (Eds.), *Test equating.* New York: Academic Press.

Morris, L. (1979). *Elusive equality.* Washington DC: Howard University Press.

Morrison, H. (1937). The curriculum and the program of studies. In H. L. Caswell & D. S. Campbell, *Readings in curriculum development,* New York: American Book Company, p. 160.

Morrison, H. C. (1926). *The practice of teaching in the secondary school.* Chicago: University of Chicago Press.

Mort, P. R. & Furno, O. F. (1960). *Theory and synthesis of a sequential sequence.* New York: Institute of Administrative Research, Teachers College, Columbia University.

Mosier, C. I. (1951). Problems and designs of cross-validation, *Educational & Psychological Measurement, 11,* 5-11.

Mosteller, F., & Moynihan, D. P. (Eds.). (1972). *On equality of educational opportunity.* New York: Random House.

Mosteller, F., & Tukey, J. W. (1977). *Data analysis and regression: A second course in statistics.* Reading, MA: Addison Wesley.

Mountcastle, V. B. (1975). The view from within: Pathways to the study of perception. *John Hopkins Medical Journal, 136,* 109-131.

Mountcastle, V. B., & Edelman, G. M. (1978). *The mindful brain: Cortical organization and the group-selective theory of higher brain function.* Cambridge: Massachusetts Institute of Technology Press.

Mulaik, S. A. (1972). *Modern factor analysis.* New York: McGraww-Hill.

Mulaik, S. A. (1970). *The foundations of factor analysis.* New York: McGraw Hill.

Mulaik, S. A., & James, J. R. (1994). Objectivity and reasoning in science and structural equatins modelling. In, R. H. Hoyle (ed.), *Structural equation modeling: Issues and applications.* Beverly Hills, CA: Sage Publications.

Muller, S. (1975). American education standards are slipping. *Today's Education, 64*(3), 50-52.

Münrterberg, H. (1898). Psychology and education, *Educational review, 16,* 103-132.

Murdock, B. B. (1993). TODAM2: A model for the storage and retrieval of item, associative, and seril-order information, *Psychological Review, 100, 2,* 183-203.

Muthen, B. O. (1989). Latent variable modeling in heterogeneous populations. *Psychometrika, 54,* 557-585.

Nandakumar, Ratna (1993). Assessing essential unidimensionality of real data, *Applied Psychological Measurement, 17,* 1, 29-38.

Narens, L. (1981). On the scales of measurement. *Journal of Mathematical Psychology, 24,* 249-275.

Narens, L., & Luce, R. D. (1976). The algebra of measurement. *Journal of Pure and Applied Algebra, 8,* 197-233.

National Assessment of Educational Progress. (1976a). Minimal competency tests. States tackle complex, 'hot' issue. *National Association for Educational Progress Newsletter, IX,* 3, 1-3.

National Assessment of Educational Progress. (1976b). Two-sides to tests: Positive, negative. *National Association for Educational Progress Newsletter, IX,* 3.

National Association for Developmental Education. (1992). Developmental education defined. Boone, NC: *National Association for Developmental Education.*

National Education Association. (1893). *Report of the Committee on Secondary School Studies.* Washington, DC: U. S. Government Printing Office.

National Governors Association. (1986). *Time for results: The Governors' 1991 report on education.* Washington, DC: Author.

National Institute of Education (1984). *Involvement in learning: Realizing the potential of American higher education.* Washington, DC: National Institute of Education Study Group on the Conditions of Excellence in American Higher Education, Author.

National Society for the Study of Education (1927). *The foundations of curriculum-making. Twenty-sixth yearbook, Part II.* Bloomington, Il.: Public School Publishing Company, pp. 19-20, 23-25.

Neeb, K., Wieberg, H. W. & Schot, F. (1984). Empirical evaluation of different procedures for the construction of criterion-referenced items and instructional tasks. *Studies in Educational Evaluation, 10*(2), 191-197.

Neill, G. (1977a). NIE considers development of national competency tests. *Phi Delta Kappan, 59*(1), 66.

Neill, G. (1977b). Two federal programs hurt by negative survey results. *Phi Delta Kappan, 59*(1), 67.

Neisser, J. (1976). *Cognition and reality: Principles and implications of cognitive psychology.* San Francisco: W. H. Freeman.

Neisser, J. (1967) *Cognitive psychology.* New York: Appleton-Century-Crofts.

Newell, A., Shaw, J., & Simon, A. (1958). Elements of a theory of human problem solving. *Psychological Review,* 65, 151-166.

Newell, A., & Simon, H. A. (1971). *Human problem solving.* Englewood Cliffs, NJ: Prentice-Hall.

Newmann, F. M. (1988). Higher order thinking in the high school curriculum. *NASSP Bulletin, 72,* 58-64.

Ng, K. C. & Abramson, B. (1990). Uncertainty management in expert system, *Institute of Electronics and Electrical Engineers Expert: Intelligent Systems and their application, 5,* 29-47.

Nie, N. H., Hull, D. H., Jenkins, J. G., Steinbrenner, K. S., & Brent, D. H. (1975). *SPSS: Statistical package for the social sciences* (2nd ed.). New York: McGraw Hill.

Niel, G. (1977). Two federal programs hurt by negative survey results, *Phi Delta Kappan,* 59, 1, p. 67.

Nist, S. L. (1985). Developmental versus remedial: Does a confusion of terms exist in higher education reading programs?, *Journal of Developmental Education, 8,* 3, 8-10.

Nitko, A. J. (1980). Distinguishing the many varieties of criteriion-referenced tests, *Review of educational research, 50,* 461-485.

Nitko, A. J. (1970, October). *Criterion-referenced testing in the context of instruction.* Paper presented at the Educational Records Bureau, National Council on Measurement in Education Symposium, "Criterion-Referenced Measures: Pros and Cons," New York. (ED 047 010).

Nitko, A. J. (1968, September). *Measurement of instructional outcome vs. measurement for instruction: A view of IPI testing procedures.* Philadelphia: Research for Better Schools. (ED 036 185).

Noble, C. E. (1952). An analysis of meaning, *Psychological Review, 59,* 421-430.

Norman, D. A. (1970). Introduction: Models of human memory. In D. A. Norman (Ed.), *Models of human memory* (pp. 1-15). New York: Academic Press.

Norman, D. A., & Rumelhart, D. E. (1975). Memory and knowledge. In D. A. Norman and D. E. Rumelhart (Eds.), *Explorations in cognition.* San Francisco, CA: W. H. Freeman, 1-32.

Norwich, K. E. (1983). To perceive is to doubt: The relativity of perception. *Journal of Theoretical Biology, 102,* 175-190.

Novak, D. (1977). *A theory of education.* Ithaca, NY: Cornell University Press

Novak, J. & Gowin, D. B. (1984). *Learning how to learn.* New York: Cambridge University Press.

Nosek, J. T. & I. Roth (1990). A comparison of formal knowledge representation schemes as a communication tool: Predicate logic vs. semantic networks, *International journal of man-machine studies, 33,* 2, 227-239.

Novick, M. R. (1973). High school attainment: An eample of a computer-assisted Bayesian approach to data analysis. *International Statistical Review, 41,* 264-271.

Novick, M. R., & Jackson, P. H. (1974a). *Statistical theories of mental test scores.* Reading, MA: Addison-Wesley.

Novick, M. R., & Jackson, P. H. (1974b). *Statistical methods for educational and psychological research.* New York: McGraw-Hill.

Novick, M. R., Jackson, P. H., Thayer, D. T., & Cole, N. S. (1971). *Applications of Bayesian methods to the prediction of educational performance. Monograph No. 42,* Circle Pines, IA: American College Testing Service.

Novick, M. R., & Lewis, C. (1974). Prescribiug test length for criterion referenced measurement. In C. W. Harris, M. C. Alkin, & W. J. Popham (Eds.). *Problems in criterion-referenced measurement. CSE Monograph Number 3* (pp. 139-158). Los Angeles: Center for the Study of Education, University of California.

Novick, M. R., Lewis, C., & Jackson, P. H. (1972). The estimation of proportions in m groups. *Psychometrika, 37,* 132-148.

Noyles, Sale, & Stalnaker (1945). *Report on the first six tests in English composition.* New York: The College Board.

Nunnally, J. C. (1967). *Psychometric theory.* New York: McGraw Hill.

Nuyen, N. A. (1986). Equating achievement across subjects: Is it possible? The Queensland experience. *Studies in Educational Evaluation, 12,* 245-250.

Oakland, T. (1972, April). *An evaluation of available models for estimating the reliability and validity of criterion referenced measures.* Paper presented at the annual meeting of the American Educational Research Association, Chicago. (ED 065 589).

Ogden, C. K. & Richards, I. A. (1923). *The meaning of meaning.* NY: Harcourt, Brace.

O'Keefe, J., & Nadel, L. (1978). *The hippocampus as a cognitive map.* London, England: Oxford University Press.

Olivas M. (1989). *The law and higher education: Cases and materials on colleges in court.* Durham, NC: Carolina Academic Press.

Olivas, M. (1979). *The dilemma of access.* Washington DC: Howard University Press.

Olsen, L. & Moore, M. (1982). *Voices from the classroom: Students and teachers speak out on the quality of teaching in our schools.* Oakland, California: Citizens Policy Center.

Olton, D. S., Becker, J. T., & Handelmann, G. H. (1983). Hippocampal function: Working memory or cognitive mapping. *Physiological*, 70-84.

Original papers in relation to a course of liberal education. (1829). *American Journal of Science and Arts, 15*, 297-351.

Osgood, C. E (1941). Ease of individual judgment-processes in relation to polarization of attitudes in the culture, *Journal of social psychology, 49*, 403-418.

Osgood, C. E (1946). Meaningful similarity and interference in learning, *Journal of experimental psychology, 36*, 132-154.

Osgood, C. E (1948). An investigatin into the causes of retroactive interference, *Journal of experimental psychology, 38*, 132-154.

Osgood, C. E (1952). *Mehtod and theory in experimental psychology*. NY: Oxford University Press.

Osgood, C. E (1956). Fidelity and reliability. In H. Quastler (Ed.), *Informatino theory in psychology*. Glencoe, Ill.: Free Press.

Osgood, C. E & Luria, Z. (1954). A blind analysis of a case of multiple personality using the semantic differential, *Journal of abnormal and social psychology, 49*, 579-591.

Osgood, C. E. & Sebeok, T. A. (1954). Psycholinguistics: a survey of theory and research problems. *Journal of abnormal social psychology, 49*, p. 275.

Osgood, C. E. & Suci, G. J. (1952). A measure of relation determined by both mean difference and profile information. *Psychological Bulletin, 49*, 251-262.

Osgood, C. E. & Tannenbaum, P. H. (1955). The principle of congruity in the productoin of attitude change, *Psychological Review, 62*, 42-55.

Osgood, C. E., Suci, G. J. & Tannenbaum, P. H. (1971). *the measurement of meaning*. Urbana, Illinois: Univeristy of Illinois Press.

Otis, A. S., & Davidson, P. E. (1913). The reliability of standard scores in adding ability. *Elementary School Teacher, 13*, 91-105.

Owen, S. A., & Ranick, D. L. (1977). The Greensville Program: A common sense approach to basics. *Phi Delta Kappan, 5*(7), 531-533.

Ozenne. D. G. (1971). *Toward an evaluative methodology for criterion-referenced measures: Test sensitivity. CSE Report No. 72*. Los Angeles: Center for the Study of Evaluation, Graduate School of Education, University of California at Los Angeles. (ED 061 263).

Page, E. B. (1977). Testing: What in he world are we arguing about. In R. M. Bossone and M. Weiner (Eds.), *Proceeding of National Conference on Testing: Major Issues*. University of New York, November, ED 152 814.

Paivio, I. P. (1971). *Imagery and verbal processes*. New York: Holt, Rinehart and Winston.

Palmer, S. E. (1975). Visual perception and world knowledge: Notes on a model of sensory cognitive interaction. In D. A. Norman and D. E. Rumelhart (Eds.), *Explorations in cognition*. San Francisco: Freeman.

Palmer, S. E. (1977). Hierarchical structure in perceptual representation. *Cognitive Psychology, 9*, 441-474.

Parker, W. (1989). Participatory citizenship: Civics in the strong sense, *Social education, 53*, 353-354.

Pask, G. (1975). *Conversation, Cognition, and Learning*. Amsterdam: Elsevier.

Paul, R. (1990). Socratic Questioning. In R. Paul (Ed.) *Critical thinking: What every person needs to survive in a rapidly changing world*. Rohnert Park, Ca.: Sonoma State University, Center for Critical Thinking and Moral Critique.

Pavlov, I. P. (1927). *Conditioned reflexes: An investigation of the physiological activity of the cerebral cortex.* New York: Oxford University Press.

Pawlik, K. (1976). *Diagnose der diagnostik.* Stuttgart: Klett.

Payne, D. A., Krathowohl, D. R., & Gordon, J. (1967). The effect of sequence on programmed instruction. *American Education Research Journal, 4*(2), 125-133.

Pearson, E. S., & Hartley, H. O. (Eds.). (1966). *Biometrika tables for statisticians, Volume 1* (3rd ed.), New York: Cambridge University Press.

Pedhazur, E. L. (1982). *Multiple regression in behavioral research.* New York: Holt, Rinehart & Winston.

Pedhazur, E. L., & Schmelkin, E. P. (1991). *Measurement, design and analysis.* Hillsdale, N.J.: Lawrence Erlbaum Associates.

Peeke, H. V., & Herz, M. J. (1973). *Habitation.* New York: Academic Press.

Pellegrino, J. W., & Glaser, R. (1979). Cognitive correlates and components in the analysis of individual differences. *Intelligence, 3,* 187-214.

Pellegrino, J. W., & Glaser, R. (1980). Components of inductive reasoning. In R. E. Snow, P.A. Federico, and W. E. Montague (Eds.), *Aptitude, learning, and instruction. (volume 1). Cognitive process analysis of aptitudes.* Hillsdale, N.J.: Erlbaum.

Pellionisz, A., & Llinas, R. B. (1980). *Tensorial representation of space-time in CNS: Sensory-motor coordination via distributed cerebellar space-time metric.* Abstracts, Tenth Annual Meeting of the Society of Neuroscience, 510.

Pellionisz, A., & Llinas, R. B. (1979). Brain modeling by tensor network theory and computer simulation. *Neuroscience,* 4, 323-348.

Pelz, D. C. & Andrews, F. M. (1966). *Scientists in Organizations.* New York: John Wiley and Sons, Inc..

Perkins, D. N. R. (1989). Selecting fertile themes for integrated learning. In H. H. Jacobs (Ed.) *Interdisciplinary curriculum: Design and implementation,* Alexandria, Va.: Association for Supervision and Curriculum Development.

Perkins, D. N., R. Allen & J. Hafner (1983). Difficulties in everyday reasoning. In W. Maxwell (Ed.) *Thinking: The expanding frontier,* Philadelphia: The Franklin Institute Press.

Perkins, K. (1984). *A comparison of instructional sensitivity indices.* Urbana, Illinois: Southern Illinois University. ED 301 576.

Piaget, J. (1971). *Genetic Epistemology,* Translated by E. Duckworth. New York: Norton.

Piaget, J. (1959). *Language and thought of the child.* Cleveland, Ohio: World.

Piaget, J. (1954). *The construction of reality in the child.* New York: Basic Books.

Piaget, J. (1950). *The psychology of intelligence.* London, England: Routledge & Kegan Paul.

Piaget, J. (1932). *The moral judgment of the child.* London, England: Routledge & Kegan Paul.

Piaget, J., & Inhelder, B. (1977). *Mental imagery in the child.* New York: Basic Books.

Pines, A. L. (1977). *Scientific concept learning in children: The effect of prior knowledge on resulting cognitive structure subsequent to A-T instruction.* Doctoral dissertation, Cornell University.

Platt, C. B., & MacWhimmey, B. (1983). Error assimilation as a mechanism in language learning. *Journal of Child Language, 10,* 401-414.

Popham, W. J. (1993). *Educational evaluation.* Needham Heights, MA.: Allyn and Bacon.

Popham, W. J. (1990). *Modern educational measurement.* Englewood Cliffs, NJ: Prentice

Hall.

Popham, W. J. (1987). Two-plus decateds of educational objectives, *International journal of educational research, 11,* 1, 31-41.

Popham, W. J. (1978). *Criterion-referenced measurement.* Englewood Cliffs, NJ: Prentice Hall.

Popham, W. J. (1974a). *Technical travails of developing criterion-referenced tests.* Paper presented at the annual meeting of the National Council on Measurement in Education, Chicago. (ED 091 421).

Popham, D. A. (1974). The assessment of learning: Cognitive and affective. Lexington, MA: D. C. Heath, 334-336.

Popham, W. J. (1971). Indices of adequacy for criterion-referenced test items. In W. J. Popham (Ed.), *Criterion-referenced measurement* (pp. 79-100). Englewood Cliffs, NJ: Educational Technology Publications.

Popham, W. J., & Baker, E. L. (1970a). *Planning an instructional sequence.* Englewood Cliffs, NJ: Prentice Hall.

Popham, W. J., & Baker, E. L. (1970b). *Systematic instruction.* Englewood Cliffs, NJ: Prentice Hall.

Popham, W. J., & Baker, E. L. (1970c). *Establishing instructional goals.* Englewood Cliffs, NJ: Prentice Hall.

Popham, W. J., & Husek, T.R. (1971). Implications of criterion-referenced measurement. In W. J. Popham (Ed.), *Criterion-referenced measurement* (pp. 17-40). Englewood Cliffs, NJ: Educational Technology Publications.

Popham, W. J., & Husek, T. R. (1969). Implications of criterion-referenced measurement. *Journal of Educational Measurement,* 6, 1-9.

Posner, M. I., & McLeod, P. (1982). Information processing models: In search of elementary operations. *Annual Review of Psychology,* 33, 477-514.

Postman, L. (1955). Short-term memory and incidental learning. In A. Melton (Ed.), *Categories of human learning.* New York: Academic Press.

Potthof, R. F. (1982). Some issues in test equating. In P. W. Holland and D. B. Rubin (Eds.), *Test equating.* New York: Academic Press.

Poucet, B. (1993). Spatial cognitive maps in animals: New hypotheses on their structure and neural mechanisms, *Psychological Review, 100, 2,* 163-182.

Pratt, J. W., Raitla, H. & Schlaifer, R. (1965). *Statistical methods for educational and psychological research.* New York: McGraw-Hill.

Pratte, R. (1988). Civic education in a democracy, *Theory into practice, 27,* 303-308.

Preece, P. F. W. (1978). Associative structure and the schema of proportionality, *Journal of Research in Science Teaching, 15,* 395-399.

Preece, P. F. W. (1976a). Associative structure of science concepts, *British Journal of Educational Psychology, 46,* 174-183.

Preece, P. F. W. (1976b). Mapping cognitive structure: A comparison of methods, *Journal of educational psychology, 68,* 1-8.

Preer, J. (1982). *Lawyers vs. educators: black colleges and desegregation in public higher education.* Westport, CT: The Greenwood Press.

Prendergast, J. (1984). *A comparsion of an a priori mathematics hierarchy with hierarchies generated from equivalent tests.* Unpublished doctoral dissertation, Boston University.

Prentice, W. C. H. (1961). Some cognitive aspects of motivation. *American Psychologist,*

16, 503-511.

President's Commission For Higher Education (1947). *Higher education for a democracy.* New York: Harper & Row.

Pruett, J. A. (1994). *The relationship of gender bias to mathematics and science achievement.* Doctoral dissertation. Grambling, LA: Grambling State University.

Pruzansky, S., Tversky, A., & Carrol, J. D. (1982). Spatial versus tree representations of proximity data. *Psychometrika, 47,* 1, 3-24.

Pryor, H. C. (1923). A suggested minimal spelling list. In G. M. Whipple (Ed.), *The 16th Yearbook of the National Society for the Study of Education* (pp. 73-84). Bloomington, IL: Public School Publishing.

Pyatte, J. (1969). Some effects of unit structure on achievement and transfer. *American Educational Research Journal, 6*(2), 241-261.

Pylyshyn, Z. (1973). What the mind's eye tells the mind's brain: A critique of mental imagery. *Psychological Bulletin, 80,* 1-24.

Quillian, M. R. (1968). Semantic memory. In M. Minsky (Ed.), *Semantic information processing.* Cambridge, Ma.: Massachusetts Institutie of Technology Press.

Quillian, M. R. (1969). The teachable language comprehender, *Communications of the Association for Computing Machinery, 12,* 459-475.

Quirk, R., & Greenbaum, S. (1973). *A concise grammar of contemporary English.* New York: Harcourt.

Randall, D. L. (1970). *Formal methods in the foundations of science.* Doctoral dissertation, California Institute of Technology.

Rakow, E. A., Airasian, P. W., & Madaus, G. F. (1976, April). *Assessing school and program effectiveness: Estimating hidden teacher effects.* Paper presented at the annual meeting of the National Council on Measurement in Education, San Francisco.

Rakow, E. A., Airasian, P. W., & Madaus, G. F.(1975, April). *A comparison of two item selection techniques for program evaluation.* Paper presented at the annual meeting of the National Council on Measurement in Education, Washington, DC.

Randall, R. S. (1972, April). *Contrasting norm-referenced and criterion referenced measures.* Paper presented for the symposium entitled "A Model for Estimating the Reliability and Validity of Criterion-Referenced Measures" at the annual meeting of the American Educational Research Association, Chicago. (ED 065 593).

Rao, C. R. (1958). Some statistical methods for the comparison of growth curves. *Biometrics, 14,* 1-17.

Rapoport, A. (1968). Mathematical models of social interaction. In R. Luce, R. Duncan, R. R. Bush, and E. Galanter (Eds.), *Handbook of mathematical psychology, Volume II.* New York: John Wiley & Sons, 497-579.

Rasch, G. (1980). *Probabilistic models for some intelligence and attainment tests.* Chicago: The Univeresity of Chicago Press.

Rasch, G. (1966, May). An item analysis which takes individual differences into account. *British Journal of Mathematical Statistical Psychology, 19*(1), 49-55.

Rasmussen, J. (1985). The role of hierarchical knowledge representation in decision making and system management. *IEEE Transactions on Systems, Man, and Cybernetics, 15,* 2, 234-243.

Rasmussen, J. (1983). Skills, rules, and knowledge: Signals, signs, and symbols, and other distinctions in human performance models. *Transactions of the International Association of Electrical and Electronic Engineers, Systems, Man, and Cybernetics,*

18, 252-263.

Raven, J. (1991). The wider goals of education: Beyond the 3 Rs, *The educational forum, 55*, 343-357.

Reckase, M. D. (1985). The difficulty of test items that measure more than one ability. *Applied Psychological Measurement, 9*(4), 401-412.

Reckase, M.D. (1981). Procedures for criterion-referenced tailored testing. Columbia, Missouri: Missouri University, Columbia, Department of Educational Psychology. (ED 209354).

Reckase, M. D. (1979). *Some decision procedures for use with tailored testing.* Paper presented at the meeting of computer assisted testing, Minneapolis, MN, ED 183 627.

Reckase, M. D., & McKinley, R. L. (1991). *The discriminating power of items that measure more than one dimension.* Iowa City, IO: Authors.

Reed, S. K., Ernst, G. W., & Banerji, R. (1974). The role of analogy in transfer between similar problem states. *Cognitive Psychology, 6*, 436-450.

Reeves, M. P. (1954). An application of the semantic differential to thematic apperception test material. Unpublished doctor's dissertation, University of Illinois, 142, 237-238.

Reich, R. B. (1989). The quiet path to technological preeminence. *Scientific American, 261*, 41-47.

Reid, J. B., & Roberts, D. M. (1978). A Monte Carlo comparison of Phi and Kappa as measures of criterion-referenced reliability. Paper presented at the annual meeting of the American Educational Research Association, Toronto, Ontario, Canada, March, 1978. (ED 159 226).

Remmers, H. H. (1954). *Introduction to opinion and attitude measurement.* NY: Harpers, 196-198.

Remmers, H. H. & Silance, E. B. (1934). Generalized attitude scales, *Journal of social psychology, 5*, 298-312.

Resnick, L. B. (1963). Programmed instruction and the teaching of complex intellectual skills. *The Harvard Educational Review, 33*(4), 439-471.

Resnick, L. B. & M. C. Wang (1969). Approaches to the validation of learning hierarchies, *Journal of Research in Science Teaching*

Restle, F., & Greeno, J. G. (1970). *Introduction to mathematical psychology.* Reading, MA: Addison-Wesley.

Reutzel, D. R. & Hollingsworth, P. M. (1990). Skill hierarchies in reading comprehension, *Reading Improvement, 27*, 1, 64-71.

Rice, J. M. (1912). *Scientific Management in Education.* New York: Hinds, Noble & Elredge.

Rice, J. M. (1893a). *The Public School System of the United States.* New York: Century.

Rice, J. M. (1893b). The public schools of Chicago and St. Paul, *The Forum, 15*, 200-215.

Riess, B. F. (1940). Semantic conditioning involving the galvanic skin reflex, *Journal of experimental psychology, 26*, 238-240.

Riess, B. F. (1946). Genetic changes in semantic conditioning, *Journal of experimental psychology, 36*, 143-152.

Rigney, J. W. (1976). *On cognitive strategies for facilitating acquisition, retention, and retrieval in training and education* (Technical Report Number 78). Los Angeles: University of Southern California.

Rigney, J. W. (1970). Learning strategies: A theoretical perspective. In F. Restle and J. G. Greeno (Eds.), *Introduction to mathematical psychology.* Reading, MA: Addison-

Wesley, 163-205.

Rist, R. S. (1990). Variability in program design: The interaction of process with knowledge, *International journal of man-machine studies, 33*, 3, 305-322.

Roberts, G. H. (1989). Personal and academic stressors affecting developmental education students. *Research and Teaching in Developmental Education 5*(2), 39-53.

Rock, I. (1957). The role of repetition in associative learning. *American Journal of Psychology, 5,* 70, 186-193.

Rogers, C. R. (1963). The actualizing tendency in relation to "motives" and to consciousness. In M. R. Jones (Ed.), *Nebraska symposium on motivation* (pp. 1-24). Lincoln: University of Nebraska Press.

Rogers, C. R. (1955). Persons or science? A philosophical question. *American Psychologist, 10,* 267-278.

Rogers, C. R. (1947). Some observations on the organization of personality. *American Psychologist, 2,* 358-368.

Rogers, C. R., & Dymond, R. F. (1954) *Psychotherapy and personality change: Co-ordinated studies in the client-centered approach.* Chicago: University of Chicago Press.

Rogers, P. H. (1989). *Predicting student success in college.* Unpublished doctoral dissertation. Department of Educational Leadership, Grambling State University.

Roid, G. H., & Haladyna, T. M. (1982). *A technology for test-item writing.* New York: Academic press.

Roid, G. H., & Haladyna, T. M. (1980). The emergence of an item-writing technology, *Review of Educational Research, 50,* 293-314.

Rokeach, M. (1973). *The nature of human values.* NY: Free Press.

Roosevelt, T. (1907). [Letter to Henry S. Pritchett.] In *Bulletin No 3 of the National Society for the Promotion of Industrial Education.* New York: National Society for the Promotion of Industrial Education, 6-9.

Rose, J. S., Ryan, J. P., & Birdseye, A. T. (1984). Instructional validity: Merging curricular, instructional and test development issues. Paper presented at the Annual Meeting of the American Educational Research Association, New Orleans, LA, April 23-27.

Ross, E. A. (1901). *Social control: A survey of the foundations of order.* New York: Macmillan.

Roth, W. M., Gabel, D., Brown, L., & Rice, D. (1992). A combined method of indscal and cognitive mapping for describing hanges in students' cognitive structure. *Educational & Psychological Measurement, 52,* 769-779.

Rouche, J. E., & J. J. Snow (1977). *Overcoming learning problems.* San Francisco: Jossey-Bass.

Roudabush, G. E. (1973, February). *Item selection for criterion-referenced tests.* Paper presented at the annual meeting of the American Educational Research Association, New Orleans. (ED 074 147).

Roudabush, G. E., & G. D. Ross. (1971, February). *Some reliability problems in a criterion-referenced test.* A paper presented at the annual meeting of the American Educational Research Asssociation, New York. (ED 050 144).

Rowan, T. C. (1954). Some developments in multidimensional scaling applied to semantic relationships. Unpublished doctor's dissertation, University of Illinois.

Ruch, G. M. (1929). *The objective or new-type examination.* New York: Scott, Foresman, and Company.

Rudolph, F. (1989). *Curriculum: A history of the American undergraduate course of study since 1936*. San Francisco: Jossey-Bass Publishers.

Ruffin, S. C. (1989). Improving urban communities and their schools: A national emergency, *National Association of Secondary School Principals Bulletin*, 73, 61-70.

Rugg, H. O. (1916). *The experimental determination of mental discipline in school studies*. Baltimore: Warwick & York.

Rumelhart, D. E., & Abrahamson, A. A. (1973). A model for analogical reasoning. *Cognitive Psychology, 5*, 1-28.

Rumelhart, D. E., Lindsy, P. H. & Norman, D. A. (1972). A process model for long-term memory. In E. Tulving & W. Donaldson (eds.), *Organization of memory*. New York: Academic Press.

Rummelhart, D. E. & McClelland, J. L. (1987). PDP models and general issues in cognitive science. In J. L. McClelland & D. F. Rumelhart, *Parallel distributed processing, Explorations in the microstructure of cognition, Volume 1: Foundations*. Cambridge, MA: The Massachusetts Institute of Technology Press (110-146).

Rumelhart, D. E., & Norman, D.A. (1981). Accretion, Tuning and Restructuring: Three Model of Learning. In J. W. Colton & R. Klatzky, *Semantic Factors in Cognition*. Hillsdale, N.J.: Lawrence Erlbaum.

Rumelhart, D. E., & Norman, D. A. (1975). The active structural network. In D. A. Norman and D. E. Rumelhart (Eds.), *Explorations in cognition*. San Francisco, CA: W. H. Freeman, 35-64.

Rumelhart, D. E., & Norman, D. A. (1975). The computer implementation. In D. A. Norman and Rumelhart, D. E. (Eds.) *Explorations in cognition*. San Francisco, CA: W. H. Freeman, 160-178.

Rumelhart, D. E., & Ortony, A. (1977). The representation of knowledge in memory. In R. C. Anderson, R. J. Spiro, & W. E. Montague (Eds.), *Schooling and the acquisition of knowledge* (pp. 99-136). Hillsdale, NJ: Lawrence Erlbaum.

Rumelhart, D. E. & Norman, D. A. (1975). The computer implementation. In, Norman, D. A. & rumelhart, D. E. (Eds.) *Explorations in cognition*. San Francisco, CA: W. H. Freeman, 160-178.

Rummel, R. J. (1970). *Applied factor analysis*. Evanston, IL: Northwestern University Press.

Russell, B. (1923). Vagueness. *Australian Journal of Philosophy, 1*.

Rysbert, J. A. (1986). Effects of modifying instruction in a college classroom, *Psychological Reports, 58*, 965-966.

Sabers, D. L., & Kania, J. G. (1972, April). *Item precision in criterion-referenced measurement*. Paper presented at the annual meeting of the National Council for Measurement in Education, Chicago.

Saccone, C., Lanave, C., Pesole, G., & Preparata, G. (1990). Influence of base composition on quantitative estimates of gene evolution. In R. F. Doolittle (Ed.), *Methods in enzymology, Volume 183: Molecular evolution: Computer analysis of protein and nucleic acid sequences*. New York: Academic Press, 571-583.

Sacerdoti, E. A. (1977). *A structure for plans and behavior*. The Artificial Intelligence Series. New York: Elsevier North-Holland.

Safrit, M. J. (1981). *Evaluation in physical education*. Englewood Cliffs, NJ: Prentice-Hall.

Safrit, M. J., Stamm, C. L. & Douglass, J. A. (1981). The consistency of mastery classification for criterion-referenced test of motor behavior: The effect of varying sample size, *Journal of human movement studies, 7,* 131-143.

Sakai, T. (1996). *Riemannian geometry, Translations of mathematical monographs, Vol. 149.* Providence, R.I.: American Mathematical Society.

Salvia, J., & Ysseldyke, J. (1985). *Assessment in special and remedial education.* Bostn: Houghton Mifflin.

Samuelson, R. J. (August, 1992). The value of college. *Newsweek, 31,* 75.

Satoh, K. (1989). Relative plausibility based on model ordering: Preliminary report. In, Z. W. Ras (ed.), *Methodologies for intelligent systems, 4,* 17-24. New York: North-Holland.

Saupe, J. L. (1966). Selecting items to measure change. *Journal of Educational Measurement,* 3, 223-228.

Savage, L. J. (1972). *The Foundations of statistics.* New York: Dover.

Sax, G. (1989). The measurement of interests, attitudes and values, *Principles of educational and psychological measurement and evaluation.* Belmont, Ca.: Wadsworth, 467-504.

Scandura, J. B. (1977). Structural approach to instructional problems. *American Psychologist, 32,* 33-35.

Scandura, J. B. (1976). *Structural learning II: Issues and approaches.* New York: Gorden and Breach.

Scandura, J. B. (1973). *Structural learning: Theory and research.* New York: Gorden and Breach.

Scandura, J. B. (1966). Prior learning, presentation order, and prerequisite practice in problem solving. The *Journal of Experimental Education, 34*(4), 12-18.

Schank, R. C. (1975). *Conceptual information processing.* Amsterdam: North-Holland.

Schott, F., Neeb, K. E., & Wieberg, J. J. W. (1981). *Lehrstoffanalyse und unterrichtsplanung. Eine praktische anleitung zur analyse von lehrstoffen, präzisierung von lehrzielen, konstruktion von lehrmaterialien, uberprüfung des lehrerfolges.* Braunschweig: Westermann.

Schubert, W. H. (1981). *Curriculum: Perspective, paradigm and possibility.* New York: Macmillan Publishing Company.

Schuell, T. J. (1968). Retroactive inhibition in free-recall learning of categorized lists. *Journal of Verbal Learning and Verbal Behavior, 7,* 797-805.

Schustack, M. W. & Anderson, J. R. (1979). Effects of anology to prior knowledge on memory for new information, *Journal of Verbal Learning and Verbal Behavior, 18,* 564-583.

Scott, W. A. (1969). Measures of test homogeneity. *Educational and Psychological Measurement,* 20, 751-760.

Scriven, M. (1991). The science of valuing. In Wm. R. Standish, Jr., T. D. Cook & L. C. Leviton (eds.) *Foundations of program evaluation: Theories of prActice.* Newbury Park, Ca.: Sage Publications, 73-118.

Scriven, M. (1972). Pros and cons about goal-free evaluation, *Evaluation Comment, 3,* p. 4.

Scriven, M. S. (1967). The methodology of evaluation. In R. E. Stake (ed.), *Perspectives of curriculum evaluation.* Chicago: Rand McNally.

Selz, O. (1922). *Zur psychologie des produktiven denkins und intuns.* Bonn, Germany:

Cohen.

Sewell, O. (1972). Incentives for inner-city teachers. *Phi Delta Kappan*, October, 129-135.

Shanker, A. (1990). The end of the traditional model of schooling-and a proposal for using incentives to restructure our public schools, *Phi Delta Kappan*, 71, 5, 345-357.

Shannon, G. A. (1986). *Usefulness of score interpretive information for examinees who fail criterion-referenced tests*. Paper presented at the annual conference of the American Educational Research Association, San Francisco. ED 294 898.

Shavelson, R. J. (1974). Methods for examining representations of a subject-matter structure in a student's memory. *Journal of Research in Science Teaching, 11*, 231-249.

Shavelson, R. J. (1972). Some aspects of the correspondence between content structure and cognitive structure in physics instruction. *Journal of Educational Psychology, 63*, 225-234.

Shavelson, R. J., Block, J. H., & Ravitch, M. M. (1972). Criterion-referenced testing: Comments on reliability. *Journal of Educational Measurement, 5*, 133-138.

Shavelson, R. J. & Stanton, G. C. (1975). Construct validation: Methodology and application to three measures of cognitive structure. *Journal of Educational Measurement, 12*, 67-85.

Shaw, A. N., & Simon, H. A. (1958). Elements of a theory of human problem solving. *Psychological Review, 65*(3), 151-166.

Sheldon, H. O. (1842). *A lecture upon the Lyceum system*. Cincinnati: Ephraim Morgan & Company.

Shepard, L. A. (1980). Standard setting issues and methods, *Applied psychological measurement, 4*, 4, 447-467.

Shepard, L. A. (1979). Setting standards. In M. A. Bunda & J. R. Sanders (Eds.), *Practices and problems in competency-based measurement*. Washington, D.C.: National Council on Measurement in Education.

Shepard, L. A. (1976). Setting standards and living with them, *Florida journal of educational research, 18*, 23-32.

Shepard, R. N. (1966). Metric structures in ordinal data. *Journal of Mathematical Psychology*, 3, 287-315.

Shepard, R. N. (1962a). The analysis of proximities: Multidimensional scaling with an unknown distance function I. *Psychometricka, 27*(2).

Shepard, R. N. (1962b). The analysis of proximities: Multidimensional scaling with an unknown distance function. II. *Psychometrika, 27*(3).

Shepard, R. N. (1957). Stimulus and response generalization: A stochastic model relating generalization to distance in psychological space. *Psychometrika*, 32, 325-345.

Shepard, R. N. & Cooper, L. A. (1982). *Mental images and their transformations*. Cambridge, Ma.: M.I.T. Press/Bradford.

Shepard, R. N., Romney, A. K., & Nerlone, S.B. (1972a). *Multidimensional scaling, theory, and applications in the behavioral sciences, Volume I: Theory*. New York: Seminar Press.

Shepard, R. N., Romney, A. K., & Nerlone, S. B. (1972b). *Multidimensional scaling, theory, and applications in the behavioral sciences, Volume II: Applications*. New York: Seminar Press.

Shiffrin, R. M., & Schneider, W. (1977). Controlled and automatic human information processing: II. Perceptual learning, automatic attending, and a general theory.

Psychological Review, 84, 127-190.

Shoemaker, D. M. (1975). Toward a framework for achievement testing. *Review of Educational Research, 45,* 127-148.

Shoemaker, D. M. (1971, March). Criterion-referenced measurement revisited. *Educational Technology,* 61-62.

Shoemaker, S. H., & Johnson, R. T. (April, 1981). *Assessing the construct validity of a criterion referenced test: A nomological network approach.* Paper presented at the Annual meeting of the American Educational Research Association, Los Angeles, ED 204 59.

Shrock, S., Mansukhani, R. H., Coscarelll, W., & Palmer, S. (1986). An overview of criterion-referenced test development. *Journal of the National Society for Performance and Instruction, 25,* 6, 3-7.

Siegel, S. (1956). *Nonparametric statistics.* New York: McGraw Hill Book Company.

Sigmond, G. (1981). *Use of judgmental procedures by groups of raters to set minimum competency standards.* Paper presented at the Annual Meeting of the National Council on Measurement in Education, Los Angeles.

Silver, E. A., & Marshall, S.P. (1990). Mathematical and scientific problems solving: Findings, issues, and instructional implications. In B. J. Jones and L. Idol (Eds.), *Dimensions of thinking and cognitive instruction.* Hillsdale, NJ: Lawrence Erlbaum.

Simmons, R. F. (1973). Semantic networks: Their computation and use for understanding English sentences. In R. C. Schank & K. M. Colby (Eds.), *Computer models of thought and language.* San Francisco, Ca.: Freeman.

Simon, H. A. (1979). Information processing models of cognition. *Annual Review of Psychology, 30,* 363-396.

Simon, H. A. (1967). Motivational and emotional controls of cognition. *Psychological Review, 74,* 29-39.

Simpson, M., & Arnold, B. (1983). Diagnostic tests and criterion-referenced assessments: their contribution to the resolution of pupil learning difficulties. *Programmed Learning and Educational Technology, 20,* 1, 36-42.

Sinclair, U. (1924). *The Goslings-A study of the American schools.* Pasadina, Ca.: Author.

Skager, R. W. (1978). *The great criterion-referenced test myth,* Center for the Study of Evaluation, Report Number 95. Paper presented at the annual meeting of the American Educational Research Association, Washington DC, April, ED 160 650.

Skaggs, G., & Lissitz, R. W. (1986). IRT test equating: Relevant issues and a review of recent research. *Review of Educatoinal Research, 56,* 4, 495-529.

Skinner, B. F. (1966). Teaching machines (1961). In S. Coopersmith (Ed.), *Frontiers of psychological research.* San Francisco: Freeman.

Skinner, B. F. (1964). The science of learning and the art of teaching. *Harvard Educational Review,* 116(2), 86-97.

Skinner, B. F. (1958). Teaching machines. *Science, 238,* 969-977.

Skinner, B. F. (1957). *Verbal behavior.* New York: Appleton.

Skinner, B. F. (1955). Are theories of learning necessary? *Psychological Review, 57,* 193-216.

Skinner, B. F. (1949). *Walden Two.* New York: Macmillan.

Skinner, B. F., Solomon, A. C., & Lindsley, O. R. (1954). A new method for the experimental analysis of the behavior of psychotic patients. *Journal of Nervous and Mental Disease, 120,* 403-406.

Slinde, J. A., & Linn, R. L. (1978). An exploration of the adequacy of the Rasch model for the problem of vertical equating. *Journal of Educational Measurement, 15*(1), 23-36.

Slobin, D. I. (1979). *Psycholinguistics (2nd ed.).* Glenview, IL: Scott-Foresman.

Smets, P. (1988). Belief functions (with discussion). In, P. Smets, A. Mamdani, D. Dubois, & H. Prade (Eds.), *Non-Standard Logistics for Automated Reasoning.* New York: Academic Press, 51-84.

Smirnov, N. (1948). Table for estimating the goodness of fit of empirical distributions. *Annals of Mathematical Statistics, 19,* 279-281.

Smith, M. (1963). *Principles and applications of tensor analysis.* NY: Howard W. Sams.

Smolensky, P. (1987). Information processing in dynamical systems: Foundations of Harmony Theory. In D. E. Rumelhart & J. L. McClelland (Eds.), *Parallel distributed processing, Explorations in the microstructure of cognition: Vol. 1: Foundations* (pp. 194-281). Cambridge: Massachusetts Institute of Technology Press.

Snedden, D. (1925). Planning curriculum research. *School and Society, 22,* 259-265, 287-293, 319-328.

Snedden, D. (1921). *Sociological determination of objectives in education.* Philadelphia: J. B. Lippincot.

Snedden, D. (1919). Cardinal principles of secondary education. *School and Society, 9,* 517-527.

Snedden, D. (1916). The "project" as teaching unit. *School and Society, 4,* 419-423.

Snedden, D. (1915). Vocational education. *New Republic, 3,* 40-42.

Snedden, D. (1912). Report of Committee on National Legislation. In *Bulletin No. 15 of the National Society for the Promotion of Industrial Education.* New York: National Society for the Promotion of Industrial Education, 126-134.

Sokolv, Y. N. (1963). *Perception and the conditional reflex.* Oxford, England: Pergamon Press.

Spada, H. (1976). *Modelle des denkens und lernes.* Bern: Huber.

Spada, C., & Kemp, W. F. (Eds.). (1977). *Formalized theories of thinking and learning and their implications for science instruction.* Huber.

Spearman, C. (1927). *The abilities of man: Their nature of measurement.* New York: Macmillan.

Spearman, C. (1904). "General Intelligence" objectively determined and measured. *The American Journal of Psychology, 25,* 202-292.

Spelt, P. F., Lyness, E., & de Saussure, G. (1989). Deveopment and training of a learning expert system for an autonomous robot. *Simulation, 53*(5), 223-228.

Spence, K. W. (1960). *Behavior theory and learning.* Englewood Cliffs, NJ: Prentice-Hall.

Spence, K. W. (1958). A theory of emotionally based drive (D) and its relation to performance in simple learning situtations. *American Psychologist, 13,* 131-141.

Spence, K. W. (1956). *Behavior theory and conditioning.* New Haven, CN: Yale University Press.

Spence, K. W. (1951). Theroetical interpretations of learning. In S. S. Stevens (Ed.), *Handbook of Experimental Psychology.* New York: Wiley.

Spence, K. W. (1944). The nature of theory construction in contemporary psychology. *Psychological Review, 51,* 47-68.

Spencer, H. (1897). *Education: Intelectual, Moral, and Physical.* NY: D. Appleton and Company.

Spencer, H. (1865). *Social Statics.* NY: D. Appleton and Company.

Spencer, H. (1861). *Education: Intelectual, Moral and Physical.* NY: D. Appleton and Company.

Sperling, G. (1960). The information available in a brief visual presentation. *Psychological Monographs, 74, Whole Number 498.*

Sperry, R. W. (1968). Hemisphere deconnections and unity in conscious awareness. *American Psychologist, 23,* 10, 723-733.

Sperry, R. W. (1966). Brain bisection and mechanisms of consciousness. In J. C. Eccles (Ed.), *Brain and conscious experience.* New York: Springer-Verlag.

Spiegelhalter, D. J. (1986). A statistical view of uncertainty in expert systems. In, W. Gale (ed.), *Artivical intelligence and statistics.* Reading, MA: Addison-Wesley, 17-55.

Spring, J. (1986). *The American school 1642-1985.* New York: Longman, Inc.

Squire, L. R. (1984). Memory and the brain. In S. Friedman (Ed.), *Brain, Cognition and Education.* New York: Academic Press.

Squire, L. R. (1981). Two forms of human amnesia: An analysis of forgetting. *Journal of Neuroscience, 1,* 635-640.

Staden, R. (1990). Searching for patterns in protein and nucleic acid sequences. In R. F. Doolittle (ed.), *Molecular evolution: Computer analysis of protein and nucleic acid sequences.* New York: Academic Press, 193-211.

Staggers, N. & Norcio, A. F. (1993). Mental models: concepts for human-computer interaction research. *International Journal of Man-Macnine Studies, 38,* 587-605.

Stagner, R. & Osgood, C. E. (1946). Impact of war on a nationalistic frame of reference: I. Changes in general approval and qualitative patterning of certain stereotypes, *Journal of social psychology, 24,* 187-215.

Stake, R. E. (1991). Retrospective on 'The countenance of educational evaluation.' In M. W. McLaughlin and D. C. Phillips (Eds), *Evaluation and education: At quarter century.* Chicago: University of Chicago Press, 67-88.

Stake, R. E. (1985). A personal interpretation, *Educational evaluation and policy analysis, 7,* 3, 243-244.

Stake, R. E. (1967). The countenance of educational evaluation, *Teachers College Record, 68,* 523-540.

Starch, D. (1918). *Educational measurement.* New York: Macmillan.

Stedman, L. (1987). It's time we changed the effective schools formula. *Phi Delta Kappan, 69,* 215-224.

Stedman, L. (1985). A new look at the effective schools literature. *Urban Education, 20,* 295-326.

Steinheiser, F. H., Jr. (1978). Criterion referenced testing: A criitical analysis of selected models.. Technical paper 306, Final report. Alexandria, VA: Army Research Institute for the Behavioral and Social Seiences. ED 169 097.

Stensvold, M.S., & Wilson, J. T. (1990). The interaction of verbal ability with concept mapping in learning from a chemistry laboratory activity. *Science Education, 74,* 4, 473-489.

Stent, G. S. (1972). Prematurity and uniqueness in scientific discovery. *Scientific American, 227,* 6, 84-93.

Sternberg, R. J. (1982). A componential approach to intellectual development. *Advances in the Psychology of Human Intelligence, 1,* 413-463.

Sternberg, R. J. (1979). The nature of mental abilities. *American Psychologist, 34,* 214-230.

Sternberg, R. J. (1977). *Intelligence, information processing, and analogical reasoning: The componential analysis of human abilities.* Hillsdale, NJ: Erlbaum.

Sternberg, S. (1969). The discovery of processing stages: Extensions of Doners' method. *Acta Psychologica, 38,* 276-315.

Sternberg, S. (1963). Stochastic learning theroy. In R. D. Luce, R. R. Bush, and E. Galanter (Eds.), *Handbook of mathematical psychology,, Vol. II.* New York: Wiley.

Stevens, A., & Rumelhart, D. A. (1975) Errors in reading: An analysis using an augmented transition network model of grammar. In D. A. Norman and D. E. Rumelhart (Eds.), *Explorations in cognition.* San Francisco, CA: W. H. Freeman, 135-155.

Stevens, S. S. (1951). Mathematics, measurement and psychophysics. In S. S. Stevens (Ed.), *Handbook of experimental psychology.* NY: Wiley, 1-49.

Stewart, J. (1979). Content and cognitive structure: Critique of assessment and representation techniques used by science education researchers. *Science Education, 63,* 395-405.

Stillwell, J. (1996). *Sources of hyperbolic geometry.* Providence, R.I.: American Mathematical Society.

Stout, W. F. (1990). A new item response theory modeling approach with applications to unidimensionality assessment and ability estimation. *Psychometrika, 55,* 2, 293-325.

Stowitschek, J., Gable, R., & Hendrickson, J. (1980). *Instrcuional materials for exceptional children: Selection, management, and administration.* Baltimore, MD: Asper Corporation.

Strayer, G. D. (1911). The abilities of special groups of high-school students in the subjects which they studied. Research within the field of education, its organization, and encouragement. *The School Review Monographs, 5* (pp. 7-15). Chicago: University of Chicago Press.

Strike, K. A., & Posner, G. J. (1976). Epistemilogical perspectives on conceptions of curriculum organization and learning. *Review of Research in Education, 4,* 106-141.

Stroud, A. H., & Sechrest, D. (1966). *Gaussian quadrature formulas.* Englewood Cliffs, NJ: Prentice Hall.

Stufflebeam, D. L. (1971). *Educational evaluation and decision making.* Itasca, Illinois: F. E. Peacock.

Subkoviak, M. J. (1978). Empirical investigation of procedures for estimating reliability for mastery tests. *Journal of Educational Measurement, 15*(2), 111-116.

Succi, G. J. (1952). A multidimensional analysis of social attitudes with special reference to ethnocentrism. Unpublished doctor's dissertation, University of Illinois.

Sundberg, N. D., & Tyler, L. E. (1962). *Clinical psychology.* New York: Appleton Century-Crofts.

Suppes, P. (1964). Modern learning theory and the elementary school curriculum. *American Educational Research Journal, 4,* 79-93.

Suppes, P., & Atkinson, R. C. (1960). *Markov learning models for multiperson interactions.* Stanford: Stanford University Press.

Suppes, P., & Morningstar, M. (1972). *Computer-assisted instruction at Stanford: Data, models, and evaluation of arithmetic programs.* New York: Academic Press.

Suppes, P., & Zinnes, J. L. (1963). Basic measurement theory. In R. D. Luce, R. R. Bush, & E. Galanter (Eds.), *Handbook of mathematical psychology, Vol.I.* New York: Wiley.

Surra, C. (1988). *TUCKROT-A program for rotation of learning curves.* Available from

Catherine Surra, University of Arizona, School of Family and Consumer Resources, Tempe, AZ 85721.

Swaminathan, H., Hambleton, R. K., & Algina, J. (1975). A Bayesian decision-theoretic procedure for use with criterion-referenced tests. *Journal of Educational Measurement, 12*(2), 87-98.

Swaminathan, H., Hambleton, R. K., & Algina, J. (1974). Reliability of criterion-referenced tests: A decision-theoretic formulation. *Journal of Educational Measurement, 11*(4), 263-267.

Synge, J. L. & Schild, A. (1949). *Tensor calculus.* NY: Dover publications.

Syz, H. C. (1926). Psycho-galvanic studies on sixty-four medical students. *British Journal of Psychology, 17,* 54-69.

Taber, J. I., Glaser, R., & Schaefer, H. H. (1965). *Learning and programmed instruction.* Reading, MA: Addison Wesley.

Tallmadge, G. K. (1985). Rumors regarding the death of the equipercentile assumption may have been greatly exaggerated. *Journal of Educational Measurement, 22,* 1, 33-39.

Tallmadge, G. K. (1982). An empirical assessment of norm-referenced evaluation methodology. *Journal of Educational Measurement, 19,* 2, 97-112.

Tan, M., & Schlimmer, J. C. (1990). Two case studies in cost-sensitive concept acquisition. *Proceedings of the Conference of the American Association for Artificial Intelligence,* 854-860.

Tannenbaum, P. H. (1953). Attitudes toward source and concept as factors in attitude change through communications. Unpublished doctor's dissertation, University of Illinois.

Tannenbaum, P. H. (1955). What effect when TV covers a congressional hearing?, *Journal Quarterly, 32,* 434-440.

Tannenbaum, P. H. (1956). The effect of background music on interpretation of stage and television drama, *Audio-visual communications review, 4,* 2, 92-101.

Tatsuoka, K. (1980). *The least-squares estimation of latent trait variables.* Paper presented at the annual conference of the American Educational Research Association, Boston, Massachusetts.

Tatsuoka, K. K., & Tatsuoka, M. M. (1983). Spotting erroneous rules of operation by the individual consistency index. *Journal of Educational Measurement, 20,* 221-230.

Tatsuoka, M. & Tatsuoka, K. (1980). *Detection of aberrant response patterns and their effect on dimensionality* (Research Report 80-4). Urbana, Illinois: University of Illinois, Computer based Education Laboratory.

Tatsuoka, M. M. (1971). *Multivariate analysis: Techniques for educational and psychological research.* New York: John Wiley and Sons.

Taylor, D. W. (1960). Towards an information processing theory of motivation. In M.R. Jones (Ed.), *Nebraska symposium on motivation.* Lincoln: University of Nebraska Press.

Taylor, F. (1919). *Principles of scientific management.* New York: Harper and Row.

Trembath, R. J. & White, R. T. (1979). Mastery achievement of intellectual skills, *Journal of experimental education, 47,* 247-252.

Terman, L. M. (1919). *The intelligence of school children.* Boston: Houghton Mifflin.

Terman, L. M. (1916). *The measurement of intelligence.* Boston: Houghton Mifflin.

Terman, L. M., & Merrill, M. A. (1960). *Measuring intelligence.* Cambridge: Houghton

Mifflin.

Thibault, J. W. & Kelley, H. H. (1967). *The Social Psychology of Groups*. New York: John Wiley & Sons, Inc.

Thissen, D. (1982). Marginal maximum likelihood estimation in the one-parameter logistic model. *Psychometrika, 47*, 175-186.

Thompson, F. (1973). Dynamics of information, *The KEY reporter, 38, 2*.

Thompson, G. H. (1927). The tetrad-difference criterion, *British journal of psychology, 8*, 271-281.

Thompson, G. H. (1951). *The factorial analysis of human ability*. New York: Houghton Mifflin.

Thompson, J. D. (1966). *Approaches to Organizational Design*. Pittsburgh, PA: University of Pittsburgh Press.

Thompson, R. F., Berger, T., & Madden, J. (1983). Cellular processes of learning and memory in mammalian CNS. *Annual Review of Neuroscience, 6*, 447-491.

Thompson, R. F., Hicks, L. H., & Shryrokov, V. B. (1980). *Neural mechanisms of goal-directed behavior and learning*. New York, NY: Academic Press.

Thorndike, E. L. (1932). *The fundamentals of learning*. New York: Columbia University Press.

Thorndike, E. L. (1918). The nature, purposes, and general methods of measurement of educational products. In G. M. Whipple (Ed.), *The measurement of educational products. Seventeenth Yearbook of the National Society for the Study of Education, Part II* (pp. 16-24). Bloomington, IL: Bloomington Public School Publishing.

Thorndike, E. L. (1913). *Educational psychology, Volume 2: The psychology of learning.* New York: Columbia University Press.

Thorndike, E. L. (1912). The measurement of educational products. *The School Review, 20*(5), 289-299.

Thorndike, E. L. (1911). Quantitative investigations in education with special reference to cooperation within this association. Research within the field of education, its organization, and encouragement, *The School Review Monographs, 1* (pp. 33-54). Chicago: University of Chicago Press.

Thorndike, E. L. (1901). Notes on child study, *Columbia University contributions to philosophy, psychology and education, 8*, Nos. 3-4. New York: Macmillan, p. 20.

Thorndike, E. L. & Woodworth, R. S. (1901). The influence of improvement in one mental function upon the efficiency of the other functions, Part I, *Psychological Review, 8*, p. 249.

Thorndike, R. L. (Ed.). (1971). *Educational Measurement* (2nd ed.). Washington, DC: American Council on Education.

Thorndike, R. L., & Hagen, E. (1969). *Measurement and evaluation in psychology and education* (3rd ed.). New York: Wiley.

Thurstone, L. L. (1938). *Primary mental abilities, psychometric monographs, number 1.* Chicago, Illinois: University of Chicago Press.

Thurstone, L. L. (1938). *Primary mental abilities. Psychometric Monographs, No. 1,* Chicago: University of Chicago Press.

Thurstone, L. L. (1932). Stimulus dispersions in the method of constant stimuli. *Journal of Experimental Psychology, 15*, 284-297.

Thurstone, L. L. (1927). A law of comparative judgment. *Psychological Review, 34*, 273-286.

Thurstone, L. L., & Chave, E. J. (1929). *The measurement of attitude.* Chicago: University of Chicago Press.

Thurstone, L. L., & Thurstone, T. G. (1941). *Factorial studies of intelligence. Psychometric Monographs, 2.* Chicago: University of Chicago Press.

Thurlow, W. R. (1950). Direct measures of discriminations among individuals performed by psychological tests. *Journal of Psychology, 25,* 281-314.

Tiegs, E. W. (1939). *Tests and measurements in the improvement of learning.* Boston: Houghton Mifflin.

Tiegs, E. W. (1931). *Tests and measurements for teachers.* Boston: Houghton Mifflin.

Timm, N. H. (1975). *Multivariate analysis with applications in education and psychology.* Los Angeles: Brooks Cole Publishing.

Tindal, G., Fuchs, L. S., Fuchs, D., Shinn, M. R., Deno, S. L., & Germann, G. (1985). Empirical validation of criterion-referenced tests. *Journal of Educational Research, 78,* 4, 203-209.

Tinsley, H. E. A. (1971). *An investigation of the Rasch simple logistic model for tests of intelligence or attainment.* Unpublished doctoral dissertation, University of Minnesota.

Tinsley, H. E. A., & Dawis, R. V. (1977). Test-free person measurement with the Rasch simple logistic model. *Applied Psychological Measurement, 1*(4), 483-488.

Tismaneanu, V. (1990). Eastern Europe: The story the media missed, *The bulletin of the Atomic Scientists,* March, 17-21.

Tolaas, J. (1986). Transformatory framework: Pictorial to verbal. In B. B. Wolman & M. Ullman (Eds.), *Handbook of states of consciousness* (pp. 31-67). New York: Van Nostrand Reinhold Company.

Tolaas, J. (1980a). Dreams, dreaming and recent intrusive events. *Journal of Altered States of Consciousness, 5*(3), 183-210.

Tolaas, J. (1980b). The magic theater and the ordinary theater: A comparison. *Journal of Mental Imagery, 4,* 115-127.

Tolman, E. C. (1959). Principles of purposive behavior. In S. Koch (Ed.), *Psychology: A study of science, Volume 2.* New York: McGraw-Hill.

Tolman, E. C. (1948). Cognitive maps in rats and men. *Psychological Review, 55,* 189-208.

Tolman, E. C. (1938). The determiners of behavior at a choice point. *Psychological Review, 45,* 1-41.

Tolman, E. C. (1932). *Purposive behavior in animals and men.* New York, New York: Appleton-Century-Crofts.

Tolman, E. C., & Honzik, C. H. (1930). Degrees of hunger; reward and nonreward; and maze learning in rats. *University of California Publications in Psychology, 4,* 241-256.

Torgerson, W. S. (1952). Multidimensional scaling I: Theory and method. *Psychometrika, 17,* 401-419.

Toulmin, S. (1972). *Human Understanding. Volume I: The collective use and evolution of concepts.* Princeton, NJ: Princeton University.

Traub, R. E. & Rowley, G. L. (1980). Reliability of test scores and decisions, *Applied psychological measurement, 4,* 4, 517-545.

Travers, J. (1950). *How to make achievement tests.* New York: Odyssey Press.

Treisman, A. (1966). Human attention. In B. M. Foss (Ed.), *New horizons in psychology.*

London, England: Pelican Original, A 775.

Trembath, R. J. & White, R. T. (1979). Mastery achievement of intellectual skills, *Journal of experimental education, 47,* 247-252.

Tsutkawa, R. K. (1992). Prior distribution for item response curves, *British Journal of Mathematical and Statistical Psychology, 45,* 51-74.

Tsutakawa, R. K., & Johnson, J. C. (1990). The effect of uncertainty of item parameter estimation on ability estimates. *Psychometrika,* 55(2), 371-390.

Tucker, L. R. (1966). Learning theory and multivariate experiment: Illustration of determination of generalized learning curves. In R. B. Cattell (Ed.), *Handbook of multivariate experimental psychology.* New York: Rand McNally, 476-501.

Tucker, L. R. (1940). The role of correlated factors in factor analysis, *Psychometrika, 5,* 141-152.

Tukey, J. W. (1977). *Exploratory data analysis.* Reading, MA: Addison Wesley.

Tulvin, E. (1972). Episodic and semantic memory. In E. Tulvin & W. Donaldson (Eds.), *Organization of memory* (pp. 382-403). New York: Academic Press.

Turbayne, C. M. (1962). *The myth of metaphor.* New Haven: Yale University Press.

Turvey, M. V. (1973). On peripheral and central processes in vision: Inferences from an information processing analysis of masking with pattern stimuli. *Psychological Review, 80,* 1-52.

Tyler, R. W. (1991). General statement on program evaluation. In M. W. McLaughlin & D. C. Phillips (Eds), *Evaluation and education: A quarter century.* Chicago: University of Chicago Press, 3-17.

Tyler, R. W. (1983). A rationale for program evaluation. In G. F. Madaus, M. S. Scriven, D. L. Stufflebeam (Eds.), *Evaluation models: Viewpoints on educational and human services evaluation.* Boston, MA: Kluwer-Nijhoff.

Tyler, R. W. (1973). *Research in science teaching in a larger context.* Columbus, OH: ERIC Information Analysis Center for Science, Mathematics, and Environmental Education. ED 076 426.

Tyler, R. W. (1971). *A viable model for a college of education.* Presentation at the Inauguration of Dean Doi, University of Rochester, October 30, ED 059 961.

Tyler, R. (1964a). America needs the experimental college. *Educational Forum, 28,* 151-157.

Tyler, R. (1964b). The interrelationship of knowledge. *The National Elementary Principal, 68,* 13-21.

Tyler, R. (1959). Conditions for effective learning. *Journal of the National Education Association, 68,* 47-49.

Tyler, R. (1953). The Core Curriculum. *Journal of the National Education Association, 62,* 563-565.

Tyler, R. (1951). Evolving a functional curriculum. *The American Journal of Nursing, 51,* 736-738.

Tyler, R. (1949). *Basic principles of curriculum and instruction.* Chicago: The University of Chicago Press.

Tyler, R. (1948). Educability and the schools. *The Elementary School Journal, 156,* 220-221.

Tyler, R. (1942). General statement on evaluation. *Journal of Educational Research, 35,* 492-501.

Tyler, R. (1930). Measuring the ability to infer. *Educational Research Bulletin, 9,* 475-

480.

Uleman, J. S., & Bargh, J. A. (1989). *Unintended thought.* New York: Guilford Press.

Ullman, M. (1973). A theory of vigilance and dreaming. In V. Zigmind (Ed.), *The oculomotor system and brain function* (pp. 455-465). London, England: Butterworth.

Ullman, S. (1977). *The interpretation of visual motion.* Doctoral Dissertation, Massachusetts Instistute of Technology.

Underwood, B. (1966). Forgetting. In S. Coopersmith (Ed.), *Frontiers of psychological research.* San Francisco: Freeman.

Underwood, B. J., & Keppel, G. (1962). One-trial learning? *Verbal Learning and Verbal Behavioir, 5,* 1, 1-13.

Uprichard, A. E. (1970). The effect of sequence in the acquisition of three set relations: An experiment with preschoolers. *Arithmetic Teacher,* 597-604.

Vandenberghe, R., Price, C., Wise, R., Josephs, O., & Frackowiak, R. S. J. (1996). Functional anatomy of a common semantic system for words and pictures, *Nature, 383,* 6597,254-256.

van der Linden, W. J. (1981). *On the estimation of the proportion of masters in criterioin referenced testing.* Enscheds, The Netherlands: Twente University of Technology, ED 310 155.

Van Patten, J., Chao, C. I., & Reigeluth, C. M. (1986). A review of strategies for sequencing and synthesizing instruction. *Review of Educational Research, 56,* 4, 437-471.

Van Ryzin, J. (1977). *Classification and clustering.* New York: Academic Press.

Vasconcellos, J. & Murphy, M. (1987). Education in the experience of being citizens, *Educational leadership, 45,* 70-73.

Vico, G. (1965). *On the study methods of our time.* Translated by E. Giantruco. New York: Bobbs-Merrill.

Vico, G. (1944). *The autobiography of Giambattista Vico.* Translated by M. H. Fisch & T. G. Bergin. Ithica, NY: Cornell University Press.

Viemot, L. (1979). Spontaneous reasoning in elementary dynamics. *European Journal of Science Education, 1,* 205-221.

Vosniadou, S., & Brewer, W. F. (1987). Theories and knowledge restructuring in development. *Review of Educational Research, 57,* 1, 51-67.

Vygotsky, L. S. (1978). *Mind in society: The development of higher psychological processes.* Cambridge, MA: Harvard University Press.

Vygotsky, L. S. (1962). *Thought and language.* New York: Wiley.

Walbesser, H. H., & Eisenberg, T. A. (1972). *A review of research on behavioral objectives and learning hierarchies. (SMEC Report).* Columbus, OH: ERIC Information Analysis Center.

Wallace, G., & Larsen, S. (1977). *The assessment of learning problems and teaching.* Boston: Allyn and Bacon

Wanner, E. (1974). *On remembering, forgetting, and understanding sentences.* The Hague: Mouton.

Ward, J. (1970). On the concept of criterion-referenced measurement. *British Journal of Educational Psychology, 40,* 314-323.

Ward, L. F. (1893). *The psychic factors of civilization.* Boston: Ginn.

Ward, L. F. (1883). *Dynamic sociology or applied social science as based upon statistical sociology and the less complex sciences, Volume 2.* New York: Appleton.

Washburne, C. W. (1922). Educational measurements as a key to individualizing instruction and promotion. *Journal of Educational Research, 5,* 195-206.

Watson, J. B. (1924). *Psychology from the standpoint of a behaviorist.* Philadelphia: Lippencott.

Watson, J. B., & Rayner, R. (1920). Conditional emotional reactions. *Journal of Experimental Psychology, 3,* 1-14.

Waugh, N. C., & Norman, D. A. (1965). Primary memory. *Psychological Review, 72*(2), 90-104.

Weber, M. B., & Argo, J. K. (1979). A study of the homogeneity of items produced from item forms across different taxonomic levels. Paper presented at the annual meeting of the Eastern Educational Research Association, Kiawah Island, SC, February, 1979. (ED 175 906).

Weiner, S. (1989). We decided to show how things can work. *Forbes,* 144, 180-188.

Weisman, J. (1993). Skills in the Schools: Now It's Business' Turn, *Phi Delta Kappan, 74,* 367-309.

Wellington, J. K. (1977). American education: Its failure and its future. *Phi Delta Kappan, 58*(7), 527-530.

Werner, H., & Kaplan, B. (1963). *Symbol formation: An organismic developmental approach to the psychology of language and the expression of thought.* New York: Wiley.

Wertheimer, M. (1945). *Productive thinking.* New York: Harper and Row.

Wesman, A. G. (1971). Writing the test item. In R. L. Thorndike (Ed.), *Educational Measurement* (pp. 81-129), Washington, DC: American Council on Education.

West, E. B. (1980). Crime in American public schools, *The public interest,* 18-42.

Westen, D. (1991). Social conition and object relations, *Psychological Bulletin, 109,* 3, 429-455.

Wheat, H. G. (1933). The nest Step for our laboratory schools away from lesson learning. *Educational Administration & Supervision, 19,* 203-218.

Wherry, R. J., & Gaylord, R. H. (1944). Factor pattern of test items and tests as a function of the correlation coefficient, content, difficulty, and constant error factors. *Psychometrika, 9,* 237-244.

Whipple, G. M. (1911). Methods, discipline, tests. Research within the field of education, its organization, and encouragement. *The School Review Monographs, 1,* 71. Chicago: The University of Chicago Press.

White, R. T. (1981). Achievements and directions in research on intellectual skills. *Australian Journal of Education, 25,* 224-237.

White, R. T. (1979a). Achievement, mastery, proficiency, competence. *Studies in Science Education, 6,* 1-22.

White, R. T. (1979b). Describing cognitive structure. In *Proceedings of the 1979 Annual Conference of the Australian Association for Research in Education,* Melbourne: Australian Association for Research in Education.

White, R. T. (1974a). The validation of a learning hierarchy. *American Educational Research Journal, 11*(2), 121-136.

White, R. T. (1974b). A model for the validation of learning hierarchies. *Journal of Research in Science Teaching,* 11(2), 121-136.

White, R. T. (1973). Research into learning hierarchies. *Review of Educational Research, 43*(3), 361-375.

White, R. T., & Clark, R. M. (1973). A test of inclusion which allows for errors of measurement. *Psychometrika, 38*(1), 77-86.

White, R. T., & Gagné, R. M. (1974). Past and future research on learning hierarchies. *Educational Psychology, 11*(1), 19-28.

White, R. T., & Glynn, S. M. (1990). *Children's mental models of gravity and their predictions of the vertical motion of objects (Report No. 6277).* Cambridge, MA: Bolt, Beranek, and Newman.

White, R. T., & Gunstone, R. F. (1980). Converting memory protocols to scores on several dimensions. In *Papers of the 1980 annual conference of the Australian Association for Research in Education.* Sydney: Australian Association for Research in Education.

Whitely, S. E. (1981). Measuring aptitude processes with multicomponent latent trait models. *Journal of Educational Measurement, 18,* 2, 67-84.

Whitely, S. E. (1980). Multicomponent latent trait models for ability tests. *Psychometrika, 45,* 4, 479-494.

Whitely, S. E. & Barnes, G. M. (1979). The implications of processing event sequences for theories of anologic reasoning, *Memory and Cognition, 7,* 323-331.

Whitely, S. E., & Dawis, R. V. (1974). The nature of objectivity with the Rasch model. *Journal of Educational Measurement, 11*(2).

Whitely, S. E. & Schneider, L. M. (1981). Information structure on geometric analogies: A test theory approach, *Applied Psychological Measurement, 5,* 383-397.

Wiersma, Wm. & Jurs, S. G. (1990). *Educational measurement and testing.* Boston: Allyn and Bacon.

Wiggins, G. (1989). A true test: Toward more authentic and equitable assessment. *Phi Delta Kappan, 70,* 9, 703-713.

Wilcox, R. R. (1980). Determining the length of a criterion-referenced test, *Applied psychological measurement, 4,* 4, 425-446.

Wilcox, R. R. (1979). Applying ranking and selection techniques to determine the length of a mastery test, *Educational and Psychological Measurement, 39,* 13-22.

Wilcox, R. R. (1977). Estimating the likelihood of a false-positive or false-negative decision with a mastery test: An empirical Bayes approach. *Journal of Educational Statistics, 2,* 289-307.

Wilcox, R. R., & Harris, C. W. (1977). On Emrick's "An evaluation model for mastery testing." *Journal of Educational Measurement, 14*(3), 215-218.

Wilhelms, F. T. (1975). What about basic standards? *Today's Education, 64*(1), 46-48.

Williams, J. C. (1978). *Human Behavior in Organizations.* Dallas, Tx.: South-Western Publishing Co.

Williams, M. D., Hollan, J. D., & Stevens, A. L. (1983). Human reasoning about a simple physical system. In D. Gentner and A. L. Stevens (Eds.), *Mental models.* Hillsdale, NJ: Lawrence Erlbaum.

Willmott, A. S., & Fowles, D. E. (1974). *The objective interpretation of test performance.* England: National Foundation for Educational Research.

Wilson, M. (1992). Objective measurement: The state of the art. IN M. Wilson (ed.), *Objective measurement: Theory into practice.* Norwood, New Jersey: Ablex Publishing Corporation, 1-8.

Wilson, M. A. & McNaughton, B. L. (1994). Reactivation of hippocampal ensemble memories during sleep, *Scinece, 265,* 676-679.

Winer, B. J. (1971). *Statistical principles in experimental design* (2nd ed.). New York: McGraw Hill.

Winograd, T. (1975). Frame representation and the declarative-procedural controversy. In D. G. Bobrow & A. Collins (Eds.), *Representation and understanding* (pp. 185-210). New York: Academic Press.

Winston, P. H. (1975). Learning structural descriptions from examples. In P. H. Winston (Ed.), *The psychology of computer vision*. NY: McGraw-Hill, 157-209.

Winzenz, D., & Bower, G. H. (1970). Subject-imposed coding and memory for digit series. *Journal of Experimental Psychology, 83,* 52-56.

Wisner, M., & Carey, S. (1983). When heat and temperature were one. In D. Gentner & A. Stevens (Eds.), *Mental models*. Hillsdale, NJ: Lawrence Erlbaum Associates.

Wolff, C. F. (1740). *Psychologia rationalis: methodo scientifica pertractata...cognitionem profutura proponuntur.* Francofurti: Lipsiae.

Womer, F. B. (1966). *Unit VII: Teacher-made tests: Writing the test.* Chicago: Science Research Associates.

Wong, S. K. M. , Yao, Y. Y., Bollmann, P. & Bürger, H. C. (1991). Axiomatization of qualitative belief structure, *Institute of Electronics and Electrical Engineers Transactions on Systems, Man, and Cybernetics, 21,* 4, 726-734.

Wood, D. A. (1960). *Test construction: Development and interpretation of achievement tests.* Columbus, Ohio: C. E. Merrill.

Wood, P. (1992). Generation and objective rotation of generalized learning curves uing matrix language products. *Multivariate Behavioral Research, 27,* 1, 21-29.

Woodbury, M. A. (1951). On the standard length of a test. *Psychometrika,* 16, 103-106.

Woodcock, R. W., & Dahl, M. N. (1976). *A common scale for the measurement of person ability and test item difficulty.* Circle Pines, MN: American Guidance Service.

Woodrow, H. (1946). The ability to learn. *Psychological Review, 53,* 147-158.

Woods, W. A. (1975). What's in a link: Foundations for semantic networks. In D. G. Bobrow and A. Collins, *Representation and understanding*. New York: Academic Press, 35-82.

Woodson, M. I. (1974). The issue of item and test variance for criterion-referenced tests, *Journal of educational measurement, 11,* 63-64.

Woodson, M. I., & Charles, E. (1974). The issue of item and test variance for criterion--referenced tests. *Journal of Educational Measurement,* 11, 63-64.

Woodson, M. I., & Charles, E. *The issue of item and test variance for criterion referenced tests.* Berkeley, CA: University of California. (Undated). (ED 017 042).

Woodson, M. I., & Charles, E. *Classical test theory and criterion referenced scales.* Berkeley, CA: University of California at Berkeley (Undated). (ED 083 298).

Woodworth, R. S. (1918). *Dynamic psychology.* New York: Columbia University Press.

Woodworth, R. S., & Scholsberg, H. (1954). *Experimental psychology.* New York: Holt, Rinehart, and Winston.

Worthing, A. G., & Giffner, J. (1943). *Treatment of experimental data.* New York: John Wiley & Sons.

Wright, B. D. (1975). *Sample-free test construction and person measurement.* American Educational Research Association presession. Unpublished manuscript.

Wright, B. D. (1967, October). *Sample-free test calibration and person measurement.* Invitational conference on testing problems. Princeton: New Jersey: Educational Testing Service.

Wright, B. D., & Bell, S. R. (1984). Item banks: What, why and how. *Journal of Educational Measurement, 21*, 331-345.

Wright, B. D., & Douglas, G. A. (1974). *Best test design.* Chicago: University of Chicago. Unpublished manuscript.

Wright, B. D., Linacre, J. M., & Schulz, M. (1990). *A user's guide to BIGSCALE.* Chicago: MESA Press.

Wright, B. D., & Mead, R. J. (1975, March). *CALFIT: Sample-free item calibration with a Rasch measurement model.* Research Memorandum 18. Chicago: University of Chicago.

Wright, B. D., & Panchapakesan, N. (1969, Spring). A procedure for sample-free item analysis. *Educational and Psychological Measurement, 29*(1), 23-48.

Wrigley, C. & Neuhaus, J. O. (1952). A refactorization of the Burt-Pearson matrix with the ORDVAC electronic computer, *British journal of psychology, statistics section, 5*, 105-108.

Wrigley, C. & Neuhaus, J. O. (1955). *The matching of two sets of factors.* Contract report, No. A-32, Task A. Urbana, Ill.: University of Illinois.

Wulfeck, W. H., Ellis, J. A., Richards, R. E., Wood, N. D., & Merrill, M. D. (1978). *The instructional quality inventory: I. Introduction and overview.* San Diego, CA: Navy Personnel Research and Development Center.

Wündt, W. (1874). *Grundzuge der physiologische phschologie.* Leipzig: W. Engelman.

Wündt, W. (1890). *Compendium of psychology.* Torino, France: Clausen.

Yerkes, R. M. (Ed.). (1921). Psychological examining in the U.S. Army. *Memoirs of the National Academy of Sciences, 15.*

Young, A., & T. Fulwiler (1986). *Writing across the disciplines.* Portsmouth, NH: Heinemann.

Young, F. W. (1972). A model for polynomial conjoint analysis algorithms. In R. N. Shephard, A. K. Romney, and S. B. Nerlove (Eds.), *Multidimensional scaling: Theory and applications in the behavioral sciences (Vol. 1)* (pp. 69-104). New York: Seminar Press.

Yule, R. *Proceedings of the Royal Society, London, LXVI*, 23.

Yussen, S. R. (1985). *The growth of reflection in children.* New York: Academic Press.

Zachert, V. & Friedman, G. (1953). The stability of the factorial pattern of aircrew classification tests in four analyses, *Psychometrika, 18*, 219-224.

References to Case Law

Adams v. Bell, 711 *F. 2d* 161, D.C. Cir. 1983.

Adams v. Bell, No. 3095-70, D.D.C. 11 March, 1983.

Adams v. Bell, No. 3095-70, D.D.C. 24 March 1983.

Adams v. Bennett, 675 *F. supp.* 688, D.D.C., 1987.

Adams v. Califano, No. 3095-70, D.D.C. 29 December 1977.

Adams v. Richardson, 356 *F. Supp.* 92, 1973.

Adams v. Richardson, 480 F. 2d. 1159, D.C. Cir 1973.

Adams v. Weinberger, 391 *F. supp.* 269, D.C.C. 1977.

Brown v. Board of Education, 347 U.S. 483, 1954.

Baxemore v. Friday, 478 U.S. 385, 1986;

Chance v. Board of Examiners, 330 *F. Supp.* 203, 1971.

Geier v. Blanton, 427 *F. Supp.* 644, 1977

Pearson v. Murray, 168 Md. 478, 182 A. 590, 1936.

Missouri ex rel. Gaines v. Canada, 305 U.S. 377, 1938.

McLaurin v. Oklahoma State Regents, 339 U.S. 637, 1950.

McKissick v. Charmichael, 187 F.2d 949, 4th. Cir. 1951.

North Carolina v. Department of Education, No. 79-217-CIV-5, Education Department, North Carolina 17 July 1981;

Sipuel v. Board of Regents 332 U.S. 631, 1948.

Sweatt v. Painter, 339 U.S. 629, 1950.

United States of America v. State of Louisiana, et al, U.S.D.C., 80-3300 §A.

Wrighten v. University of South Carolina, 72 F. supp.

Subject Index

Multidimensional, 45, 192, 214
Network, 17, 21, 177, 178, 185, 188, 191, 193, 195, 201
Neuropsychological, 191, 193
Nonlinear, 35, 183, 223, 231
Nontraditional, 165, 207
Norm referenced, v, viii, 3, 13, 15, 17, 22, 23, 29-31, 38, 39, 41-43, 45,
        46, 51, 52, 56, 62-64, 67, 69, 72-74, 78-80, 82, 87, 88, 98, 151,
        153, 156, 158, 247
Normal, 3, 4, 51, 55, 61, 65, 104, 106, 107, 113-115, 122, 125, 127, 133,
        135, 138, 140, 142, 145, 146, 239-242
Normal curve, 3
Objective, 22, 45, 52, 84, 86-88, 152-154, 156, 160, 163, 258-262
Objective assessment, 52
Objective measurement, 22
Observations, 35, 36, 67, 68, 123, 158, 220-222, 225, 243, 248-250
Organizational goals, 259, 270
Outcome, 4, 5, 18, 19, 23
Outcomes, x, 5, 17-19, 117, 165, 169, 170, 201
Paradigms, 15, 29, 31, 39, 51, 78, 91, 109, 116, 117, 164, 171, 191, 193,
        198, 215, 221, 247, 248, 259, 270
Parameter, vii, viii, 40-44, 59, 79, 83, 84, 86, 88, 90, 95, 96, 98, 100, 101,
        108, 119, 195, 206-209, 213, 220, 228, 237
Parameter estimates, 84, 206, 207
Parameter estimation, 98, 206-208, 213, 220
Parameter space, 195
Perception, viii, xi, 180, 192, 198, 255, 256
Performance, 1, 3, 17, 19, 21, 23, 45, 46, 110, 151-159, 162, 163, 165,
        167-169, 249, 257
Phenomenological, 34, 191, 213
Placement, 16, 17, 19
Potential energy, 196, 235, 236
Probability, 33, 35-37, 39, 41-43, 48, 51, 57, 67, 73, 76, 77, 79-83, 107,
        119, 130, 139-141, 144, 145, 148, 194, 195, 203, 204, 206, 207,
        209, 215, 236, 238, 241, 242, 263
Processors, 34, 177, 178, 213
Proficiency, vii, 1, 4, 16, 17, 33-38, 45-48, 75, 79, 91, 114, 122, 153, 154,
        156, 157, 159, 165, 170, 201, 202, 248, 249, 257, 259, 261, 263
Proficiency space, 36, 37
Program, v, xi, xii, 5, 14-23, 28, 29, 31, 53, 54, 61, 66, 72, 84, 89, 99, 117,

About the Author

Professor Robert M. Hashway, Ph.D. is currently a professor of education at Grambling State University. He holds degrees in electronic engineering and mathematics as well as educational research, measurement and evaluation. Professor Hashway has been one of the leading researchers in developmental education for the past twenty five years. As a professor of physics, chemistry and electronics at Roger Williams University, he designed and developed multimedia approaches for training engineers in the use of advanced instrumentation. In 1970, he was one of the first professors in the United States to incorporate microcomputers in the classroom at the college and secondary levels. As the nation's first state director of developmental education for the Massachusetts State College System he developed the Nation's first multimodality computer managed developmental program to be implemented on a statewide basis. As chief executive officer of Microware Inc. and their associated Advanced Concepts Learning Centers he developed processes to facilitate lifelong learning for executives, educators, rift employees and; the underprivileged learner. He provided technical assistance to develop the only developmental education doctoral program in the United States at Grambling State University where Professor Hashway is the ranking professor. He has published over 200 articles and monographs in the field of developmental education as well as five related books (*Objective Mental Measurement, Foundations of Developmental Education,* the *Handbook of Developmental Education,* and *Developmental Assessment* published by the Greenwood Publishing Group as well as *Cognitive Styles* published by the Mellon Research University Press). Professor Hashway has received numerous honors for leadership in Higher Education as well as the recipient of the 1997 Presidential Award for Excellence in Educational Research from the Eastern Educational Research Association, and is included in *Who's Who in America.* Professor Hashway is a reviewer for *Teacher Education, Teaching Education, Multivariate Behavioral Research, Review of Research in Education, and Structural Equation Modeling.* Professor Robert M. Hashway, Ph.D. is editor of the *Educational Research Quarterly* and the *Research to Improve Learning,* and past editor of the *Journal of Learning Improvment* and *Eastern Educational Researcher,* as well as the *North Eastern Educator.*